Bauhaus Futures

Bauhaus Futures

edited by Laura Forlano, Molly Wright Steenson, and Mike Ananny

The MIT Press
Cambridge, Massachusetts
London, England

This book was set in ITC Stone Serif Std and ITC Stone Sans Std by Toppan Best-set Premedia Limited. Printed and bound in the United States of America.

Library of Congress Cataloging-in-Publication Data

Names: Forlano, Laura, 1973- editor. | Steenson, Molly Wright, editor. | Ananny, Mike, editor.
Title: Bauhaus futures / Laura Forlano, Molly Wright Steenson, and Mike Ananny [editors].
Description: Cambridge, MA : The MIT Press, 2019. | Includes bibliographical references and index.
Identifiers: LCCN 2018059704 | ISBN 9780262042918 (hardcover : alk. paper)
Subjects: LCSH: Design--Philosophy. | Bauhaus. | Design--Social aspects. | Design--Forecasting.
Classification: LCC NK1505 .B38 2019 | DDC 709.05/1--dc23 LC record available at https://lccn.loc.gov/2018059704

10 9 8 7 6 5 4 3 2 1

Contents

List of Illustrations

Black-and-White Figures

Color Plates

Acknowledgments

We would like to thank our many contributors for their enthusiasm for this project, especially on the ambitious schedule that allowed *Bauhaus Futures* to be published in time for the 100th birthday of the Bauhaus school. We have learned so much from you and your multifaceted perspectives. We are grateful for the financial support of Denis Weil and the Institute of Design (ID) at Illinois Institute of Technology, Dan Martin and the College of Fine Arts at Carnegie Mellon University, and Josh Kun and the Annenberg School for Communication and Journalism at the University of Southern California, all of which helped to make this book a reality. The late Walter Nathan, a member of ID's Board of Advisors for over 20 years, expressed excitement about this project during its most nascent stage; he will be greatly missed. Martin Thaler, one of the book's contributors, taught a course called "Bauhaus Futures" in Spring 2017 at the IIT Institute of Design, an inspiration for the title of this book. We appreciate the support of Joi Ito at the MIT Media Lab for his curiosity about the project, and are thankful to Doug Sery and Amy Brand at the MIT Press for taking an interest in this book from the beginning. Olaitan Awomolo joined us as a research assistant at the perfect time and helped to pull the volume together.

Laura Forlano would like to thank Helen Nissenbaum and the Digital Life Initiative at Cornell Tech and Urs Gasser and the Berkman Klein Center for Internet and Society at Harvard University for providing vital and engaging communities during her sabbatical year. Molly Wright Steenson wishes to thank her community at Carnegie Mellon University. Mike Ananny wishes to thank Stanford's Center for Advanced Study in the Behavioral Sciences and the Berggruen Institute for fellowship support during the volume's preparation. Mike and Molly would like to thank Laura for hatching and leading this project. And finally, we would all like to thank our life partners for their support as we pursued the Bauhaus into the future.

Introduction

Laura Forlano, Molly Wright Steenson, and Mike Ananny

What would keep the Bauhaus up at night if it were practicing today?

The excitement over new experiments with machine learning, drones, or genetic material? The speculative futures imagined in the latest "climate fiction" novel or film? The closing of thousands of retail stores and shopping malls? The power of new genres of mass, computational propaganda? The role of private technology companies in shaping social association and political mobilization? All of these concerns underpin contemporary conceptions of aesthetics and ethics at the intersection of design, technology, and humanity, the central concern of the Bauhaus school. Where does a Bauhaus approach live today? Who are the current pioneers of experimental laboratories and practices? How do these sites reinscribe or resist Bauhaus traditions? What are the central questions of our time? And where might we be in another 100 years?

100 Years Ago: 1919

The Bauhaus—founded by Walter Gropius in Weimar, Germany in 1919—was an interdisciplinary and international school of design, described as an "experimental laboratory for the building of the future."[1] While the school had only a 14-year tenure, its influence can be found all over the world. It is best known for its integration of research, teaching, and practice; its experimentation with materials; its holistic understanding of the relationship between nature and technology; its commitment to the democratization and affordability of well-designed products and buildings; its pragmatic approach to collaboration with industry; and, its open-minded, diverse, and heterogeneous approach to ideas, theories, methods, and styles. In fact, as this book illustrates, despite the school's widespread influence and legacy, there was no single Bauhaus; a critical examination illustrates its varied multiplicity.

The Bauhaus was forced to close in 1933 under political pressure from the National Socialists because the school's international and universal appeals to good design posed challenges to the government. The Bauhaus faculty and students departed (often fleeing the Nazis) for over 29 countries—most notably to the New Bauhaus in Chicago (now the Institute of Design at Illinois Institute of Technology) and Black Mountain College in North Carolina, as well as the Red Bauhaus in Russia and the White City of Tel Aviv, Israel. The school's emphasis on simplicity, modularity, and minimalism can be found in the design of everything from housewares, product design, furniture, and even entire rooms (such as the Frankfurt Kitchen, part of the broader Neues Bauen movement that coincided with the Bauhaus) to architecture, housing developments, neighborhoods, and cities; from textiles and fashion to wallpaper and websites. In fact, the Bauhaus's mobility—moving first from Weimar to Dessau in Germany, and then in the United States and a global diaspora—and its ability to reconstitute itself in different political and economic contexts and geographies serves as a precedent for today's fluid circulation of ideas, scholars, designers, and practitioners.

The Bauhaus is frequently used to frame the concerns of a particular point in time. Among the many such frames, there is a Bauhaus of firsts (the first Weimar exhibition in 1923, the first major US exhibition in 1938 at the Museum of Modern Art)[2] in which the Bauhaus represents the meshing of human and machine, design for mass production, and what the 1938 *Bauhaus 1919–1928* MoMA catalog called a "new and modern kind of beauty."[3] There is the Bauhaus of left-wing politics, but also the Bauhäusler who worked in some capacity with the Third Reich.[4] There is the Bauhaus of emigration and exile, as some Bauhäusler, including director Hannes Meyer, left Germany for the Soviet Union, or fled Europe to the United States or other countries, as Xanti Schawinsky did. There is the resulting Bauhaus diaspora in the United States, Israel, Mexico, and beyond, and the Bauhaus of institutions that followed in its wake, Black Mountain College, the IIT Institute of Design, and twenty-first-century variants like the Interaction Design Institute Ivrea in Italy. There is the Bauhaus Dessau, located in the former East Germany, and the nuances it brought to the German history of industrial design.

And then there is the Bauhaus after 1989, after the fall of the Berlin Wall. As environmental remediation began around Dessau in the early 1990s, an ecological reading of the Bauhaus was born that reflected concerns of environmental writers and green thinkers. This particular history extended beyond the Bauhaus itself, connecting the history of *Siedlungen* (housing developments) to the city planner and landscape architect Leberecht Migge, a proponent of subsistence farming. The Bauhaus of women, many of whom were largely ignored throughout Bauhaus history, are now getting their due through a series of exhibitions and publications, not least at the Bauhaus Archiv and Museum für Gestaltung in Berlin. And there is the Bauhaus as a reflection of German history itself, as Kathleen James-Chakraborty notes.[5]

This list is by no means a comprehensive accounting of Bauhaus historiography, and even to begin such a list is to suggest all of its exclusions. To the point of this volume, the Bauhaus is a way of thinking through things, through pedagogy, through design. There are the many studies of the Bauhaus as a utopia and as the producer of utopias from the late 1980s forward. Could it be said that this volume belongs to that lineage? The Bauhaus is so successful as an idea—as Ludwig Mies van der Rohe said, and as many others have quoted—because "Only an idea spreads so far."[6]

100 Years Later: 2019

One hundred years later, many of the core questions and values that concerned the Bauhaus remain relevant. Coinciding with the 2019 Bauhaus centennial, this book includes work by leading scholars, designers, and practitioners from a range of fields including art, architecture, and design, media studies and communication, and science and technology studies to consider the Bauhaus's influences in light of contemporary debates around the political, ethical, and aesthetic relationships between design, technology, and humanity. Most visibly spurred in the West by Brexit and Trump's election, scholars, designers, and practitioners today are grappling with political, economic, and social climates in significant flux. Nationalism is again in tension with cosmopolitanism; the consolidation of elite wealth and power is juxtaposed to ideals of democratic distribution and equitable participation; and forces of environmental exploitation continue to challenge more holistic and sustainable relations between humans and nonhumans.

This book continues a long-standing multidisciplinary, interdisciplinary, and transdisciplinary conversation. The importance of such a dialogue is reinforced both by the Bauhaus school's resistance to specialization as well as by the explicit need today for scholarship, practice, and advocacy that embed an integrative approach. As editors, our own academic backgrounds and work cross many traditional disciplinary boundaries—from studies of languages, communication, and cultures to media, design, architecture, and computing. Our contributors represent an even broader range of disciplines and pursuits both within as well as outside the academy. We believe this diversity of perspectives is essential for reflecting on both the well-known and the forgotten legacies of the Bauhaus. Furthermore, this reflection is necessary in order to craft the emergent and vital and, at the same time, incomplete and imperfect design practices of the future. We expect scholars and practitioners in many design-related fields (including graphic design, product design, interaction design, service design, organizational design, strategic design, systems design, architecture, and urban planning) as well as many others to take up the many topics, questions, and approaches proposed in this book and broaden this critical reflection on design pedagogy, history, contemporary practice, and futures.

As the title suggests, *Bauhaus Futures* is not a historical account of the Bauhaus school but rather a provocation for the many possible futures of design. While scholarship on the Bauhaus has often focused on its history and/or on specific disciplines within design and architecture, we deliberately invited more speculative accounts and reflections on the Bauhaus legacy. Scholarly critique and more generative, artistic practices—referred to as speculative or inventive methods—often reside in different worlds.[7] The book combines history, theory, critique, and analysis with these art, design, and experimental practices, visions, and utopias. It is simultaneously about design and uses design as a method and as a mode of inquiry to raise critical questions about the world. In a world obsessed with novel solutions and the rush toward particular, techno-determined futures, *Bauhaus Futures* urges us to pause and reflect on the Bauhaus, and then to create and value alternative knowledges, practices, and futures for the field of design.

From a theoretical perspective, we engage concepts, issues, and ideas about cultural, sociotechnical, political, economic, and environmental legacies, continuities, and discontinuities of modernism and the Bauhaus. As we chart pathways for design scholarship, practice, and advocacy in this volume and beyond, we are particularly excited by these questions: How might reflections on the Bauhaus help us unpack the black box of design in a range of related disciplines? What are the emergent collective, cooperative, and collaborative relations among scholarship, design, and practice in connection with industry, commercialism, and markets? How are concepts like the posthuman and the more-than-human, robots and automation and the cyborg relevant to the field of design, and how might they elaborate on the Bauhaus search for "New Man, New Architecture and New Living"?

The Bauhaus school was forever experimenting with the materials, technologies, and machines of its time. Bauhäusler were inspired by the idea that "technical innovation could alter the form of life" and that only with "constant contact with advanced technology, with the diversity of new materials and new methods of construction [can] the creative individual ... [develop] a new attitude to design" driven by inextricable connections among environments, machines, lived experiences, and political ideologies.[8] Indeed, the calls of the early twentieth-century Bauhaus to see and create design as an intertwined social, technical, and political project continue in many of today's creative cultures.

But today these social, technical, and political concerns look very different. They are shaped by contemporary debates—both popular and scholarly—that reconstruct the meanings of issues such as perception, vision, and representation; knowledge and expertise; freedom and constraints; measurement, standards, and classification; human, nonhuman, and the natural environment; epistemologies, ontologies, and ethics; form, function and aesthetics; norms, values and responsibilities; subjectivity and identity; embodiment and materiality—among many other categories that are being redefined in the present era.

Since much of our own scholarly work focuses on understanding and engaging with histories and futures of emerging technologies and their implications for cities, infrastructures, architecture, design, journalism, media systems, and even human bodies themselves,[9] we are particularly interested in the development of methodologies that allow for such experimentation along the lines of the following prompts: How are experiments with new materials leaving clues about designers' envisioned social, political, economic futures—e.g., in algorithms, bots, big data, platforms, drones, implants, virtual and augmented reality, surveillance infrastructures, machine learning and artificial intelligence, self-driving cars, genetic material, quantum particles? Conscious of the Bauhaus's pragmatic approach to industry engagements, how is today's power to shape political outcomes distributed—often unevenly—among technology creators, critical scholars, and social justice activists who must increasingly convene in and around online spaces often driven by inscrutable, large-scale, commercially driven and monopolistic algorithmic systems? What kind of change is realistically possible in such sociotechnical landscapes? How are the conceptual, speculative, and imaginative resources typically associated with art appearing in contemporary disciplines of social science, design, and engineering? How are alternative possible futures being explored and prototyped? What new aesthetics are emerging at the intersection of art, design, and technology? What are their political valences, and how do they challenge traditional divides between aesthetics and ethics?

The book also has a more radical aim in that it seeks to address the many ways in which the last hundred years of design history, the field of design today and the many things that are designed (including digital, computational systems), continue to ignore issues such as gender, race, ethnicity, class, sexuality, and disability. Recent conversations about decolonizing design and feminist design practices as well as social justice and the emergent conception of design justice contribute to the growing awareness of the need for more critical accounts of the Bauhaus legacy, as well as a rethinking of existing modes of knowledge production and creative practice in the field of design.[10] Unless they are remedied, these absences in design scholarship, pedagogy, and practice contribute significantly to existing structural inequalities and insure that the world of the future will be very much the same as the one we live in today. We are especially interested in asking: What did the Bauhaus misunderstand or get completely wrong? Who has been included in or excluded from Bauhaus histories, and what are the consequences of these omissions? Where are the lesser-known and unknown sites of the Bauhaus diaspora? How can the Bauhaus ambition of universal, cosmopolitan design be understood with respect to indigenous knowledge production? What are the limits of the Bauhaus? And how might the design field (and thereby the worlds that we design) reflect a greater commitment to social and economic justice?

100 Years Later: 2119

Where might we be in 100 years? Or even 1,000 years?

Through their critical engagement with the Bauhaus legacy as well as their speculative and creative approaches, the diverse contributions in this book suggest a range of exciting questions for the design field and many adjacent areas. At the same time, as in the Bauhaus school, there are many questions and issues that are missing from this account. While many of the chapters have engaged deeply with emerging computational technologies, fewer have addressed the urgent need to rethink existing design scholarship, practice, and advocacy in the context of the Anthropocene, sustainability, and the realities of climate change. We close this section with a few of these still unanswered questions: How might we begin to reconnect theories about emerging technologies with those about the natural environment? How might we understand the way in which humans adapt to new conditions, whether technological or environmental? How might we design futures that reflect principles of social and environmental justice, supporting a diversity of economies, societies, and worlds? What are the roles of utopian ideals that travel far and wide in time and space, such as those of the Bauhaus, with respect to more locally situated practices? Who will maintain, repair, and care for these worlds?

Overview

This book is arranged in six sections organized around common themes: history, pedagogy, race and social justice, making and materiality, bodies and gender, and emerging technologies and futures. Each section features chapters that follow more traditional academic formats alongside others that are more experimental in nature, including interviews and plays, manifestos and diagrams, as well as detailed accounts of art and design practices. In some cases, these chapters make visible aspects of the Bauhaus history that have been lost or forgotten, reinterpreted through different bodies of theory. In other cases, contributors trace the lineage from the Bauhaus to contemporary examples. And, finally, many pieces offer speculations and provocations about what might be next for the field of design, and even for the world itself.

To some extent, the themes of these six sections follow the outlines of the field of science and technology studies (STS), which understands design and technology not as neutral artifacts but as sites of struggle where different conceptions of knowledge, expertise, identity, standardization, labor, and freedom all play out when humans and nonhumans meet. To the extent that such broad concerns and objects of study depend upon meetings where human actions (intentions, designs, deployments, interpretations, resistances) and positivist, computational processes (operationalizations, calculations, automations) complement and collide, the very meanings of "technical," "social," and "political" are continuously made and remade. Following STS scholar Latour's view that "technology is society made durable,"[11] critical technologists and technological critics must not just debunk existing computational arrangements—they must also invent and experiment with novel sociotechnical realities of their own, with the goal of "mediating, assembling, gathering"[12] new relationships at human-nonhuman intersections.

The book's first section, "Situating the Bauhaus in Design History," includes two chapters reflecting on the history of the Bauhaus curriculum as well as contemporary feminist pedagogy. **Ramia Mazé** examines the ways in which the Bauhaus (and subsequent design pedagogies such as Pelle Ehn's 1998 Manifesto for a Digital Bauhaus) produced blueprints for design education around the world. She illustrates the ways in which the "norms and forms" of institutional structures shape the field of design, replicating structural inequalities around gender and power, and argues for feminist approaches that resist existing models while enacting alternatives. **Fred Turner** considers the history of the Bauhaus as "an emblem of the hope that design would create the kind of society politics could not," and as a search for a new kind of worker, citizen, and society. He argues that the legacy of the Bauhaus can be seen in the United States and around the world in everything from products to furniture and even the Burning Man festival, which "celebrates the fusion of art and technological craft and means to model an alternative and freer society." The techno-utopian emphasis on creatively collaborative production, innovation, and design that pervades business and higher education today shares much with the original tenets of the Bauhaus school.

The second section, "Critical Pedagogies, Imaginaries, and Memes," reflects on the history of the Bauhaus curriculum as well as on contemporary parallels in existing institutions and organizations, experimental practices such as worldbuilding, as well as speculative proposals for design education. **Joi Ito**, **Natalie Saltiel**, and **Andre Uhl** reflect on the similarities between the Bauhaus and the MIT Media Lab, including its interdisciplinarity, the use of advanced technologies and materials, the focus on social impact, and the integration of design, style, and practice. In particular, they ask how the Media Lab might learn from earlier design traditions in order to inform self-adaptive complex systems, nonlinear and organic processes, and computational design. Turning to the history of Black Mountain College, **Carol Strohecker** describes memetic ways in which the Bauhaus DNA traveled throughout the region in North Carolina, "making kin" in a series of related organizations to suggest a new evolution for global culture in the twenty-first century. Through a speculative email from the future, **Stuart Candy** and **Jeff Watson** redefine Walter Gropius's Bauhaus ("School of Building") manifesto as a present-day "School of Worldbuilding," alluding to their approach to designing futures. The proposed school deploys "technologies of play and performance" through games, narratives, situations, and contexts. For a student in the school, imagination, exploration, and experimentation are a "way of life." Next, based on the original circular Bauhaus curriculum that signified a quintessential modernist approach to design, **Carl DiSalvo** creates a set of three diagrams that serve as contemporary imaginaries of the Bauhaus. The diagrams include "A Pedagogy for a 21st Century Bauhaus, Silicon Valley," "A Pedagogy for a Postcapitalist Bauhaus," and "A Pedagogy for a Bauhaus for the Anthropocene." These diagrams both celebrate the contributions of the Bauhaus and engage with the limits of this approach to design education in the twenty-first century.

The third section, "'Problems' and Politics of Race and Social Justice," interrogates the core Bauhaus values around humanist universalism, the design of everyday life, pluralism, and experimentalism, inverting and extending these concepts in order to engage with critical approaches to design that center on race and justice. **Elizabeth Chin** argues that design's whiteness—aesthetically, racially, and culturally—is both outcome and symptom of the limits of Bauhaus values of humanist universalism. Through the Laboratory of Speculative Ethnology, Chin draws on Afro- and ethnofuturism to work beyond whiteness, using performance, materials, aesthetics, and writing to challenge existing design normativities that originated in the Bauhaus. **V. Mitch McEwen** reveals the ways in which the Bauhaus frames everyday life as a problem to which science, invention, technology, and computation offer possible responses. McEwen analyzes the "problem of the problem," engaging the ways in which the United States invented the Negro as a problem, so that the Negro can be understood as the American Bauhaus. Drawing on her own experience as a design scholar in a technical university, **Nassim Parvin** argues for building design practices that incorporate social justice and democracy in order to confront contemporary challenges. In particular, she draws on Walter Gropius's vision, which embedded pluralism and experimentalism, and in particular architectonics—the concept that design could be understood as a new liberal art of technical culture—to argue on behalf of the yet unfulfilled Bauhaus promise of design as a liberal art. **Tim Parsons** and **Jessica Charlesworth** trace the lineage of socially motivated practice in the field of design from the left-leaning Bauhaus school to the current approaches of critical and speculative design. Specifically, these practices use design to provoke questions rather than as an instrument for economic growth. They draw on their "Catalog for the Post-Human," a discursive tool about the future of work that hypothesizes that workers may be required or expected to augment themselves in order to stay competitive in the future.

The fourth section, "Materialities of Making," takes designed things—technologies, products, prototypes, and buildings—as the focus, illustrating how to put fieldwork, ideologies and values, histories and futures into conversation. **Jeffrey Bardzell**, **Shaowen Bardzell**, and **Silvia Lindtner** describe the design artifacts—models, prototypes, products, pieces of hardware, and so on—that they have encountered in their fieldwork on design and innovation in China and Taiwan. They let these artifacts tell the stories from the field, including the intentions of their designers as well as the aesthetic and ideological aspirations of the regions in which they came into being. Drawing on the history of two iconic Bauhaus designs—a teapot and a lamp—**Denisa Kera** and **Joanne Pouzenc** rethink the present expectations, uses, and misuses of prototypes represented by contemporary cultures around making and technology. Engaging with examples from Silicon Valley, Maker Faire, and IKEA, they illustrate how today's do-it-yourself kits and prototypes echo the original Bauhaus tensions among experiment, vision, and production while introducing contemporary paradoxes between mass production and authentic, handmade crafts. **Martin Thaler** examines the IIT Institute of Design's original core principles on teaching design and their application to the design of contemporary products through a graduate workshop course on product design. Based on research on the key Bauhaus tenets, he and his students defined five actionable design principles for today, which they used to design new future product concepts in the areas of furniture, lighting, and housewares. **Trudi Lynn Smith**, **Kate Hennessy**, and **Oliver Neumann** present a series of images of the Bauhaus building in Dessau, using them to advance the concept of "anarchival materiality" as a generative force of entropy in archives. They offer an alternative reading of the Bauhaus that takes fugitivity, precarity, and dynamism (rather than longevity and stasis) as central logics.

The fifth section, "Embodiment in Feminist Circuits and Cyborgs," grapples with the Bauhaus's patriarchal history by reflecting on the alternative values and practices in the textile and weaving work of women through contemporary examples, speculative dialogues, and theoretical interventions. **Daniela K. Rosner** and **Alex S. Taylor** trace feminist precarity through the work of Anni Albers and other weavers of the Bauhaus, who are central (but underrecognized) figures. They examine how Albers emphasized difference, uncertainty, and vulnerability in her design practice, looking to materials, tools, and designs as the constitutive elements for multiple worlds in the making. **Shannon Mattern**'s interview with **Taeyoon Choi**, cofounder of the School for Poetic Computation (SFPC), explores the school's philosophical links to the Bauhaus and in particular to its weaving workshop as well as to Anni Albers's weaving workshop at Black Mountain College. These historical practices around textiles and computation, which can be traced to the Jacquard loom, offer a design precedent for a feminist theory of design that explores the tensions between craft and automation, mind and body, and analytical and creative expression. In light of the patriarchal structure of the Bauhaus, **Luiza Prado de O. Martins** imagines a conversation between two figures: the designed Bauhäusler body—the Bauhaus Automaton—and the post/decolonial cyborg described and identified by scholars Chela Sandoval and Joseba Gabilondo. In particular, the Bauhaus designed for a specific kind of body—mechanized, automated, and ultimately directed toward masculinity—and thereby ignored femininity, non-Westernness, and alternative modernities. **N. Adriana Knouf** explores the liminal space between art and craft that was a hallmark of the Bauhaus through her practice-based research on the integration of handmade paper and electronics. Her engagement with papermaking highlights the affordances of different material substrates including fiber choice, fiber preparation, sheet forming, and drying in order to combine older ways of making with contemporary capabilities and materialize the utopian ethos of the Bauhaus.

The sixth and final section, "Emerging Technologies, Techno-utopian Aesthetics, and Interactions," offers critical engagements with foundational design concepts such as representation, color, production, and interaction alongside contemporary examples such as LED lighting, digital fabrication, algorithmic architecture, and the future of interaction design. Drawing on images of the use of color in advertising signs from the 1940s to the present, **Alice Arnold** examines the history of color from a technological and cultural perspective, from the Bauhaus through to the use of LED lighting today. She explains the impact of the new color and light economy on color perception, visual culture, and urban environments. **Michael J. Golec** examines the history of lock technologies alongside contemporary examples in order to understand the significance of New Bauhaus instructor György Kepes's concept of dynamic iconography, defined as the ability for design to make visible the "complexities of the modern world." Specifically, he discusses Gothic locks as well as today's "smart" locks with attention to values and design criteria such as transparency, seamlessness, and dematerialization. **Matthew Hockenberry** engages with the logistical legacies of the Bauhaus and their implications for the future of remote production in artistic practice and industrial manufacturing. He considers the Bauhaus as a site of investigation into the possibilities of distribution, mobility, and assembly and argues that its legacy is a form of design that is suspect due to its obfuscating and instrumental qualities. **B. Coleman** traces the history of Bauhaus aesthetics through to today's algorithmic architecture, focusing on questions of materiality and modes of production in concert with the production of an aesthetic and ideological mode. In particular, generative, computational architecture allows for the creation of "unique" objects, which were formerly associated with craft and craftsmanship. In response to our prompt about the techno-utopian Bauhaus, with their commitment to "a new unity" between art and technology, **Robert Wiesenberger** interviews two editors of the journal *Logic*, **Ben Tarnoff** and **Moira Weigel**, about the place of critical conversations about technology. In particular, the journal is concerned with questions around the building, functioning, financing, and use of technology, having taken on topics including justice, scale, and failure. Importantly, they ask about technologies: Whom do they enrich, and whom do they impoverish? What futures do they make feasible, and which ones do they foreclose? **Karen Kornblum Berntsen** and **Paul Pangaro** draw on cybernetician Gordon Pask's theory of conversation and his *Colloquy of Mobiles* project in order to propose fundamental design principles for the field of interaction design, which is challenged to integrate the tangible and the intangible. Pask's project, which was originally exhibited in 1968 and recreated in 2018, exposes the fundamental nature of designing for interaction.

Notes

1. See https://www.bauhaus100.de/en/past/overview/whatwasthebauhaus.html, accessed July 27, 2017.

2. The first US exhibition of the Bauhaus was at Harvard in 1930. See Robert Wiesenberger, "The Bauhaus and Harvard," Harvard Art Museums, https://www.harvardartmuseums.org/tour/the-bauhaus/slide/6339.

3. Herbert Bayer, Ise Gropius, and Walter Gropius, *Bauhaus, 1919–1928* (New York: Museum of Modern Art, 1938), front flap.

4. Kathleen James-Chakraborty, "Beyond Cold War Interpretations: Shaping a New Bauhaus Heritage," *New German Critique* 39, no. 2 (2012), 14.

5. Ibid.

6. Ludwig Mies van der Rohe quoted in Sigfried Giedion, *Walter Gropius* (New York: Dover, 1992).

7. Celia Lury and Nina Wakeford, *Inventive Methods: The Happening of the Social* (New York: Routledge, 2012); Janet Vertesi et al., "Engaging, Designing and Making Digital Technologies," in *The Handbook of Science and Technology Studies*, ed. Ulrike Felt et al. (Cambridge, MA: MIT Press, 2016).

8. Peter Galison, "Aufbau/Bauhaus: Logical Positivism and Architectural Modernism," *Critical Inquiry* 16, no. 4 (1990), 716.

9. Laura Forlano, "Decentering the Human in the Design of Collaborative Cities," *Design Issues* 32, no. 3 (2016); Molly Wright Steenson, *Architectural Intelligence: How Designers and Architects Created the Digital Landscape* (Cambridge, MA: MIT Press, 2017); Mike Ananny, *Networked Press Freedom: Creating Infrastructures for a Public Right to Hear* (Cambridge, MA: MIT Press, 2018); Laura Forlano, "Data Rituals in Intimate Infrastructures: Crip Time and the Disabled Cyborg Body as an Epistemic Site of Feminist Science," *Catalyst: Feminism, Theory, Technoscience* 3, no. 2 (2017).

10. Elizabeth (Dori) Tunstall, "Decolonizing Design Innovation: Design Anthropology, Critical Anthropology, and Indigenous Knowledge," in *Design Anthropology: Theory and Practice*, ed. Wendy Gunn, Ton Otto, and Rachel Charlotte Smith (New York: Bloomsbury, 2013); Luiza Prado de O. Martins, "Privilege and Oppression: Towards a Feminist Speculative Design," paper presented at the Design Research Society, Umea, Sweden, 2014; Sasha Costanza-Chock, "Design Justice, AI, and Escape from the Matrix of Domination," *Journal of Design and Science* (2018).

11. Bruno Latour, "Technology Is Society Made Durable," in *A Sociology of Monsters: Essays on Power, Technology and Domination*, ed. John Law (London: Routledge, 1991).

12. Bruno Latour, "Why Has Critique Run out of Steam? From Matters of Fact to Matters of Concern," *Critical Inquiry* 30, no. 2 (2004), 248.

I Situating the Bauhaus in Design History

1 Design Education Practice

Reflections on Feminist Modes and Politics

Ramia Mazé

As I write this in 2018, the centennial of the founding of the Bauhaus is already in preparation. The *Bauhaus100* website lifts up a particular image and narrative of the school, celebrating it as an "experimental laboratory for the building of the future." Indeed, the Bauhaus has long been a model for many ideals and institutions of design. My closest encounter with the Bauhaus has been through experience of one such model, the "Digital Bauhaus" framed by Pelle Ehn in 1998. Ehn's was a manifesto underpinning the institutions through which I entered into research and doctoral education in Sweden, after my previous study and practice in architecture and design. Now is a pivotal time—the centennial of the Bauhaus is an opportunity to reflect on legacies of the Bauhaus and blueprints for design education today. It's a call to consider possible and, even, our preferred futures of design education. What do we want for the next 100 years, what do we want to be different, and how can we go about "building the future"?

Raising the question of difference, of different or preferred futures, is also a call for criticality. Through my years as a designer and then as a researcher, I have come to appreciate the role and power of critical theory and practice. One role of critical theory is to examine everyday life, to ask how particular norms, hegemonies, and in/exclusions are constructed and (re)produced. Practices of critical historiography ask such questions of the past, and critical futures studies interrogate the future. Further, feminist critical modalities explicitly explore how things could be otherwise. Taken into practice, theory is not neutral—in questioning, in naming and framing, it may destabilize how things were before and open new possibilities for thought and action.

Now is a time for such criticality in design education, for identifying what could and should be different, for aspiring and acting toward our preferred future. Here I explore some of the everyday building blocks of design education, namely those of design canon and curricula, academic and research convention. In order to explore these critically, and in relation to difference, I take a feminist perspective. By "feminism" here I refer not only, or even primarily, to issues of gender and gender inequality. Feminist theory has become a powerful tool for interrogating the multiple, intersecting variables comprising the human condition, social relations, and societal hierarchies which result in inequality as experienced by many people and cultures. In this respect, design has indeed progressed over the past 100 years. We've been making critical, feminist and decolonial theories of our own, adapting these to our practices as designers, educators, and researchers, and building, as architectural theorist Hélène Frichot puts it, "feminist design power tools."[1]

In this essay, I write in the first person, from my own experience and work, referencing many others by name. For me, this is a feminist approach to writing. Donna Haraway articulates all knowledge as, unavoidably, situated, embodied, and partial,[2] an understanding that has been crucial not only for feminist theory but also for "research through practice" in design. Positioning myself and others is my refusal of the so-called "God trick" of supposed universality and neutrality.[3] It's also a way to express a personal stake in, among other things, Bauhaus futures.

Design Canon and Educational Curricula

In "building the future," the past and present are necessarily implicated. The future is not empty—it will be occupied by the legacies and consequences of preexisting worldviews, structures, institutions, policies, and practices.[4] These are historically rooted and, whether by habit or intent, continually reproduced. As the present turns into the future, minute by minute, there is nonetheless a potential to think and do differently, to contest and reform those things that condition, determine, and occupy the future.[5] Indeed, as philosopher Elizabeth Grosz argues,[6] a particular, political potential of the future lies in the possibility to conceptualize difference, to gain a critical distance from the past and present and, thereby, to build different possible futures.

From this perspective, I would like to reconsider the conjunction of "Bauhaus" and "futures," to reflect on the relation of the past to futures that might be possible and, indeed, that I might prefer. On further perusing the *Bauhaus100* website, the title of one webpage gets to the point, asking "What exactly was the Bauhaus?" This is followed immediately on the page by a historical group photo, the "Bauhaus Masters on the Roof of the Bauhaus Building" (figure 1.1). The conjunction of title and image suggests that one answer to the question is that the Bauhaus is very much embodied in particular people. After this first impression, my next assessment is of the appearance of the group, which consists almost entirely of formally attired men. The second

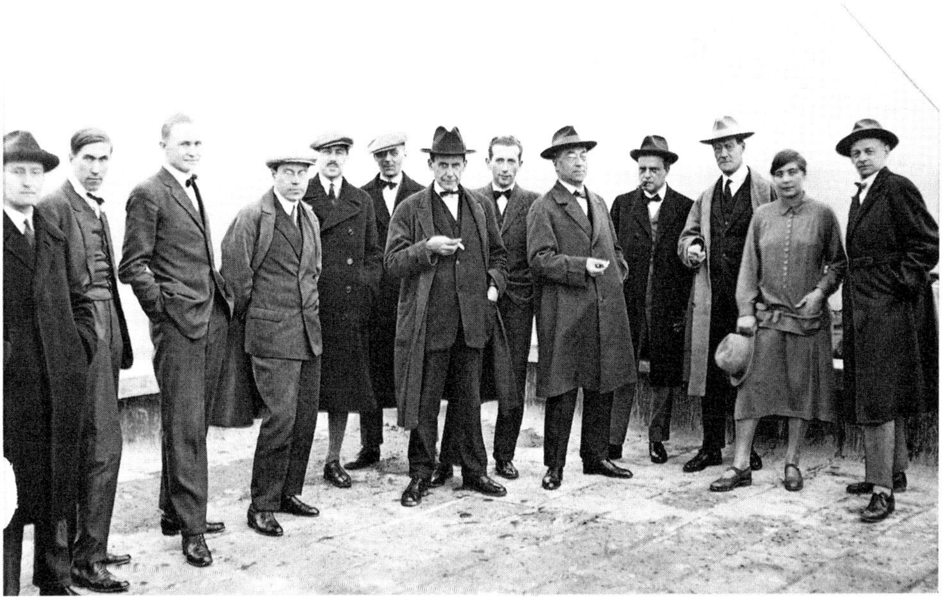

Figure 1.1
"Die Bauhausmeister auf dem Dach des Bauhauses in Dessau," 1926. Photographer unknown. Josef Albers, Hinnerk Scheper, Georg Muche, László Moholy-Nagy, Herbert Bayer, Joost Schmidt, Walter Gropius, Marcel Breuer, Wassily Kandinsky, Paul Klee, Lyonel Feininger, Gunta Stölzl, Oskar Schlemmer. Bauhaus-Archiv Berlin / Musée National d'Art Moderne/ Centre de Création Industrielle, Centre Georges Pompidou, Paris, legs Nina Kandinsky.

from the right in the photo, Gunta Stölzl, is the only woman counted among the 13 "Masters."

Such inequality, which is so apparent when people's bodies are captured on film, was endemic to the Bauhaus and, furthermore, explicitly intended within its institutional structures and policies, for example in admissions. Katerina Rüedi, a historian of the Bauhaus, writes:

> Weimar legislation had given women equality of access to study. In 1920, therefore, there were 78 male and 59 female students at the Bauhaus whereas Gropius had originally anticipated 100 men but only 50 women. As the two genders continued to apply in equal numbers, the entry of women students at the Bauhaus was restricted. Women paid higher fees (180 marks for women and 150 marks for men) and were limited in numbers. In a 1920 decision, Gropius and the Council of Masters adopted differential admission in order to prevent equal numbers at the school: "selection should be more rigorous right from the start, particularly in the case of the female sex, already over-represented in terms of numbers."[7]

Referencing the work of historian Magdalena Droste, Rüedi notes

> Gropius' reluctance to conduct any "unnecessary experiments" (a euphemism for equal access) and his recommendations that women should be sent directly from the Introductory course to the weaving workshop, with pottery and bookbinding as other possible alternatives ... no women were to be admitted to study architecture at the Bauhaus.[8]

This may seem outrageous to us. We might too easily dismiss this as archaic, a policy quickly relegated to history that is simply unacceptable in our academic institutions today. However, this should not—must not—stop us from interrogating specific instances as part of wider phenomena, including legacies and consequences that may continue into the present and, potentially, into the future. Such instances cannot be merely relegated to the past, nor are they compensated for by pointing out exceptions to the rule—though, certainly, there are "lost histories" of women at the Bauhaus such as Gunta Stölzl that should be told.[9] Indeed, researching and revealing oppressed or omitted stories, thereby "making the invisible visible," are important roles of critical historiography.[10]

A more recent and, at least for me, even more discomforting example in design is that of Rosa Taikon. When Taikon passed away in 2017, my colleague, design historian Christina Zetterlund, wrote her obituary for the national newspaper *Svenska Dagbladet*.[11] Taikon's story is close to home, since she was a student during the 1960s at Konstfack College of Arts Crafts and Design in Sweden, where both Zetterlund and I later worked. The obituary recounts Taikon's substantial and historical contributions as a late-modernist jewelry artist. Its title also signals a wider impact: "Taikon's work was part of her struggle." Taikon's work builds upon her education but also upon her Swedish Roma family and cultural heritage—which is, arguably, a Swedish heritage, since Roma have lived in Sweden for 500 years. Zetterlund highlights this point, stating: "She is undoubtedly one of the most outstanding Swedish jewelry artists." Nor was Taikon's achievement about becoming "normalized" into the mainstream. Through her degree at Konstfack, Taikon gained access and invitations to exhibit in major galleries and museums in Sweden and globally. Her exhibition at Sweden's National Museum in 1969 included her own work, that of her sister Katarina Taikon, and an extensive section on the history of the Swedish Roma, including serious human rights abuses. Thus, Taikon's work might be understand as a critical art/design practice, and, further, a practice of activism and political struggle.

"Rosa Taikon was the only well-known Roma silversmith in Sweden," notes Zetterlund in the obituary, continuing, "She had no successors, either at Konstfack or any other art school in Sweden." This is not due to admissions policy—Swedish institutions have equality structures/policies in place, and Konstfack faculty, students, and alumni pioneer gender, queer, and "norm-critical" approaches to the arts.[12] Yet, like most of our design institutions in Europe and the United States, it remains predominantly white, middle- and upper-class. Institutions of design education condition the demographic patterns within the discipline and society, producing qualified graduates for professional practice and cultural organizations, which further employ, fund, and give prizes in ways that often reproduce taught, enculturated and established norms, values, and demographics. The model of a design student, of a designer, of "good" design is self-perpetuating. Zetterlund argues elsewhere that the absence of multiple types of designers and subjectivities in design history reproduces norms that deter those of more diverse backgrounds from applying to design schools.[13] Making Taikon's work at the National Museum and at Konstfack visible in the media and in design history serves to highlight the continuing absence of Roma and other minorities within the national archives, in the design canon, and in our academic institutions.

Admissions and recruitment policies in academia continue to be the subject of profound cultural, moral, and legal struggles. These have also been the subject of research on the persistent phenomena of inequality, for example recent evaluation of more than two decades of unprecedented gender equity polices at the Massachusetts Institute of Technology (MIT).[14] Despite measurable improvements, inequalities persist there and elsewhere, prompting soul-searching and further perspectives on the so-called "pipeline problem."[15] Focus on the "pipeline" entails increasing the number of qualified people from underrepresented groups and removing barriers to the development of career paths and to progression to higher levels within institutions. Associated policies tend to target structural factors at gateway or turning points such as entrance exams, application evaluation, and promotion processes. In this respect, the increased number of women in institutions of higher education (reaching a female majority in many of our arts and architectural institutions today) is important and necessary. However, and despite increasing numbers of historically underrepresented groups at lower levels in academia and in early career stages, the pipeline continues to leak dramatically.[16] Inequalities persist at higher organizational levels and in advanced career stages. One conclusion is that pipeline approaches are necessary but not sufficient. This can also motivate a consideration of bias, discrimination, and deterrence as effected not only structurally but through subtle and everyday micropractices, social interactions, networks, and norms as well as through symbolic and psychological dimensions.

In relation to design education, Danah Abdullah's doctoral work makes several valuable theoretical and practical contributions to "decolonizing" institutional structures and everyday practices.[17] Her topic is design educational institutions in Jordan, which are conditioned by and reproduce the "neo-patriarchal" state. For Abdullah, "neo-patriarchy" spans from macrostructures—society, the state, and the economy—to microstructures—the individual psyche, personality, and the family. It also positions male supremacy, i.e., patriarchy, in concert with the socioeconomic organization of modernity, including industry and other originally Western European economic models. Abdullah studies the varied forms that neo-patriarchy takes in design educational institutions and curricula. She examines issues of access, considering entrance exams, fees, and "privileges of the King" (i.e., seats for students from certain sectors of society); power, academic freedom and language; course lists and study plans (including how these re/produce Western/capitalist paradigms); and power in the classroom, including models of teacher- versus student-centered pedagogy. Crucially, she makes suggestions for how to intervene into the macro (bureaucratic/juridical structures) and micro (curricula and pedagogy).

A particularly interesting example along these lines is the process of decolonization under way at the Ontario College of Art and Design (OCAD), Canada's biggest art and design university, under the leadership of Dori Tunstall. This and other Canadian institutions aim not only at equality but equity in order to redress the historical colonization and oppression of indigenous peoples and territories. The recent "Open Call for Indigenous Applicants" for five tenured/tenure-track faculty positions is interesting both as a structural policy (a pipeline approach to increasing candidates and potentially equity through a targeted call) but also in terms of more subtle variables. Previous gender studies have revealed how the composition and form of job ads affect whether or not women apply, which can be affected by seemingly trivial things such as wording, tone, punctuation, and lists, which elicit different responses between genders.[18] The OCAD ad is carefully composed to frame traditionally exclusive/excluding categories such as academia, design, and research more broadly than "normal" through terms such as "university of the imagination," "visual culture," and "Indigenous knowledge systems." The ad was further accompanied by Tunstall's personal social media campaign reaching out more broadly than the institutional website and providing practical tips concerning application to academic posts.

Decolonization at OCAD goes beyond conforming to the Ontario Human Rights Code, implemented through gateway and pipeline policies aimed at broadening representation in the faculty, board, and student body. The issue has been opened and discussed extensively within an institution-wide cultural and organizational change. Concepts stemming from indigenous communities (such as *mnaadendimowin*) have been developed and integrated into a governing principle of "respectful design,"[19] which is stated in the high-level university mission as well as in the nitty-gritty of criteria used in grading and graduating students. Thus, and beyond the gateway terms for entering the institution, faculty and students continue within radically transformed structures (including budgets, evaluation criteria, and performance indicators and subtle or "soft" variables such as institutional brand, content of curricula and courses, cultural values, and ethos).

These examples articulate modalities of institutional critique, which can open for contesting the terms in which design is constituted and practiced. Historians such as Rüedi sift through meeting notes and bureaucratic documentation accumulated within institutional archives, unearthing particular decisions with far-reaching consequences. Zetterlund and others reveal overlooked or hidden figures within design, recording and making public alternative histories. An important task of critical historiography is to trouble (rather than merely celebrate and reproduce) design history and those designers canonized in our past and present history books, museum archives, and educational syllabi.

These examples make institutional critique explicit as a set of possible practices through which not only to contest and but to reform design. Within her work, Taikon might be understood as an activist; acknowledging the privilege accompanying enrollment at Konstfack, she used her access to the National Museum to expand what and who might count in design. This is an important example of institutional "criticism from within" design practice, and the example also surfaces further practices available to design researchers and educators. Obituary writing can be understood as a form of institutional critique reaching a broad public, raising awareness of policies, structures, and, importantly, the "soft" norms governing our design institutions. Writing job ads, in the case of OCAD, seems to be a careful and critical practice with measurable outcomes. Indeed, and beyond mere reproduction of top-down national policies, OCAD demonstrates a more comprehensive process of institutional self-critique and change, through which design definitions, cultures, and future generations of designers may be transformed.

Everyday practices within academic life, such as writing, bring the idea (and ideals) of institutional critique within reach. In my Nordic context, sociologist Liisa Husu has been a pioneering scholar of covert and subtle forms of discrimination and interventions in response. Her book *Sexism, Support and Survival in Academia*[20] is required reading in the mandatory course I took for academic promotion. Sara Ahmed's related and well-known scholarship details the "diversity work" in academia that often starts involuntarily, as a result of experiencing discrimination.[21] Reclaiming slurs, such as "feminist killjoys," the title of her popular blog, she also attends to the typically unrewarded and stigmatized diversity work as an ongoing "phenomenological practice" enacted in daily practical reflections, struggles, and actions that take place within the mundanities of academia. For example, Ahmed evokes a practice of institutional critique that I find relevant to design—citation:

> I would describe citation as a rather successful reproductive technology, a way of reproducing the world around certain bodies. The reproduction of a discipline can be the reproduction of these techniques of selection, ways of making certain bodies and thematics core to the discipline, and others not even part.[22]

I have been developing my own "critical citation practice." Influenced by "critical design" during my postgraduate studies at the Royal College of Art (RCA) in London, as my career has developed as a researcher, educator, administrator, and academic leader, I have attempted to transpose criticality into practices associated with these roles as well. I have become increasingly reflexive and meticulous about whom I cite and reference in my syllabi, presentations, and publications. For example, my preparation process often involves listing potential citations in spreadsheets to examine and to make more conscious choices concerning gender and culture (im)balances.

I was shocked the first time I tried this during a book project with Johan Redström, Zetterlund, Matilda Plöjel, and Lisa Olausson.[23] I was writing at the time about how climate change disproportionately affects certain cultures, generations, genders, and geographies, and how design can reproduce such inequalities. When I paused in the process to scrutinize my bibliographic references, I found these dominated by white, Western, male authors. As I decided to rectify this, I started developing a practice of nerdy, quantitative counting, but also, importantly, I started a more qualitative journey to find and engage with more authors from different backgrounds. In the process, I encountered a wealth of new examples and sources that have fundamentally transformed my work. Plöjel, the book designer, perceived this shift, and we tried to reflect this in the graphical form of the article. In addition to the normal appended list of references, and alongside my own text and other illustrations on each page of the article, sources were represented visually as reproductions of book spines including author names. Thus, my alternative design canon became even more visible.

As designers, educators, administrators, and researchers, we all, daily, may contest and reform the design canon, understood here literally as the doctrine, dogma, and lineage of key figures and works comprising design. Career advancement comes with an increase in authority and privilege, and I try to recognize this with more critical practices. Now, in my position as an academic in Finland, though it is one of the most gender-equal countries in the world, I find persistent inequalities are still apparent despite substantial policy and structural measures.[24] Husu calls our attention to hidden forms of discrimination in academia, in which women, parents, and others encounter closed cultures, gendered distributions of labor, and impenetrable social hierarchies, experienced as bias, exclusion, isolation, and obstacles blocking their career paths. These compound to the extent that, in the end, there remains only a dramatically gendered pattern of "professors and 'leavers.'"[25] For me, citation is a contributing practice, among many others, which I can effect. It is, apparently, normal for both men and women to cite equally qualified female authors less frequently than males.[26] While writing the article mentioned above, I found myself reproducing a practice that contributes to systematically discriminating and excluding others like me from advancing within academia. This has done much more than "kill joy" for me; this kind of critical institutional practice has transformed my ideals, knowledges, and the basic content of my everyday practice.

Academic and Research Conventions

This returns me to my firsthand encounter with the model of a "Digital Bauhaus" more than half a century after the original was founded—that is, my own experience of a Bauhaus future. 2002 marked a career milestone when Monica Bueno and I presented our first academic conference paper about our critical and participatory design project with an elder community.[27] The conference keynote, "Neither Bauhäusler nor Nerd: Educating the Interaction Designer,"[28] was by participatory design pioneer Pelle Ehn, who would later become my doctoral supervisor. This was the time when my postgraduate field of study at the RCA, rather ambiguously named "Computer-Related Design,"[29] was becoming named, institutionalized, and widely called upon by industry as "interaction design." Ehn's keynote referred to his previously published "Manifesto for a Digital Bauhaus,"[30] a founding document for a new interaction design curriculum at Malmö University and for two new research studios of the Interactive Institute in Malmö, Sweden. In 2001, I had moved to Sweden to work at the Interactive Institute in Göteborg and gravitated toward a research career, eventually completing my doctorate through Malmö University.[31] In response to the institutional model of the MIT Media Lab in the United States, the Interactive Institute was founded as Sweden's national research institute modeling transdisciplinary knowledge production combining art and technology and addressing the public and societal challenges.

Articulating the original Bauhaus as a social and progressive experiment in his "Manifesto for a Digital Bauhaus," Ehn highlighted its moral as well as aesthetic foundations. However, he argues that its "'soft' ideas of participation and democracy" dissipated as World War II loomed and key Bauhaus figures emigrated. A footnote references *From Bauhaus to Our House*, satirical author Tom Wolfe's self-proclaimed "late colonial history" of design, which recounted how emigres were honored in the United States as "The White Gods."[32] Bauhaus founder Walter Gropius became head of Harvard's architecture school, where Marcel Breuer joined him; László Moholy-Nagy opened the New Bauhaus in Chicago that evolved into the Institute of Design; and Josef Albers opened a rural Bauhaus in North Carolina at Black Mountain College. Wolfe does not mention the lone female master at the Bauhaus, Gunta Stölzl.

By 1998, Ehn targeted the "nerd generation and the third culture." He argued for building upon the studio-based pedagogies of the original Bauhaus but additionally emphasized transdisciplinarity and "Scandinavian design that unites a democratic perspective emphasizing open dialogue and active user participation."[33] These were evident in research projects developed within the context of the Interactive Institute studios,[34] along with an orientation, articulated in Ehn's 2002 keynote, in relation to the critical design of my RCA tutors and authors of *Design Noir*,[35] Anthony Dunne and Fiona Raby. Ehn concludes:

> Design noir is not glamourous with great utopias and modern heroes as the Bauhaus, but it still has a humanist stance and a consciousness about political dilemmas that can take us beyond modern design and challenge both the Bauhäusler and the nerd as the interaction designer of tomorrow.[36]

Against this backdrop, my doctoral research took shape at the Interactive Institute. Indeed, the institute was a testbed for developing design and artistic research in Sweden as a whole. At the time, there was no doctoral program that would accept and fund arts practitioners as researchers, and we at the institute prototyped early examples of "research through practice."[37] Eventually, our approaches and many of my colleagues shifted to more formal institutions such as educational programs at universities, funding programs at national research foundations and research conferences and publications in design and the arts.[38] This was part of a larger wave, spanning several decades in Nordic, European, and other regions, of practitioners entering institutions of higher education and research, inventing and reforming academic structures and norms. Critical practitioners, more specifically, have contested the institutionalized practices, doctrinal conventions, and material forms that research takes. Examples in Sweden include the doctoral work of myself and Otto von Busch[39] and my colleagues at the Interactive Institute, Kristina Lindström and Åsa Ståhl. We all conducted "research through practice," a modality of knowledge production that I articulated in my doctorate as "criticism from within" the materiality, methods, and modality of design practice.[40] Further, the doctoral dissertation became a site for expressing, experimenting with, and expanding critical practice, challenging the form of the book itself.

The work of Lindström and Ståhl is particularly interesting in this respect. They were researchers at the Interactive Institute, who then applied with the same coauthored research proposal to two different departments (Interaction Design and Media & Communication Studies, respectively) at Malmö University. This is highly unconventional in institutional terms—but it is in the transdisciplinary spirit of the Digital Bauhaus. Their proposal was accepted, they were assigned different supervisors (Pelle Ehn and Bo Reimer, respectively) and they proceeded to embark on several years of "research through design" together in their project "Threads—a Mobile Sewing Circle." Their final dissertation was written, publicly defended and published as a single, coauthored book.[41] It was comprised of multiple coauthored and peer-reviewed articles published in well-reputed journals and conferences, with inserted introductory, concluding, and interim texts. The form of the book as well as the writing style and authorial "voice" were carefully and critically positioned, drawing upon feminist technoscience theories that informed not only their project but the composition of the dissertation itself. Particularly striking to me was how their theorized position on knowledge as jointly produced was reflected in shifts between single-authored ("I") and collective ("we") in the book and in the defense.

Their work exemplifies relevant philosophies and epistemologies of Ehn's manifesto and the ambitions of our institute to engage in institutional self-critique and organizational change. The voice "we" reflects the spirit of a "third culture" conception of knowledge *co*-production. Lindström and Ståhl extend but also challenge philosophical underpinnings of "research through practice," such as pragmatist positions adopted from Donald Schön concerning knowledge as produced through embodied and material action. They seem to depart from the cognitivist assumptions of his scholarship; instead they emphasize knowledge as emerging in between people and things, relationally and socially through *inter*action. To formulate their epistemological position, they draw upon feminist theorists of science and technology such as Donna Haraway and Karen Barad. Through the work of Barad and María Puig de la Bellacasa, they also challenge and develop notions of criticality, moving beyond the Frankfurt School theories influencing the critical design of Dunne & Raby to theorize their work in terms of feminist concepts of relation, concern, and care. Lindström and Ståhl thus theorize, cross, and reconfigure boundaries between knowledges, disciplines, methods and even bodies and beings. This is an example of how feminist modes of criticality may not only interrogate but also project, activate, and enact alternatives. Their alternative articulations of research practices and academic conventions constitute a major departure from doctoral study typically constituted as individualistic and monodisciplinary.

At the time in Sweden, there was not only a shift of the arts and associated practices into academia but also reconsideration of more institutionalized and established research traditions. Notably, at the Royal Institute of Technology (KTH) School of Architecture in Stockholm, doctoral students experimented with writing and teaching as practices of knowledge production. The subject of Katja Grillner's dissertation was eighteenth-century landscape architecture, for example, but its contribution was not only historical but methodological.[42] She developed a narrative and dialogical mode of writing as a hermeneutical research method for the field of architectural history and theory. Subsequently, Grillner's doctoral student, Katarina Bonnevier, completed her dissertation as a study of historical architectural subjects.[43] Bonnevier integrated dialogical methodologies with activism, design, and theater, which are theorized and positioned as critical (queer feminist) practices. Bonnevier articulates herself within an emerging tradition of "PhD by architectural design," which parallels "research through practice" in design.

Brady Burroughs, who was supervised mainly by Frichot and secondarily by Grillner, completed her dissertation building upon and further developing these epistemologies and methodologies. Additionally, in Burroughs's case, teaching was the site of critical (queer feminist) practice, in which knowledge was produced through experiments with curricula, pedagogical methods, and course materials. In the classroom, for example, she explored alternative relations of power and authority, including coproduction of the course syllabus with students, and experiments with subjectivity and voice through theater, masquerade, writing, and social media. She documents efforts to alter the power dynamic of the architectural jury, or "crit," which is a primary vehicle for indoctrinating students into the working culture, social dynamics, and hierarchies (predominantly patriarchies) of the architectural profession.[44] Some of these methods were also applied and developed "live" within an interim evaluation of her research, for which I was the opponent, and in the final public defense. The multiple subjectivities and epistemological standpoints informing her research, articulated through fictional personas, are expressed as three authors, Beda Ring, Brady Burroughs, and Henri T. Beall, on the book cover and colophon of her dissertation.[45]

These examples of doctoral work and dissertations develop dialogical forms of creative and critical practice, thus extending social and relational conceptions of knowledge production to the writing process and form of the dissertation. Grillner, Bonnevier, and Burroughs situate this in relation to a tradition of feminist writing, for example as articulated by Mona Livholts.[46] They experiment with subject/author positions, identities, and voices, playing with and blurring theory/practice and high/low literary forms and boundaries. In addition, these demonstrate multiple and interacting practices in knowledge (co-)production, including design practices (such as making, prototyping, and testing), historiographical practices, writing practices, and even naming/referencing/citational practices. These are further practical examples of institutional critique, thus contributing to potential "feminist design power tools," accessible in our everyday work as design academics.

The academic book norm has become an important site for my own work in collaboration with several of these scholars. I have been reconsidering the activity of making a book ("bookmaking")[47] as a critical and feminist practice of design in two different academic book projects: *Share This Book* with Redström, Zetterlund, Plöjel, and Olausson,[48] and *Feminist Futures of Spatial Practice* with Meike Schalk and Thérèse Kristiansson,[49] which includes collaborations with and contributions from Bonnevier, Burroughs, Frichot, Grillner, and more than 30 others from across architecture, the arts, art history, curating, cultural heritage studies, environmental sciences, futures studies, film, visual communication, design and design theory, queer, intersectional, and gender studies, political sciences, sociology, and urban planning. To elaborate more specifically through one example, *Feminist Futures* can be understood to query the codified format of an edited, peer-reviewed academic book.

To conceptualize "bookmaking," I looked both to practices of critical design and to critical and/or feminist theory. Critical (graphic) designers such as Dexter Sinister and James Goggin reconfigure the scope of criticality within their work. Dexter Sinister, the joint identity of David Reinfurt and Stuart Bailey, do produce books. But their practice also takes the form of the "Just-In-Time Workshop & Occasional Bookstore," a space and time for anyone to learn and self-produce graphic design, and with a lending-library and community-building intent. This alternative production and distribution model is "best described as a self-conscious model: both a regular design studio and a tool to question the nature of a design studio."[50] Goggin considers the 99% non-design activity involved in running a design company as critical, including the daily details of administering, contracting, lecturing, curating, editing, distributing, and "press-passing."[51] The mundane action of doing criticality is emphasized in his company name, Practise, in which the British spelling with an "s" exclusively denotes a verb (whereas "practice" can be a noun or a verb).

Feminist architectural theorist Jane Rendell further interrogates writing, curating, and making edited books or anthologies as feminist spatial practices, arguing that the edited book is an ideal site for investigating movements between disciplines and between theory and practice.[52] This was enacted physically and socially in "Anthology Works," an event organized by FATALE (in which Bonnevier, Burroughs, Grillner, and Schalk are the main members) featuring Rendell as a keynote. Participants, including myself, took part in a series of activities exploring the notion of "anthology" from different disciplinary positions. The anthology and other academic practices have normativities and exclusions. The anthology as, essentially, a structure for selecting, giving voice to, and citing particular texts and authors can become feminist or decolonial when done by or with others, and otherwise. An example was Grillner's activity "Architecture Writing Workshop,"[53] which unfolded at the event as role play and dialogue among participants through the medium of extracted quotations from a historical canon of feminist texts. Not only the content of the texts but the format of the activity itself was positioned as feminist. In the activity, texts were selected and sequenced, collectively and performatively, in an embodied and dialogic way creating relations or interiority among differently situated knowledges, and in which subaltern authors outside of the mainstream canon were voiced and heard by each and all together. This can be seen as a microcosm of our "bookmaking" in *Feminist Futures*.

Feminist Futures of Spatial Practice is the culmination of a process set into motion within the "Introduction to Architecture and Gender" course module offered at KTH. A more extensive account is provided elsewhere of how the course was set up, including its location and position toward the university, admissions policy, and pedagogical methods, conceived as a "pedagogical queering-tool" involving a series of critically debated microdecisions and standpoints.[54] A community and a critical mass of content formed around and through the course. Thus, a book project and process were initiated. Criticality in the book was enacted through mundane practices related to academic conventions such as: selection, positioning, sequencing, and voices of contributors; review and editorial processes including language, spelling, and style guides; balance and distribution of theory and practice as well as labor and resources during the process; and terms, materiality, and ownership within book publishing and distribution.[55] To pick one practice to further exemplify here, we reconceptualized review as a kind of "peer review in the round," performed face to face, in dialogue and collectively (figure 1.2).

Five "roundtable" sessions were organized in 2014, in which contributors to the course were invited to develop contributions for the book. Roundtables took the form of intimate conversations of texts circulated in advance, closely read and carefully commented by participants and a designated "peer reviewer." Peer review is a key mechanism to ensure quality in the academic system in which many of us work. Standard "blind" peer review is argued to serve gender and other measures of equality in publishing, though certainly not unequivocally, and even the most rigorous standards may be subject to nepotism and sexism.[56] While peer review standards are important to build and maintain, there is no singular, unassailable solution to ensuring quality and

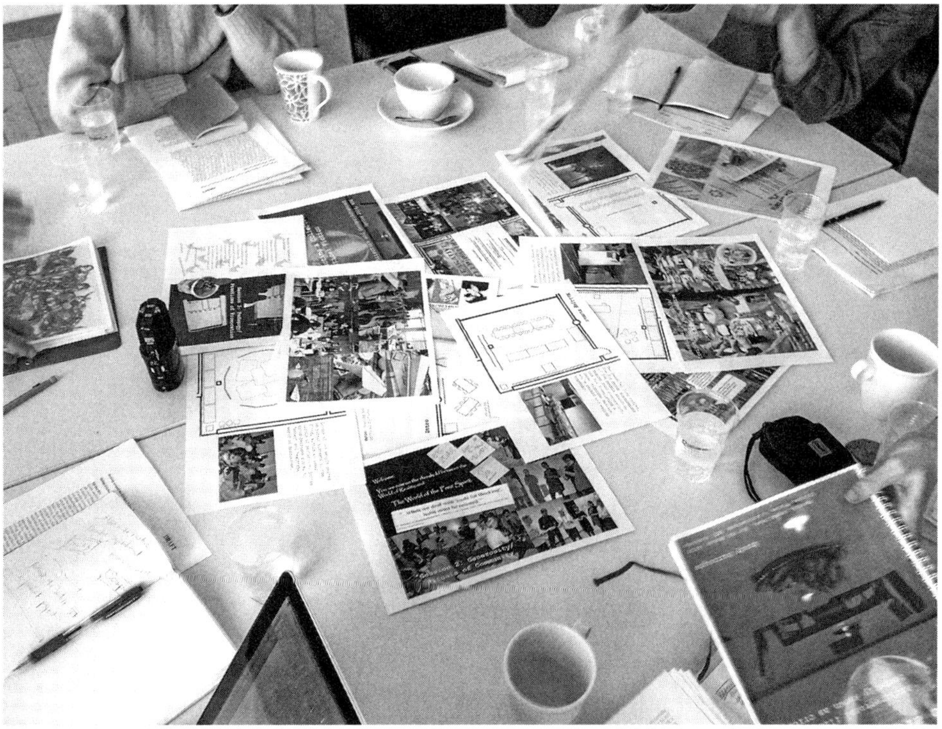

Figure 1.2
Peer review in the round, roundtable with Ramia Mazé, Katja Grillner, Meike Schalk, Maryam Fanni, Hélène Frichot, and Brady Burroughs. Photograph by Ramia Mazé, 2014.

equality in review. In *Feminist Futures*, we sought quality and equality through other means suited to the community and project. We were inspired by feminist pedagogy, including what Nel Janssens terms "the pleasure of conversation" and what Doina Petrescu terms "feminist collective reconstructions."[57] In the roundtables, we came from different backgrounds, disciplines, and positions within academia or practice—rather distant social/cultural locations that could potentially pose a danger of inequality or hierarchy. Each participant had shared with all a chapter draft, which meant each was equally vulnerable and each had a common stake in both receiving and giving feedback. Giving and receiving feedback in person, as a conversation and around a table, entailed that critique became dialogic and mutualistic, articulated from distinctly different but mutually respectful positions. The external "peer reviewer" in our session acted as kind of moderator, rather than as an evaluator, listening in the conversations for common issues articulated from different perspectives.

Peer review in *Feminist Futures* had a pedagogical purpose as a kind of peer learning, in contrast to other purposes such as critique or evaluation. Unexpected commonalities and differences emerged within the peer review conversations, which thus constituted a kind of interpersonal or collective knowledge-making. After the roundtables, each draft further evolved through several cycles of further review with the three book editors, in which reviewing continued as an increasingly precise form of dialogue. As editors, we also contributed with chapters and were thus reviewed by the others, enhancing our sensitivity to the personal and power relations enacted within review processes. This reflection and transparency throughout the process was attuned not only to articulating but to listening carefully, more than in standard review or editorial processes. An implication is a more careful and multifaceted editorial position, and the evolution of chapters that ever more precisely in argument, language, and form expressed the author(s) own position and voice. In practice, there was never a "universal" nor neutral position but rather a safe space created spatially (in the room, around the table, and consequently continuing in more distant and written exchanges). Within the roundtables, and the "bookmaking" as a whole, there was an intense and continual "being-in-relation" continuously performed, a continual self-transformation and peer learning.

Concluding Thoughts

I and my two coeditors of *Feminist Futures* came to academia from different practice backgrounds, each grappling with our positionality and power in relation to our disciplines (no small feat considering our transdisciplinary experiences), within the institution more generally, and in relation to our predecessors and future generations. Nor are we alone in this, as can be understood through the scholarship of Husu and Ahmed and as articulated by philosophers Isabelle Stengers and Vinciane Despret in their book *Women Who Make a Fuss*.[58] As for Stengers and Despret, an immediate problem for us today is that, unlike for our predecessors at the Bauhaus, it can be hard to see or recognize when and where we are oppressed. Covert and subtle forms of inequality are not easily visible in a group photograph. Many of us, and especially women and others in the minority, are too often told not to "make a fuss." Mainstream design, the design profession, and our established cultural and educational institutions are resistant to change and may favor abstract and often uncritical conceptions of "innovation" and "progress." Here the idea of the future is critical—we cannot know what needs to be different (or "innovated") nor what direction we prefer ("progression") without making a fuss. We must pause to reflect on the past and present.

Critical and feminist practices question and contest, but also project, activate, and enact alternative norms or future ideals. The how and when, as well as by and for whom, of such practices is also important. Even as we expand our collection of "feminist design power tools," these are always situated and directed, and must also be subject to critical questions. Nevertheless, in our everyday practices present and future overlap, moment by moment, as we critically learn from the past and actively live out alternatives and preferred futures—for example, as "embodied utopias" and through "practicing otherwise."[59] We encounter glass walls and ceilings, which we try to pierce or make our own. Critical historiography and design studies (for example through feminist or decolonial perspectives) help to understand underlying worldviews, ontologies, and ideologies. These are daily reproduced in canons, curricula, and other forms, which in turn in/exclude and shape students, teachers, and potentially ourselves. We may experience an inevitable "mainstreaming," or indoctrination, to existing structures and policies. But there is also at least some power in our everyday micropractices, in collaborating, co-producing knowledge, in building collectivity, in becoming toward others and preferred futures.

I have argued here that we can act, each of us, from within our everyday practices, as part of larger sociopolitical entities, in the here and now, and affect the future. I've traversed examples of critical/feminist practices of design history, education, and research. For me, and from multiple standpoints in my everyday—as a woman, a designer, an educator, a researcher, an author, a jury member, and so on—there are possibilities for asking critical questions, for being reflexive and intentional about the differences and futures I try to affect. Each time I cite others, make a syllabus, supervise students, collaborate with peers, write and make books, there exists the possibility to do things differently, to become closer to my preferred future. In *Feminist Futures*, we argue that feminist futures are "becoming" when common projects—e.g., a canon, curriculum, project, or conversation—not only momentarily produces an alternative space, but effects new connections and social relations that can alter ingrained patriarchal structures as many of us still experience them.

Notes

1. Hélène Frichot, *How to Make Yourself a Feminist Design Power Tool* (Baunach: Spurbuchverlag, 2016).

2. Donna Haraway, "Situated Knowledges: The Science Question in Feminism and the Privilege of Partial Perspective," *Feminist Studies* 14, no. 3 (1998), 575–599.

3. Sandra Harding, *Sciences from Below: Feminism, Postcolonialities and Modernities* (Durham: Duke University Press, 2008). Cf. Jane Rendell, "How to Take Place (but Only for So Long)," in *Altering Practices: Feminist Politics and Poetics of Space*, ed. Doina Petrescu (London: Routledge, 2006), 69–88.

4. Ramia Mazé, "Politics of Designing Visions of the Future," *Journal of Futures Studies* (forthcoming, 2018).

5. Ramia Mazé and Josefin Wangel, "Future (Im)Perfect: Exploring Time, Becoming and Difference in Design and Futures Studies," in *Feminist Futures of Spatial Practice*, ed. Meike Schalk, Thérèse Kristiansson, and Ramia Mazé (Baunach: Spurbuchverlag), 273–286.

6. Elizabeth Grosz, *Architecture from the Outside* (Cambridge, MA: MIT Press, 2001).

7. Katerina Rüedi, "Bauhaus Dream-House: Imagining the (Un)gendered and (Un)disciplined Social Body," in *Proceedings of the 87th ACSA Association of Collegiate Schools of Architecture Annual Meeting* (1999), 111. Cf. Katerina Rüedi Ray, *Bauhaus Dream-House: Modernity and Globalization* (London: Routledge, 2010).

8. Rüedi, "Bauhaus Dream-House," 111.

9. Mariángeles García, "The Lost History of the Women of the Bauhaus," trans. Marina Gosselin, *Arch Daily*, May 22, 2018, https://www.archdaily.com.

10. Leonie Sandercock, ed., *Making the Invisible Visible: A Multicultural Planning History* (Berkeley: University of California Press, 1998).

11. Christina Zetterlund, "Taikons konst var en del av hennes kamp," trans. Christina Zetterlund, *Svenska Dagbladet*, Mar 7, 2017, https://www.svd.se.

12. Camilla Andersson, Karin Ehrnberger, and Maja Gunn, eds., *Norm Form* (Stockholm: ARKDES National Center for Architecture and Design, 2017).

13. Christina Zetterlund, "Just Decoration? Ideology and Design in Early-Twentieth-Century Sweden," in *Scandinavian Design: Alternative Histories*, ed. Kjetil Fallan (London: Berg, 2012), 103–116.

14. Lotte Bailyn, "Academic Careers and Gender Equity: Lessons Learned from MIT," *Gender, Work and Organization* 10, no. 2 (2003), 137–153.

15. Kristin Monroe and William Chiu, "Gender Equality in the Academy: The Pipeline Problem," *Political Science and Politics* (April 2010), 303–308.

16. Monroe and Chiu, "Gender Equality." Cf. Courtney Gasser and Katharine Shaffer, "Career Development of Women in Academia: Traversing the Leaky Pipeline," *Professional Counselor* 4, no. 4 (2014), 332–352.

17. Danah Abdullah, "Design Otherwise: Towards a Locally-Centric Design Education Curricula in Jordan" (PhD diss., Goldsmiths University College London, United Kingdom, 2017).

18. Danielle Gaucher, Justin Friesen, and Aaron Kay, "Evidence that Gendered Wording in Job Advertisements Exists and Sustains Gender Inequality," *Journal of Personality and Social Psychology* 101, no. 1 (2001), 109–128.

19. Dori Tunstall, "On Respectful Design," accessed August 16, 2018, https://www2.ocadu.ca/keyword/resepectful-design.

20. Liisa Husu, *Sexism, Support and Survival in Academia* (Helsinki: University of Helsinki, 2001).

21. Sara Ahmed, *On Being Included: Racism and Diversity in Institutional Life* (Durham: Duke University Press, 2012).

22. Sara Ahmed, "Making Feminist Points," accessed August 1, 2018, http://feministkilljoys.com.

23. Ramia Mazé, "Who Is Sustainable?," in *Share This Book*, ed. Ramia Mazé, Lisa Olausson, Matilda Plöjel, Johan Redström, and Christina Zetterlund (Stockholm: Axl Books, 2013), 83–124.

24. European Commission, *SHE FIGURES 2015* (Luxembourg: Publications Office of the European Union, 2016). Cf. Kristina Rolin and Jenny Vainio, "Gender in Academia in Finland: Tensions between Policies and Gendering Processes in Physics Departments," *Science Studies* 24, no. 1 (2011), 26–46

25. Husu, *Sexism, Support and Survival in Academia.*

26. Vincent Larivière, Chaogun Ni, Yves Gingras, Blaise Cronin, and Cassidy Sugimoto, "Bibliometrics: Global Gender Disparities in Science," *Nature* 504, no. 7079 (2013), 211–213; see also Danica Savonick and Cathy Davidson, "Gender Bias in Academe: An Annotated Bibliography of Important Recent Studies," accessed August 16, 2018, http://blogs.lse.ac.uk/impactofsocialsciences/2016/03/08/gender-bias-in-academe-an-annotated-bibliography.

27. Ramia Mazé and Monica Bueno, "Mixers: A Participatory Approach to Design Prototyping," in *Proceedings of the Conference DIS Designing Interactive Systems* (2002).

28. Pelle Ehn, "Neither Bauhäusler nor Nerd: Educating the Interaction Designer," in *Proceedings of the Conference DIS Designing Interactive Systems* (2002).

29. Gillian Crampton Smith, "Computer-Related Design at the Royal College of Art: 1997 Graduation Projects," *Interactions* 4, no. 6 (1997), 27–33.

30. Pelle Ehn, "Manifesto for a Digital Bauhaus," *Digital Creativity* 9, no. 4 (1998), 207–216.

31. Ramia Mazé, *Occupying Time: Design, Technology and the Form of Interaction* (Stockholm: Axl Books, 2017).

32. Tom Wolfe, "The White Gods," in *From Bauhaus to Our House* (New York: Farrar, Straus & Giroux, 1981).

33. Ehn, "Manifesto for a Digital Bauhaus."

34. Lone Malmborg, "The Digital Bauhaus: Vision or Reality?," *Digital Creativity* 15, no. 3 (2004), 175–181.

35. Anthony Dunne and Fiona Raby, *Design Noir: The Secret Life of Electronic Objects* (Basel: Birkhäuser and August Media, 2001).

36. Ehn, "Neither Bauhäusler nor Nerd."

37. Pelle Ehn and Peter Ullmark, "Educating the Reflective Design Researcher," in *Practice-Based Design Research*, ed. Laurene Vaughan (London: Bloomsbury, 2017), 77–86.

38. Cf. Rolf Hughes, Catharina Dyrssen, and Maria Hellström Reimer, "Artistic Research Today and Tomorrow," *Årsbok Konstnärlig FoU* (Stockholm: Swedish Research Council, 2011); Catharina Dyrssen, Kristina Hagström-Ståhl, Lars Hallnäs, Hans Hellsten, Åsa Unander-Scharin, Johan Sandborg, and John Sundholm, "The Future of Swedish Research: Overview 2014 Artistic Research" (Swedish Research Council, Stockholm, 2014); Susannah Helgeson et al., eds., *D! Designforskning för nytänkande, innovation och hållbar tillväxt* 22 (2014)

39. Joyce Yee, "Methodological Innovation in Practice-Based Design Doctorates," *Journal of Research Practice* 6, no. 2 (2010).

40. Mazé, *Occupying Time*. Cf. Ramia Mazé and Johan Redström, "Difficult Forms: Critical Practices of Design and Research," *Research Design Journal* 1, no. 1 (2009), 28–39.

41. Kristina Lindström and Åsa Ståhl, "Patchworking Publics-in-the-making" (PhD diss., Malmö University, Sweden, 2014).

42. Katja Grillner, "Ramble, Linger and Gaze: Dialogs from the Landscape Garden" (PhD diss., KTH Royal Institute of Technology, Sweden, 2000).

43. Katarina Bonnevier, "Behind Straight Curtains: Towards a Queer Feminist Theory of Architecture" (PhD diss., KTH Royal Institute of Technology, Sweden, 2007).

44. Brady Burroughs, "Architectural Flirtations, Formerly Known as Critique: Dethroning the Serious to Clear Ground for Generous Architectural Conversations," in Schalk, Kristiansson, and Mazé, *Feminist Futures of Spatial Practice*, 225–238. Cf. Dana Cuff, *Architecture: The Story of Practice* (Cambridge, MA: MIT Press, 1992).

45. Beda Ring, Brady Burroughs, and Henri T. Beall, "Architectural Flirtations: A Love Storey" (PhD diss., KTH Royal Institute of Technology, Sweden, 2016).

46. Mona Livholts, ed., *Emergent Writing Methodologies in Feminist Studies* (London: Routledge, 2011).

47. Ramia Mazé, "Bookmaking as Critical and Feminist Practice of Design," in *Proceedings of the Design Research Society Conference DRS* (2018).

48. Mazé, Olausson, Plöjel, Redström, and Zetterlund, *Share This Book*.

49. Schalk, Kristiansson, and Mazé, *Feminist Futures of Spatial Practice*.

50. Dexter Sinister, "On Self-Initiated Projects as an Alternative Platform," in *Iaspis Forum on Design and Critical Practice—The Reader*, ed. Magnus Ericson et al. (Berlin: Sternberg Press / Iaspis, 2009), 267.

51. James Goggin, "Practice from Everyday Life," in *Graphic Design: Now in Production*, ed. Andrew Blauvelt and Ellen Lupton (Minneapolis: Walker Art Center, 2011), 32–40.

52. Jane Rendell, "Critical Spatial Practice: Curating, Editing, Writing," in *Issues in Curating Contemporary Art and Performance*, ed. Judith Rugg and Michele Sedgwig (London: Intellect, 2007), 59–75.

53. Hélène Frichot, Katja Grillner, and Julieanna Preston, "Feminist Practices: Writing around the Kitchen Table," in Schalk, Kristiansson, and Mazé, *Feminist Futures of Spatial Practice*, 171–198.

54. Meike Schalk, Ramia Mazé, Thérèse Kristiansson, and Maryam Fanni, "Introduction," in Schalk, Kristiansson, and Mazé, *Feminist Futures of Spatial Practice*, 13–23.

55. Mazé, "Bookmaking as Critical and Feminist Practice of Design."

56. Christing Wennerås and Agnes Wold, "Nepotism and Sexism in Peer-Review," *Nature* 387, no. 6631 (1997), 341. Cf. references in Savonick and Davidson, "Gender Bias in Academe."

57. Nel Janssens, "Collective Sense-Making for Change," in Schalk, Kristiansson, and Mazé, *Feminist Futures of Spatial Practice*, 151–158; Petrescu, *Altering Practices*.

58. Isabelle Stengers and Vincienne Despret, *Women Who Make a Fuss* (Minneapolis: Univocal Publishing, 2014).

59. Grosz, *Architecture from the Outside*; Petrescu, *Altering Practices*.

2 What Was the Bauhaus? And What Can It Teach Us Today?

Fred Turner

In April 1919, in the small city of Weimar, Germany, architect Walter Gropius took up an office in the former home of the Weimar Academy of Fine Art. He had just taken charge of a new, state-sponsored school for art and design, the Staatliche Bauhaus. In a pamphlet decorated with a woodcut of a star-dappled Gothic cathedral he announced his intentions:

> Architects, sculptors, painters—we all must return to the crafts! ... Let us then create a new guild of craftsmen, without the class distinctions that raise an arrogant barrier between craftsman and artist! Together let us desire, conceive, and create the new structure of the future which will embrace architecture and sculpture and painting in one unity and which will one day rise toward heaven from the hands of a million workers like the crystal symbol of a new faith.[1]

In that single paragraph, Gropius set an agenda that would shape first European, then American, and ultimately global art and design for a hundred years. Anyone who has walked into a modern office has seen Marcel Breuer's steel tube chairs; anyone who has visited Tel Aviv or Cambridge, Massachusetts, or any number of other cities, has seen the glass-and-concrete handiwork of Bauhaus-trained architects.

Yet the influence of the Bauhaus has extended far beyond its ubiquitous design sensibility. From its inception, the Bauhaus has been an emblem of the hope that design would create the kind of society politics could not. The life of the Bauhaus as an institution precisely tracked that of the Weimar Republic, the chaotic democracy that preceded Hitler's Third Reich. From 1919 to 1933, the Bauhaus lived on the largesse of government subsidies, individual donations, and to some degree the sale of its own designs. This foundation allowed the school to model a new kind of multidisciplinary community—artistic, technological, and social all at once. Though the school employed far fewer women than men, and though it informally encouraged women to concentrate in areas such as weaving and dance, the school was one of the first in

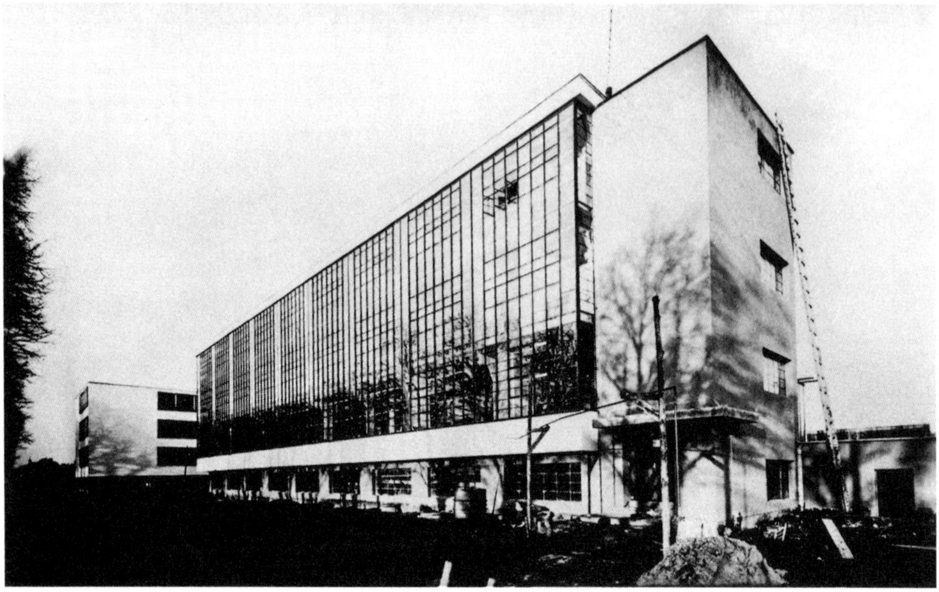

Figure 2.1
The Bauhaus building in Dessau, Germany, and the "Bauhaus Manifesto and Program" published in 1919 by Walter Gropius. © 2018 Artists Rights Society (ARS), New York / VG Bild-Kunst, Bonn.

Germany to admit men and women on an equal basis.[2] The school's curriculum and social style quickly came to define the modern art school. Through both, Gropius and his colleagues hoped to produce a new kind of person. Professionally, this "New Man," as he was often called, would be able to blend the arts and crafts. Psychologically, he would be a person who could draw on feelings, sensations, and reason all at once, and so be able to keep himself whole and sane before the onslaught of industrial modernity. For the founders of the Bauhaus, the New Man was meant to be a new kind of citizen, and the Bauhaus itself was meant to be a living, breathing model of a newly democratized society.

In the late 1930s, as Hitler consolidated his power, Gropius and many of his colleagues fled to the United States. When they did, they brought the social, psychological, and professional ideals of the Bauhaus with them. They transformed the Bauhaus into a prototype for institutions as diverse and influential as Black Mountain College and the Aspen Institute. Their teachings reshaped key parts of engineering education in America, most notably at the Illinois Institute of Technology and MIT. Across the Cold

Umfang der Lehre.

Die Lehre im Bauhaus umfaßt alle praktischen und wissenschaftlichen Gebiete des bildnerischen Schaffens.

A. Baukunst,
B. Malerei,
C. Bildhauerei

einschließlich aller handwerklichen Zweiggebiete.

Die Studierenden werden sowohl handwerklich (1) wie zeichnerisch-malerisch (2) und wissenschaftlich-theoretisch (3) ausgebildet.

1. Die handwerkliche Ausbildung – sei es in eigenen, allmählich zu ergänzenden, oder fremden durch Lehrvertrag verpflichteten Werkstätten – erstreckt sich auf:
   a) Bildhauer, Steinmetzen, Stukkatöre, Holzbildhauer, Keramiker, Gipsgießer,
   b) Schmiede, Schlosser, Gießer, Dreher,
   c) Tischler,
   d) Dekorationsmaler, Glasmaler, Mosaiker, Emallöre,
   e) Radierer, Holzschneider, Lithographen, Kunstdrucker, Ziselöre,
   f) Weber.

Die handwerkliche Ausbildung bildet das Fundament der Lehre im Bauhause. Jeder Studierende soll ein Handwerk erlernen.

2. Die zeichnerische und malerische Ausbildung erstreckt sich auf:
   a) freies Skizzieren aus dem Gedächtnis und der Fantasie,
   b) Zeichnen und Malen nach Köpfen, Akten und Tieren,
   c) Zeichnen und Malen von Landschaften, Figuren, Pflanzen und Stilleben,
   d) Komponieren,
   e) Ausführen von Wandbildern, Tafelbildern und Bilderschreinen,
   f) Entwerfen von Ornamenten,
   g) Schriftzeichnen,
   h) Konstruktions- und Projektionszeichnen,
   i) Entwerfen von Außen-, Garten- und Innenarchitekturen,
   k) Entwerfen von Möbeln und Gebrauchsgegenständen.
3. Die wissenschaftlich-theoretische Ausbildung erstreckt sich auf:
   a) Kunstgeschichte – nicht im Sinne von Stilgeschichte vorgetragen, sondern zur lebendigen Erkenntnis historischer Arbeitsweisen und Techniken,
   b) Materialkunde,
   c) Anatomie – am lebenden Modell,
   d) physikalische und chemische Farbenlehre,
   e) rationelles Malverfahren,
   f) Grundbegriffe von Buchführung, Vertragsabschlüssen, Verdingungen,
   g) allgemein interessante Einzelvorträge aus allen Gebieten der Kunst und Wissenschaft.

Einteilung der Lehre.

Die Ausbildung ist in drei Lehrgänge eingeteilt:

I. Lehrgang für Lehrlinge,
II. „ „ Gesellen,
III. „ „ Jungmeister.

Die Einzelausbildung bleibt dem Ermessen der einzelnen Meister im Rahmen des allgemeinen Programms und des in jedem Semester neu aufzustellenden Arbeitsverteilungsplanes überlassen.

Um den Studierenden eine möglichst vielseitige, umfassende technische und künstlerische Ausbildung zuteil werden zu lassen, wird der Arbeitsverteilungsplan zeitlich so eingeteilt, daß jeder angehende Architekt, Maler oder Bildhauer auch an einem Teil der anderen Lehrgänge teilnehmen kann.

Aufnahme.

Aufgenommen wird jede unbescholtene Person ohne Rücksicht auf Alter und Geschlecht, deren Vorbildung vom Meisterrat des Bauhauses als ausreichend erachtet wird, und soweit es der Raum zuläßt. Das Lehrgeld beträgt jährlich 180 Mark (es soll mit steigendem Verdienst des Bauhauses allmählich ganz verschwinden). Außerdem ist eine einmalige Aufnahmegebühr von 20 Mark zu zahlen. Ausländer zahlen den doppelten Betrag. Anfragen sind an das Sekretariat des Staatlichen Bauhauses in Weimar zu richten.

APRIL 1919.

Die Leitung des
Staatlichen Bauhauses in Weimar:
Walter Gropius.

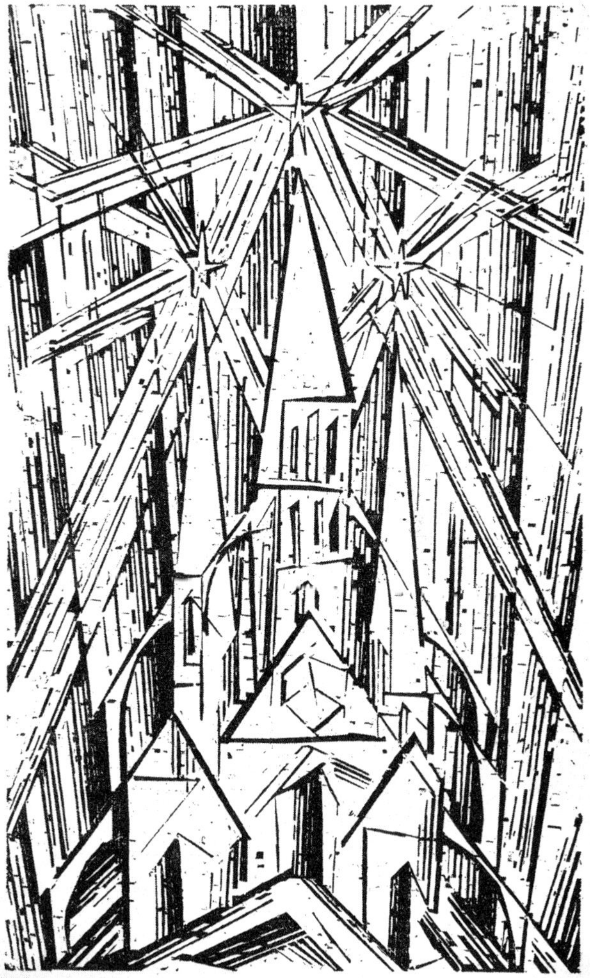

Figure 2.1 (continued)

War, they helped normalize the integration of art and technology and at the same time helped promote the importance of a new kind of worker who could bring these areas together. By the 1960s, the New Man who had emerged from the rubble of World War I, the multitalented artist-scientist-craftsman who would change the world through creativity and design rather than politics, had become a model for the multimedia artists of downtown Manhattan and the commune-builders of the American counterculture. And he is still very much with us today.

The Bauhaus in Weimar

From the beginning, Gropius anchored the Bauhaus's search for a new society and for a new kind of citizen in older struggles to humanize industrial production. The Bauhaus had deep roots in the arts and crafts tradition of William Morris and John Ruskin.[3] Morris and Ruskin sought to combat the alienating effects of industrialization by embracing handicraft, everyday utility in design, and rich, often handmade materials. Gropius too saw the blending of art and craft as a way to improve everyday life, but he also celebrated the machine and the factory. Before he came to the Bauhaus, Gropius belonged to the Deutscher Werkbund, a community of artists, designers, and industrialists who sought to improve the design of everyday goods with the aid of mechanical production and so to provide goods of the highest quality to ordinary citizens. Gropius believed that industrial technologies could transform production by empowering artists to make a new kind of work, and could transform consumption by making that work available to ordinary people. In short, machines could be tools of democratization.

Such ambitions meshed nicely with the founding goals of the Weimar Republic. The republic's constitution, written not far from the Bauhaus and published in August 1919, transformed the German Reich into a parliamentary democracy. The republic's first leaders emphasized industrial reforms, ensuring workers the rights to an eight-hour workday and collective bargaining. At the Bauhaus, Gropius tried to instill a similarly egalitarian culture. Students dressed informally and served on the school's governing council. Faculty were not called "professor" but the far less magisterial "master." From the start, Gropius tried to set painters and craftsmen on equal footing. He imagined that students and their teachers would engage in "mutual planning of extensive, Utopian structural designs—public buildings and buildings for worship—into the future."[4]

In Weimar, the Bauhaus had no way to pursue Gropius's architectural vision because it lacked an architectural workshop. The school's early years also produced relatively few examples of what we now consider canonical Bauhaus style. What they did produce, however, was a new way of training the artist-craftsman. Every student at the Bauhaus was required to take a six-month "preliminary course" taught by the painter and mystic Johannes Itten. The preliminary course was unlike anything offered by ordinary art schools at the time. Itten was a follower of the neo-Zoroastrian sect of Mazdaznan, a group devoted to the pursuit of self-realization and the development of spiritual community through vegetarianism, breathing exercises, fasting, and sexual self-control. In his course, Itten fused the Mazdaznan emphasis on the body with the development of artistic skills. He created a series of exercises in which students explored colors and textures and their interrelations. Before they tried to paint or draw or otherwise represent the world, Itten wanted his students to feel their materials in their bodies. He required them to practice breath control and meditation, and to move their bodies in patterns suggested by the shapes with which they were working.

Itten aimed to create more than a new kind of worker. "The Preliminary Course concerns the student's whole personality," explained a 1922 Bauhaus pamphlet, "since it seeks to liberate him. ... The personality of each student is allowed to develop freely in his work in order to enable him to contribute to the practical realization of the common idea."[5] At its most basic, the preliminary course sought to elicit the indwelling creativity of individual students and help them apply it. Yet threaded through this ideal was a fundamentally political project and one that the early Bauhaus shared with other modernist movements. Itten's students were to free their personalities in order to serve the "common idea." That is, their individual integration of personal and professional skills was meant to model and help bring into being a more integrated and authentic social order. At a time when party politics had become a matter of life and death across Germany, the preliminary course proposed artistic training as a mechanism for fostering individual psychological change, and through it, collective political improvement.

When Gropius and others tired of Itten's mysticism and forced him to resign in 1922, the Hungarian artist László Moholy-Nagy took his place at the head of the preliminary course. Moholy had come from Berlin, where he painted severely abstract canvases and experimented with photograms, a type of cameraless photography. He shared Itten's faith in the transformative powers of art, but he also celebrated the liberating power of industrial technology. "Everyone is equal before the machine," he wrote in 1922. "I can use it, so can you. It can crush me; the same can happen to you. There is no tradition in technology, no class-consciousness. Everyone can be the machine's master or its slave."[6]

Together with Josef Albers, a recent Bauhaus graduate, Moholy transformed the preliminary course. Moholy and Albers did continue to urge students to form themselves as whole people and to use their training to do it. They also retained and celebrated the political thread that ran through Itten's pedagogy. Henceforth however, there would be no more Mazdaznan mumbo jumbo. Instead, students would learn to design for and within an industrial society. "Individualism is not primarily a school concern, for individualism stresses particularity and separateness," wrote Albers. "It is the task of the school to integrate the individual into the society and the economy and to have him partake in the activities of his time."[7]

Moholy and Albers were not alone in their turn toward industry. In 1922, a Dutch artist named Theo van Doesburg had come to Weimar and begun teaching his own classes, outside the school. Van Doesburg was a leader of a new Dutch movement, De Stijl, alongside painter Piet Mondrian. Van Doesburg and Mondrian promoted a pared-down aesthetic favoring sharp geometric forms and solid colors—an aesthetic much more in synch with the mechanical forms of modern industry than with the neomedieval handicrafts of Ruskin and Morris. Thanks in part to van Doesburg's influence, as well as increasing pressures on the school to train designers who could work more closely with manufacturers, the Bauhaus began to change. Gropius stopped talking about crystal symbols and started talking about the need to embrace heavy industry. "I seek unity in these [artistic and industrial] ways of life," he wrote in a circular sent to the Bauhaus faculty in February 1922. "Why is it that we can appreciate equally well the form of a well-built automobile, an airplane, and a modern machine as individual works of art beautifully formed by creative hands? It is by no means our nature to reject one or the other."[8]

The Bauhaus was a state-sponsored institution, though, and even as it reached out to industry, it remained vulnerable to political pressure. In the spring of 1924, members of the German Völkische movement, a precursor to the Nazis, pushed the parliament of Thuringia, where Weimar was located and whose Ministry of Education funded the school, to cut back on its funding. They questioned the number of faculty the school employed, the school's cosmopolitan orientation, and especially the "moral qualities of the Director."[9] Gropius mounted a robust defense, pointing to the number of students trained, the exhibitions of student work, and the international reputation of Bauhaus faculty, but the Thuringian ministers were unsatisfied. By the end of the year, the right wing had become a majority in the parliament and had cut the school's funding to such a degree that it was forced to close.

The Bauhaus Moves to Dessau

The closure of the Weimar Bauhaus marked the end of its early, experimental phase and the beginning of the period for which it remains best known today. The newly conservative Weimar no longer wanted the Bauhaus, but other cities competed to house the school. Led by airplane designer and industrialist Hugo Junkers, a coalition of businessmen from the city of Dessau, not far from Berlin, won out, and in 1925 Gropius and his colleagues set up shop there. For a time, the economic and political pressures of Weimar eased. Thanks to a close collaboration with Junkers as well as municipal and state authorities, the Bauhaus enjoyed a sudden abundance of funding. Gropius hired new professors, a number of whom had graduated from the Weimar Bauhaus. The school began publishing a newsletter and a book series. It established its first architecture department. And perhaps most important of all, it opened a new campus designed by Gropius: a single, interlinked complex of buildings that gleamed with white-painted brick and vast expanses of glass. One wing had several floors of workshops and classrooms; another featured offices. A six-story dormitory for students towered over the whole, with balconies on every floor. A two-story bridge connected two of the buildings, with offices on its first floor and space for an architecture department and Gropius's own office above. The complex also included a large exhibition space, a theater, a cafeteria, and a gym—any of which could be reached, like any other part of the campus, simply by following the halls. No one need ever step outside.

The new campus instantly became a visible symbol of the ways Gropius and his colleagues had repurposed the school's founding ideals. More than 1,500 visitors from all over Europe attended its opening in December 1924. What they saw was both a hypermodern piece of architecture and an infrastructure for a highly collaborative community of artists and designers. The new campus was a self-contained world, with everything a person needed to keep body and soul together, and with the easiest of access to friends. Xanti Schawinsky, a student at the time, recalled that Gropius's campus created an easy comradery: "All you had to do to call a friend was to step out onto your balcony and whistle," he wrote.[10] It might not have been a Gothic cathedral, but the new campus seemed to many to have finally brought into being the kind of intimate community of purpose promised in 1919.

The campus also signaled a reorientation of the Bauhaus mission. The turn away from romanticism, mysticism, and handicraft that had begun in Weimar exploded into a full-on embrace of architecture, heavy industry, and modern mass production. Alongside the core campus complex, Gropius designed and oversaw the construction of six semidetached townhouses for Bauhaus faculty. These houses were entirely fitted out with products from Bauhaus workshops, and their interiors were painted by their new inhabitants. They quickly became international models of what modern living might look like. So too did Herbert Bayer's new typeface, which appeared on all Bauhaus publications. The traditional German script then in general use featured elaborate curls and other decorative flourishes, and a complex pattern of capitalization. Bayer's typeface was as clean and cool as a bar of aluminum—no flourishes, not even any capital letters—and wondrously easy to read.

Not everyone was thrilled with the school's new direction. "Architecture became the new principal field of study," explained T. Lux Feininger, the son of the man who had etched the Gothic cathedral for the pamphlet of 1919. "The new unity of art and technology came to a standstill. ... The dreams of a regeneration of society hardened into specialization. Authority, structure, re-entered the scene."[11] It might be more accurate to say that the ideal of the unity of art and technology simply scaled up to include architecture and publishing. But the tone of the school did change. Local officials had reminded Gropius and his colleagues that at the end of the day, they would need to justify the city and the state's investment by intensifying their collaborations with industry. In part for that reason, Gropius centralized his authority. The collaborative decision-making of the early Weimar years disappeared. Masters were called professors once again.

The effort to form a new kind of worker only intensified, however, and the preliminary course remained the centerpiece of Bauhaus teaching. Moholy and Albers may have shown little concern for their charges' spiritual growth, but they continued to require their students to become adept in working with a wide array of materials. These encounters were meant to simultaneously engage the whole range of the students' senses and train them for the array of professional possibilities then emerging.[12] Their internal, psychological wholeness and their professional flexibility would free them to embrace the industry that had alienated so many before them. The New Man must "achieve a natural balance of intellectual and emotional power" wrote Moholy; only then, wrote Gropius, could "the work of the new man ... become an organic part of unified industrial production."[13]

For models students needed only to look at the first generation of Bauhaus professors to have been trained by the Bauhaus itself. Marcel Breuer could paint and make furniture; Herbert Bayer could design buildings and whole publication programs. Most of the Dessau faculty were men—of the school's thirty-five professors, only six were women, and only one of those women, Gunta Stölzl, a professor of weaving, had been trained at the Bauhaus.[14] Yet almost all of the first Bauhaus graduates could paint, draw, photograph, design appliances, costumes, and posters, and weave a rug. Visitors to the Dessau campus could see individual examples of student work, and if they toured the faculty housing, they could see how Bauhaus designs could be used to create a unified aesthetic environment. At Dessau, architecture largely remained the province of male instructors and students, but the buildings were filled with industrial designs created by men and women alike. These designs continue to define Bauhaus style today. Marianne Brandt's semi-globe teapot and her arch-necked desk lamp; Anni Albers's weavings; Josef Albers's color block paintings; Oskar Schlemmer's geometric designs for the theater; the abstract paintings of Paul Klee, Wassily Kandinsky, and Moholy-Nagy; and above all, the architecture of Walter Gropius—between 1925 and its closure in 1933, the Bauhaus created much of the visual vocabulary of twentieth-century modernity.

To an increasingly nationalistic, right-wing German government, however, the cosmopolitanism of the Bauhaus had begun to seem traitorous. Never mind that the Bauhaus put Germany at the center of the international design world. To fascists, the Bauhaus had become an emblem of anti-Aryan community. The story of how the Bauhaus changed as the Nazis came to power is long and complex and has been well told elsewhere.[15] To understand the Bauhaus's lingering importance for our own time, it is enough to note that in Dessau, and in the end for a few tumultuous months in Berlin, the school and its leaders had to battle on two fronts: one, to continue to bring the Bauhaus vision to life in the world of art and design; and two, to keep the Bauhaus funded and functioning as an institution. In 1928, Gropius left the school to pursue his own architecture practice and Hannes Meyer, a well-known Marxist, became its leader. Meyer lacked Gropius's political tact and offended many inside and outside the school. In 1930, he was replaced by the architect Ludwig Mies van der Rohe. By that time, the political conflicts that had long surrounded the school had infiltrated its student body. In 1932, a Communist faction even demanded the elimination of the preliminary course.

Mies fought ferociously to save the school. But the political climate made that impossible. Nazi critics attacked from all sides. The Bauhaus was a nest of Bolsheviks said some, a nest of Jews said others. Even the flat roofs of Bauhaus buildings were suspect—after all, said the fascists, northern countries needed peaked roofs; only the non-Aryan nations of warmer climes did not.[16] In 1932, a group of Nazi representatives from the Dessau city council toured the Bauhaus. Two days later, their leader published an article entitled "What Will Become of the Bauhaus?" in a local newspaper. He answered his own question thus:

> The disappearance of this so-called "Institute of Design" will mean the disappearance from German soil of one of the most prominent places of Jewish-Marxist "art" manifestation. May the total demolition follow soon and may on the same spot where today stands the somber glass Palace of oriental taste, the "aquarium" as it has been popularly dubbed in Dessau, soon rise homesteads and parks that will provide German people with homes and places for relaxation. "The robe has fallen, the Duke must follow."[17]

The New Man in the New World

And so he did. By the summer of 1933, the Bauhaus had closed its doors for good. The end of the Bauhaus as an institution, however, dramatically enhanced the reach and influence of its ideals. In the late 1930s, many former Bauhaus professors emigrated to the United States. Alongside refugee German intellectuals such as Theodor Adorno and Max Horkheimer, and together with American artists, industrialists, and academics, they transformed American cultural life. Gropius went to Harvard, where he became chair of the university's department of architecture. Mies van der Rohe migrated to Chicago, designed much of the campus of the Illinois Institute of Technology, and then went on to architect such icons of modernism as the 1958 Seagram building in Manhattan. László Moholy-Nagy went to Chicago, where he founded what was first called the New Bauhaus and later the IIT Institute of Design. Moholy's student György Kepes first joined him there, then moved to MIT, where he established one of the most influential postwar arenas for art-and-technology collaborations, the Center for Advanced Visual Studies (CAVS). Herbert Bayer went to New York, where he developed important exhibitions for the Museum of Modern Art and designed advertisements for Walter Paepcke's Container Corporation of America. Ultimately he played a key role in helping Paepcke turn the small town of Aspen, Colorado, into a center of American intellectual life.

To map the Bauhaus community's impact on American life after World War II would take an entire volume.[18] American architecture, advertising, engineering education, museum display—all changed dramatically under the influence of individual Bauhaus emigres. Collectively however, the emigres brought with them two key elements of the German Bauhaus, one organizational and the other psychological. Into a Cold War America in which many dreaded the powers of bureaucracy, Bauhaus emigres brought antibureaucratic models of organization based on artistic and technological collaboration and egalitarian social ideals. And to an America preoccupied with the psychological fragmentation and alienation of what novelist Sloan Wilson called "the man in the gray flannel suit," they introduced the New Man, psychologically integrated, multiskilled, independent, and democratic.

Perhaps the easiest place at which to see the impact of these two contributions is Black Mountain College. Today the rural North Carolina school, which operated from 1933 to 1957, is remembered as the epicenter of midcentury American avant-garde painting, dance, and poetry. This is no surprise given that its students included figures such as painter Robert Rauschenberg, sculptor Kenneth Snelson, filmmaker Stan VanDerBeek, and writer Francine du Plessix Gray. Its faculty was just as illustrious, featuring at one time or another the poet Charles Olson, the painter Willem de Kooning, architect Buckminster Fuller, and composer John Cage. But when Josef and Anni Albers arrived in 1933, Black Mountain was a small college devoted to providing a general education in line with the liberal educational philosophy of John Dewey.

Like Dewey, the designers of Black Mountain's curriculum put art at the center of human experience. The school's founding president, John Andrew Rice, hired Josef Albers to run the school for that reason. Albers arrived speaking hardly any English. When students asked him what he would teach, he often answered "To open eyes!"[19] He quickly began teaching courses in painting and basic design that grew directly from his work in the preliminary course at the Bauhaus in Dessau. He taught students to see colors in relationship to one another, to feel their way into different materials, and to imagine themselves as builders of a new, more democratic society. "I don't think there was one comment he made pertaining to the visual world that he didn't intend to pertain to the human world," one of his students recalled. "He told us over and over that there is no meaning to teaching art unless it is a teaching for how to live your life. This was not a little side note. It was fundamental to his teaching."[20]

Albers's teaching carried with it the legacy of the Bauhaus vision of the New Man, as did the work of his fellow emigres. In 1938, the director of the New Bauhaus in Chicago, László Moholy-Nagy, updated his 1928 book *The New Vision* for American audiences and published it in English. He cited John Dewey and American Progressives as inspirations for his teaching philosophy and explicitly tied the goals of the Weimar Bauhaus to his work in Chicago.[21] The aim of all his teaching, he wrote, was to make a new kind of person. As he put it, "Not the product, but man, is the end in view."[22] In Germany, the New Man was meant to salvage the world through industry. In America, he was meant to do the same thing, but in a liberal-democratic context. "The revolutionist should always remain conscious that the class struggle is, in the last analysis, not about capital, nor the means of production," wrote Moholy in *The New Vision*. "In actuality it concerns the right of the individual to a satisfying occupation, work that meets the inner needs, a normal way of life and a real release of human powers."[23] John Dewey couldn't have said it better.

At Black Mountain College, Albers took the doctrine of the New Man one step further toward American liberalism. In his 1942 memoir, the school's founding president, John Andrew Rice, recalled that "Black Mountain was to be education for democracy." The definition of the kind of democracy it would exemplify, however, owed at least as much to the Bauhaus as to any American individualism. "The democratic man, we said, must be an artist," wrote Rice. "The integrity, we said, of the democratic man, was the integrity of the artist, an integrity of relationship."[24] At Black Mountain College, as at the Bauhaus, students would be introduced to multiple materials and multiple modes of perception and would become multiply skilled in ways that served the arts and industry. But as they mastered the relationships among materials and among their own senses, they would also develop the kinds of emotional flexibility

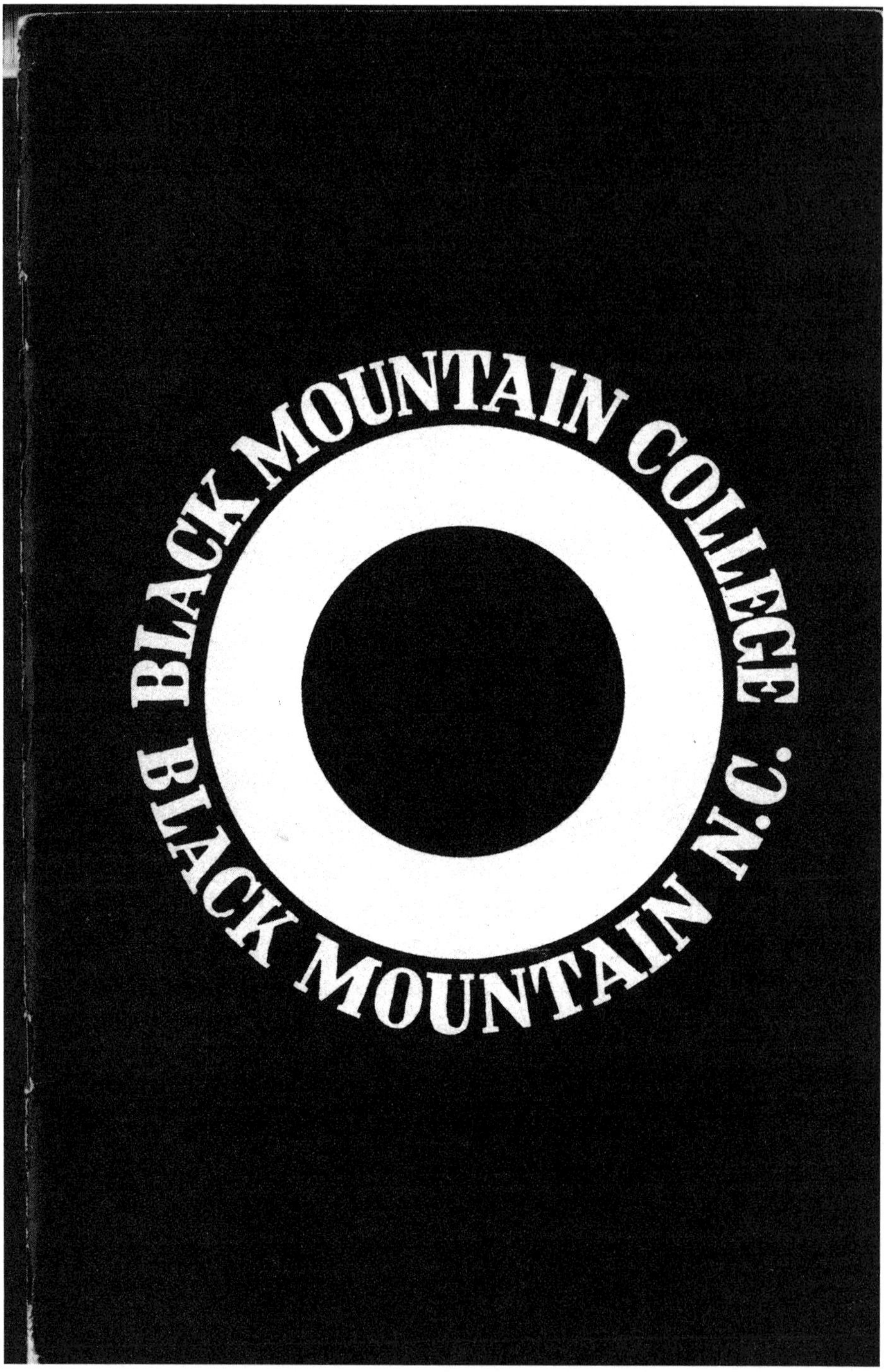

Figure 2.2

Black Mountain College logo and Josef Albers's drawing class, ca. 1939–1940. Courtesy of the Western Regional Archives, State Archives of North Carolina.

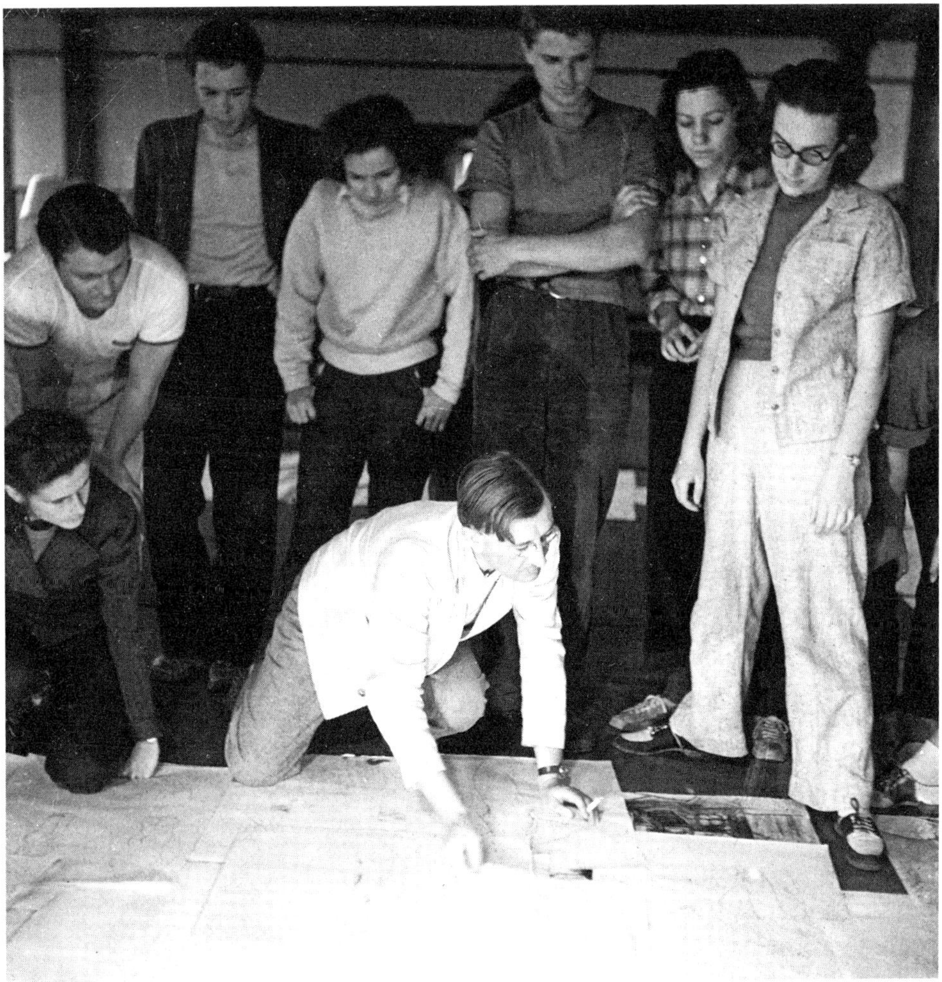

Figure 2.2 (continued)

and collaborative individualism that would turn the College into a model of a new, less hierarchical America. In his Black Mountain versions of the preliminary course, Albers even talked about colors and forms as if they were citizens in an ideal liberal democracy. They should "know about each other" and "pay attention to each other," he said. They "should not exist for themselves." They should "cooperate ... integrate ... get along."[25]

Albers headed Black Mountain College from 1933 to 1949, and in those years the school became, like the Bauhaus itself, an emblem of an alternative way of organizing egalitarian sociability. While the tensions of World War II and the early Cold War swirled through American society at large, Black Mountain College modeled a world in which art and design and attention to the senses produced the kind of collaborative, benevolent polity that state-level politics had so clearly failed to establish. In later years, Albers's students and colleagues would take pieces of that model with them into the heart of the New York art world and the San Francisco counterculture. Buckminster Fuller's geodesic dome, which he prototyped at Black Mountain in the summer of 1948, became the preferred form of housing on the communes of the 1960s. The Happening, a performance art form pioneered by John Cage at Black Mountain in 1952, became a quintessential genre of political theater. And the notion that a democratic community could be formed by turning away from politics and back toward the senses, toward expression, and toward design as a way of organizing activity defined much of the American counterculture.

Conclusion

Today the legacy of the Bauhaus can be seen everywhere from the floors of furniture stores to the desert sands of the Burning Man Festival in Nevada. We have become so accustomed to the geometric modernism of Bauhaus teapots and lamps that we no longer have any idea where they came from, or that they even have an origin at all. For its part, the Burning Man Festival looks like just another spectacular eruption from the creative volcano that is the San Francisco Bay area. But dig a little deeper and you can see the Bauhaus influence—in the geodesic domes in the dust and above all in the collaborative production of technology-centered art that drives so much of the event. Like the Bauhaus, and like Black Mountain College, Burning Man celebrates the fusion of art and technological craft and means to model an alternative and freer society.

Though few may remember the Bauhaus as an institution, its governing beliefs suffuse our culture today. Creativity, collaboration, innovation, design—these are the watchwords of higher education and the corporate sector around the globe. The kind of interdisciplinary training the Bauhaus pioneered has gone mainstream, not just for artists but for computer scientists, product designers, marketers, and engineers. The hope of blending work and play and of transforming the workplace into a model of egalitarian community that once animated the Bauhaus now lights up the California headquarters of Google and Facebook.

And that should give us pause. When Itten and Moholy and Albers taught the preliminary course, they hoped that their students might help create a society that mirrored their classrooms. Such a society would be collaborative, person-centered, and expressive. It would take advantage of the latest developments in manufacturing and design. And it would operate on its own terms, far from the concerns of states. In reality, however, the freedom of such a society depended even then on the strength of political institutions. The Bauhaus came to life alongside the Weimar Republic and depended for its survival on the munificence of the republic's democratically elected representatives. Likewise, Black Mountain College could not have survived in the post-war years without tuition paid by students using the G.I. Bill. And for all its much-hyped entrepreneurship, Silicon Valley's computers and software would never have come into being without several generations of research supported and managed by the federal government.

In this context, the fate of the original Bauhaus, like the fate of the Weimar Republic, reminds us that individual genius, small group collaboration, and even the exquisite design of systems and tools will never be sufficient foundations for democracy. The Bauhaus was founded on the belief that the pleasure of art and technology, properly united, could defuse the tensions of politics and perhaps even replace them. But its struggles as an institution and the means of its demise tell us something different. They remind us that if we want to have the kind of society the Bauhaus fought for, not to mention the kind of beauty it brought into the world, we will need to embrace both the unity of art and technology and the agonistic struggles of democratic politics.

Notes

1. Walter Gropius, "Program of the Staatliche Bauhaus in Weimar," published by the Staatliche Bauhaus, Weimar, April 1919; rpt. in Hans Maria Wingler, *The Bauhaus: Weimar, Dessau, Berlin, Chicago* (Cambridge, MA: MIT Press, 1978), 31.

2. Ulrike Müller, Ingrid Radewaldt, and Sandra Kemker, *Bauhaus Women: Art, Handicraft, Design*, English-language ed. (Paris: Flammarion, 2009), 7–15. See also Alice Rawsthorn, "Female Pioneers of the Bauhaus," *New York Times*, March 23, 2013, https://www.nytimes.com/2013/03/25/arts/25iht-design25.html.

3. There are many excellent histories of the Bauhaus. I've drawn extensively on two: Frank Whitford, *Bauhaus* (London: Thames and Hudson, 1984), and Éva Forgács, *The Bauhaus Idea and Bauhaus Politics* (Budapest: Central European University Press, 1995). Excellent accounts of the Bauhaus's early years can also be found in Elaine S. Hochman, *Bauhaus: Crucible of Modernism* (New York: Fromm International, 1997); Herbert Bayer, Walter Gropius, and Ise Gropius, *Bauhaus, 1919–1928* (New York: Museum of Modern Art, 1938); Hans Wingler, "Origin and History of the Bauhaus," in Wingler, *The Bauhaus*, xviii-11; and Magdalena Droste, *Bauhaus, 1919–1933* (Cologne: B. Taschen, 1998).

4. Gropius, "Program of the Staatliche Bauhaus in Weimar," quoted in Wingler, *The Bauhaus*, 32.

5. "Exhibition of the Work of Journeymen and Apprentices in the Staatliche Bauhaus Weimar, April-May 1922," rpt. in Wingler, *The Bauhaus*, 54. It is clear that the Bauhaus's founders shared an aspiration for wholeness with contemporary Gestalt psychologists, many of whom were working in Berlin. Yet there is little evidence that Gropius and his colleagues in fact engaged with Gestalt psychology directly. See Karen Koehler, "More Than Parallel Lines: Thoughts on Gestalt, Albers, and the Bauhaus," in *Intersecting Colors: Josef Albers and His Contemporaries*, ed. Vanja Malloy (Amherst, MA: Amherst College Press), 45–64.

6. László Moholy-Nagy, "Constructivism and the Proletariat," May 1922; quoted in Whitford, *Bauhaus*, 128.

7. Josef Albers, "Creative Education," from "Sixth International Congress for Drawing, Art Education, and Applied Art in Prague, 1928," rpt. in Wingler, *The Bauhaus*, 142.

8. Walter Gropius, "The Viability of the Bauhaus Idea: Notes of February 3, 1922," rpt. in Wingler, *The Bauhaus*, 51.

9. Walter Gropius, "The Staatliche Bauhaus and the Thuringian Landtag," from the newspaper *Deutschland* (Weimar), no. 114, April 24, 1924; rpt. in Wingler, *The Bauhaus*, 84–85.

10. Schawinsky, quoted in Forgács, *The Bauhaus Idea*, 134.

11. T. Lux Feininger, quoted in Whitford, *Bauhaus*, 186.

12. As art historian Éva Forgács has argued, the Dessau Bauhaus focused less on the construction of a single *Gesamtkunstwerk* and more on developing student-artists as wholes in themselves. See Forgács, *The Bauhaus Idea*, 142–143.

13. László Moholy-Nagy, *Von Material zur Arkitektur* (1928), quoted in Forgács, *The Bauhaus Idea*, 142; Walter Gropius, *The Scope of Total Architecture* (1962), 20; quoted in Forgács, *The Bauhaus Idea*, 143.

14. Müller, Radewaldt, and Kemker, *Bauhaus Women*, 14 and 43–49.

15. For starting points, see Whitford, *Bauhaus*, 192–196, and Peter Hahn and Christian Wolsdorff, *Bauhaus Berlin: Auflösung Dessau 1932, Schliessung Berlin 1933, Bauhaüsler und Drittes Reich: Eine Dokumentation* (Weingarten: Kunstverlag Weingarten, 1985).

16. Whitford, *Bauhaus*, 195. For an account of the aesthetic of the flat roof, see Adolf Behne and Paul Westheim, "Zur Äesthetik des flachen Daches," *Das neue Frankfurt*, no. 7 (1926–1927), 163–164; rpt. as "The Aesthetics of the Flat Roof," in Anton Kaes, Martin Jay, and Edward Dimendberg, *The Weimar Republic Sourcebook* (Berkeley: University of California Press, 1994), 449–450.

17. Hoffman (no first name), "What Will Become of the Bauhaus?" *Anhalter Tageszeitung*, July 10, 1932; rpt. in Wingler, *The Bauhaus*, 177.

18. Pieces of the story have already been well told. For starting points, see James Sloan Allen, *The Romance of Commerce and Culture: Capitalism, Modernism, and the Chicago-Aspen Crusade for Cultural Reform* (Chicago: University of Chicago Press, 1983); Gwen Finkel Chanzit and Daniel

Libeskind, *From Bauhaus to Aspen: Herbert Bayer and Modernist Design in America* (Boulder, CO: Johnson Books, 2005); Frederick A. Horowitz and Brenda Danilowitz, *Josef Albers: To Open Eyes: The Bauhaus, Black Mountain College, and Yale* (London: Phaidon, 2006); Victor Margolin, *The Struggle for Utopia: Rodchenko, Lissitzky, Moholy-Nagy, 1917–1946* (Chicago: University of Chicago Press, 1997); Reinhold Martin, *The Organizational Complex: Architecture, Media, and Corporate Space* (Cambridge, MA: MIT Press, 2003); Jill E. Pearlman, *Inventing American Modernism: Joseph Hudnut, Walter Gropius, and the Bauhaus Legacy at Harvard* (Charlottesville: University of Virginia Press, 2007); Franz Schulze, *Mies van der Rohe: A Critical Biography* (Chicago: University of Chicago Press, 1985); Fred Turner, *The Democratic Surround: Multimedia and American Liberalism from World War II to the Psychedelic Sixties* (Chicago: University of Chicago Press, 2013). For the influence of Bauhaus artists and designers in Europe and the Soviet Union, see the essays collected in Philipp Oswalt, ed., *Bauhaus Conflicts, 1919–2009: Controversies and Counterparts* (Ostfildern: Hatje Cantz, 2009).

19. Josef Albers, quoted in Frederick A. Horowitz, "What Josef Albers Taught at Black Mountain College and What Black Mountain College Taught Josef Albers," *Journal of Black Mountain College Studies* 11 (Spring 2011), http://www.blackmountainstudiesjournal.org/volume-11-spring-2011/1-9-frederick-a-horowitz/.

20. Unidentified student of Josef Albers, quoted in Horowitz, "What Josef Albers Taught."

21. László Moholy-Nagy, *The New Vision: Fundamentals of Design, Painting, Sculpture, Architecture*, trans. Daphne M. Hoffmann, rev. ed. (New York: W. W. Norton, 1938), 17 and 19.

22. Ibid., 14.

23. Ibid., 16.

24. John Andrew Rice, *I Came out of the Eighteenth Century* (New York: Harper, 1942), 328; quoted in Turner, *The Democratic Surround*, 134.

25. Albers, quoted in Horowitz, "What Josef Albers Taught."

II Critical Pedagogies, Imaginaries, and Memes

3 Designing Participation

Rethinking the Bauhaus's Legacy at the MIT Media Lab

Joi Ito, Natalie Saltiel, and Andre Uhl

> What the Bauhaus of the 1920s was to steel, glass, and the assembly line, the Media Lab at the Massachusetts Institute of Technology (MIT) is to the subtle structures of electronics and communications in the high-tech 1980s.
>
> —"Inventing the Future at MIT," *New Scientist*, November 12, 1987 (review of *The Media Lab: Inventing the Future at MIT*, by Stewart Brand)

> The Media Lab is a style of thought, one characterized by ... iconoclasm, irreverence and plurality.
>
> —Nicholas Negroponte, quoted in "The New New Thing," *Times Higher Education*, December 8, 2011

What are the terms of the future today? A century after the founding of the Bauhaus, how and where do we look for visions forward? The Bauhaus, as it emerged from a historical context defined by political upheaval and instability, sought a holistic constructivism through a radical rethinking and dissolution of disciplinary boundaries. Through reexamination of modes and materials of production, the Bauhaus attempted to reimagine the creative capacity and potential of the institution. Similarly, the Media Lab unites a diverse array of themes, practices, and approaches under one roof with the intent to foster cross-pollination and crossover of intellectual, scientific, and artistic exploration.

The Bauhaus experimented with the cutting-edge technologies of its era, materials of craft including glass, metal, and wood. Today our potential media have expanded to include biological materials, code, algorithms, multidimensional modeling, and systems design. When you combine these elements with the building processes of craftspeople, industrial mass production, 3D printing, organic growth, and self-assembly, you get a very different kind of output. The way we think about how that output affects and interacts with society was a question that confronted Bauhaus designers and continues to engage designers today. What we create, and what we choose to create, cannot and should not be divorced from the contexts, both social and historical, in which we work. The Bauhaus's origins and evolution were responses to a historical era defined by political and ideological extremism, anxiety of rapid industrialization and technological change, and social instability.[1]

The Media Lab's ongoing development is shaped by our own eras, from the techno-optimism of the digital revolution toward a renewed focus on ethics and equity. The Lab has benefited from the freedom and independence of the undirected funding provided by its consortium funding structure. This structure has allowed us to use technological advances to engage with the world outside of academia. Unlike purely academic organizations, the Media Lab seeks to translate thoughtful and creative endeavors beyond theory and into practice. Past projects have included the E Ink used in e-readers (and, more recently, in smart signs that help municipalities communicate with citizens); rainbow holograms; touch screens; and a forerunner of Google Maps. More recently, research groups at the Lab have created advanced prosthetic limbs, sought ways to advance justice on Earth through technologies developed for space, invited diverse communities to improve family leave and breast pump technologies, and studied the relationship between climate change and human well-being. These are projects influenced by our current social and political climate, and are designed to transcend the laboratory and engage directly with their communities; the Lab's future work will continue to evolve with the cultures around it.

*

> The Bauhaus strives to bring together all creative effort into one whole, to reunify all the disciplines of practical art—sculpture, painting, handicrafts, and the crafts—as inseparable components of a new architecture. The ultimate, if distant, aim of the Bauhaus is the unified work of art—the great structure—in which there is no distinction between monumental and decorative art. (Walter Gropius, "Bauhaus Manifesto")

The Bauhaus perceived a new aesthetics of industrial production methods and design practice. Its early idealistic mission to reunify all the disciplines was an expression of technological and democratic optimism for a "new structure of the future."[2] As both the Bauhaus and the Lab can attest, launching such an ambitious program is rarely straightforward. In the Lab's case, securing the support of MIT and the School of Architecture and Planning allowed us the freedom to experiment, grow, and flourish. While many projects at the Lab continue to integrate formal practical and theoretical learnings from the study of architecture, the freedom of the Lab's system has allowed our work to evolve in diverse and disparate directions. Both the physical and intellectual dimensions of the Media Lab exist in a kind of "negative space," free of the deterministic and solid structures of academic disciplines and single-focus labs. One of the metaphors we use to describe the "space" of research created at the Media Lab is that of a huge piece of paper holding nearly infinite possibilities for connection. The paper is covered in black dots representing disciplines. The vast areas of white space between these dots represent what we call *antidisciplinary* space. Although many people would like to play in this white space, few academic departments provide funding, encouragement, or tenure consideration for research without a disciplinary anchor in one of the black dots—and preferably, in *only one* of the black dots. Many currently pressing issues, however, require a completely new way of thinking and doing, which is only possible if one goes beyond the notion of disciplines.

The Lab's structure encourages researchers to work horizontally across fields and take the high risk of an unconventional approach. It promotes collaboration between fields, rather than the hyperspecialization that can make communication difficult. It is an "avoidance of all rigidity; priority of creativity; freedom of individuality, but strict study discipline,"[3] which was also embraced in the founding ideology of the Bauhaus. It's an approach that values undirected research, encouraging members of the Media Lab community to ask questions that haven't been asked, and begin building prototypes even before they know exactly what they're for. As a surprising number of breakthrough inventions are found while looking for something else, as peripheral vision and intentional serendipity can maximize discovery, this focus on doing and building often yields surprising new discoveries.

The Bauhaus successfully harnessed industrial production methods while developing a new design language;[4] the Media Lab, over its history, has integrated computing and digital technologies into a distinct practice of production that regularly expands to encompass new technologies and techniques. From its inception, when Nicholas Negroponte presented former MIT President Jerome Wiesner with his vision of a laboratory that was also an academic department—a place for both science and art, where research was inseparable from learning—the Media Lab has attempted to integrate seemingly disparate influences. Its founders included Negroponte (an architect) and Wiesner (an electrical engineer), but also Marvin Minsky ("the father of artificial intelligence"), Seymour Papert (an early pioneer of children's computer science and protégé of constructivist Jean Piaget), and Muriel Cooper (MIT Press art director and the founder of MIT's Visible Language Workshop).[5]

The continued lineage of this vision can be seen in the Krebs Cycle of Creativity developed by Neri Oxman, the head of the Lab's Mediated Matter research group. It

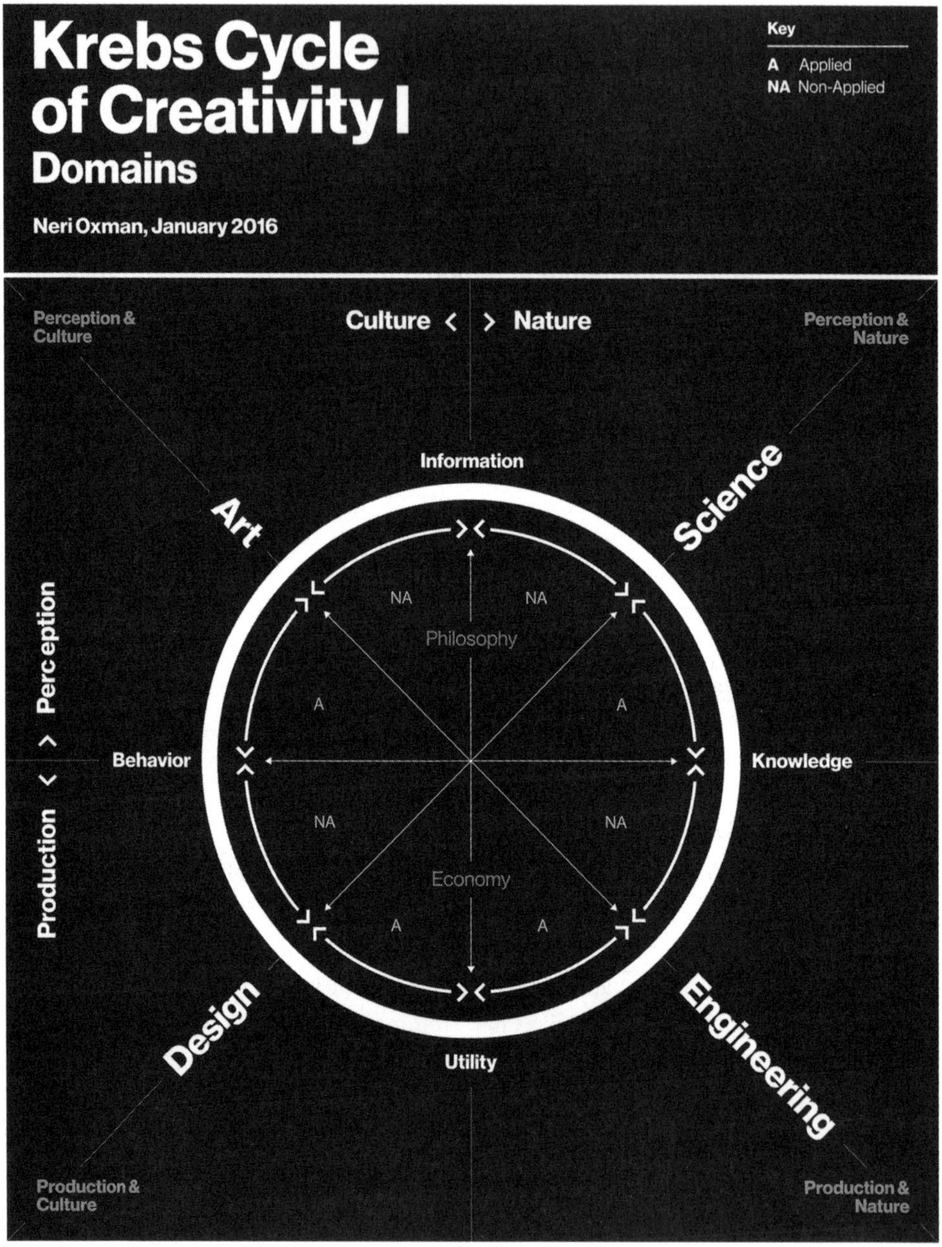
Krebs Cycle of Creativity I
Domains
Neri Oxman, January 2016
Key
A Applied
NA Non-Applied
Perception & Culture
Culture < > Nature
Perception & Nature
Information
Art
Science
NA
NA
Philosophy
A
A
Production < > Perception
Behavior
Knowledge
NA
NA
Economy
A
A
Design
Engineering
Utility
Production & Culture
Production & Nature

Figure 3.1

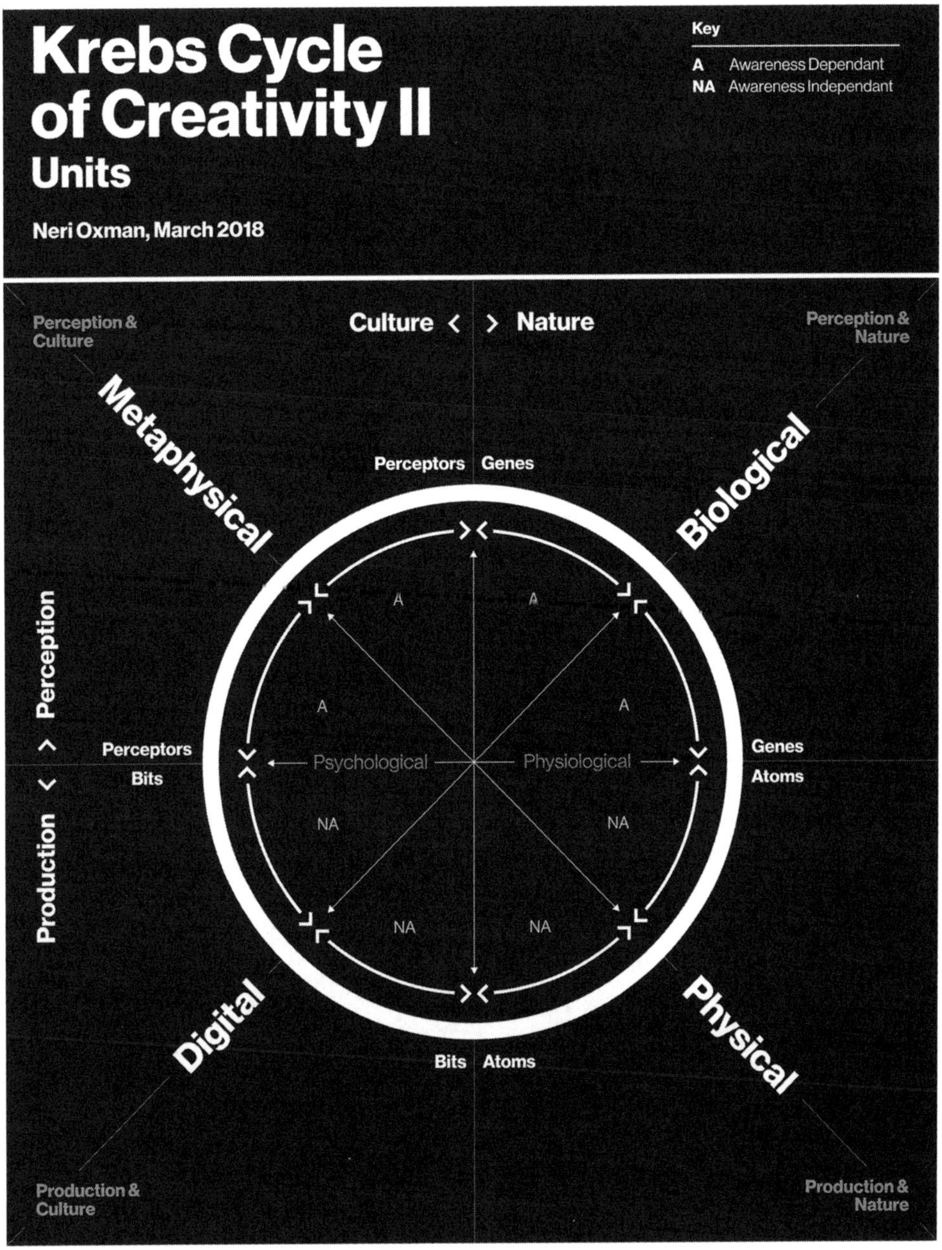
Krebs Cycle
of Creativity II
Units
Neri Oxman, March 2018
Key
A Awareness Dependant
NA Awareness Independant
Perception & Culture
Culture < > Nature
Perception & Nature
Metaphysical
Biological
Perceptors Genes
A
A
A
A
Perception > < Production
Perceptors
Bits
Psychological
Physiological
Genes
Atoms
NA
NA
NA
NA
Digital
Physical
Bits Atoms
Production & Culture
Production & Nature

Figure 3.2

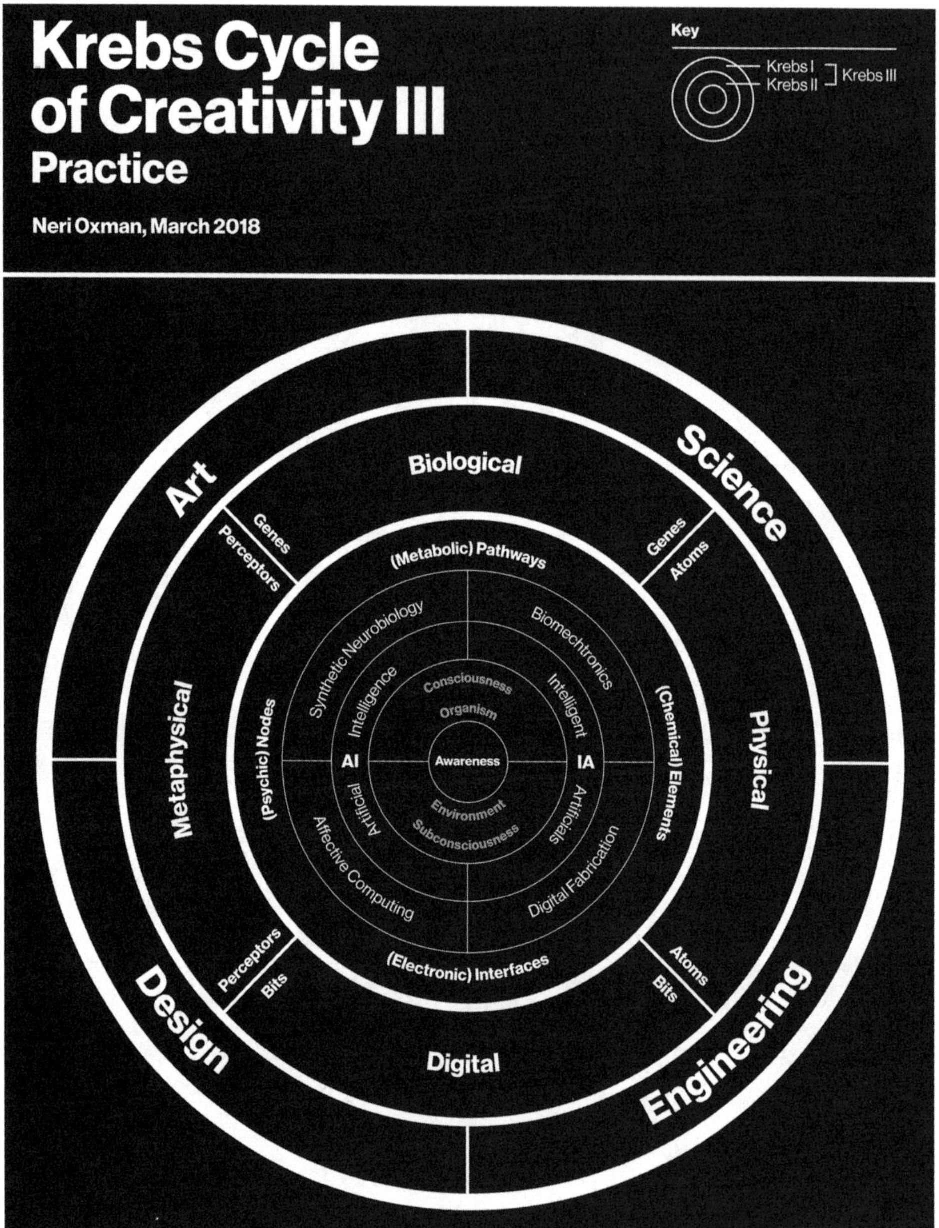
Krebs Cycle of Creativity III
Practice
Neri Oxman, March 2018
Key
Krebs I
Krebs II
Krebs III
Art
Science
Design
Engineering
Biological
Physical
Digital
Metaphysical
Genes
Perceptors
Atoms
Bits
(Metabolic) Pathways
(Chemical) Elements
(Electronic) Interfaces
(Psychic) Nodes
Synthetic Neurobiology
Biomechtronics
Digital Fabrication
Affective Computing
Intelligence
Intelligent
Artificials
Artificial
AI
IA
Consciousness
Organism
Awareness
Environment
Subconsciousness

Figure 3.3

illustrates a system of creative energy based on the interplay of science, engineering, design, and art. Science takes information and turns it into knowledge, engineering takes knowledge and turns it into utility, design takes utility and turns it into meaning and behavior, and art takes that meaning and behavior and transforms it back into information. In order for research to be meaningful and impactful, it requires all of these connections to be vital. While the link between art and science is often the weakest, it is potentially the most powerful. The Media Lab's flexibility and receptive stance to change and evolution can help encourage more connections of that type.

This synergy of art and technology is not the only parallel that links the Bauhaus and the Media Lab—we are also bound together by the use of the most advanced technologies and materials of the era, the desire to impact society, and the search for a new culture and sensibility suitable for the time. A century ago, there was a clearer separation between the artificial and the organic; today, domains like synthetic biology and artificial intelligence increase our opportunities to design and deploy directly into the realm of "nature," and in many ways even to "design" nature. Thus, the distinctions between the natural and the artificial have blurred or even disappeared.

*

Every period in history is defined by a paradigm that arises from its materials and particular opportunities and threats. 1985, when the Media Lab was founded, was an optimistic moment for digital technology, promising to empower individuals by giving them voice and agency and enriching garage and dorm room entrepreneurs in the process—shifting power from stodgy, restrictive institutions to young and radical entrepreneurs. Alan Kay was telling us that "you predict the future by inventing it." And many of that era's predictions have come true. We have supercomputers in our pockets in the form of smart phones, artificially intelligent assistants, autonomous vehicles, and a global network of nearly instantaneous communication and knowledge transmission. News has thrown off the yoke of legacy media organizations, allowing the new emergent voices of the internet to reign. Democratic elections have wrestled themselves free of the control of traditional political machines.

However, the consequences of the amazing transformations that many believed would foster love, peace, and prosperity are more complicated than we ever imagined. In too many ways, the optimism of the past three decades has been undermined and darkened by the effects and successes of our technological inventions. The intervening years have given us the time and distance to reflect upon the choices and responsibilities we incurred by "inventing the future." We now see that the paradigms of transformation and growth cannot fail to ask: "Good for whom over what time scale?" The young entrepreneurs may have conquered the rigid organizations, but they have failed to replace them with viable alternatives. As a result, they have contributed to the pervasive mistrust and destabilization of once respected social and political institutions. Despite our optimism, our inventions and technologies affected the world's complex social, political, and cultural systems in ways we did not intend or anticipate.

*

At a time when the influence of science and technology is increasing in scope and significance, how do we begin to rethink the place of humanity and the relationship between ourselves and our creations? The practitioners of Bauhaus theory carried their political and aesthetic values into realizing their visions; where do we embed our agency in confronting the challenges that we face today? The Media Lab has long taken up the mantle of nontraditional work at the intersection of art, design, science, and technology, but as we enter a new era marked by political instability and the promise of imminent technological disruption, we need to rethink the tools, practices, and outputs of our research and production.

New mediums and interventions enable a new scope of possibilities, but they also present us with new questions and responsibilities. By redirecting the development of design to the future of science, we may be able to encourage the emergence of a new kind of design and science, where designers and scientists are no longer central planners but rather participants within the systems they inhabit.

At the Media Lab, students are encouraged to design across scales and to reflect on how their decisions simultaneously impact various layers, from microbial to astrophysical to sociopolitical and technical inequities. Since it is impossible for designers and scientists to deterministically control such complex self-adaptive systems, it is crucial to develop a sensibility about one's role as a participant in them. Increasingly, we must perceive, understand, and take responsibility for our impact both within and across systems. As the boundaries between the natural and the artificial collapse, we must be conscious of how these systems affect each other and how our impact on them often causes unintended consequences for us. As participants, we can engage with each of these systems so long as we remain aware and perceptive of the systems we are in. A participant concept of design is a fundamental reevaluation of modernist modes of thinking, which presumed that we could "invent the future" with direction and intentionality. It demands a shift from exercising control toward embracing integration, questioning how relationships between the parts define the mechanisms of a system, and understanding how each system interacts and forms relationships with other systems. It necessitates reciprocity between designers, communities, and end users. And ultimately it entails the inclusion of voices and options that have too often been overlooked and disregarded

As designers across scales, we recognize the shortcomings of the common notion that growth is the solution to everything. Rather, growth can be the cause of system failures in many contexts. In a healthy system, regulatory mechanisms manage inflows and outflows, but evolution optimized for growth leads to the development of runaway positive feedback loops that exceed many of those regulatory mechanisms and causes entire systems to become dangerously unbalanced. The most pressing issues of this century, including climate change, health crises, and social inequality, must be considered earlier in the process of technological development. We need to expand the scope of the conversation and engage scholars from the humanities and the social sciences to help us reflect and consider the social and ethical implications of technological inventions and interventions.

In the early days of the Media Lab, the constructivist approach it favored excluded most social scientists who studied and discussed things but didn't *build* things. In our time period, where opportunities have become problems, participant design must be inclusive and learn how to design for the benefit of an entire system. This will involve engaging many of the disciplines, institutions, and controls that we previously disregarded as impediments or irrelevant. Today, many of our research groups have social scientists tightly integrated into their labs. We have ethicists working with genomics researchers to empower indigenous peoples to control the use of CRISPR gene drive in their environments, lawyers working with machine learning experts to mitigate the negative impact of algorithms in the criminal justice system, and ethnographers working with satellite engineers to advance justice in Earth's complex systems.

In turning away from solutionist ways of thinking, participant designers must wrestle with a universe of deep questions. The most important of these is how to design for the benefit of an entire system and not only for maximum growth and the benefit of a handful of players in it. Who does the system benefit, and over what time scale? How do we integrate thoughtful and ethical design early on in our practice? In what ways do we need to reconfigure the incentives that we have helped to develop through the technologies we have designed and deployed? The Bauhaus and the Media Lab have both promoted integration and inclusivity among disciplines, but what can the Media Lab learn from the radical willingness of the Bauhaus to evolve when we reconsider redesigning our methods of production?

While the Bauhaus created a space for the human element and human exploratory practices to make contact with modern materials and fabrication capabilities, the Media Lab is now on a mission to develop and thoughtfully design interfaces between nature, technology, and society that support balance and sustainability. We are still at the beginning, but it is exactly the nonduality of these apparent opposites that becomes tangible in a nondisciplinary space and will set the tone for a new culture of flourishing at the Media Lab and beyond.

Notes

1. Elaine S. Hochman, *Bauhaus: Crucible of Modernism* (New York: Fromm International, 1997).

2. Walter Gropius, "Bauhaus Manifesto and Program" (1919), https://dessaubauhaus.wordpress.com/page/2/.

3. Ibid.

4. Hochman, *Bauhaus: Crucible of Modernism.*

5. Cooper was also responsible for the design of *The Bauhaus* (Cambridge, MA: MIT Press, 1969).

4 Situating *Machenhäuser*

Carol Strohecker

> The Bauhaus was not an institution with a clear program—it was an idea, and Gropius formulated this idea with great precision. ... The fact that it was an idea, I think, is the cause of this enormous influence the Bauhaus had on every progressive school around the globe. You cannot do that with organization, you cannot do that with propaganda. Only an idea spreads so far.
>
> —Ludwig Mies van der Rohe[1]

Characteristics of the Bauhaus curriculum and learning environment emigrated with Walter Gropius, Josef Albers, and others as they left Germany and settled in new homes. Concepts and practices that distinguished the Bauhaus gradually appeared at other schools and took root according to conditions of new locales. Themes from the Bauhaus continue to resound among art, design, manufacturing, labor, education, community, and life. Perhaps these interrelating themes could now inform learning environments deliberately aiming to develop cooperative and resilient global culture.

The recent evolution of Arizona State University (ASU) might be seen as an initial foray. Projecting transformative potentials for higher education in terms of scale and risk, ASU president Michael Crow charts a progression from Greek academies to European medieval universities, German and American research universities, and American land grant universities, toward the emergence of a broadly inclusive, entrepreneurial "new American university."[2]

An earlier context for Bauhaus themes began with William Barton Rogers envisioning a "new polytechnic institute,"[3] founded as the Massachusetts Institute of Technology (MIT) two days before the start of the Civil War. American land grant universities were spawned a year later as a response to industrialization, with the 1862 Morrill Act providing federal resources for states' broad education of their citizenry. The focus on "agriculture and the mechanic arts"[4] is reflected in the stated purposes of contemporaneous institutions. Many schools included farmland and agricultural research; some focused on development of technologies and manufacturing techniques based in urban settings. As these institutions developed, industry progressed while trade and labor unions struggled to ensure decent pay, reasonable hours, and safe environments for workers. Disputes and power plays sharpened socioeconomic class divisions.

Massachusetts designated MIT as one of its land grant universities. Ellen Swallow Richards became the first woman to graduate from MIT, in 1873—four years before a group of women in Rhode Island founded a museum and school to enrich culture and methods associated with industrial manufacturing, particularly of textiles and silver-based jewelry and ware.[5] Through an emphasis later echoed by Walter Gropius, these founders of the Rhode Island School of Design (RISD) aimed to infuse the functional concerns of industry with aesthetic sensibilities.

In 1890, the second Morrill Act emphasized preparation of teachers and prohibited distribution of the federal funds to schools "where the distinction of race or color is made in the admission of students."[6] Two years later, the first African-American to graduate from MIT moved to Tuskegee Institute, where preparation for the "mechanical industries" included architectural drawing and design.

Across the ocean, in heavily industrialized regions of Germany, the Bauhaus flourished from 1919 to 1933. Like RISD's founders, Gropius wanted to infuse craft-based manufacturing with knowledge and sensibilities from the fine arts. His agenda was not only aesthetic, however: he wanted to blur boundaries of socioeconomic classes, as well as of arts and crafts. He aimed to develop a values-based culture of learning that would generate objects and places improving everyday life for all people. Through mass production, the middle classes would create things to nurture body and spirit—things that would be beautiful as well as functional. The "arrogant barrier between craftsmen and artists"[7] would dissolve.

The Bauhaus curriculum, therefore, ranged across scales and media, to encompass painting, textiles, sculpture, architecture, interior design, typography, and graphic design, as well as "industrial" design. Through these modalities, students explored line and shape, material and form, proportion and scale, space and movement, pattern and rhythm, light and color, even optical illusions. A sense of purpose came from the belief that things for people to use and places for them to inhabit should reflect "life itself," thus requiring the artist/designer to have "an intimate knowledge of biological, social, technical and artistic problems."[8] This curriculum could not sanction narrow specialization.

Furthermore, Gropius asserted, "to make a unity out of all these different branches of human activity, a strong character is required." As individuals engaged their broad studies and creative endeavors, dialogues in the immediate context would enrich and improve designed outcomes, while the surrounding culture would sift through the results over time. Ultimately, subsequent generations would determine criteria defining persistent quality. These critical acts would come to characterize a healthy society in which "diversity is ... the very source of true democracy."[9]

To enact this beneficent curriculum, students worked on what we would now call "real-world problems": Gropius and colleagues brought commissioned work into the learning environment so students could come to understand the human needs, as well as economics, conditioning their creative work. Students, teachers, and clients all engaged in the critical dialogue. This entrepreneurial approach, as well as Gropius's insistence on inclusiveness, remarkably foreshadow Michael Crow's "new American university":

> I tried to put the emphasis of my work on integration and co-ordination, inclusiveness, not exclusiveness, for I felt that the art of building is contingent upon the co-ordinated teamwork of a band of active collaborators whose co-operation symbolizes the co-operative organism of what we call society.[10]

Perhaps an even more recognizable version of the Bauhaus experiment has evolved since the 1970s, as the MIT Media Lab emerged in tandem with personal computers and the internet. The Media Lab enacts an updated version of Gropius's vision, collaborating with a range of companies and dubbing the broad-ranging creative context "antidisciplinary."[11] As a student there,[12] I participated in the 1985 dedication of the Wiesner Building and initiated discussions among peers concerned with censorship, authorship, ownership, and other ethical issues coming to light in those early days of networked computing. Later I was among researchers at the partnering Media Lab Europe (MLE), involving in projects of my "Everyday Learning" group collaborators from different disciplines, sectors, cultures, and generations. Over the years I have evolved my own spin of arts, design, sciences, and engineering,[13] and their interaction with production, labor, education, community, and life.

Moving from MLE's base in Dublin, I arrived in the Piedmont region of North Carolina, about 138 miles (222 kilometers) east of where Josef and Anni Albers had settled when entering the United States 73 years earlier. In 1933, the Bauhaus had closed as Adolf Hitler came to power in Germany. Luminaries including Gropius, László Moholy-Nagy, and the Alberses fled the Nazis: Gropius went to England and then Harvard; Moholy-Nagy to England and then Chicago; and the Alberses to the Blue Ridge Mountains of North Carolina, where Black Mountain College (BMC) was beginning to form. The iconoclastic educator and BMC cofounder John Andrew Rice had sent Josef Albers a telegram inviting him to join the BMC faculty. "I do not speak one word English," replied Albers. "Come anyway," said the return telegram.[14] The Alberses found a welcoming context at BMC, near Asheville.

Several lines of thought converged as BMC developed during the next 24 years: the importance of Albers's version of the Bauhaus curriculum and John Dewey's educational philosophies have long been recognized; influences from BMC's surrounding geography and culture perhaps less so. Surely one of these influences was the Asheville Farm School (AFS), founded in 1894. North Carolina had designated two land grant universities and the AFS was not one of them; nevertheless, its mission to engage members of a community in learning means of production for their own sustenance was compatible with the mission of community-facing agricultural colleges that had received resources through the Morrill Act. The AFS added a hands-on approach to learning that has sustained since its transitions in 1942 to a coed junior college and in the mid-1960s to the four-year Warren Wilson College. That school's profile echoes BMC themes, through the "philosophy of integrated work, community engagement, and academics" in the setting of a student-run, working farm and the notion of "campus as" classroom/laboratory/studio.[15]

In the early twentieth century, timber from the mountainous area around Asheville and the foothills to the east fed development of a thriving furniture industry. By 1913 the town of High Point hosted the Southern Exposition,[16] which rivaled manufacturing centers in the North and eventually lent sophisticated woodworking to the repertoire for artist/crafters at BMC. Whether laboring over an exquisite cabinet or making a necklace with acorns and other found objects, BMC residents experimented with materials, techniques, and intellectual turf as fertile as Cecil soil and as malleable as red Cecil clay.

As the High Point Furniture Market was burgeoning, Columbia University professor John Dewey published *Democracy and Education*. This 1916 work is an exploration of the importance of interactions between citizen and community, self and society, in forming and appreciating public opinion. Rice and Dewey likely met in 1931, at a conference in Florida on the Curriculum for the Liberal Arts College.[17] They maintained a dialogue for the next several years, as BMC matured and Dewey became one of its advisors. In 1934, Dewey published *Art as Experience*, explaining art as the "capacity to work a vague idea and emotion over into terms of some definite medium."[18] In his 1938 *Experience and Education*, Dewey elaborated themes of art and expression, identifying "two principles which are fundamental in the constitution of experience: the principles of interaction and of continuity."[19] This contrapuntal relation resonates with Gropius's idea of culture extending through time to provide a stabilizing, quality-assessing context for expressions of individual creativity.

Also in 1934, Moholy-Nagy's articulation of his *New Vision* set the agenda for the "New Bauhaus," now the IIT Institute of Design in Chicago. Maintaining focuses on material (surface treatment, painting), volume (sculpture), and space (architecture), he echoed Gropius in invoking democratic values, foundations of artistic expression, and their reliance on coordinated experience. As if in dialogue with Dewey, Moholy-Nagy emphasized the importance of individual experience to learning and education. He further clarified that learning through self-expression depends on awareness of one's own developing capacities. Jonathan Fisher notes, in turn, that "constant reflection, coupled with intelligently directed action was ... the basis for the general curriculum of Black Mountain College." Proximity to the AFS, along with sheer necessity, may have influenced how this "action" manifested:

> Students' lives at Black Mountain included much more than just study. There were always other projects and other work to be done, including farm work, textile work like the weaving of curtains, administrative tasks like college bookkeeping and even the construction of the Studies Building designed and overseen by Bauhaus architect, Walter Gropius. ... This relatively flat, decentralized organizational structure, in which every student and teacher was expected to contribute not only to the academic life but also to the manual labor which sustained the school was firmly rooted in John Dewey's belief that educational experiences should never be artificially delimited.[20]

At BMC, "living" and "learning" were intertwined: "as much real education took place over the coffee cups as in the classrooms. ... The usual distinctions between curricular and extracurricular activities, between work done in a classroom and work done outside it, were broken down. ... From the beginning Black Mountain emphasized the social responsibilities that come from being part of a community, yet tried to see to it that personal freedom wouldn't be sacrificed to group needs."[21] This "commitment to a radically more democratic organizational structure"[22] constituted both founding vision and day-to-day practice at BMC.

Albers held the comparable view that "all creative work moves between the two polarities: intuition and intellect, or possibly between subjectivity and objectivity."[23] Like Dewey, Albers characterized education in terms of the importance of students' direct personal experience and their freedom to experiment. And like Moholy-Nagy, Albers grounded his educational principles on explorations of "the possibilities and limits of materials."[24] He wanted to "'open the eyes' of students by disrupting ingrained habits of perception and considering forms apart from their conventional associations, reduced to their basic characteristics (line, shape, material, color). His strategies of 'defamiliarization,' such as drawing with the non-dominant hand, mirror writing, exploring optical illusions, and representing 'negative' spaces ... are now an accepted part of the academic training of visual artists."[25] Such exercises develop self-awareness as well as artistic finesse, helping the student prepare for negotiating relations between self and society.

Albers especially enjoyed juxtaposing colors to demonstrate how they change value in relation to each other: "when you really understand that each color is changed by a changed environment, you eventually find that you have learned about life as well as about color."[26]

Albers, Dewey, and Rice all pointed to such larger lessons from artistic experimentation. Albers asserted that art connects to every realm of human interest. By providing new ways of seeing and encouraging self-reflection, it could spark interest in science or any topic and build character. Rice, also, espoused this more general view:

> In the process of working with paints, sounds, and words, Rice thought the student might well express something of his inner being, but in his view, the far more important educative aspects of the "art-experience" lay elsewhere—in the discovery of "integrity." ...
>
> He was not chiefly interested in producing painters, musicians, poets, but in making democrats, people capable of choosing what it was they proposed to believe in, what was going to be their world. ...
>
> The integrity an artist learns when dealing with materials, translates into an integrity of "relationship with oneself and with other men."[27]

Having inherited sensibilities from the Bauhaus, BMC demonstrated how self and society could advance through service-oriented community action coupled with rigorous scholarly and creative work. In essence, this is the mission of today's land grant universities. As BMC enacted these ideals, they came to influence the development of nearby educational and artistic organizations. BMC faculty and visitors helped to condition the culture around Asheville,[28] which persists as a mecca for those interested in beautifully crafted forms.[29] Sometimes members of the BMC community traveled eastward to Raleigh, contributing to North Carolina State University's School (now College) of Design and places along the way.

In 2006, I arrived in the state's Piedmont Triad area, roughly halfway between Asheville and Raleigh. The cities of High Point, Greensboro, and Winston-Salem define this north-central part of North Carolina, just as Raleigh, Durham, and Chapel Hill define the Research Triangle to the east. My biases toward "learning by doing" and the value of interdisciplinary, intersectoral, intergenerational environments to support learning through creative processes—formulated through work at MIT's Media Lab, which itself inherited from the Bauhaus (as well as from Piaget and other seminal thinkers)—had been reasonably well received in Europe's cosmopolitan and high-tech contexts. North Carolinians seemed also to accept these ideas, though they inflected them with even stronger emphases on community and materiality. Here I found well-developed notions of self-reliance in the context of a self-sustaining community and respect for intense focusing on physical processes for handling and manipulating materials. I came to understand these preferences and the proliferation of arts organizations in terms of BMC's history and its Bauhaus lineage.

In 1949, while BMC was in full swing, a local Junior League raised $7,200 to form the Arts Council of Winston-Salem and Forsyth County, said to be the first locally established arts council in the United States.[30] At least one of its founders was later involved in forming the National Endowment for the Arts (NEA). Also in Winston-Salem is SECCA (the Southeastern Center for Contemporary Art), which has evolved through three phases since 1956 to become a national-level promoter and exhibitor of visual arts.[31] SECCA had a moment of infamy in 1989, as debates about the use of NEA funds to display photographs by Robert Mapplethorpe raised issues of censorship.[32] Winston-Salem also hosts the Piedmont Craftsmen, a competitive guild of craft artists and collectors founded in 1963.[33] That same year, North Carolina's governor Terry Sanford and renowned author John Ehle convinced the state's General Assembly to create a performing arts conservatory, now known as the University of North Carolina School of the Arts.[34] The lobby of one of its buildings displays a quote from Sanford: "I would like to scratch on the wall, somewhere at the North Carolina School of the Arts, neatly and in artistic style of course: 'This institution is unorthodox and heretical.'" After BMC's closure, it took only six years for its zeitgeist to find a new home—and a Galaxie 500 heading east on Route 40 could get there in a couple of hours.

In 2003, members of the Piedmont Triad community responded to downturns in the furniture, textiles, and tobacco manufacturing industries by identifying design as the basis of a strategy for community economic development.[35] They envisioned a design center to become part of an urban research park reclaiming warehouses and other abandoned structures, to revitalize the urban landscape while educating people about creative processes—particularly supported by digital technologies.[36] The Center for Design Innovation (CDI) resulted from this concerted effort. CDI is now organized as a multicampus consortium within the UNC public university system.[37] As CDI's inaugural director,[38] I catalyzed creative projects ranging across disciplines and involving members of area businesses, state and local governments, and nonprofit organizations. Students worked with artists and designers, biologists and biotech researchers, engineers and computer specialists, dancers and musicians. Programmatic themes included urban farming, bike trails, "STEM to STEAM," data visualizations, and various forms of social and economic entrepreneurship. Current focuses include motion capture and special effects for dynamic media.

This is the context, more than any other, that taught me what a community can achieve when people articulate a common goal and pull together to accomplish it. I had lived in coastal areas all my life, yet this is the context in which I first heard the expression "All boats float on a rising tide." In parallel with the effort to finance and co-create a center for community-based learning through creative processes and digital techniques, there were painfully honest, self-reflective exercises challenging race-related health disparities and other inequities. This was a community actively engaged in reinventing itself, through an ever-expanding array of individuals stepping forward to participate. BMC and the Bauhaus continue to reverberate through the "can-do" attitude of this community and the sustenance of convivial relationships between people and their tools and environments.

One young entrepreneur who founded a local fair-trade coffee shop and a wine bar—for which he made beautifully hand-crafted wooden furnishings—is fond of saying, "The journey is the destination." He might as well be related to Rice, who believed educators have a responsibility to "show [the young] that ... the only thing on which they can rely with assurance is the experience of the quest."[39] BMC encouraged individual, self-aware creativity in the context of community as an analog for life in a healthy democracy, and BMC's nearby descendants continue to enact that principle. They seem instinctively to understand that achieving an effective balance relies on continually shifting emphases on the part and the whole, the self and the culture, and tending to relations between the two. Prolonged favoring of one over the other or ignoring connections between them could threaten progress, if not survival, and tip beyond democracy toward more extreme individualism or socialism.

At one point in CDI, anticipating focuses on computer-based imaging techniques as we rallied collaborators to organize the 2010 instantiation of the Design, Art, and Technology Symposium,[40] I was initially surprised when volunteers from the community opted for a theme around food production and preparation. But then I realized how deeply, in this culture, agriculture and gardening are contexts for learning and food is a medium for expression, a binder of community, and a currency for interpersonal exchange. I was at the table with spiritual descendants of BMC and, through them, the Bauhaus.

Culture circles forward. It is intriguing to note the 2012 essay in which an MIT student calls for symmetric completion of that institution's land grant mission, by acknowledging the convergence of "agriculture" and "mechanic arts" (in the language of the 1862 Morrill Act):

> The current global agricultural system constitutes the nexus of biological, chemical, civil, environmental and mechanical engineering. ...

> At this time of realignment of our institutional initiatives, it behooves President Reif, Provost Kaiser, and the faculty to consider the addition of a course of study and research in agricultural science and engineering as a way to meet the word of the law and justify MIT's designation as a land grant institution, but more importantly, to begin to engage in this great challenge of our time.[41]

Industrial advances prompted societal changes that led to the Morrill Act and the founding of America's land grant universities. These advances also contributed to the emergence of the Bauhaus. Through art-inspired, practically informed design, the Bauhaus strived to reduce class inequity and spin a context for individuals and community in democratic balance. Students' engagement in creative work would help them to understand their own abilities and values. Today we are again seeing rapid technological advancement, while the reach of each subculture in our global society is expanding. Unfortunately, themes of 1930s Germany seem to be recurring as well: fear of an unknown economic future, fear of the unfamiliar, perhaps fear of fear itself. As in pre-World War II culture, class distinctions underlie current fears—yet now we are losing sleep over class differences so extreme the Bauhaus could have imagined them only in caricature. And we are moving too slowly in figuring how to cooperate in order to address global-scale environmental shifts.

As if circling back to Gropius, in 2018 the National Academies of Sciences, Engineering, and Medicine issued a call for integration of disciplinary knowledge in higher education.[42] This "integration" represents a departure from universities' tendency to self-organize based on grouping relatively narrow specializations. Facing grand challenges such as causes and effects of climate change, we can only hope that this call is not too little, too late:

> Though causal evidence on the impact of integration on students is limited, it is this committee's consensus opinion that further effort be expeditiously exerted to develop and disseminate a variety of approaches to integrated education and that further research on the impact of such programs and courses on students be supported and conducted.[43]

If we are now too little, too late in avoiding climate change, our collective inability in recent decades to communicate effectively about dangerous trends, possible alternatives, and necessary mitigations may be partly to blame. Dennis Meadows, former leader of the MIT team who prepared the 1972 *Limits to Growth* report for the Club of Rome,[44] claims "it is too late for sustainable development."[45] He bemoans the difficulty of communicating to achieve broad understanding of scientific phenomena. The 1972 report concluded with this daunting caution:

> If the present growth trends in world population, industrialization, pollution, and resource depletion continue unchanged, the limits to growth on this planet will be reached sometime within the next one hundred years.[46]

In both the report and widely disseminated versions intended for a lay audience, the authors explained why the growth of population and industrial output is inherently exponential; showed that exponential growth quickly rises to any conceivable limit; described computer scenarios demonstrating that the currently prevailing growth policies would lead to overshoot and collapse (not asymptotic approach to limits); and suggested that changes in those policies "could lead to a sustainable state, if the changes dealt with both cultural and technical issues and were implemented soon."[47] Millions of copies of *Limits* sold worldwide, and over the years there have been many efforts to further disseminate the results and educate the public.[48] Yet, unfortunately, today's situation is consistent with the collapse scenarios. Meadows laments:

> The public has difficulty with subtle and conditional messages. ... With roughly half of our scenarios being equilibrium, you would imagine that over the last forty years, roughly half of the media illustrations of our work would show the equilibrium runs. But you would be wrong. I have never—I think, in forty years, I have never seen any newspaper, any journal, any television program, show the equilibrium scenarios from our runs. They focus on overshoot and collapse ... nuanced, conditional discussions are not what the media likes. We're not the only ones to suffer from this. The climate scientists, these days, face exactly the same problem. People can deal with weather predictions because they're short-term and demonstrably provable—or not—but when a climate scientist gets up and starts talking about scenarios ... it's very, very difficult for the media to give any sort of realistic and educational summary of the work.[49]

How can we convey complexities and subtleties inherent in scientific work, given the sound bite mentality of mass media and the still primitive state of our ability to communicate globally? We need to communicate deeply and on a global scale, and we have no Esperanto to rely on. Perhaps we are missing opportunities in the broad recognizability of visual imagery. Techniques for producing photographs, illustrations, movies, and animations yield potentials for richly meaningful renditions of ideas; yet eye candy proliferates. And, evidently, many people are gullible by fake news, much of which relies on images deliberately constructed to warp or deceive.

Along with developing integrated research efforts and educational settings, we need *Machenhäuser* focused on evolving visual vernaculars through which we can represent difficult concepts with fidelity and sophistication. Might we find a method in returning to Bauhaus explorations of line and shape, material and form, proportion and scale, space and movement, pattern and rhythm, light and color? Could nurturing self-reflective practice, in balance with community service, now support an emergent web of diverse and robustly democratic cultures—in contrast to islands of fearfully insulated, self-protective interests?

In addition to building from Bauhaus fundamentals and defamiliarization strategies, we could explore extensions of globally recognizable logotypes; Scott McCloud's theses about combining the verbal, visual, and spatial;[50] and data visualizations as elucidated by Edward Tufte[51] and practiced by the likes of Ben Fry[52] and the *New York Times*.[53] Our challenge—likely unreachable but perhaps worth setting as a high bar—would be figuring how to expand from emoji and Xu Bing's wordless "book that anyone can read"[54] to purely visual equivalents of classics such as *Hamlet* and *The Origin of Species*. Each situation for such an ambitious *Machenhaus* would present its own local conditions, both historic and cultural, modulating the perpetuation of Bauhaus principles and ideals. But all of these environments would aim to support students in their development of character and discernment, along with visual strategies, as they become self-aware global citizens cooperating to make a better world.

Notes

1. Hans M. Wingler, *The Bauhaus: Weimar, Dessau, Berlin, Chicago* (Cambridge, MA: MIT Press, 1978), vii.

2. Michael M. Crow, "Building an Entrepreneurial University," based on remarks made at the Third Annual Kauffman Foundation-Max Planck Institute Entrepreneurship Research Conference, Munich, June 8, 2008, accessed August 26, 2018, https://president.asu.edu/sites/default/files/Building%20an%20Entrepreneurial%20University%20(Germany)%20060808%20Kauffman-Planck%20Conference_0.pdf.

3. "MIT Facts: Top Ten MIT History Facts," MIT Libraries-Archives, accessed August 26, 2018, https://libraries.mit.edu/mithistory/mit-facts/.

4. "Morrill Act (1862)," information excerpted from Milestone Documents in the National Archives, National Archives and Records Administration, accessed August 26, 2018, https://www.ourdocuments.gov/doc.php?flash=true&doc=33.

5. "Mission and History," RISD Museum, accessed August 26, 2018, https://risdmuseum.org/about/mission_history.

6. "Second Morrill Act Redux: America's 1890s Land Grant Universities Academic Excellence," United States Department of Agriculture, National Institute of Food and Agriculture, July 15, 2015, accessed August 26, 2018, https://nifa.usda.gov/blog/second-morrill-act-redux-america's-1890s-land-grant-universities-academic-excellence.

7. "Bauhaus," The Art Story Foundation, accessed August 26, 2018, https://www.theartstory.org/movement-bauhaus.htm.

8. Walter Gropius, *The Scope of Total Architecture* (New York: Collier, 1943/1937), 18.

9. Ibid., 13.

10. Ibid., 19.

11. "About the Lab: Mission & History," MIT Media Lab, last updated May 16, 2018, https://www.media.mit.edu/about/mission-history/.

12. "Alumni," MIT Media Lab, accessed August 26, 2018, https://www.media.mit.edu/people/alumni/.

13. "Network for Sciences, Engineering, Arts and Design." SEAD, accessed August 26, 2018, http://sead.viz.tamu.edu.

14. Martin Duberman, *Black Mountain: An Exploration in Community* (Evanston: Northwestern University Press, 1972), 42.

15. "History," Warren Wilson College, accessed August 26, 2018, https://www.warren-wilson.edu/about/history/.

16. "The Evolution of the High Point Market: Roots of the Market," *Furniture Today*, April 25, 2009, accessed August 26, 2018, http://www.furnituretoday.com/article/359027-the-evolution-of-the-high-point-market/.

17. Jonathan Fisher, "The Life and Work of an Institution of Progressive Higher Education: Towards a History of Black Mountain College, 1933–1949," *Journal of Black Mountain College Studies* 6 (2014), accessed August 26, 2018, http://www.blackmountainstudiesjournal.org/volume-6-alma-stone-williams-race-democracy-arts-and-crafts-and-writers-at-bmc-summer-2014/6-fisher-halfway-formatted-use-other-version/.

18. John Dewey, *Art as Experience* (New York: Perigee Books, 1934), 75.

19. John Dewey, *Experience and Education: The Kappa Delta Pi Lecture Series* (New York: Collier/Macmillan, 1938), 51.

20. Fisher, "The Life and Work of an Institution of Progressive Higher Education."

21. Martin Duberman, *Black Mountain*, 25–27.

22. Fisher, "The Life and Work of an Institution of Progressive Higher Education."

23. Ibid.

24. Ibid.

25. "Josef Albers: American Painter, Poet, Sculptor, Teacher, and Theoretician," The Art Story Foundation, accessed August 26, 2018, http://www.theartstory.org/artist-albers-josef.htm.

26. Martin Duberman, *Black Mountain*, 54–56.

27. Ibid., 39–40.

28. "Welcome to the Southern Highland Craft Guild," Southern Highland Craft Guild, accessed August 26, 2018, https://www.southernhighlandguild.org.

29. "Asheville: Discovery, Inside and Out," ExploreAsheville.com, accessed August 26, 2018, https://www.exploreasheville.com/things-to-do/arts/.

30. "About Us," The Arts Council of Winston-Salem and Forsyth County, accessed August 26, 2018, http://intothearts.org/about/.

31. "About," Southeastern Center for Contemporary Art, accessed August 26, 2018, http://secca.org/about.php.

32. Alan G. Artner, "The Eye of the Storm: Mapplethorpe's Unblinking Vision Sparked a Continuing Battle over Art," *Chicago Tribune*, December 31, 1989, accessed August 26, 2018, http://articles.chicagotribune.com/1989-12-31/entertainment/8903220038_1_sam-wagstaff-robert-mapplethorpe-janet-kardon/2.

33. "History," Piedmont Craftsmen, accessed August 26, 2018, http://piedmontcraftsmen.org/about/history/.

34. "We Promise This. You'll Do What You Love," University of North Carolina School of the Arts, accessed August 26, 2018, http://www.uncsa.edu.

35. "Northwest North Carolina Comprehensive Economic Development Strategy / Forsyth County Economic Development Strategy" (AngelouEconomics, Austin, December 2003), accessed August 26, 2018, http://www.cdiunc.org/Info/2003ForsythStrategy.pdf.

36. "Report: Design Center Study. Presented to: Northwest Piedmont Council of Governments" (AngelouEconomics, Austin, September 2005), accessed August 26, 2018, http://www.cdiunc.org/Info/2005DesignCenterStudy.pdf.

37. "About the Center," Center for Design Innovation, accessed August 26, 2018, http://cdiwsnc.org/splash/, http://www.cdiunc.org.

38. Chris Richter, "Designing Woman Seeks to Shape Triad Economy," *Business North Carolina*, People, January 2007, updated September 16, 2011, http://businessnc.com/designing-woman-seeks-to-shape-triad-economycategory/.

39. Mary Emma Harris, *The Arts at Black Mountain College* (Cambridge, MA: MIT Press, 1987), 59.

40. "DATS'10: Design, Art and Technology Symposium," Center for Design Innovation, accessed August 26, 2018, https://www.uncsa.edu/pressreleases/Releases2010/Sept10/DATS10.pdf.

41. Addison Killean Stark, "Living Up to MIT's Land Grant Commitment," *The Tech*, September 21, 2012, accessed August 26, 2018, https://thetech.com/2012/09/21/killean-v132-n39.

42. "Branches from the Same Tree: A National Convening on the Integration of Arts, Humanities, and STEMM in Higher Education," National Academies of Sciences, Engineering, and Medicine, accessed August 26, 2018, http://sites.nationalacademies.org/pga/bhew/branches/.

43. David Skorton and Ashley Bear, eds., "The Integration of the Humanities and Arts with Sciences, Engineering, and Medicine in Higher Education: Branches from the Same Tree," National Academies of Sciences, Engineering, and Medicine; Policy and Global Affairs; Board on Higher

Education and Workforce; Committee on Integrating Higher Education in the Arts, Humanities, Sciences, Engineering, and Medicine, Consensus Study Report, 2018, accessed August 26, 2018, https://www.nap.edu/catalog/24988/the-integration-of-the-humanities-and-arts-with-sciences-engineering-and-medicine-in-higher-education.

44. Dennis L. Meadows, Donella H. Meadows, Jorgen Randers, and William W. Behrens, *The Limits to Growth* (New York: Universe Books, 1972); Club of Rome, "The Limits to Growth," accessed August 26, 2018, https://www.clubofrome.org/report/the-limits-to-growth/.

45. Dennis L. Meadows, "Perspectives on the Limits of Growth: It Is Too Late for Sustainable Development," Smithsonian Institution, February 29, 2012, accessed August 26, 2018, https://www.youtube.com/watch?v=f2oyU0RusiA.

46. Dennis L. Meadows, "Dennis Meadows—Why Didn't We Learn?," speech at the Annual Global Conference of the Club of Rome, Berlin, November 24, 2016, accessed August 26, 2018, https://www.youtube.com/watch?v=xa5-t6kA7L0.

47. Meadows, "Perspectives on the Limits of Growth."

48. Donella H. Meadows, Jorgen Randers, and Dennis L. Meadows, *Limits to Growth: The 30-Year Update* (White River Junction, VT: Chelsea Green, 2004).

49. Meadows, "Perspectives on the Limits of Growth."

50. See Scott McCloud, *Understanding Comics: The Invisible Art* (Kitchen Sink Press, Northampton, 1993); *Reinventing Comics: How Imagination and Technology Are Revolutionizing an Art Form* (New York: Paradox Press/HarperCollins, 2000); McCloud, *Making Comics: Storytelling Secrets of Comics, Manga and Graphic Novels* (New York: William Morrow/HarperCollins, 2006).

51. "The Work of Edward Tufte and Graphics Press," accessed August 26, 2018, https://www.edwardtufte.com/tufte/.

52. Ben Fry, *Visualizing Data: Exploring and Explaining Data with the Processing Environment* (Sebastopol, CA: O'Reilly Media, 2008).

53. "TR&D," The New York Times Research & Development group, accessed August 26, 2018, http://nytlabs.com.

54. Xu Bing, *Book from the Ground: From Point to Point* (Cambridge, MA: MIT Press, 2014).

5 The School of Worldbuilding[1]

Stuart Candy and Jeff Watson

The School of Worldbuilding[2] responds to the question "How might we design a better world?" by turning it on its head: "How might we world a better design?"[3]

The School of Worldbuilding is a *ludus*, a place-process or situation that facilitates certain kinds of play. Just as it is possible to frame a playful situation so as to exploit or injure, as in the case of a street corner hustler running a cup-and-ball game, so too can other framings of play make possible discovery, invention, and epiphany. The core technologies of the School are thus framing technologies—that is, technologies of play and performance: methods for instantiating the kinds of situations that enable participants to encounter, create, and operationalize new imaginaries.[4]

The School of Worldbuilding is not as interested in what we can do in imaginary worlds as it is in what we might do with or through or occasionally in spite of them, in this world.[5]

The School of Worldbuilding sees the educator not as a purveyor of content, but as a certain kind of game master. It sees the student not as a receptacle, but as a certain kind of player.[6]

The School of Worldbuilding's central curriculum is not only a transmedia practice, but also a transreality one. Of what use is a proliferation of worlds, in itself?[7] After all, the power of any imaginary lies in its contrapuntal interplay with our experience of "reality," shedding light on what we desire and fear, creating tensions, opening doors, changing what we can see and do—during the imaginative play itself, or when we awaken, or look up from the page, or rise from our seats as the credits roll.[8] The significance of worldbuilding is understood not to consist in the creation of alternative worlds as such, as an end in and of itself; rather, its significance is in the creation of portals.

The School of Worldbuilding reveals, unravels, and revels in diverse purposes, from the joy and generativity of sheer spectacle to the rigors and results of practical problem-solving. The embrace of disparate agendas avoids their being co-opted and instrumentalized to only one end.

The School of Worldbuilding is political because the imagination itself is political.[9] Power and authority contour and transform social imaginaries just as those imaginaries contour and transform power and authority. Indeed, domination and liberation alike depend on the imagination. What revolution ever started anywhere but in the imagining of a different world? And what tyranny ever lasted without mastery over imaginal resources?[10]

The School of Worldbuilding is an arena of shared interest and exchange between otherwise fragmented design practices, and a popular vernacular uniting activities ranging from playful exploration to urgent change-making. These include literature and poetry, cinema, arts and crafts, architecture, game and sport design, anthropology, philosophy, cooking, engineering, psychology, psychopharmacology, activism, gardening, futures, parenting, law, myth, and magic.[11]

The School of Worldbuilding confers no degree. To be a student of worldbuilding is to commit to exploration and experimentation as a way of life.[12] Graduation is not only impossible: it is undesirable. To graduate from the School is to fail out of it.

The School of Worldbuilding has no required courses. All courses are electives. All programs are extracurricular. The sole prerequisites are senses; especially of humor, adventure, and justice. If lacking these, a willing student can cultivate them, and should in any case, for their own good.

The School of Worldbuilding has no tuition or entry requirements. The imagination belongs to everyone, and so does the School.[13]

The School of Worldbuilding has no campus. It is a movable liminal space, becoming something different—and supporting different becomings—as it moves. Occasionally, the School can be found just beneath the Library of Babel. There was a time when the School and the Library were the same thing. But the Librarian and the Magister ultimately had a falling out. The Librarian wanted simply to catalog possible worlds, but the Magister wanted to *do something* with them.[14]

The School of Worldbuilding tells its students on the first day: every action matters—and the foundations of action can be found in the imagination. All organizations, indeed all human endeavors, are imaginary—until they aren't. The most fundamental lesson the School has to share is that imaginary artifacts, personas, assemblages, networks, and economies can serve to instantiate portals of potential or *world seeds* within existing systems. Thus the School's motto: "Art into Reality."[15]

The School of Worldbuilding sees that wherever our prospects seem to converge or narrow, the task becomes to offer alternatives by means of the guerrilla intervention and the unsolicited gift.[16]

The School of Worldbuilding is particularly concerned with the practice of social dreaming;[17] the tending and fruition not of individual genius but of group *scenius*.[18] Even when it pretends to be, and notwithstanding persistent fantasies to the contrary, a world is never for, or by, *one*.

The School of Worldbuilding recognizes "worldbuilding" as the product of a particular cultural context, while also understanding that the impulse it expresses has existed in all places, all cultures, and all human consciousness since time immemorial.[19]

The School of Worldbuilding repudiates the Western habit of disembodiment: the body knows things that escape the sharpest mind.

The School of Worldbuilding's pedagogy honors poetic intuition and other forms of tacit knowledge over procedural fidelity.[20] It is medium-agnostic, since there are at least as many ways one might build a world as there are possible worlds to be built.[21]

The School of Worldbuilding serves as a catalyst to diverse ends. Earnest, exhaustive undertakings aspiring to permanence are just one end of a wide spectrum that admits cathedral and bazaar alike.[22] Thus, outcomes differ as mandates and timescales vary. Some worlds are durable alternate realities with civilization-scale reach, elaborated and inhabited over many generations, spawning their own worlds in turn, like the fabled tower made up of turtles all the way down.[23] Other worlds are perfectly ephemeral, mere sketches or gestures, rungs on a ladder only ever to be climbed once, like the relationships of comic performers devised onstage in real time, suddenly revealing a truth to laughter, and then vanishing.[24]

The School of Worldbuilding's central design material, context, and site of intervention is narrative. Having been called into existence by the needs of the stories of which it forms part, the School is duly constituted to disappear once its roles have been fulfilled.

Classes begin immediately.

Notes

1. This document arrived without comment or introduction in the Situation Lab's email inbox at 11:25am EST on May 18, 2018. Yet, strangely, and quite inexplicably, it was timestamped thirty years into the future: May 18, 2048. After consulting with our tech support team, we learned further unusual details: first, that the message was sent using a 256-bit internet protocol that is not currently in use anywhere by anyone; and second, that the physical location specified by this

protocol appears to be in a remote southern extreme of the Indian Ocean. Whether the product of a prank, a technical error, or some kind of post-Large Hadron Collider temporal distortion, we have been unable to ascertain. In any event, the text has proven a source of inspiration for all of us at the Lab, and given its relevance to the subjects discussed in this volume, we have decided to share it here in its entirety. We have also taken the liberty of responding to select elements via footnotes, in an effort to illustrate or enrich the often provocative statements of the email's unidentified authors. The main text remains otherwise unchanged.

2. As Bauhaus ("the School of Building") founder Walter Gropius wrote in his school's inaugural manifesto, "[the] ultimate goal of all art is building" (Gropius, 1919).

3. This line echoes the slogan of the mid-2000s design initiative Massive Change: "[It's] not about the world of design; it's about the design of the world" (Mau, 2004, back cover).

4. In antiquity, the Latin word *ludus* was used to refer not only to board games such as the proto-checkers *ludus latrunculorum* (Tilley, 1892) or the well-known festival games and spectacles hosted at the Circus Maximus (*ludi circensis*), but also to a wide variety of spatio-processual structures that shaped or facilitated playful activities. Thus, Roman schools, contexts where the children of elites would prepare for their adult lives through rehearsal and play, were known as *ludi litterarii* (Booth, 1970); similarly, gladiatorial training camps, where performers would practice their dangerous craft under the nip-denotes-the-bite (Bateson) aegis of play, were called *ludi gladiatorii*: the largest of all such schools being the *ludus magnus* near the Flavian Amphitheatre in Rome (Neubauer et al., 2014). Importantly, these structures did not require a physical plant: they could be entirely conceptual, as in the case of a poetic *ludus*, which provided poets and other speakers with performative scripts that functioned as scaffolds for creative action (Miller).

5. The first *Whole Earth Catalog* famously began: "We are as gods and might as well get used to it" (Brand, 1968, p. 2, although the quote often appears "... might as well get good at it"). Some decades later, the stakes of the Anthropocene more clearly in focus, the declaration had been revised: "We are as gods and HAVE to get good at it" (Brand, 2009, p. 1). We cannot tell here whether the manifesto's authors are truly ontological pluralists, that is, espousing the reality of many alternative worlds.

6. For activist and educator Paulo Freire, democracy suffers when education is reduced to "an act of depositing, in which the students are the depositories and the teacher is the depositor." In such a situation, which Freire famously calls the "banking model" of education, "the scope of action allowed to the students extends only as far as receiving, filing, and storing the deposits. They do, it is true, have the opportunity to become collectors or catalogers of the things they store. But in the last analysis, it is the people themselves who are filed away through the lack of creativity, transformation, and knowledge in this (at best) misguided system." The authors here seem to agree with Freire when he asserts that knowledge "emerges only through invention and re-invention, through the restless, impatient, continuing, hopeful inquiry human beings pursue in the world, with the world, and with each other" (Freire, 1970/2000).

7. We note that this seemingly rhetorical question may invite actual, and conflicting, answers.

8. A realization foreshadowed by the ascent in the late 2000s of idioms for influencing reality by using fiction, as in the apparently paradoxical practices of "experiential futures," "science fiction prototyping," and "design fiction." Bruce Sterling: "Design fiction is not design with science fiction in it; it is design with some of science fiction's ontological awareness that reality is mutable." (Sterling in Durfee and Zeiger, 2018, pp. 18–26).

9. The political not only shapes the imaginal; it *depends* on it. Chiara Bottici: "If we understand politics as whatever pertains to life in common and the decisions concerning its fate, the link is quite clear. Politics coincides with the sphere of public life and therefore includes all that concerns the social and the political. Politics thus understood depends on the imaginal because it is only by imagining it that a public comes into being" (Bottici, 2014, p. 90). See also Duncombe, 2007.

10. Simply put, art and politics can never be separated. To suggest otherwise is to deny the impact of acts of imagination on the material and psychosocial world, and the ways that those impacts can produce or reproduce power relations. Filmmaker Boots Riley: "Art for [art's] sake is never for [art's] sake—it's for the sake of the status quo" (Riley, 2018).

11. Architect and educator Ann Pendleton-Jullian describes such "shared arenas of interest and exchange" as "innovation ecotones." In environmental science, an ecotone is a place "where two distinct ecosystems overlap or grade into one another." Such systems can "contain an abundance of diverse species and a complex set of exchange dynamics" compared to more stable and less-graded ecosystems such as those that might be found in the very center of a forest. It is at the confluence of many streams of being that novelty and discovery emerge, in education and evolution alike (Pendleton-Jullian, 2009, p. 2).

12. The ambitious ideal of the *Gesamtkunstwerk*, or total artwork, here starts to take on a coloration somewhat closer to the Hungarian term *életművész*, literally "life-artist": one who lives her life as a work of art—and perhaps thereby brings into being a different kind of world.

13. This admissions policy appears especially inclusive, and appropriately so, in relation to younger students. "Think of the times, as a child, when you were lost in play for hours, adopting roles and characters, playing in the sand, and making complex worlds. The ability to focus is not the issue: it is a question of what is worth focusing on" (O'Donnell, 2018, p. 25).

14. See Borges, 1941/2000.

15. A curious parallel here to the Bauhaus motto, dating back to its 1919 founding: "Art into Industry" (Winton, 2007).

16. Numerous echoes detected, including "semiological guerrilla warfare" (Eco, 1986, pp. 135–144); "unsolicited architecture" (Hyde and Moore, 2010); futures as "a game of dissenting visions" (Nandy, 1996, p. 637); and "the gift" (Hyde, 2007).

17. See Dunne and Raby, 2013.

18. Brian Eno: "Genius is individual, scenius is communal" (Jeffries, 2010).

19. Despite its engineering connotations, "building" here is clearly intended to encompass a multitude of processes, including the hermeneutic operations of readers, players, and other kinds of participants. As Mark J. P. Wolf notes, much of worldbuilding consists of the creation of a "*world gestalten*," that is, "a structure or configuration of details [that] implies the existence of an imaginary world, and causes the audience to automatically fill in the missing pieces of that world, based on the details that they are given" (Wolf, 2012).

20. Antoine de Saint-Exupéry (attrib.): "If you want to build a ship, don't drum up the men to gather wood, divide the work and give orders. Instead, teach them to yearn for the vast and endless sea" (O'Toole, 2015).

21. The term "procedural fidelity" points toward the use of structured play processes that enable the systematic building of worlds. Examples of such processes include imagination games such as *Microscope* (Lame Mage Productions, 2011), *Dialect* (Thorny Games, 2018), and the Situation Lab's own generative game-tool, *The Thing from the Future* (2014). "Poetic intuition," on the other hand, could be exemplified by the worldbuilding practices of a creator like Ursula K. Le Guin: "I did not plan these worlds and people. I found them, gradually, piecemeal, while writing stories" (Le Guin, 2003).

22. See Raymond, 2001.

23. The entire nation-state system, for instance, is built on a centuries-old imaginary substrate. See Anderson, 2006.

24. Here the authors evoke a distinction analogous to the central one outlined by philosopher James Carse in *Finite and Infinite Games* (Carse, 2011). Further, the reference to real-time performance suggests playful curricular strands in both improvisation (Halpern et al., 1994; Johnstone, 2015) and live action role-playing (Stenros and Montola, 2010; Saitta et al., 2014).

References

Anderson, B. 2006. *Imagined Communities: Reflections on the Origin and Spread of Nationalism*. Rev. ed. London: Verso.

Bateson, G. 1976. *Steps to an Ecology of Mind*. New York: Ballantine Books.

Booth, A. D. 1970. "The Stage and Division of Roman Education: A Study of the Relationship between the Teaching of the Ludi Magister and the Grammaticus." PhD diss., McMaster University, Hamilton, Ontario, Canada. Retrieved from http://digitalcommons.mcmaster.ca/opendissertations/5065.

Borges, J. L. 2000. *The Library of Babel*. Boston: David R. Godine.

Bottici, C. 2014. *Imaginal Politics: Images beyond Imagination and the Imaginary*. New York: Columbia University Press.

Brand, S., ed. 1968. *Whole Earth Catalog*. Retrieved from https://monoskop.org/images/0/09/Brand_Stewart_Whole_Earth_Catalog_Fall_1968.pdf.

Brand, S. 2009. *Whole Earth Discipline: An Ecopragmatist Manifesto.* New York: Viking.

Carse, J. 2011. *Finite and Infinite Games.* New York: Simon and Schuster.

Duncombe, S. 2007. *Dream: Re-imagining Progressive Politics in an Age of Fantasy.* New York: New Press.

Dunne, A., and F. Raby. 2013. *Speculative Everything.* Cambridge, MA: MIT Press.

Durfee, T., and M. Zeiger. 2018. *Made Up: Design's Fictions.* New York: ArtCenter Graduate Press; Barcelona: Actar.

Eco, U. 1986. *Travels in Hyper Reality: Essays.* Trans. W. Weaver. New York: Harcourt Brace Jovanovich.

Freire, P., and D. Macedo. 2000. *Pedagogy of the Oppressed, 30th Anniversary Edition.* Trans. M. B. Ramos. New York: Bloomsbury.

Gropius, W. 1919. "Manifesto and Program of the Weimar State Bauhaus." Retrieved from https://www.bauhaus100.de/en/past/works/education/manifest-und-programm-des-staatlichenbauhauses/index.html.

Halpern, C., D. Close, and K. Johnson. 1994. *Truth in Comedy: The Manual of Improvisation.* Colorado Springs: Meriwether.

Hyde, L. 2007. *The Gift: Creativity and the Artist in the Modern World.* New York: Vintage.

Hyde, R., and T. Moore. 2010. "Unsolicited Architecture." Bootleg of *Volume*'s "Unsolicited" issue produced for AIA Conference, Sydney. Retrieved from http://cargocollective.com/roryhyde/Unsolicited-Bootleg.

Jeffries, S. 2010. "Surrender. It's Brian Eno." *The Guardian*, April 28. Retrieved from http://www.theguardian.com/music/2010/apr/28/brian-eno-brighton-festival.

Johnstone, K. 2015. *Impro: Improvisation and the Theatre.* Abingdon, UK: Routledge.

Le Guin, U. K. 2003. *The Birthday of the World: And Other Stories.* Reprint ed. New York: Harper Perennial.

Mau, B., et al. 2004. *Massive Change.* London: Phaidon.

Miller, P. A. 2006. "The World of Roman Song: From Ritualized Speech to Social Order." *American Journal of Philology* 127(4), 607–611.

Nandy, A. 1996. "Bearing Witness to the Future." *Futures* 28(6–7), 636–639.

Neubauer, W., C. Gugl, M. Scholz, G. Verhoeven, I. Trinks, K. Löcker, ... and M. Van Meirvenne. 2014. "The Discovery of the School of Gladiators at Carnuntum, Austria." *Antiquity* 88(339), 173–190.

O'Donnell, D. 2018. *Haircuts by Children: And Other Evidence for a New Social Contract.* Toronto: Coach House Books.

O'Toole, G. 2015. "Teach Them to Yearn for the Vast and Endless Sea." *Quote Investigator*. Retrieved from https://quoteinvestigator.com/2015/08/25/sea/.

Pendleton-Jullian, A. 2009. "Design Education and Innovation Ecotones." Knowlton School of Architecture, Ohio State University. Retrieved from https://fourplusone.files.wordpress.com/2010/03/apj_paper_14.pdf.

Raymond, E. S. 2001. *The Cathedral and the Bazaar: Musings on Linux and Open Source by an Accidental Revolutionary*. Cambridge, MA: O'Reilly.

Riley, B. 2018. "Art for arts sake is never for arts sake- it's for the sake of the status quo." Tweet, August 3. Retrieved from https://twitter.com/BootsRiley/status/1025469650220400640.

Saitta, E., M. Holm-Andersen, and J. Back, eds. 2014. *The Foundation Stone of Nordic Larp*. Knutpunkt. Retrieved from https://nordiclarp.org/w/images/8/80/2014_The_Foundation_Stone_of_Nordic_Larp.pdf.

Stenros, J., and M. Montola. 2010. *Nordic Larp*. Fëa Livia. Retrieved from http://tampub.uta.fi/handle/10024/95123.

Tilley, A. 1892. "Ludus Latrunculorum." *Classical Review* 6(8), 335–336.

Winton, A. G. 2007. "The Bauhaus, 1919–1933." Retrieved from https://www.metmuseum.org/toah/hd/bauh/hd_bauh.htm.

Wolf, M. J. P. 2012. *Building Imaginary Worlds: The Theory and History of Subcreation*. New York: Routledge.

6 Diagrams for Another Bauhaus

Carl DiSalvo

In 1922 Walter Gropius produced a diagram representing the curriculum at the Bauhaus. Building, or "Bau," was at the center of the diagram, the core of all endeavors. Around this were arrayed a series of workshops and the subjects of the preliminary course. In reading the diagram we see what skills and materials were considered essential, and in what progression learning was to occur as expertise was developed. A bit over a decade later László Moholy-Nagy created a similar diagram for the curriculum of the New Bauhaus. Moholy-Nagy's diagram takes the same basic form, but there are significant changes in content. For Moholy-Nagy's pedagogy, technology and early forms of media were important components of the curriculum.

Like many diagrams, those summarizing the Bauhaus pedagogy are obvious. What they communicate is the content for a set of courses arranged in sequence over the span of a school's program. What the diagrams connote, however, extends these words and phrases and time demarcations to express a set of themes in relation to one another, and through these themes and relations insight into beliefs about what design education ought to include and how design education ought to be ordered. Admittedly, it is a leap from a model of design education to a model of the world, but it is leap worth taking. Moreover, it is a leap in line with the modernist design project. As a pedagogy, the Bauhaus program is more than just an outline for education; it can also be interpreted as a framework for conceptualizing the making of the artificial. Put another way, the pedagogy can be interpreted as an answer to the question *What do we need to know in order to make the world?*, which itself is a reflection on the question *How is the world made?* Like so much pedagogy, and for that matter like so much design, the answer to that question is culturally and temporally specific. What Gropius and Moholy-Nagy offer through these diagrams and the pedagogies they express straddles the universal and the particular. It would be more precise to say that each diagram answers the questions *What do we need to know in order to make the world, here and now?* and *How is the world made, here and now?*

The newer diagrams shared here continue this line of expression. Each diagram expresses a different perspective on what a design pedagogy might be in the early twenty-first century. Each diagram conveys a distinct view on making the made world, manifest through a set of subjects, themes, and relations. For some audiences the content may be foreign, whereas for others it might seem familiar, perhaps again obvious. There's been a bit of play with the structure of the diagrams, but not too much: the diagrams are still intended to show a set of nested fields and matters, relative to one another. The choice of the perspectives expressed in these diagrams is admittedly idiosyncratic. My intention is to highlight what I consider to be significant standpoints in contemporary design: both positions and vectors that mark where design is now and where it may be going.

There are important differences in these diagrams from those original diagrams of Gropius and Moholy-Nagy. The diagrams shared here are not schematics of any design curriculum currently in place (at least not that I am aware of). Instead, each is a blend of topics drawn from a variety of sources. Rather than considering them as representations of what is, it would be more appropriate to see them as sketches of an ongoing inquiry into what might be. The diagram "A Pedagogy for a 21st Century Bauhaus, Silicon Valley" is the most straightforward of the set and nearest to contemporary practices of making the artificial: it expresses what might be a curriculum for design in a world imbued by computation, its subjects and fields found in the headlines of today's media, business, and technology journalism. This is a pedagogy for those designers creating the digital systems and services that shape so much of our contemporary life. Of all the pedagogies it is the most obvious, and of all the diagrams it is the simplest. We might find aspects of this pedagogy in the more technology-focused design curricula, or in fact in the curricula of the more daring computer science programs.

The diagram "A Pedagogy for a Postcapitalist Bauhaus" shifts perspective and draws from a consideration of the work of J. K. Gibson-Graham, envisioning their theory and practice into a design pedagogy. In this hypothetical pedagogy and its accompanying diagram, distinctions between fields and subjects are lessened and themes mingle together, following the pluralism characteristic of postcapitalist theory and practice. Thus, there are no separations between the fields and subjects within each concentric ring, and each ring contains both methods and materials. What is at the center of this pedagogy is "Becoming"—this is not a simple four-year program but rather a lifetime of making other worlds possible. Aspects of such a pedagogy can be found in the work of emerging designers and design educators, such as that of Fabio Franz and Bianca Elzenbaumer and their collective Brave New Alps.

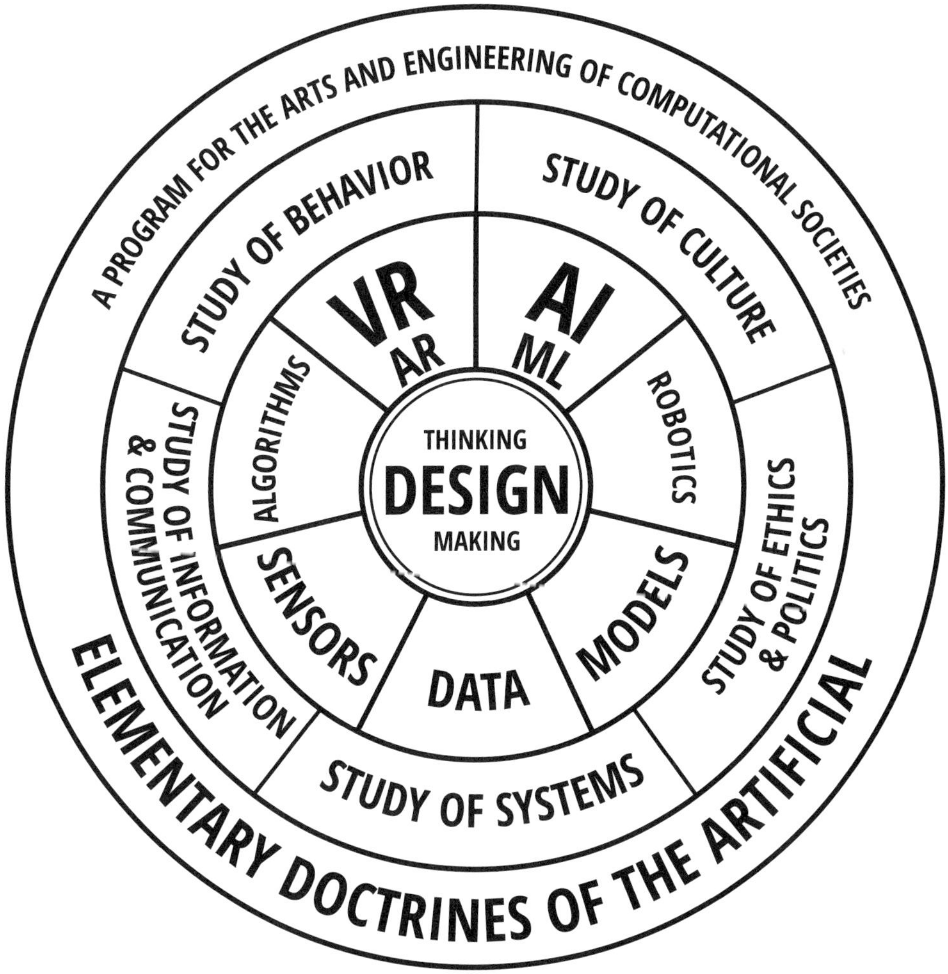

Figure 6.1
"A Pedagogy for a 21st Century Bauhaus, Silicon Valley."

Finally, the diagram "A Pedagogy for a Bauhaus for the Anthropocene" looks to contemporary theorists, designers, and artists to articulate a set of themes that we might need for designing within an epoch of instability and uncertainty brought about by climate change, particularly as inspired by the work of Timothy Morton, Anna Tsing, Elizabeth Povinelli, Tony Fry, Anne-Marie Willis, Rich Pell, Åsa Ståhl, and Kristina Lindström. This is not a pedagogy to solve or mitigate climate change through design, but rather a program for designing in order to live with and within

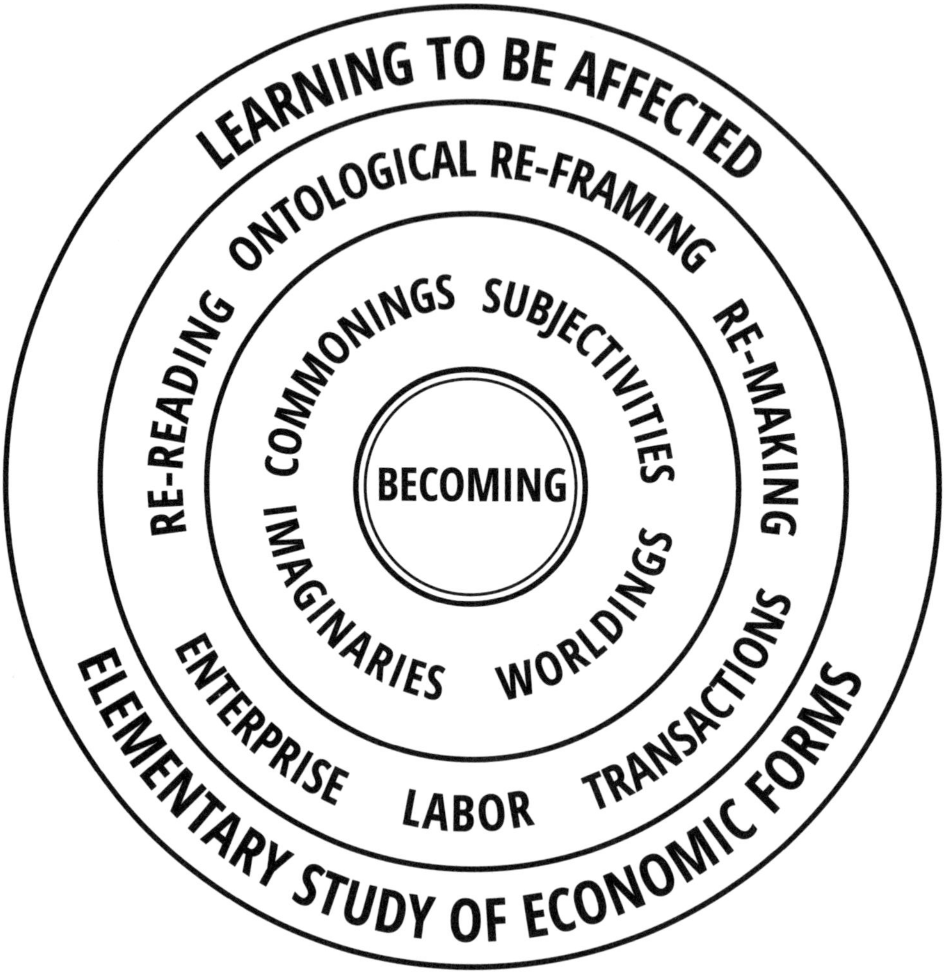

Figure 6.2
"A Pedagogy for a Postcapitalist Bauhaus."

this moment of profound ecological and accompanying social and philosophical transformations. This may be a less obvious diagram, and it certainly would be a pedagogy in flux. The structure of this diagram is intentionally fractured as movement between the subjects and themes is not linear, and the very notion of progress is called into question.

It would be fair to critique these diagrams for so closely following the structure and pattern of the original Bauhaus diagrams. After all, one might argue, perhaps a better

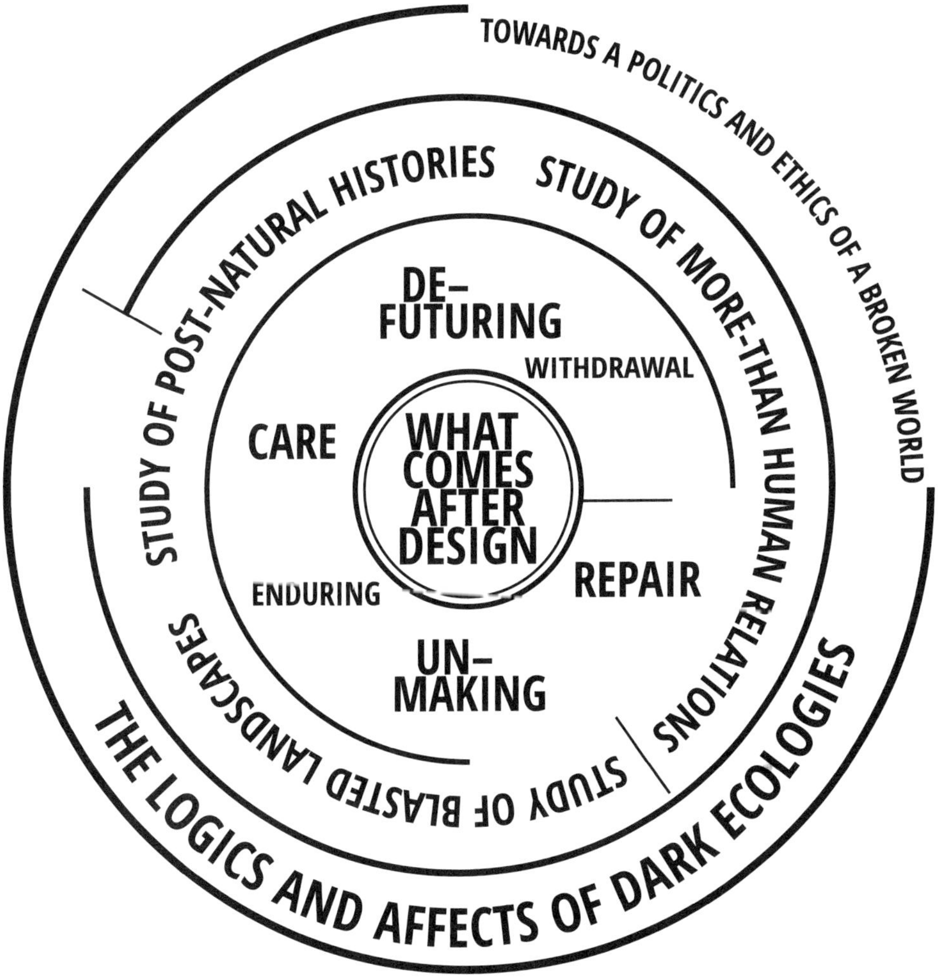

Figure 6.3
"A Pedagogy for a Bauhaus for the Anthropocene."

structure for a design pedagogy in the early twenty-first century might be a network or a stack or bubbles or spheres. By reproducing these diagrams, are you not reproducing some of the very tenets of modernism that warrant resistance or outright rejection? Perhaps that is the case. I decided to keep the structure and pattern not out of deference to history or tradition, but because I found the challenge of thinking a different Bauhaus with and through this structure and pattern to be a worthwhile conceptual and aesthetic effort.

What the Gropius and Moholy-Nagy diagrams provide is something to reflect on, a designed thing meant to express something essential to design. The pedagogies they capture and communicate continue to have impact today. We can find traces of those original Bauhaus programs and their underlying beliefs in schools of design across the globe. While the particulars of the subjects in those original diagrams are dated, what remains valuable is the belief that design pedagogy is important because it both shapes and reflects how we make the made world. At this moment of the hundredth anniversary of the Bauhaus, one question to consider is how we might want to make the made world *differently*. Experimenting with design pedagogy is one way to put that question into practice.

Works That Inspired These Diagrams

Franz, F., and B. Elzenbaumer. *Brave New Alps*. http://www.brave-new-alps.com.

Fry, T. *A New Design Philosophy: An Introduction to Defuturing*. UNSW Press, 1999.

Gibson-Graham, J. K. *A Postcapitalist Politics*. Minneapolis: University of Minnesota Press, 2006.

Gibson-Graham, J. K., J. Cameron, and S. Healy. *Take Back the Economy: An Ethical Guide for Transforming Our Communities*. Minneapolis: University of Minnesota Press, 2013.

Maeda, J. "Design in Tech Report 2018." Available at https://designintech.report.

Morton, T. *Dark Ecology: For a Logic of Future Coexistence*. New York: Columbia University Press, 2016.

Pell, R. *The Center for PostNatural History*. https://www.postnatural.org.

Povinelli, E. A. *Economies of Abandonment: Social Belonging and Endurance in Late Liberalism*. Durham: Duke University Press, 2011.

Ståhl, Å., and K. Lindström. *Hybrid Matters*. https://hybridmatters.net.

Tsing, A. L. *The Mushroom at the End of the World: On the Possibility of Life in Capitalist Ruins*. Princeton, NJ: Princeton University Press, 2015.

Willis, A. M. "Ontological Designing." *Design Philosophy Papers* 4, no. 2 (2006), 69–92.

III "Problems" and Politics of Race and Social Justice

7 Bauhaus and the People without Design History

Elizabeth Chin

Coming out of Mexico's Museo Nacional de Antropología, my mind is reeling from the 11 galleries full of stunningly designed pottery, textiles, buildings, and burials spanning centuries and centuries of cultures astonishing in their breadth and depth and beauty. Turning left, I head toward Mexico City's colonial center. As I pass the Museum of Modern Art, a large billboard announces the celebration of (merely) 100 years of Swiss design. The billboard features a much larger-than-life image of a Swiss Army knife. Standing here, no doubt several feet above Aztec archaeological remains, I find myself thinking of the book *Europe and the People without History*, by anthropologist Eric Wolf.[1] Wolf argued that we threatened to turn to many ideas into things, and in so doing risked constructing versions of human history and the human present founded on mistaken notions of the realness of our own invented realities. If Wolf was concerned with the divide between those who "have" history (EuroAmericans) and those who do not (everyone else), this essay digs into the divide between those who "have" design (EuroAmericans) and those who do not (everyone else). Similarly stark, similarly reified, and similarly problematic, Bauhaus futures must grapple with problematic Bauhaus histories, particularly histories that exclude the bulk of the world's people from having design in any meaningful way.

The history of design is often portrayed as primarily being a history of the Bauhaus, what led up to it, and what has emerged since. There is remarkably little investigation into the predecessors of the Bauhaus,[2] and the social histories of the Bauhaus take for granted that design is German, or Swiss, or International—but not African, or Melanesian, or Inuit. Part of Wolf's point was that the so-called West was never an isolated phenomenon; an actor in history, it has also been acted upon. The indigenous, the colonized, the native, it turns out, have created the West in form and character in deeply important ways, even as those whose histories celebrate their own becoming deflect or deny the existence of such cultural miscegenation.

The particular forms of universalist humanism that emerged after World War II sought to deny the legitimacy of fascism and eugenics without integrating radical challenges to EuroAmerican culture and values. If Eric Wolf insisted that those people relegated to anthropology have always been central to global dynamics, black feminism has critiqued humanist ideas of humanity as "liberal monohumanism's *homo oeconomicus*."[3] This universalist conception of the human, one implicit in so much design work, is premised upon EuroAmerican, bourgeois notions of what it means to be (or to qualify as) human. This is a definition that serves certain interests, draws from certain histories, and privileges certain futures; educated and European, the refugee Bauhaus pioneers who arrived in the United States were exactly what the so-called world community had in mind when they created the United Nations and the idea of universal human rights. As current refugee crises in Europe show, "we" didn't mean *those* people. Sylvia Wynter's caustic questioning of the use of this universal "we" is worth remembering.[4] From a black feminist perspective the "we" invoked so often is, in fact, exclusionary: Wynter argues that the human "is therefore wrought with physiological and narrative matters that systematically excise the world's most marginalized."[5] As such, the clean-edged attempt at a universal humanism that arose in response to the real potential for total annihilation was, ironically (yet predictably), a white utopia, embodied in and thus an oxymoron to those who reside beyond whiteness. Wynter emphasizes that this is a version of the human that naturalizes capitalism, in the process also naturalizing those elements that arose in service of the emergent industrial global economy—notably commodity slavery and the rise of racial notions defining blackness (as the key instance of non-whiteness) as beyond humanity.

We weren't there.[6] *Not on the campus, not in the studios, the libraries, at the lectures, holding the brushes or adzes, smoothing the wood, casting the concrete. But we were there. Where we were. You were where you were. We were irrelevant to you. And you to us.*

Tempests and Teapots

If anthropology invented the holistic concept of culture, the Bauhaus was similarly interested in the design of everyday life through cultural objects.[7] In product catalogs from the 1920s, tea services, coffee pots, and ashtrays figure prominently as objects intended for use in these everyday lives. That the Bauhaus offered vessels for coffee, tea, sugar, and tobacco as unremarkable household items in the 1920s is somewhat miraculous, given that only 100 years before each of these was to some degree a rarity, a treasure, exotic. In an aesthetic move that became a hallmark of Bauhaus focus on form, function, material, and craftsmanship, the catalog photographs portray these objects as context-free. Yet neither the materials from which these things were constructed nor the substances they were created to contain were free from history. Tea, sugar, and coffee all were foodstuffs connecting Europe to at least three different continents; tobacco is a new world domesticate; ebony was certainly imported from either Africa or Asia, and silver, too, came from abroad. Drawing from the works and perspectives in the analysis of political economy offered by Eric Wolf and Sydney Mintz,[8] it is worth considering these objects as moments in vast historical trajectories that connect people and cultures across time and space. If Bauhaus values included what Sidney Lawrence[9] calls "truth to materials," that truth was certainly utterly ahistorical.

Nearly every one of the raw materials meant to be contained by these objects, and those from which they were made, were tied up with the enslavement of Africans, with colonization, with displacement of indigenous peoples, and with forced labor of Indians and Asians. As Sidney Mintz showed so elegantly in *Sweetness and Power*,[10] sugar is deeply caught up in the mutual creation and entanglement of new and old worlds, new and old regimes, wars, and dilemmas. The mass availability of those sweet crystals was accomplished through the mass enslavement of Africans, the development of plantation economies, the growth of export throughout the triangle of trade, and the global integration into the same industrial economy that the Bauhaus sought to embrace.

The everydayness of a sugar bowl concentrates within it the degree to which the power of new economies had successfully transformed lives across the globe. Germany produced beet sugar, but after the First World War exports disappeared. Meanwhile Cuba's sugar crop grew from about 475,000 tons in 1882 to over 4 million in 1920 and Indonesia's grew fivefold.[11] When it comes to coffee, Brazil produced three-quarters of the world's coffee by the end of the nineteenth century, and was also a major exporter of sugar; both crops required slave labor into the late 1800s.[12] As Mintz emphasizes, sugar paired with tea transformed the British working class, and the tea trade was a major connection between Europe and Asia.

In several of the tea and coffee services, ebony handles add an exotic flair. Imported from Ceylon, India, Sri Lanka, and western Africa, ebony had for a century or two been a luxury wood. In Mauritius, ebony was exploited by the Dutch to the point of extinction; the British took over, building up sugar plantations, engaging slavery, and when that failed, importing workers from India and Asia.[13] With its striking black color, ebony had become a racialized material by the early twentieth century. Man Ray's 1926 photograph *Noir et Blanche* featured an African Baule mask in ebony juxtaposed against the face and form of a white model in a way that both breaks down cultural and racial oppositions while reinstating them;[14] while members of the Bauhaus may not have seen this photograph, ebony artifacts—with their emergent racialized meanings—would have been easy to encounter. Black bodies, too, were on display in a range of performances in Germany, consumed by audiences for their supposed primitiveness and backwardness, even as those performers were sophisticated in leveraging kinship networks to secure their positions.[15]

For its part, the silver from which these objects were made most likely came from the New World where silver exports far outstripped European production: between 1900 and 1925, Europe produced only 6.3 percent of world silver compared to 74.5 percent in North America and 8.45 percent in South America.[16]

This very quick examination of connections between these Bauhaus objects and "other" places takes for granted that the people who toiled to produce, transport, and deliver the commodities are as important as the products. As such these people are not precursors to progress, development, history, and design: neither history nor design could exist without those it defines as out of bounds. Wolf's point is that the boundary between those who have is both arbitrary and incorrect; Wynter's is that the very concept of the human (history or design) is constructed in a way that is monocultural, but that this is an "origin story" and as such has no greater claim to truth than any other origin story.

You could not imagine us. Failure to imagine. Us. Oh, you thought for the whole world, the whole rounding planet. Smooth planes and unadorned surfaces for everyone. Democratic, free from sticky smelly guts the remains in the trenches the borders. Negative space becomes a thing. Helvetica for all! (That came later, I know.)

Design and the Social

By the 1950s, Bauhaus-inflected discussions of architecture and design had moved away from such questions as social housing and were focused on "man in an abstract, or at least ahistorical, sense."[17] That abstract and ahistorical "man" is precisely the *homo oeconomicus* so soundly criticized by Wynter. This stance was honed in the United States, where such figures as Philip Johnson and Alfred H. Barr at MoMA forwarded a vision of the Bauhaus that "did everything in their power to eliminate [the] original discourse [of the Bauhaus]. ... The sole intention of the American promoters of the New York exhibition was to present the best and newest examples of aesthetic progress as a fashion trend."[18] As design's marriage with capitalism and commodity culture was cemented, its capacity for critical analysis of capitalism was blunted.

Today, as design aspires to intervene in the realm of the social, providing solutions and innovating around wicked problems, the most persistent Bauhausian influence is precisely the history-free, individualist hero narrative forwarded by Johnson and Barr, espoused by MoMA, and practiced today in many design programs. Most conspicuously absent is the communist, communal ethos initially espoused by Gropius. Missing, too, is the radical pedagogy that today might be called transdisciplinary.

Today design moves toward proclaiming that everything can be designed, with a growing commitment to intervening in the social.[19] Yet design too rarely questions the larger global and structural systems of inequality that create the problems it seeks to solve. Continuing to focus on ahistorical humanity, the specific histories that have given rise to blackness (and its colored companions) do not exist. Furthermore, design's disdain for the indigenous, the vernacular, the "untrained" or "unprofessional" continues unabated, primarily through a failure to critically reconsider aesthetics or what constitutes good design in the first place. Techno-utopia has no downside; it will go the last mile, providing connectivity, information, and humanitarian aid, lighting up hovels and huts the world over. Social justice has, for all intents and purposes, been absorbed into a Baudrillardian ecstasy of communication, a world for which there is no outside,[20] but a world to which blackness is nonetheless alien. (To be fair, some are more hopeful than I am, especially Arturo Escobar.)[21]

Transcendence is yours. We who are stuck in place we who have no space behind us no histories—so you say—have no choice but to march forward to move into the present but where are we in the future? It is a future for everyone you say. Where am I in there? Where are my kin? How is it that the sameness you see could be a utopia? Your wish is revealed as a hunger for genocide but not bloody or messy or ugly. Nevertheless, I name it: genocide. Your innermost desire your wished-for thing. The love of your life.

Designers tend to approach the global south in terms of lack: what "they" don't have, or what "they" need. One need only survey the surfeit of water filter projects to get a sense of this dynamic. The narrative is this: young, (white) man goes to Africa or anyplace Africa-like and discovers what masses of people already know: clean water is not widely available. "They need clean water," he thinks. "I shall design something that provides this to them." It is important to stop here and take note that said young man is responding to his own sense of need, his own shock, his own discomfort. He has not, for instance, asked people what their priorities or desires might be. Their need is obvious, manifest, it needs no interrogation. His destiny is to solve their problem. Predictably, he designs a water filtering device, often small and hand-held not because this is the best design per se, but because this is what is most convenient—and affordable prototype-wise—for *him*. Note that said device cannot possibly provide clean water in the quantities regularly required by a household, much less a village. (Note to *homo oeconomicus*: further product development and capitalization are required for that.) Young man uses this project to fill out his resume, or perhaps as a thesis project, and wins prizes. The object looks great, it works. It never goes into production. Or, like Life Straw, it is used primarily by campers and hikers and survivalists, but does not alter the basic infrastructural and political conditions that make access to clean water a pressing problem for so much of the world's people. In short, the innovative solution has not solved any problem at all (save for that of the young man's need for both recognition and a job); his humanitarianism is perversely premised on failed states caught up in postcolonial conflicts whose outlines are hazily irrelevant to the design problem.[22]

For those tempted to protest that I am being unfair, my retort is first that project after project follows this narrative nearly to exactness with such headlines as "Students Develop Low Cost Water Filtering System for African Nation";[23] second, that the pictures speak for themselves, belonging nowhere so much as they belong on the Humanitarians of Tinder blog post;[24] third, that this flattened narrative is the equivalent of the narrative "they need"; and so my question to you, in the fashion of Jamaica Kincaid, is: How does it feel to be so cruelly represented?[25] Or, to call on Chimamanda Adichie, why is this dangerous, single story of "their" need and "our" help so difficult to dislodge?[26] One part of the answer might be that the naturalization of capitalism makes social entrepreneurs and design for good inevitable outcomes of Wynter's *homo oeconomicus*, heroes in a design origin myth that begins with the Bauhaus.

Niemeyer's obeisance to the master Le Corbusier was the kind of old school gentility upon which the United Nations was founded. The deference and respect is enshrined in the moderate awkwardness of Le Corbusier's General Assembly tucked up under Niemeyer's tall, tall tower. What respect is reserved for the Manahatta, upon whose lands these buildings have been erected? Who celebrates the singular genius of Mohawk ironworkers who raised up the steel skeleton of Niemeyer's tower toward brightening skies? Why the tower and not a long house or totem pole?

Even as design moves into the massive systems of UN organizations—UNICEF's Innovation unit is a case in point—it lacks critical engagement with the very political forces that created and destroyed the Bauhaus. If designers want into the water business, they need to dive into real problems, not just the ones that allow them to do good and to create solutions for problems that might be better left unsolved. Why not deal with the introduction of cholera to Haiti, post-earthquake, by Nepalese peacekeepers whose privies were not only poorly constructed but did not even meet the UN's own sanitation standards? Since 2010, nearly 10,000 Haitians have died of cholera, in a nation that was formerly cholera-free.[27] Refusing to acknowledge culpability, the United Nations has instead set up a $400 million fund, soliciting voluntary contributions which have only trickled in and are far from reaching the target.

Here the workings of *homo oeconomicus* are stark: relatives of those felled by the UN cholera debacle must seek financial restitution for the loss of humanity for which the UN is responsible, as if money can compensate the loss of life, the shredding of kinship, the destruction of family lines. Protecting its own edifice through the instrument of diplomatic immunity, the UN asserts the inhuman yet fully humanist position that those who are there to help cannot be held to account even if their efforts go terribly wrong. The irony that Haiti should be the site of this neoliberal crisis is hard to miss: in 1804 after becoming the first black republic in world history, Haitians were forced to pay restitution to France for its loss of lands and property. Having been enslaved, those who had won their freedom by fighting for it now had to pay restitution to their enslavers. Today, they must ask to be paid by the humanist organization that is responsible for tens of thousands of deaths. This is, indeed, a wicked problem, and it is one that cannot be unsnarled without understanding blackness, and the continuing compulsions of white supremacy in the face of black survival and rebellion.

Post-Bauhaus Color Theory

Decolonizing design will mean leaving much of the Bauhaus behind, a radical recentering of aesthetics, form, and materials into cultural logics that have lain outside the universe of design from the start.[28] There will be no decolonized design until the native, the indigenous, the alien reshape design's ideologies and output. (If it's any consolation, anthropology realized this a really long time ago but has yet to fully come to terms with this problem, so it's not as if I expect massive change any time soon.)[29]

Let's begin with this principle: rethink white and black. Whiteness is not made up of all the colors, since anybody knows what you get when you mix all the paints together is closer to black that white. That which is white deflects all color in order to preserve its purity and its place. Blackness takes in color. Takes it all in, it's all in, it's all in there, scooped up and packed and please stop packaging it, that appropriation thing is older than Mammy and her daughter Aunt Jemima, crustier than a coon.

There is of course the inclusive version of whiteness, a fantasy of rainbows and unicorns with glitter sprinkles coming out of their flying butts. In this rainbow version of whiteness, deflection is framed as "I don't see color" and what diversity boils down to is really about the many ways to be white. Just ask the head of diversity at Apple—or look at the Truly Me line of American Girl Dolls. Skin tone: Dark 6; Medium 10; Fair 32. Read it and weep or lose sleep: which is you? But wasn't I supposed to be talking about color and not whiteness? See how this happens?

Conclusion

I don't blame the Bauhaus for being of its time, but I cannot help kicking the shins of those designers whose feet are encased in the steel-enforced concrete of Bauhausian values even now. When I encounter design today I'm feeling it like I'm like an HGTV host stalking into a 1950s-era home and announcing, "everything needs to be updated!" I am an evil villainess (a dragon lady, that is) who aspires to world domination. Actually, I'm a woman of color who has something to say. It helps to aspire to world domination in order to get a word in edgewise: Bwahahahaha, and I take a drag on my cigarette, provided to my outstretched hand by a minion. I look down my nose at those knobby-kneed designer guys, stripped down wearing nothing but their concrete shoes, polished and smooth, reified ideas that will drag them down to the bottom of this sea of humanity they conjured from their own enlightenment history, one in which I do not exist.

Behind me the future reaches to tap my shoulder. My history faces me unfurled across stories past and passed and passed along. To me. Here is the reason you cannot see it: you are facing the wrong direction. Turn around. It's not that hard. For you even a sideways glance brings vertigo so strong you stumble and, angry, you cast the blame at me because I pointed in the right direction. You don't know you cannot see the whole world. You think the world is what you see before you.

Close your eyes.

Jump on in, the water is fine.

Notes

1. Eric Wolf, *Europe and the People without History*, 2nd ed. (Berkeley: University of California Press, 2010).

2. Alina Payne, "Bauhaus Endgame: Ambiguity, Anxiety, and Discomfort," in *Bauhaus Construct: Fashioning Identity, Discourse and Modernism*, ed. Jeffrey Saletnik and Robin Schuldenfrei (London: Routledge, 2009), 247–265.

3. Katherine McKittrick, ed., *Sylvia Wynter: On Being Human as Praxis* (Durham: Duke University Press, 2015), 10.

4. Sidney Mintz, *Sweetness and Power* (New York: Viking Penguin, 1985).

5. McKittrick, *Sylvia Wynter*, 9.

6. In these italicized sections, I turn to performative writing in an effort to incorporate voices and modalities beyond that of academic argumentation.

7. Payne, "Bauhaus Endgame."

8. Mintz, *Sweetness and Power.*

9. Sidney Lawrence, "Declaration of Function: Documents from the Museum of Modern Art's Design Crusade, 1933–1950," *Design Issues* 2, no. 1 (1985), 65–77, https://doi.org/10.2307/1511530.

10. Mintz, *Sweetness and Power.*

11. William M. Case, "Sugar Reports" (United States Department of Agriculture, 1961), 7, http://usda.mannlib.cornell.edu/usda/nass/SugaMarkSt//1960s/1961/SugaMarkSt-08-00-1961.pdf.

12. Wolf, *Europe and the People without History*, 332.

13. Peter Burroughs, "The Mauritius Rebellion of 1832 and the Abolition of British Colonial Slavery," *Journal of Imperial and Commonwealth History* 4, no. 3 (May 1, 1976), 243–265, https://doi.org/10.1080/03086537608582463.

14. Whitney Chadwick, "Fetishizing Fashion/Fetishizing Culture: Man Ray's 'Noire et Blanche,'" *Oxford Art Journal* 18, no. 2 (1995), 7.

15. Robbie Aitken and Eve Rosenhaft, *Black Germany: The Making and Unmaking of a Diaspora Community, 1884–1960* (Cambridge: Cambridge University Press, 2013), 143.

16. Charles White Merrill, "Summarized Data of Silver Production," Report, Digital Library, 1930, 3, https://digital.library.unt.edu/ark:/67531/metadc40312/.

17. Frederic J. Schwartz, "The Disappearing Bauhaus: Architecture and Its Public in the Early Federal Republic," in *Bauhaus Construct: Fashioning Identity, Discourse and Modernism*, ed. Jeffrey Saletnik and Robin Schuldenfrei (London: Routledge, 2009), 74.

18. Joachim Krausse, "Surfaces for a Technically Obsolete World: R. Buckminster Fuller, Shelter Magazine, and the Opposition to the International Style," in *Bauhaus Conflicts 1919–2009: Controversies and Counterparts*, ed. Gerda Breuer et al. (Ostfildern: Hatje Cantz, 2010), 95.

19. Terry Irwin, "Transition Design Seminar 2," *Terry Irwin* (blog), December 21, 2015, https://medium.com/@Terry_Irwin/transition-design-seminar-2-d1ca2c84db75#.g7u7gg6lp.

20. Matthew Holt, "Baudrillard and the Bauhaus: The Political Economy of Design," *Design Issues* 32, no. 3 (Summer 2016), 55–66, https://doi.org/10.1162/DESI_a_00399.

21. Arturo Escobar, "Transiciones: A Space for Research and Design for Transitions to the Pluriverse," *Design Philosophy Papers* 13, no. 1 (January 2, 2015), 13–23, https://doi.org/10.1080/14487136.2015.1085690.

22. Peter Redfield, "Bioexpectations: Life Technologies as Humanitarian Goods," *Public Culture* 24, no. 1 (January 1, 2012), 157–184, https://doi.org/10.1215/08992363-1443592.

23. Michelle Sarver and S. Gouri Srinidhi, "Students Develop Low-Cost Water Filtering System for African Nation," 2013, https://phys.org/news/2013-01-students-low-cost-filtering-african-nation.html.

24. Lori Zimmer, "Hamster Ball-Shaped Solarball Uses the Sun to Purify Water," accessed February 2, 2018, https://inhabitat.com/hamster-ball-shaped-solarball-uses-the-sun-to-purify-water/; Clint Williams, "Clean Drinking Water in Africa May Be a Barrel Spin Away," MNN—Mother Nature Network, 2013, https://www.mnn.com/leaderboard/stories/clean-drinking-water-in-africa-may-be-a-barrel-spin-away; Belinda Waymouth, "Eco-Minded Kids + Water Filtration in African Slum = Ingenious Reincarnation of Plastic Bottles," *Huffington Post* (blog), March 19, 2015, https://www.huffingtonpost.com/belinda-waymouth/ecominded-kids-water-filtration-in-african-slum_b_6899280.html; Hippo Roller, "Water Purification Design for Hippo Rollers Wins Awards • Hippo Roller," *Hippo Roller* (blog), July 28, 2017, https://www.hipporoller.org/2017/07/water-purification-design-awards-hippo-rollers/.

25. Jamaica Kincaid, *A Small Place* (New York: Penguin, 1988).

26. Chimamanda Ngozi Adichie, "The Danger of a Single Story," 2009, https://www.ted.com/talks/chimamanda_adichie_the_danger_of_a_single_story.

27. Rick Gladstone, "U.N. Brought Cholera to Haiti. Now It Is Fumbling Its Effort to Atone," *New York Times*, June 26, 2017, sec. Americas, https://www.nytimes.com/2017/06/26/world/americas/cholera-haiti-united-nations-peacekeepers-yemen.html.

28. Elizabeth (Dori) Tunstall, "Decolonizing Design Innovation: Design Anthropology, Critical Anthropology, and Indigenous Knowledge," in *Design Anthropology: Theory and Practice*, ed. Wendy Gunn, Ton Otto, and Rachel Charlotte Smith (London: Bloomsbury Academic, 2013), 2114–2230.

29. Delmos Jones, "Towards a Native Anthropology," *Human Organization* 29, no. 4 (1970), 251–259.

8 Negro | Bauhaus

Design and Politics of Experimental Life

V. Mitch McEwen

> European scholars envy our opportunities and it must be said to our credit that great interest in the observation of social phenomena has been aroused in the last decade—an interest of which much is ephemeral and superficial, but which opens the way for broad scholarship and scientific effort.
>
> —W. E. B. DuBois, *The Study of the Negro Problems* (2)

A century ago in the United States, the most experimental framework for understanding everyday life as a problem was not a discipline (like art or design) but a subject: the Negro. While the Bauhaus in Western Europe invented design of everyday life as a problem, the United States invented the Negro as a problem.

The key to unpacking any transformation in the twentieth century may be to assess what gets schematized as a problem. Whatever is schematized as a problem becomes, eventually, open to the operations of scientific practice, the social scientific, material invention, new reporting devices, and, of course, computation. The Bauhaus may be considered a school and movement and set of practices for schematizing everyday life as a problem. This reading of the Bauhaus could chart a line to the Eameses and other American modernisms of the mid-twentieth century, as well as a projective sense of how technology may reshape everyday life in this century.

However, there is something a bit perverse in deploying the Bauhaus as a model to schematize contemporary priorities and projections. To the extent that the Bauhaus acted as a counter to the imperial ambitions of the Beaux-Arts, as a move toward verifiable claims in the studio rather than historical referents, reifying the Bauhaus as a historical construct to exalt and guide us into the future would be—at the paradigm level—to destroy it. One of the paradigmatic shifts of staging design studio as "experimental" is to erase the assumed continuity between an archive of historical traditions and projective design techniques of the present.

In the opening decades of the twentieth century, both the Negro and the Bauhaus refigure everyday life as something already experimental, even technological.

The Negro, then, is the American Bauhaus. Which means, by a perverse transitive property, the Bauhaus becomes overwhelmingly defined by Blackness. My text traces this in relation to design and technology with segues in urban space. To follow this line of thought I am turning to W. E. B. DuBois on the Negro problem, Frantz Fanon on the Negro, as well as Wendy Chun on race and technology and Anni Albers on design at the Bauhaus.

Consider first the markedly similar language by which W. E. B. DuBois lays out the method of *The Philadelphia Negro* and Anni Albers introduces her collection of work *On Weaving*. Both avoid the guide, the historical survey, the sweeping summary, in favor of *evident facts* treated *somewhat minutely*.

First, DuBois:

> The study as taken up here divides itself roughly into four parts: the history of the Negro people in the city, their present condition considered as individuals, their condition as an organized social group, and their physical and social environment. To the history of the Negro but two chapters are devoted—a brief sketch—although the subject is worthy of more extended study than the character of this essay permitted. ... All these subjects are treated usually for the Seventh Ward somewhat minutely, then more generally for the city, and finally such historical material is adduced as is available for comparison.[1]

Secondly, Albers:

> Perhaps I should start out by saying that this book is not a guide for weavers or would-be weavers, nor is it a summary of textile achievement, past or present. It is incomplete in that it does not take up many of the facets that together constitute the enormous field that is weaving. ... My concern here was to comment on some textile principles underlying some evident facts.[2]

What is it about the minutiae that does productive work here? There is a liberation from the deductive, from the need to adhere to overarching principles or the "lessons of history." What is it about this that feels already experimental—before the content, the matter, the facts even arrive at the formation?

Before addressing this, this experiment, let us address first more directly the notion that the Negro, the raced subject, or race itself, could engage this question. Wendy Chun posits race as not (only) a narrative—as in social fiction—but a technology.

> At a certain level, the notion of race as technology seems obvious. ... Race in these [racist] circumstances was wielded—and is still wielded—as an invaluable mapping tool, a means by which origins and boundaries are simultaneously traced and constructed and through which the visible traces of the body are tied to allegedly innate invisible characteristics.[3]

Race operates as a technology for organizing social relationships, a technology that—as tends to be the case for advanced technologies—generates a slew of other technologies. These include maps, census tables, and various media to racialize bodies in space.

Of course, the technology of race is not explicitly concerned with design. It would be more familiar to think of design in relation to identity or expression, along the lines of character or type. This familiarity, however, repeats the dynamic of race as technology—a technology for making type in the human condition. In other words, it is, perhaps, because race is such an effective technology for augmenting our humanity with types that we relate design and type to character, at all.

Within A(n) Office, the practice I co-lead, our own architecture and urban design work is largely sited in majority-black cities and/or immigrant contexts. In this work, we attempt to expand architecture's relationship to social codes and material facts, disregarding the augmented reality of type. Methexis, an ongoing speculative project (figure 8.1), creates models of tens of thousands of houses owned by the Detroit Land Bank Authority. A commissioned neighborhood project in Detroit (figure 8.2) entails a study of individual houses amidst land collectively managed, whether through quasi-public entities, commercial coordination, or ad hoc practices. Both projects, at different scales, deploy algorithms for designing a hunch of what might exist, what might remain of patterns built into the city, rather than a definite object. Design becomes a way of seeing what already exists, not only a means to master or shape something.

What Frantz Fanon terms "The Fact of Blackness" he introduces this way: "I came into the world imbued with the will to find a meaning in things, my spirit filled with the desire to attain to the source of the world, and then I found that I was an object in the midst of other objects."[4] In architecture this finding of one's blackness becomes less bleak, even dryly liberating. It becomes a way of working in the midst of other objects.

Let us turn again to Anni Albers—this time for another way of thinking what design does (figure 8.3).

> If, then, it appears that our stamp is or should be an immediate or implicit lucidity, a considered position, a reduction to the comprehensible by reason or intuition in whatever we touch (confusion always gets a negative rating), we have established a basis for designing—designing in any field. From city planning to the planning of a house or a road, from the composing of music to the formulation of a law, the weaving of a fabric, or the painting of a picture—behind the endless list of things shaped is a work of clarification, of controlled formulation.[5]

Design here is not defined by application of use, certainly not by scale of object. Instead, design in this rubric of the Bauhaus appears as a considered position, and the

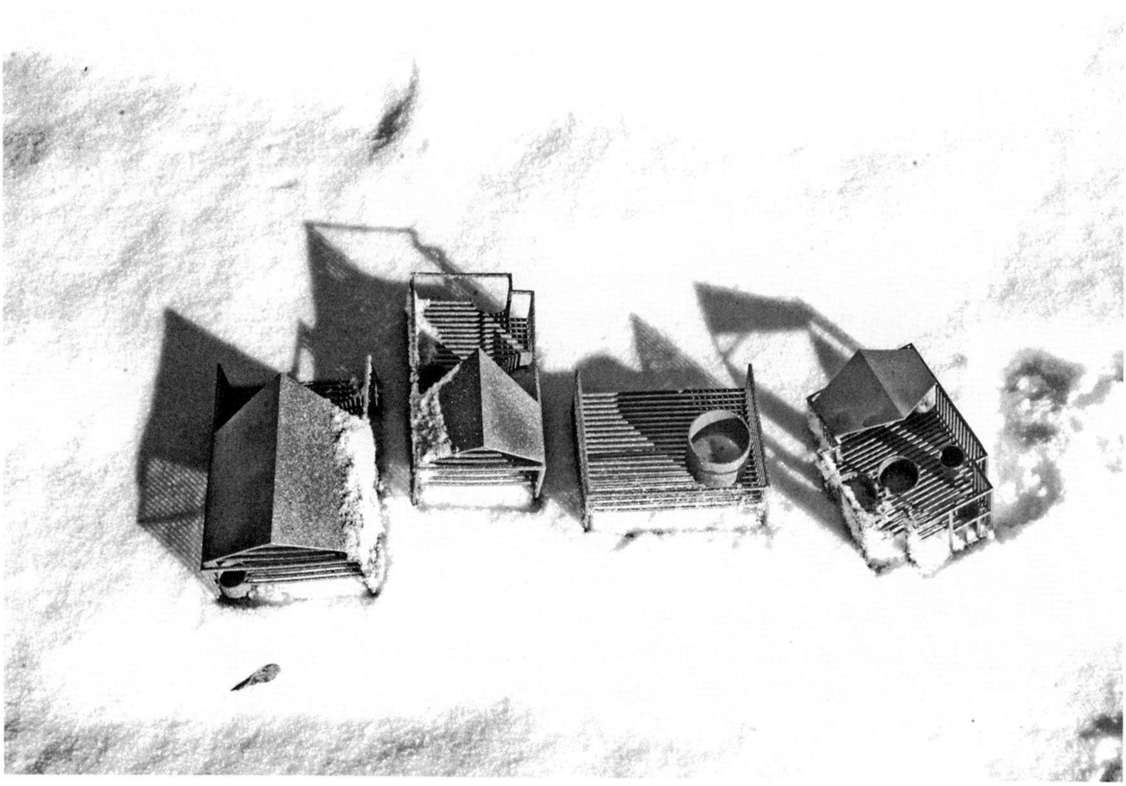

Figure 8.1
Photograph from Methexis series, speculative studies by A(n) Office based on balloon frame houses owned by the Detroit Land Bank Authority.

work that it does is the work of clarification or "controlled formulation." This clarification happens in the midst of formulation, of becoming, in relation to a *position* that is *considered*. This is the kernel of what appears in the Bauhaus paradoxically as standardization, material exploration, performance practice, and social experiment, all at once. As historian Lucia Allais quips: "Daily life at the Bauhaus was anything but ordinary: Everything was an experiment."[6]

Considering this, my focus on weaving at the Bauhaus presumes a relevance of ideation and process across the pedagogical units of the Bauhaus. The following statement would apply just as much to painting or architecture: "Only active participation in solving the changing problems of life and home makes it possible to keep the educational and cultural work of the Bauhaus weaving workshop vital and progressive."[7] The

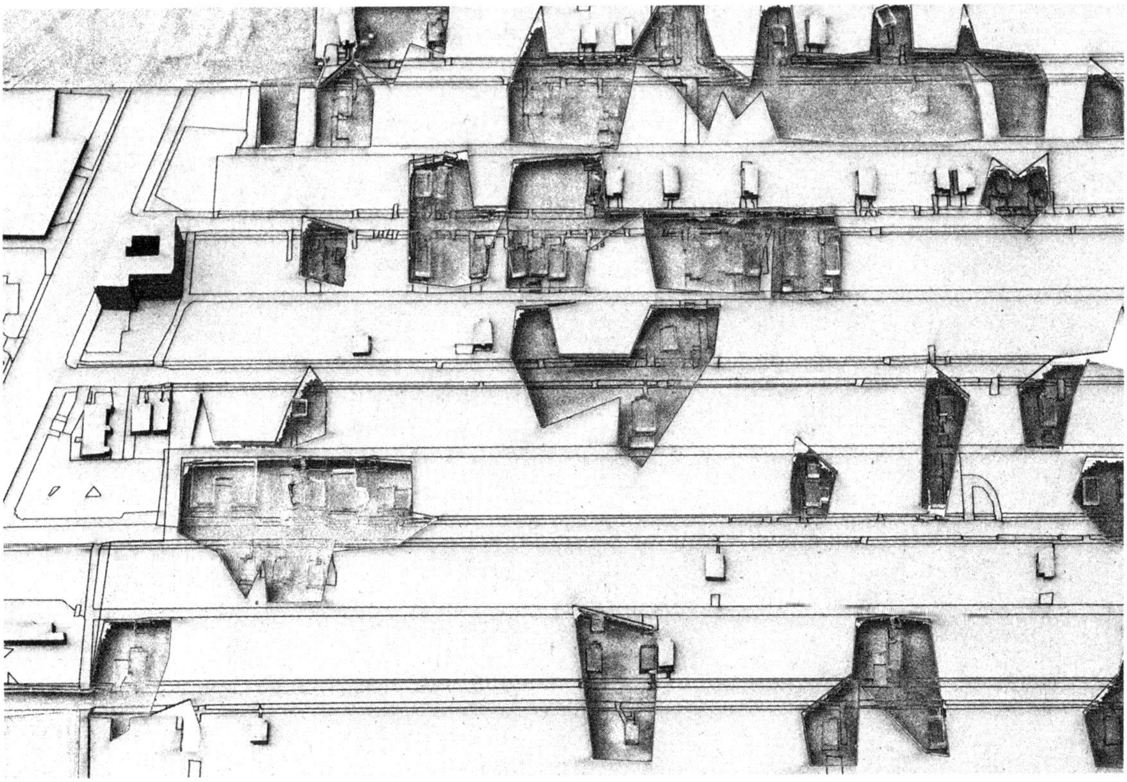

Figure 8.2
Jefferson Chalmers neighborhood strategy for City of Detroit. Study model by A(n) Office depicting archipelagos of individually owned houses within territories of collectively managed land.

changing problems of life and home launch the scaleless work of the Bauhaus in a way that opens a nonhierarchical reading of the institution. Reading the logic of the Bauhaus through weaving then refuses the institution's own sexist politics, while presuming the sincerity of its manifesto.

But to return to the Negro. Following decades of understanding that race does not exist biologically, we have a conundrum when we break through the shared common assumptions to explain what race is. A common way of explaining race relies on narrative: race can be understood as a social fiction. The Negro as a *problem* can then be understood as one of many narratives that circulate in society, albeit a narrative capable of garnering the authority to reconfigure labor markets, divide cities, and normalize mass incarceration. This slipping between the social scientific and the social fictitious

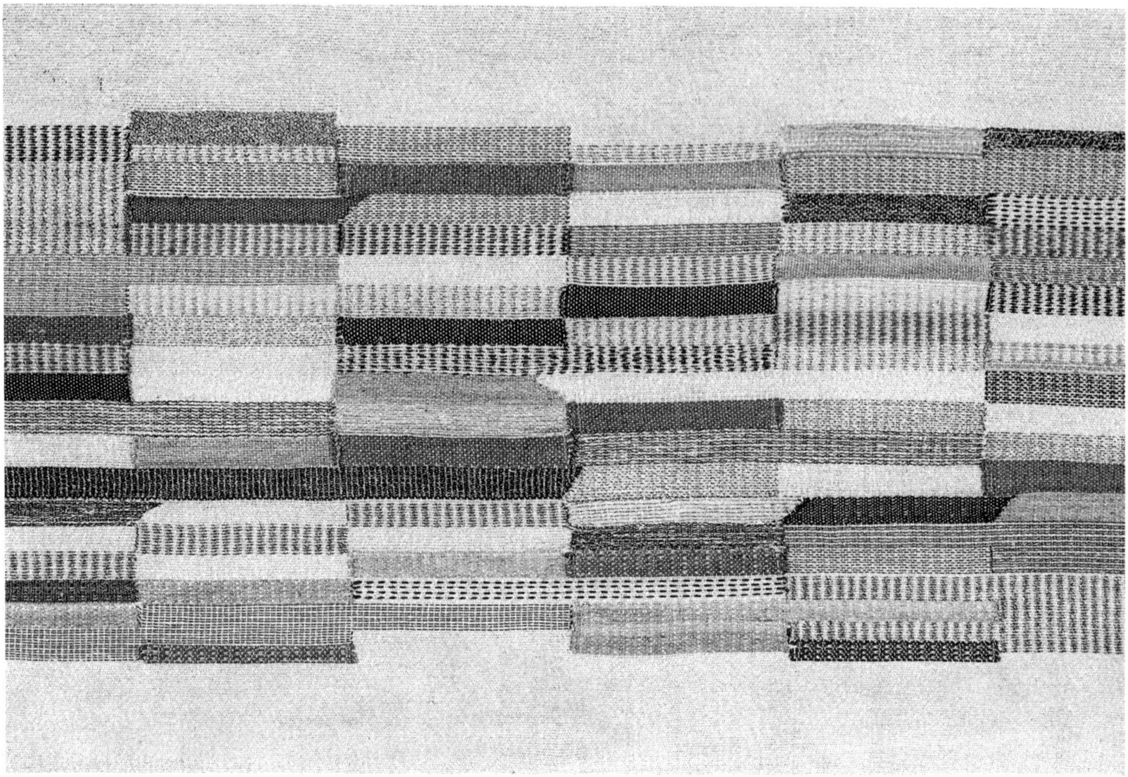

Figure 8.3
Anni Albers, Untitled. © 2018 Artists Rights Society (ARS), New York / ProLitteris, Zurich.

presents a knotted situation deserving of the most astute anthropological, legal, cultural, and social analysis.

These questions might not be so far removed from core paradigms of the Bauhaus. Design pedagogy historian Zeynep Çelik Alexander quotes Oskar Schlemmer in a 1921 letter to Gropius stating: "Bauhaus is 'building' something quite different from what was planned—human beings."[8] When DuBois mentions the envy that he imagines early twentieth-century European scholars to have for case studies located in the United States, he is talking of something not so different. The building and unbuilding of human beings as Negros through violent extraction of labor, displacement, ghettoization, and exclusion from democracy runs parallel to the invention of sociology and the mapping techniques of modern planning.

We might think race through the realm of the tentacular, the way Donna Haraway encourages us to stay with the trouble.

> The tentacular ones tangle me in SF. Their many appendages make string figures; they entwine me in the poiesis—the making—of speculative fabulation, science fiction, science fact, speculative feminism, *soin de ficelle*, so far.[9]

This, however, is not work that enters easily into architecture. Fortunately, neither is that the lens of the Negro that I am discussing here. I am not attempting to define race, nor the full arc of the history, potential, or meaning of Black America. The goal here is, rather, to consider some evident facts and treat them somewhat minutely.

To return, in this manner, to the Negro. Let us—for the sake of experiment—consider the Negro as not only a mode of technology, but more specifically a mode of design. To borrow the Bauhaus rubric as Anni Albers presents it, we can ask the following questions around this design technology:

How does the Negro engender an immediate or *implicit lucidity*?

What *touches* the Negro?

What does the Negro render *comprehensible*, and what is *reduced* to achieve this comprehension?

What is the *confusion* that the Negro avoids, and how does the Negro divert the *"bad ratings"* that confusion would provoke otherwise?

What are the *things shaped* by the Negro, and how does the Negro do *work of clarification, of controlled formulation* on these things?

To the extent that we can schematize a performance of the Negro along the lines of these questions, we will, according to Albers, have established a basis for the technology of the Negro to do design work in any field—"From city planning to the planning of a house or a road."

To address the first matter on the list, one can turn to Frantz Fanon. *How does the Negro engender an immediate or implicit lucidity?* In *Black Skin, White Masks*, Fanon famously analyzes how the Negro immediately implies the penis.

> In the midst of associational tests, I inserted the word *Negro* among some twenty others. Almost 60 per cent of the replies took this form:
>
> *Negro* brought forth biology, penis, strong, athletic, potent, boxer, Joe Louis, Jesse Owens, Senegalese troops, savage, animal, devil, sin.[10]

For our purposes here, the specificity of organ and its connotation are less significant. More significant is the operation of association. (To recap: you, the reader, are humoring my hunch that we might locate an American mode of twentieth-century design experimentation in the Negro, one as radically experimental as the Bauhaus, but virtually unrecognized as such.) Fanon, here, reveals Negro to be an associative technology—one capable of clustering associations to a word or a body or other media and amplifying associations, beyond that of part-to-whole relations or a matrix of orders. The Negro as a modus operandi of design, then, demands the method of the "associational tests" and portends an associational or networked reading of society, media, and cultures.

To return to the Bauhaus—let us now drop this pretense that the Bauhaus and the Negro can be considered as parallel entities in distinct geographies. The Bauhaus, of course, encounters the Negro. It would be easy to list here the ways that Bauhaus work performs the associative net that Fanon explicates around the Negro. There are "African" objects, such as the chair by Marcel Breuer and Gunta Stölzl. There are black line markings associated to jazz and its "freedoms." It would be easy to accuse the Bauhaus of a sweetly naive racism (distinct, obviously, from the streamlined genocidal racism of the Nazi party).

What is more germane to this discussion is to consider the design logic implicated more broadly by these moments. If part of the design work of the Negro is to shape things and do the work of clarification, then what does an object like Breuer's and Stölzl's African Chair clarify? The "character" of the African Chair clarifies the extent to which character—especially its absence—matters at the Bauhaus. There is no German Chair, certainly no European Chair. The pretense of universality achieved in Bauhaus design aligns itself with the erasure of historical, geographic—which is to say racial—character. Of course this pretense, itself, is the pretense of a European universal invented partially through the subject position of the Negro. The African Chair clarifies this *shape of things*, how the formulation of design objects without figural referents, historical patterns, and geographically associated users depends, ultimately, on "other" geographies.

The greatest encounter between the Bauhaus and the Negro could probably be located in the erasure of huge swaths of North American cities. In this Hilberseimer drawing (figure 8.4) we find the means by which the Negro becomes an urban planning technology. This drawing implies a collaboration between the Bauhaus and the Negro, albeit one attenuated through time and radically distributed in authorship. The archival title of the drawing is "Effect of H-Bomb on the size & distribution of cities." The drawing demarcates blast range, freshwater lake area, and the territory of major cities as hatched areas. The potential of the gridded dots dominates the page, a maneuver of erasure or displacement hidden in plain sight. The matrix offers up a hyperrationalization of Broadacre City—its principles reduced through Bauhaus methods to the most minimal spatial assumptions, almost a geometric proof. Plain sight, plains site,

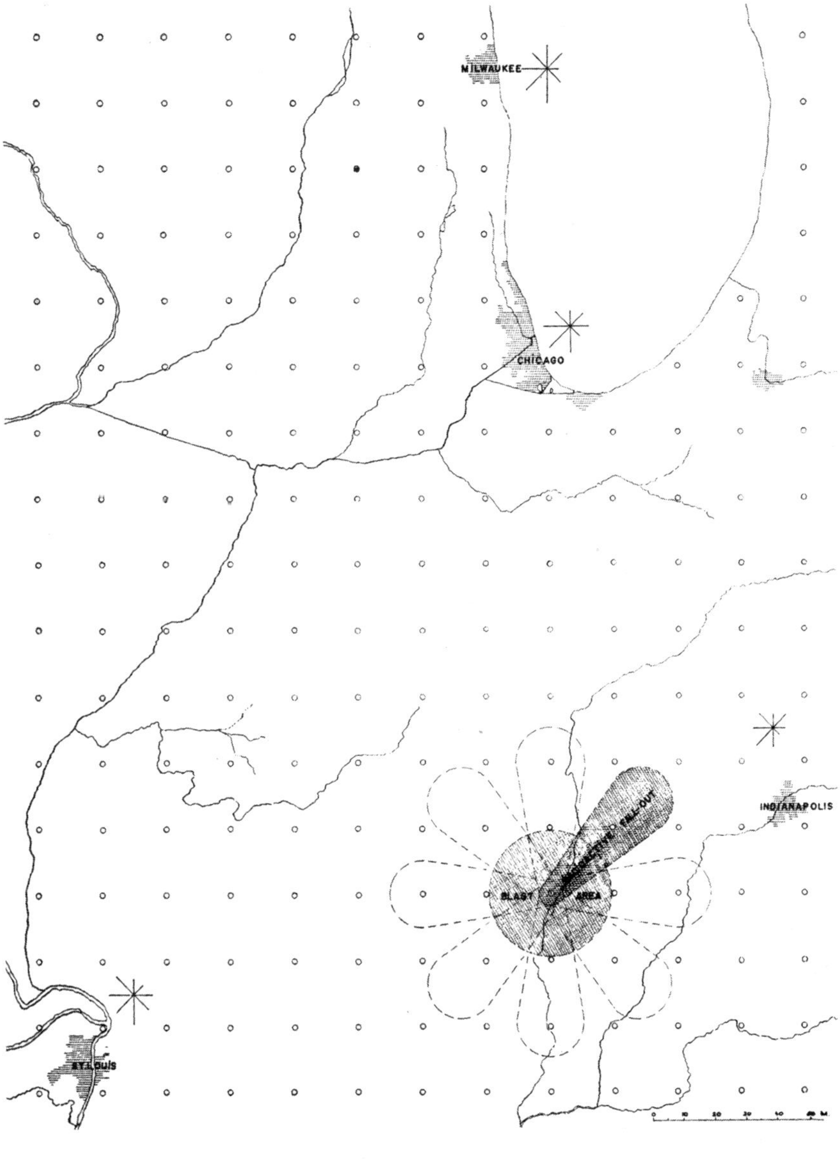

Figure 8.4

"Effect of H-Bomb on the Size and Distribution of Cities," 1955. Ludwig Hilberseimer. Ludwig Karl Hilberseimer Papers, Ryerson & Burnham Archives, The Art Institute of Chicago. Digital File # 070383.PlanforDecentral_600dpi.

plane site: the Midwest is plainly replotted, becoming not so distinct from a pattern on a loom.

Of course, the implementation of this flat decentralization in actual urban space demanded extensive territory claims, eminent domain and slum clearance, demolition and displacement. Urban renewal decimated neighborhoods across the country, landing on Negro neighborhoods rather than a regularly spaced grid. The Negro shapes, clarifies, controls the formulation of this slow-motion firebombing called urban renewal: "From city planning to the planning of a house or a road."

I want to highlight that to consider the Negro as significant to design methods as the Bauhaus—perhaps more significant—does not reduce the Negro to concept. This argument implies, rather, that evident facts in the living of Black life, in specific places and in specific ways, participate in inventing a Negro as a subject of the everyday and domain of experimental life. In addition, the Negro-as-problem, the history and legacy of this formulation that cuts across sociology, urbanism, data collection, governance, and social imagination, remains grossly unconsidered as a logic of design and a generator of technology. If the destruction of the H bomb could travel through Hilbeseimer's measured abstraction and locate itself through the presence of Negro life, then what abstract measurement and contested facts might be transformative today?

In this century, perhaps the abstract work of technology in architecture will be useful less as a means to reshape the look of things, and more so as a means to *reduce* some transformative process to the *comprehensible*. Let us also be aware that, for some of us, this is something that we experience as done to us—being reduced to comprehensible for/by/to others. There is design intelligence in that reduction. Perhaps the most important question today—100 years after the Bauhaus and in an era when the significance of the Negro as problem resurges in the form of the Arab, the immigrant, the Muslim, the Black—is how architecture will participate in a *considered position*, and whose position will be considered at all.

Notes

1. W. E. B. DuBois, *The Philadelphia Negro: A Social Study* (Philadelphia: University of Pennsylvania, 1899), 8–9

2. Anni Albers, *On Weaving* (1965; Princeton, NJ: Princeton University Press, 2017), "Introductory Note."

3. Wendy Hui Kyong Chun, "Introduction: Race and/as Technology; or, How to Do Things to Race," *Camera Obscura* 24, no. 1 (May 1, 2009), 10

4. Frantz Fanon, *Black Skin, White Masks*, trans. Charles Lam Markmann (1967; New York: Grove Press, 1988), 82

5. Albers, *On Weaving*, 54

6. Lucia Allais, email to author, March 3, 2018.

7. Gunta Stölzl, "The Development of the Bauhaus Weaving Workshop, 1931," available at http://www.bauhaus-imaginista.org/files/Gunta%20Sto%CC%88lzl_development%20of%20the%20Bauhaus%20weaving%20workshop_2:1931.pdf.

8. Zeynep Çelik Alexander, "*Mass* Gestaltung," in *Superhumanity: Design of the Self*, ed. Nick Axel, Beatriz Colomina, Nikolaus Hirsch, Anton Vidokle, and Mark Wigley (Minneapolis: University of Minnesota Press, 2018), 75.

9. Donna J. Haraway, *Staying with the Trouble: Making Kin in the Chthulucene* (Durham: Duke University Press, 2016), 31

10. Fanon, *Black Skin, White Masks*, 128

9 Building on Bauhaus

Design as the Liberal Art of the Twenty-First Century

Nassim Parvin

The Bauhaus is recognized for its influential role in shaping design practice, giving form to modern styles of architecture, textiles, and a wide range of industrial and graphic products. But is the Bauhaus mode of thinking still relevant to twenty-first-century design? If so, what were its key characteristics and how could they inform contemporary design education, practice, and inquiry?

To answer these questions we might begin with one of the most significant contributions of the Bauhaus: Walter Gropius's recognition of design as an *architectonic master art*, one that could be understood as *a new liberal art of technological culture* (Buchanan 1995, 35–43). Recognizing design as a master art entails seeing it as more than mastery of a set of materials or a series of techniques, and instead as a structured way of thinking and acting capable of (re)framing problems and conceiving the kinds of syntheses that manifest in products, arguments, and courses of action. For this, designers need to ground their work in an understanding of the fundamental plurality of principles and ways of knowing the world, transcending disciplinary boundaries and collapsing the arbitrary distinction of theory and practice.[1]

Rooted in the premise of design as a liberal art, in this chapter I distinguish three threads that connect the Bauhaus to design education and practice today, outline how these threads fit within a vision of twenty-first-century design education practice, and illustrate one instantiation of how these threads might interlace.

The first thread captures the Bauhaus's fundamental responsiveness to the social, political, and technological realities of its time. Indeed, the Bauhaus found its raison d'être in fundamental changes in industrial methods that both revolutionized the production of everyday goods and produced far-reaching transformations in the quality and organization of work and life. The Bauhaus's aim of uniting art and technology—which sought to take advantage of industrial production efficiencies to free workers from tedious manual labor while creating high-quality affordable industrial products that fit meaningfully and beautifully in various everyday use contexts—was a key element of this responsiveness.

> Thus the Bauhaus was inaugurated in 1919 with the specific object of realizing a modern architectonic art, which like human nature was meant to be all-embracing in scope. It deliberately concentrated primarily on what has now become a work of imperative urgency—averting mankind's enslavement by the machine by saving the mass product and the home from mechanical anarchy and by restoring them to purpose, to a sense of life.[2]

Following this thread to twenty-first-century design education and practice underlines the fundamental nature of an ongoing assessment and reassessment of the problematic global and local situations to design. We might identify the design of industrial production sites as an example, questioning how they impact quality of life and work both within and without their bounds. Or we might consider global issues such as extreme poverty, environmental degradation, forced migration, or misinformation, as well as possible alternatives such as sustainable food production methods that meet local needs within specific geographic locations, culturally meaningful modes of democratic governance, digital and visual literacies, or preservation of indigenous modes of knowledge-making and sharing.

Such an expansive scope and scale for design practice entails engagement with a vast array of subject matters that demand depth of research and expertise in line with the recognition of design as a master art with no subject matter (Buchanan 1995). But what kind of education might prepare students to be responsive to such complex problems?

Answering these questions foregrounds two other threads that connect the Bauhaus to the architectonic art of design today. These threads are discernable in Moholy-Nagy's later revival of the Bauhaus as documented by Alain Findeli (1990, 2001). The first thread involves the recognition of the paradox of *the vocational and the humanistic* (Findeli 1990, 7), the manifestation of which often surfaces in discussions of design education. The vocational turns up in arguments that emphasize the need for students' mastery of a set of skills and technical competencies, such as proficiency in a specific medium (e.g., sketching, model-making, or programming) or a set of methods (ranging from observational and ethnographic to statistical and quantitative). The humanistic is found in the need to educate designers on the philosophic grounding and purposes of design, focusing on its broader place in the ecology of culture and recognizing it as a universal master art. How might the pluralism of values serve design practice, and how can design serve our understanding of ethics and politics (JafariNaimi et al. 2015; Buchanan 2001a)? In what ways does technoscience shape the circulation of power and resistance (Pollock and Subramaniam 2016)? What does it take to (re)center design on the principle of people mattering (Hargraves 2018)?

While ongoing debates on the above paradox often fall into an either/or dynamic, the Bauhaus's legacy is a reminder that a productive dialectic of the two sides is essential: one that enables students to balance poetics (i.e., the internal integrity of the product known through its form, function, manner of production, and materials) with ethics and politics (i.e., its immediate and long-term impact on the communities it affects):[3]

> The first thing that we demand of a wall is that it shall stand up. If it stands up, it is a good wall, and the question of what purpose it serves is separable from that. And yet even the best wall in the world deserves to be pulled down if it surrounds a concentration camp. (Orwell 1968, 161)

Cultivating a productive dialectic between the two sides outlined above brings to the fore the third thread that is integral to the architectonic art of design—the virtue of *seeing everything in relationship*. This thread manifests in design practice by integrating analytic and synthetic modes of thinking. Findeli explains this through Moholy-Nagy's concept of *organic functionalism*:

> The functionalist aspect denotes a careful analytic, essentially scientific process whereby the students gather all pertinent information about their design problems in order to define the function that the design has to perform, not only in purely material and technological terms, but also in biological, psychophysical, and social terms. ... The organic aspect on the other hand is what makes the method phenomenological instead of strictly rationalistic and positivistic; this synthetic stage of the design process is achieved by intuition, because the complexity of the problem is beyond the reach of the sequential and verbalized process of the intellect. (1990, 12)

The kinds of analysis and synthesis that are markers of design as a liberal art are not aimed at establishing neutral building blocks that can construct apolitical universal solutions, as envisioned by some later instantiations of the Bauhaus idea especially during its Dessau years (Galison 1990). Rather they seek to identify and foreground practical, ethical, and political issues that matter in the framing and approach to problems by anticipating how possible courses of action may unfold. For this, students need to be able to put theories in relationship and distinguish their fundamental philosophic differences (e.g., positivist vs. phenomenological) and set those apart from surface-level controversies or a kind of dogmatic relativism (i.e., everyone has their own point of view, rendering any inquiry into values pointless in the end).[4]

On the analytic side, the concept of *entanglement* arising out of feminist theory serves well to illustrate the virtue of seeing everything in relationship, especially of seeing the full impact of design interventions. Indeed, feminist theory and feminist science and technology studies (STS) have played key roles in recent years in capturing the nuanced interrelationships of the scientific and technological, individual and social, and ethical and political in part by taking seriously people and modes of knowing that have been traditionally eliminated from scholarly discourses; attending to experiences of those marginalized; and challenging dualities taken as given in Western thought such as those of mind/body, theory/practice, individual/community, and form/function.[5]

On the synthesis side, the virtue of seeing things in relationship not only manifests in the kind of insight that is captured in the *act of connecting elements not obviously belonging together*, as identified by Moholy-Nagy. It also results in a deep sense of responsibility and humility in which design is recognized as the work neither of a lone genius with special talents nor of detached experts with claims to neutrality but rather as a mode of citizenship: as cultural participation in ongoing conversation and inquiry to uphold human dignity and human rights, well aligned with the conception of a master art deeply rooted in the knowledge of its grounding principles.

Weaving the Threads: An Illustration in Design Education and Practice

As an instance of interlacing the three threads, I describe the outlines of an educational experiment at Georgia Tech. In the Spring of 2016, I paired an advanced seminar course titled Critical Theory, Social Justice, and Philosophy of Design with a design studio titled Sweet Auburn: Birthplace of Ideas. Undergraduate, master's, and PhD students from a range of backgrounds (e.g., biology, marketing, and digital media) enrolled. The impetus behind combining a studio and a seminar was to connect the theoretical and practical, helping students see the substantial connection of design strategies with the larger ethical and political issues at stake aligned with understanding design as a liberal art rooted in a recognition of the plurality of principles. In other words, I designed this educational experience deliberately to put the vocational and humanistic into conversation.

The seminar course centered on classical and contemporary social justice theories. We read utilitarian, pragmatic, idealist, and feminist theories, tracing the fundamental plurality of their distinct philosophies. We discussed how they each make sense in their particular ways and more importantly how they can serve as *companions* to enrich understanding and analysis of particular design cases. The Atlanta BeltLine, a revitalization effort that transforms old railroads to walking and biking paths, emerged as a productive example for our class conversations.[6]

The studio was designed to highlight theoretical issues as practical design matters. Given the offering of the courses though the School of Literature, Media, and

Communication, the studio projects centered on the interrelated themes of communication, interaction, and storytelling. These themes were specific enough to draw in students with diverse special interests, such as urban planning, smart cities, visualization, and mapping, and broad enough to facilitate discussions on a wide-ranging set of social justice issues such as freedom of movement in the city or the politics of recordkeeping and mapping.

Students worked on two projects both centered on the close interplay of analytic and synthetic modes of thinking, the thread of seeing everything in relationship. Aligned with the social justice theme, the first project asked students to design typographic expressions of Maya Angelou's poem "Still I Rise," which captures lived experiences of oppression and resistance. The poetic quality of the piece underlines the arbitrary distinction of content and form, highlighting their intertwined nature. What is the content of the form of the poem, we asked? What is the form of its content? These questions enabled students to balance analytical issues such as choice of words, composition, and rhythm, along with their design counterparts such as typography and the quality of graphic elements, with the experience of the poem. Of each prototype we asked whether and how it was responsive to the poem, poet, and old and new audiences. In this manner we explored the poetic quality of visual/verbal languages in relationship to the ethical and political weight of design decisions and whether and how they might do justice to the spirit of the poem.

While the first project was designed to make students comfortable with design strategies, the second sought to take them out of their comfort zones, partly by not offering a concrete problem formulation or a design brief. It asked students to immerse themselves in a neighborhood in Atlanta and conceive of possibilities that are responsive to its current rather complex situation and might, in one way or another, advance social justice as they saw it. Specifically, students were asked to explore the Sweet Auburn[7] historic district; learn about its history and present situation; and consider how its past and present trajectories (both real and imagined) surface, shape, reinforce, or challenge social justice issues. As students conceived of problems and projects, they were able to see how their particular convictions of justice shaped their ways of framing the situation and conceiving design solutions. Through discussion and critiques that explicitly engaged theories of justice, they were gradually able to question those convictions, turning them into *hypotheses* (JafariNaimi et al. 2015) open to active inquiry. This in turn reshaped characterization of the situation and made them rethink the validity and effectiveness of possible design interventions.

Aligned with the ethos of participatory and co-design, the course also facilitated conversations with community partners surfacing various issues through their diverse

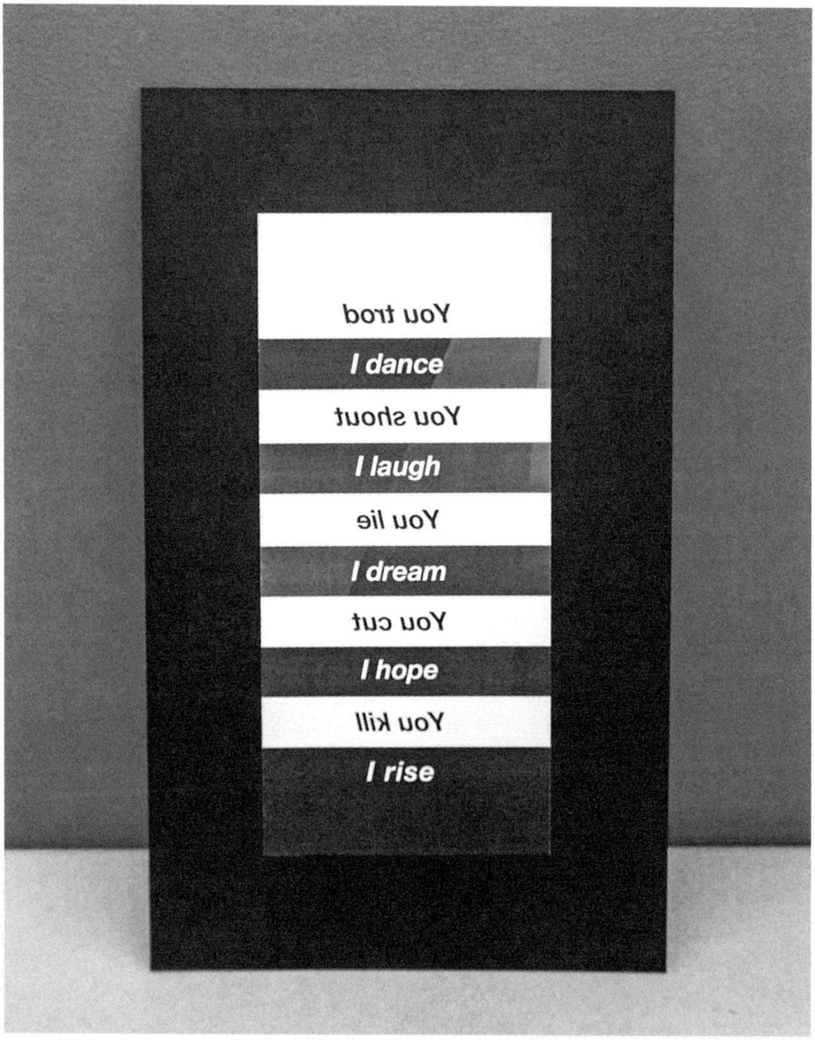

Figure 9.1
Student interpretation of the poem "Still I Rise." Design and image credits: Horyun Song.

perspectives. Students were encouraged to work in close collaboration with Sweet Auburn cultural institutions, advancing Martin Luther King's principle of *nonviolent social change* and the spirit of Sweet Auburn as the *birthplace of ideas*. This also enabled discussions of the ethics and politics of working with communities, facilitating first-hand experiences of the methodological dimension of justice formalized through readings such Linda Tuhiwai Smith's *Decolonizing Methodologies* (2013) and my own "Doing Justice to Stories" (Parvin 2018).

Together, the two projects enabled a mastery of design methods and techniques closely intertwined with reflection on philosophic groundings of design especially as related to social justice. The parallel unfolding of the theory and studio courses enabled students to experience the collapse of the theory/practice duality. They drew on their design work to reflect, challenge, and extend the theories while at the same time drawing on their theoretical understanding of social justice as the starting point for critical reflection of their designs. In doing so, the courses aligned with an understanding of design as a master art as described earlier.

The impact of such an educational experience is difficult to capture. We can look for evidence in how students grow in their thinking, the kinds of projects they take up and those they decide to forgo, their analyses of those projects, as well as the impact of those projects on the ground. Open-ended surveys and interviews reflected students' increased sense of creative self-efficacy, enhanced understanding of the relevance and value of the humanities in design and engineering, and increased tendency and intention to seek out interdisciplinary collaboration.[8] Students' initial proposals ranged in aim and scope across all disciplines of design inclusive of information, interaction, and systems and service design, such as proposals for new infrastructures or policies that were later modified to fit the available timeframe and resources. Final projects reflected this diversity. They included interactive documentaries, exhibitions of historic events, and digital archives of people and places missing from mainstream narratives of history. Their individual essays engaged a wide range of design issues such as the consequences of privatization of public land, the uses of Twitter by feminist activists in South Korea, and the appropriation of Chinese cuisine in United States.

The Bauhaus recognition of design as the liberal art of the twenty-first century stands out as a remarkable one that has yet to be realized to its full potential. Indeed, the design activity assigned to the often-overlooked contributions of the women of the Bauhaus, that of weaving, might capture the holistic approach to design-based inquiry that connects the Bauhaus to contemporary design practice and education. Together, the threads identified in this chapter serve as a starting point for engaging the

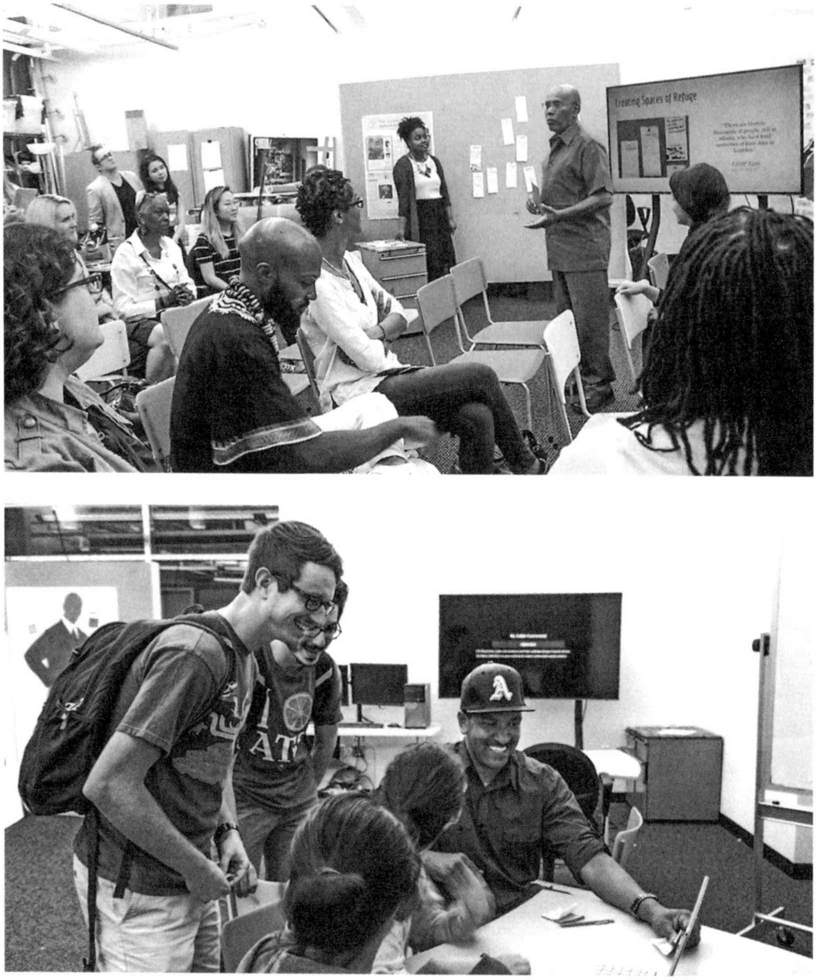

Figure 9.2
Photos capturing the close collaboration of community partners with students and their active participation in studio critiques.

complexity of wicked problems and highlighting how design might serve as a mode of inquiry into those problems.

Acknowledgments

Special thanks to my students who participated in the course with open minds and hearts, my teaching assistant Horyun Song, and guest lecturers who generously offered their time and expertise. I am deeply grateful to my community partners, especially Dan Moore Sr., Dorthey Hurst, Benjamin Graham, Tanya Graham, and the APEX Museum, for their support and collaboration. The classes were supported through the Digital Integrative Liberal Arts Center (DILAC) initiative, funded by the Mellon Foundation, Office of the Dean at Ivan Allen College, Georgia Tech.

Notes

1. Readers interested in this discussion may refer to Richard McKeon's essay "The Uses of Rhetoric in a Technological Age" (1971) for an outline of the characteristics, qualities, and significance of such a master art, with specific attention to rhetoric and technology. Richard Buchanan (2001b) builds on this essay, developing the argument for design as a master art that can overcome "the fragmentation of knowledge gained in the specializations of science and the humanities" (189).

2. Walter Gropius, "My Conception of the Bauhaus Idea," in *The Scope of Total Architecture* (New York: Collier, 1962), pp. 19–20, as cited in Buchanan (1995, 35–36).

3. "To perceive this dualism as a dialectic, to transform this antagonism into a constructive dynamic, unquestionably constituted Moholy-Nagy's fundamental issue and philosophy in Chicago" (Findeli 1990, 8).

4. For a discussion of the need for and challenges of teaching pluralism, see Booth (1986). The kind of *pragmatic pluralism* that Booth argues for is well suited for design given its emphasis on particular cases and how each philosopher might be a *companion* (ibid., 476) to help students in their effort to frame and reframe design problems.

5. The 2018 special issue of the journal *Diseña* is devoted to educational experiments that connect STS and design studio. Examples include Farías and Sánchez Criado (2018), Varga (2018), and Mattozzi (2018).

6. Students related to the Beltline strongly because of its palpable effects directly connected to social justice issues (e.g., improving the city's walkability while being a gentrifying force) and being close to home, given that it was first proposed in 1999 by a Georgia Tech master's student. Other productive examples included urban benches designed to drive the homeless away (Rosenberger 2017), and the One Laptop per Child project (Medina et al. 2014).

7. Sweet Auburn, a neighborhood a few miles south of Georgia Teach, emerged as a prominent place of business, cultural, and political activity among African Americans during the segregation era. The civil rights movement, however, had a paradoxical effect on this thriving neighborhood, as the residents spread around the Atlanta area. The construction of a highway further divided the neighborhood. Twice thus far, the area has been declared the most endangered historic place in America by the National Trust. It is now going through another wave of change due to its proximity to downtown and a renewed interest from businesses and real estate developers.

8. The two courses were explicitly set up as educational research to examine and evaluate the impact of humanities courses on undergraduate education in a technical university. The evaluation was conducted by Dr. Brandi Campbell Villa (Belay Consulting).

References

Booth, Wayne C. 1986. "Pluralism in the Classroom." *Critical Inquiry* 12, no. 3 (1986): 468–479.

Buchanan, Richard. 1995. "Rhetoric, Humanism, and Design." In Richard Buchanan and Victor Margolin, eds., *Discovering Design: Explorations in Design Studies*, 23–66. Chicago: University of Chicago Press.

Buchanan, Richard. 2001a. "Children of the Moving Present: The Ecology of Culture and the Search for Causes in Design." *Design Issues* 17, no. 1: 67–84.

Buchanan, Richard. 2001b. "Design and the New Rhetoric: Productive Arts in the Philosophy of Culture." *Philosophy and Rhetoric* 34, no. 3: 183–206.

Farías, Ignacio, and Tomás Sánchez Criado. 2018. "Re-learning Design: Pedagogical Experiments with STS in Design Studio Courses." *Diseña* 12: 14–29.

Findeli, Alain. 1990. "Moholy-Nagy's Design Pedagogy in Chicago (1937–46)." *Design Issues* 7, no. 1: 4–19.

Findeli, Alain. 2001. "Rethinking Design Education for the 21st Century: Theoretical, Methodological, and Ethical Discussion." *Design Issues* 17, no. 1: 5–17.

Galison, Peter. 1990. "Aufbau/Bauhaus: Logical Positivism and Architectural Modernism." *Critical Inquiry* 16, no. 4: 709–752.

Hargraves, Ian. 2018. "Care and Capacities of Human-Centered Design." *Design Issues* 34, no. 3: 76–88.

JafariNaimi, Nassim, Lisa Nathan, and Ian Hargraves. 2015. "Values as Hypotheses: Design, Inquiry, and the Service of Values." *Design Issues* 31, no. 4: 91–104.

Mattozzi, Alvise. 2018. "Teaching Everything in Relationship: Integrating Social Sciences and Design in Teaching and Professional Practice." *Diseña* 12: 104–125.

McKeon, Richard. 1971. "The Uses of Rhetoric in a Technological Age: Architectonic Productive Arts." In Lloyd F. Bitzer and Edwin Black, eds., *The Prospect of Rhetoric*, 44–63. Englewood Cliffs, NJ: Prentice-Hall.

Medina, Eden, Ivan da Costa Marques, and Christina Holmes, eds. 2014. *Beyond Imported Magic: Essays on Science, Technology, and Society in Latin America*. Cambridge, MA: MIT Press.

Orwell, George. 1968. "Benefit of Clergy: Some Notes on Salvador Dali." In *The Collected Essays, Journalism, and Letters of George Orwell*, ed. Sonia Orwell and Ian Angus, 156–165. Boston: David R. Godine, 2019.

Parvin, Nassim. 2018. "Doing Justice to Stories: On Ethics and Politics of Digital Storytelling." *Engaging Science, Technology, and Society* 4, 515–534.

Pollock, Anne, and Banu Subramaniam. 2016. "Resisting Power, Retooling Justice: Promises of Feminist Postcolonial Technosciences." *Science, Technology and Human Values* 41, 951–966.

Rosenberger, Robert Joseph. 2017. *Callous Objects: Designs against the Homeless*. Minneapolis: University of Minnesota Press.

Smith, Linda Tuhiwai. 2013. *Decolonizing Methodologies: Research and Indigenous Peoples*. London: Zed Books.

Varga, Hannah M. 2018. "On Design and Making with STS." *Diseña* 12: 30–51.

10 From the Bauhaus to Speculative Design

A Lineage of Socially Motivated Practice

Tim Parsons and Jessica Charlesworth

Reflecting on a Legacy

As we approach the centenary of the founding of the Bauhaus in Weimar in 1919, and finish celebrating 80 years since it came to Chicago in the form of the New Bauhaus in 1937, as designers and educators we have cause to reflect on its legacy and interpretation. Here in Chicago, both the Illinois Institute of Technology's Institute of Design (which emerged from the New Bauhaus) and the School of the Art Institute of Chicago (an institution that arguably maintains a closer relationship to the original Bauhaus ethic of designing through making) held events to contemplate and interrogate the relevance of the Bauhaus to contemporary design practice.[1] While each event had its own flavor, and offered some useful lenses through which to view the continuing echoes of the Bauhaus today, they also revealed ways the Bauhaus has become shorthand for several clichéd ideas about design—ideas that do not accurately reflect its theoretical underpinnings.

The most pervasive of these clichés is that the Bauhaus was predominantly about style. Even respected commentators such as Donald Norman are prepared to dismiss the entire legacy as one based on "form," "style," and "simplicity of appearance." In his essay "Then and Now: The Bauhaus and 21st Century Design," Norman attacks the Bauhaus for dealing only in beautiful things and ignoring usability. He writes "I do not find it relevant to the complex issues we face today."[2] This reductionist reading reveals a common design educational misstep—discussing form as if it is severed from utility and meaning. Usability may not have been called out specifically in the Bauhaus curriculum, but it is evident in the nature of the designs themselves. Furniture became uncluttered and lightweight. Graphic designs favored bold colors and sans-serif typography. Architecture foregrounded light and open space. As Magdelena Droste writes in her extensive history of the school, "As automatically as students turned to elementary forms and primary colors when starting out on a design, so too they addressed the question of function. Their aim was not style or applied art, but form appropriate to function."[3]

The Politics of Style

The Bauhaus principles that led to the elegant, pared-down designs of the objects, spaces, buildings, and graphics produced by its teachers and students were the formal manifestation of deeply held socialist political beliefs. Historian and critic Peter Dormer reminds us that the chosen style was a calculated contrast:

> If the dominant style of the old, non-socialist establishment had been plain and functional, then I am sure that the aesthetic riposte of the socialist or democratically inclined designers would have been towards elaboration, figuration and decoration. The point is that you can argue either style both ways: both can be seen as oppressive, both can be seen as democratic. You can say you are being honest about the object's role, or that you are bringing decoration and metaphor to the people. You can almost toss a coin.[4]

What has happened since the Bauhaus closed is that the meaning of the work it produced—loosely identified as the International Style—has dramatically shifted. What once provided a direct critique of bourgeois establishment taste was co-opted by corporations and assimilated to become the default aesthetic of capitalist consumption.

From glazed skyscrapers to MacBooks, the aesthetic lineage is clear, yet the political values have flipped. Therefore, if we are to speculate on what the Bauhaus would be concerned with today, were it still in existence, we should surely do so through the lens of the political leanings of its faculty and student body. Considering that these were toward the left, it is possible to position the Bauhaus on a timeline of socially oriented endeavors that track back via the Deutscher Werkbund to William Morris and John Ruskin and the arts and crafts movement, and forward through to the 1960s and radical design, arriving at the critical and speculative design practices that have emerged recently.

Socially Motivated Design

To a greater or lesser extent, all of these tendencies had social justice as a motivating factor. Ruskin and Morris railed against the inhuman conditions of nineteenth-century factories, and yearned for the maker to be freed from tyranny via the pleasure of craftsmanship. The first Bauhaus director Walter Gropius wished to flatten the hierarchy between the artist and craftsmen, uniting the disciplines to improve the quality of all built things. His successor Hannes Meyer saw that embracing the study of science and mechanized production was necessary for the artist-craftsman to evolve into a designer able to improve living standards through the economies of scale generated by volume manufacturing. And once modernism's formal vocabulary had become mainstream, a new generation of designers and theorists began to critique its monotony as a representation of an ultimately inhumane capitalist system, run on Taylorist principles and driven by built-in obsolescence.

With the postwar reconstruction that boosted design and manufacturing in Italy, there emerged three clear approaches to design practice that were underpinned by political ideologies. MoMA curator Emilio Ambasz described these as "conformist," "reformist," and that of "contestation."[5] The more radical of these approaches, which rejected the capitalist system and wished to reform or contest it, sowed the seeds for subsequent avant-garde design movements that are still influential today. The fundamental idea of these groups was that design should, first and foremost, serve people rather than industry. These designers recognized that objects did not exist in a vacuum—that there is an interconnected web of relationships and power structures connecting everyone involved in producing and using an object, and that the "design" of this web of relations should be considered part of the designer's role. And while it was not always within their reach to make major changes to these power structures, designers realized they could use the tools of their trade—the making of images and objects—to propose alternatives. Many of these "radical" designers—the likes of Superstudio, UFO, and Archizoom—largely turned their backs on designing for production and worked toward visualizing new theories.

An important touchstone of this period is Global Tools, an education project that explored alternative directions for design practice. Global Tools, which constituted over 30 members of Italy's radical design scene, held educational gatherings, operating more like an informal school than a design collective. As Catherine Rossi points out, Global Tools "were informed by a Marxist ideology that criticized the stultifying effects of alienation on man's creative abilities."[6] The "radical designers" of this period recognized that rather than simply questioning the form and function of an object within a framework of production and consumption, design could further be used as a means of questioning those systems. Having grasped design's ability to manifest fictional spaces and props, practitioners began using these to present scenarios about design, technology, and human nature.

Superstudio, a group of architects and designers from Florence, were one of a handful of design groups asked to propose an installation for the exhibition "Italy, the New Domestic Landscape" at the Museum of Modern Art in New York in 1972. Their response was to imagine an extraordinary future utopia. It was, they said,

> a reconsideration of the relations between the process of design and the environment through an alternative model of existence. ... We can imagine a network of energy and information extending to every properly inhabitable area. Life without work and a new "potentialized" humanity are made possible by such a network.[7]

Superstudio used an endless grid as a metaphor for this distribution of information and resources and superimposed this grid across a range of landscapes, collaging photographs to suggest visions of this new utopia. While it is easy to see that aspects of the project have come to pass in the form of the World Wide Web, the value of their ideas was not in whether they came true but in their ability to open up the world of speculation to designers and architects and allow them a space to "dream." The idea that designers could step away from the detailed and sometimes tedious work of conceiving, modeling, and specifying forms for everyday objects, and think about the broader structures that generated that kind of work, was hugely empowering and directly influenced the emergence of speculative and critical design in the 1990s and 2000s.

Professors Anthony Dunne and Fiona Raby coined the term "critical design" in the late 1990s during their time as researchers in the Computer Related Design Research Studio at the Royal College of Art in London. While they don't claim to have invented a new category, it has become a popular label for design that elicits debate. In his first book *Hertzian Tales*, Dunne references Raymond Geuss's *The Idea of a Critical Theory* in which Geuss explains: "Critical theories aim at emancipation and enlightenment, at making agents [i.e., the public] aware of hidden coercion, thereby freeing them from that coercion, and putting them in a position to determine where their true interests lie."[8] It is this emancipatory quality that sets many of today's speculative and critical design projects firmly within the lineage of socially motivated practices going back to the Bauhaus, Morris, and Ruskin. But whereas Morris, Ruskin, and the Bauhaus teachers and students were keen to use design as a tool to foster change through the improved design and distribution of utilitarian objects and the processes used to create them, radical design and speculative and critical design focus on design's provocative and communicative abilities.

What binds together the various strains of radical, critical, and speculative design, according to Carl DiSalvo, is "the use of designerly means to express foresight in compelling, often provocative ways, which are intended to engage audiences in considerations of what might be."[9] These designerly means combine research, structural tropes, and design proposals with presentation strategies that range from publications to exhibitions and events. Once free of the capitalist need to sell "product," speculative and critical design—like radical design that preceded it—is able to ask uncomfortable ethical questions about design, technology, and labor.

"Catalog for the Post-Human"

To illustrate how a contemporary project—through the approach of speculative design—extends the artistic engagement with technology for social ends that was evident in the work of the Bauhaus, we present an example produced by our studio Parsons & Charlesworth (see plates 1–2).

In 2014, we were supported by the Open Society Foundations (OSF), an international grant-making organization that promotes social justice, to conduct a design research project about the ethical implications of the emerging technologies of today on the future of work. The project was supported by the OSF's US Programs Future of Work inquiry, which brought together a diverse cross-disciplinary group of thinkers to address some of the biggest questions about how work is transforming and what working will look like 20–30 years from now. The inquiry explored how the transformation of work, jobs, and income will affect the most vulnerable communities, and what can be done to alter the course of events for the better.

Focusing on human enhancement technologies (HETs—technologies that temporarily or permanently overcome the limitations of the human body), our contribution had two components, a research report that drew attention to the range of HETs being actively used, or explored in the lab, and a faux sales catalog featuring a variety of fictional "everyday" products and services that our research suggested could emerge and impact the future of work.

The sales catalog, entitled "Catalog for the Post-Human,"[10] offered an instrument to help labor advocates ask questions and imagine new possibilities around the issues underrepresented workers may face in a future where they could be expected to augment themselves in order to stay competitive. The catalog was designed to reveal potential implications for the working lives of marginalized communities of workers in the near future.

The sales catalog format provides a platform to present fictional products in a nonhierarchical manner, in such a way as to enable the viewer to infer the social and political context in which such products would exist. Our catalog intentionally mimicked the approach of the now defunct *Skymall* airline mail order catalog in which often bizarre objects were described as vital necessities. This enabled us to extrapolate some of the less-well-known technologies without their proposed application jarring with those around them. Unlike a museum exhibition, where the curator's intervention suggests the ideas presented have been vetted, the sales catalog format allows unmediated ideas to be assessed at face value by the viewer.

The intention was for OSF to use the catalog in focus groups and workshops with labor advocates, where the questions it provoked could prompt discussion and debate. HETs inhabit a critical space in the debate about technology displacing work because they problematize the divide between technology (conventionally considered in mechanical and digital terms, but now including a vast range of artificial intelligence, biological, and advanced material technologies) and people. With many areas of the workforce becoming increasingly reliant on technology to gain competitive advantage, the issues are not merely about jobs being replaced by technology but the implications of people "becoming" technology in order to remain employable.

Along the lines of Dunne's argument about critical reflections, this project raised the following key questions:

- Therapies that have been developed to help those with a particular condition are often implemented by otherwise healthy individuals to enhance themselves. Might healthy individuals be encouraged or forced, either by employers or a competitive marketplace, to augment their abilities by using physical or cognitive enhancing "smart" drugs (steroids, Adderall, Ritalin and Modafinil)?
- Neurostimulation or Noninvasive Brain Stimulation (NIBS) is a set of technologies that feature in products already on the market that are able to modulate the stimulation of nerve cells in the brain areas beneath the skull. With some of these technologies already proven to monitor and improve brain function, could wearing such devices become common? Could such a shift initiate a potentially invasive culture of employee brain surveillance?
- Similarly, wearable devices now allow users to track their exercise and eating habits in a way that can help them improve health. They can also use analytics to predict psychological disorders such as depression and track their ability to get things done. Technologies introduced for such personal sensing are migrating to the workplace. Developments include wearable body sensors that enable companies to monitor and train their employees' ability to interact with customers and respond appropriately to social verbal cues. Do such technologies provide legitimate instructional resources or represent an invasion of privacy?
- Sense hacking is a term used to describe the way we shape the experience of the external world by adapting, extending and augmenting our senses using technology. Like drug therapies, sense technologies have traditionally been used to correct apparent deficiencies such as hearing loss. However, technologies are emerging that would enable augmentation of senses beyond that conventionally accepted as "normal." As workplace competitiveness increases in some sectors, will sense

augmentation become a route to competitive advantage, and what concerns might this raise in terms of workplace ethics?

In total, over thirty product ideas were presented in the catalog, described with a fictional name, sales blurb, and illustration that was either a digital collage or a 3D rendering. Examples that raised the questions above include a cochlear implant system disguised as earrings to provide improved hearing (figure 10.1), a transcranial direct current stimulation headset and productivity monitoring software, to observe, encourage, and induce productive concentration in knowledge workers (figure 10.2), and a vending machine that tailored employees' nutritional and pharmaceutical intake to their workplace needs (figure 10.3).

By suggesting that the objects were produced by a variety of vendors and brought together in the catalog, it was possible to vary the political leanings implied by their creation. While some of the concepts signified a dystopian future where commerce exploits its workforce by imposing oppressive technologies upon them, others enabled

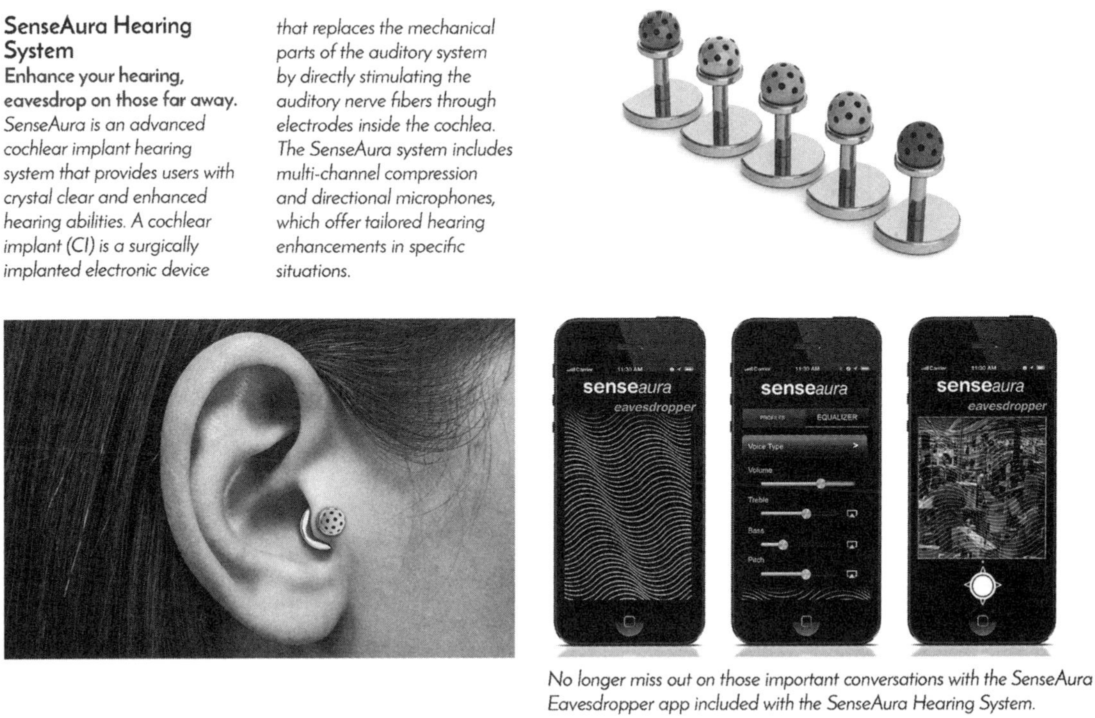

Figure 10.1
"SenseAura Hearing System," from "Catalog for the Post-Human," 2014.

Hed-Tek™ Transcranial Direct Current Stimulation

Transcranial direct current stimulation (tDCS) is a technology in which low electrical currents are applied to the skull through one or more electrodes, to modulate neuronal excitability in brain areas beneath the skull. It has proven results in increasing mental flow and the skillful operation of machinery. Hed-Tek™ offers an extensive range of tDCS products for personal and corporate use.

Hed-Tek™ tDCS Headsets

State-of-the-art anodal or cathodal stimulation of the prefrontal cortex using 2 x 2 focused electrode array. IOS and Android App controls current for a variety of operational modes.

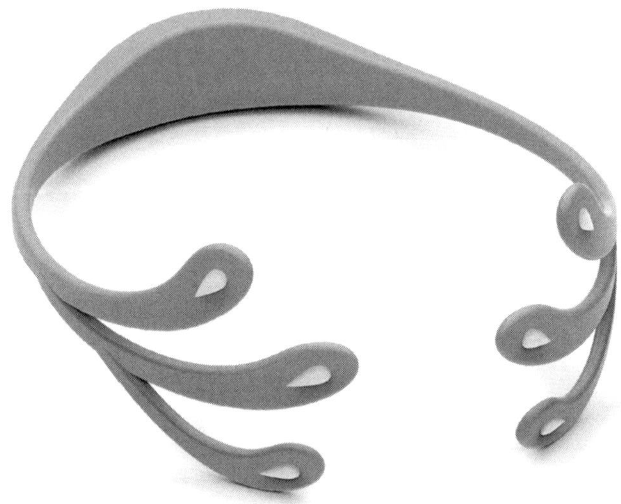

Figure 10.2
"Hed-Tek Transcranial Direct Current Stimulation Headset," from "Catalog for the Post Human," 2014.

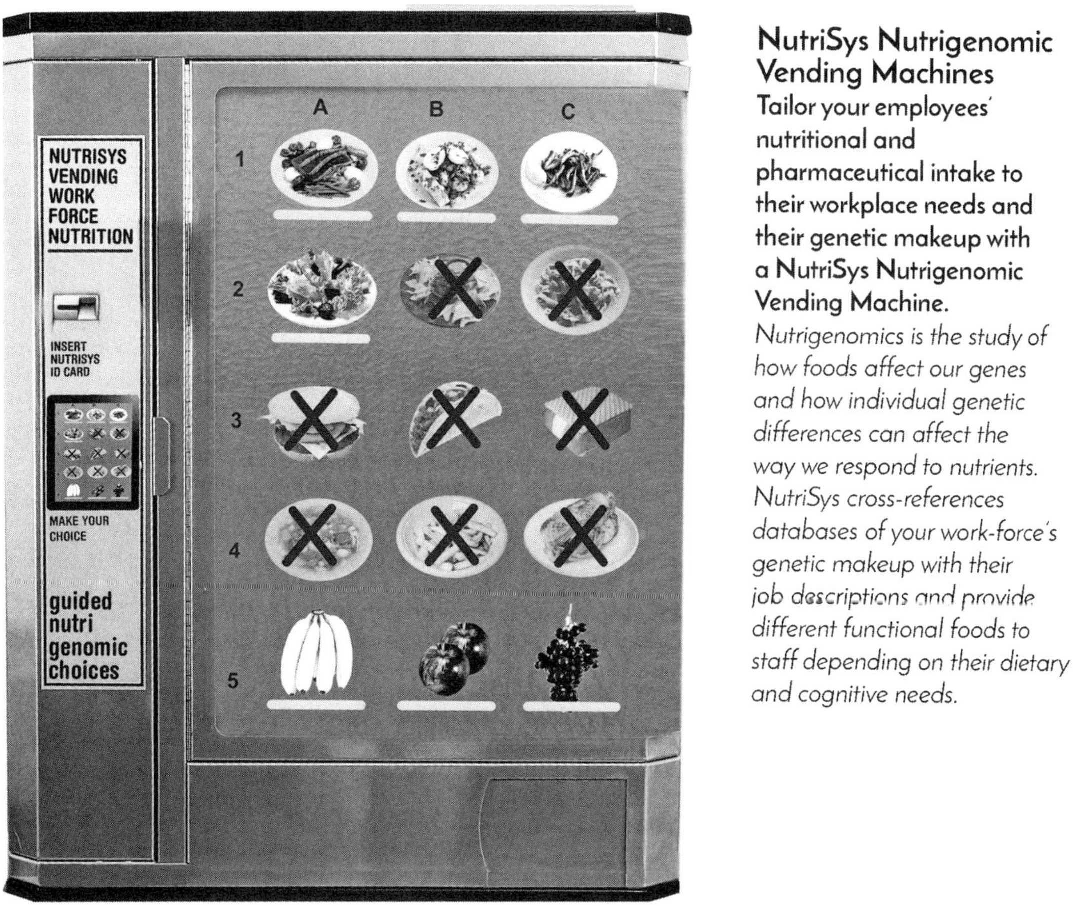

Figure 10.3
"NutriSys Nutrigenomic Vending Machine," from "Catalog for the Post Human," 2014.

workers to take back control or gain competitive advantage. A diversity of technologies was applied to the fictional concepts, ranging from those that exist in currently marketed products to those still being developed in the lab. While some are more far-fetched than others, the aim was to create concepts that were sufficiently double-edged to cause debate while remaining believable.

Along with these design fictions and the research document, we presented a list of the potential implications of the adoption of human enhancement technologies for the future of work, and in particular those likely to cause concern for labor advocacy groups. The list is too long to include here, but two examples are that employers may feel forced to make employees use HETs to keep up with pressure from competitors, and that "clean advocates" (non-HET users) may be discriminated against.

An expansion of the "Catalog for the Post-Human" project is currently in the works, with the intention to further explore relationships between work, automation, human enhancement technologies, and their impacts on human rights, through building real prototypes and orchestrating public engagement events. We aim to set up a series of futures workshops and collaborate with specialists to construct new scenarios that bring the issues to life.

The Future of Speculation

Experts writing about the future of technology in relation to societal structures, such as Adam Greenfield and Peter Frase, contrast predictions of a postcapitalist leisure society in which we will all have a universal basic income and working hours will be reduced to a minimum, with an increasingly oppressive context where automation and investments in artificial intelligence continue to marginalize and disenfranchise unrepresented workers. In this context, it is speculative design and not its problem-solving forebear that is best placed to provide provocative interventions that educate the public and guide workplace policy. With technology having evolved to a point where our lives are dramatically mediated by it, speculative design is a tool that can produce a vital critical counterpoint to its market-driven application.

However, speculative design, as an approach, despite its lineage, is still not widely recognized by the general public, with most projects confined to design museum exhibits and specialist print or online publications. It needs more venues, more protagonists, more proponents, and more critics to broaden its reach and strengthen its effectiveness. It has also come under pressure to justify its value, as Carl DiSalvo points out:

> One limit of speculative design, then, is the extent to which it foments or supports substantive reflection on alternate presents and possible futures. This limit is not determined by any one strategy, but rather by the efforts of the designers employing the strategy. So, it is not that spectacle is without value. There *is* value in base provocation as it can serve to jolt us from assuredness and complacency, if only momentarily. It can spark a curiosity that might be pursued, but to be truly provocative is to rouse to action.[11]

If speculative design is to foster real social change of a kind that would bear out its position in the history of socially motivated design work discussed here, its protagonists, supporters, and critics will have to work together to ensure its audience really is "roused to action." Not everyone will agree that the Bauhaus teachers, if they were here today, would be speculative designers, but those keen to apply an artistic engagement with technology to today's social issues should not overlook speculative design as a potent tool to educate, emancipate, and motivate change. In advocacy groups, socially motivated speculative designers find a natural client-partner, and in those designers such clients find a passionate group of practitioners committed to finding ways to use design as a tool for promoting social justice. What could be more relevant to the complex issues we face today?

Notes

1. "Bauhaus Futures," October 26, 2017, hosted by IIT Institute of Design; and "Bauhaus Legacy? Demystifying the Bauhaus in Chicago and Beyond," September 20, 2017, supported by the Goethe Institute and hosted by the Department of Art History, Theory & Criticism at the School of the Art Institute of Chicago.

2. Donald Norman, "Then and Now: The Bauhaus and 21st Century Design," jnd.org, accessed February 2, 2018, https://www.jnd.org/dn.mss/then_and_now_the_ba.html.

3. Magdelena Droste, *Bauhaus, 1919–1933* (Cologne: B. Taschen, 1990), 79.

4. Peter Dormer, *Meanings of Modern Design: Towards the Twenty-First Century* (London: Thames and Hudson, 1990), 20.

5. Emilio Ambasz, ed., *Italy, the New Domestic Landscape* (New York: Museum of Modern Art, 1972), 19–20.

6. Catherine Rossi, "Between the Nomadic and the Impossible: Radical Architecture and the Cavart Group," in *The Italian Avant Garde, 1968–1976*, ed. Alex Coles and Catherine Rossi (Berlin: Sternberg Press, 2013), 48.

7. Superstudio, "Counterdesign as Postulation:Superstudio," in Ambasz, *Italy, the New Domestic Landscape*, 242.

8. Anthony Dunne, *Hertzian Tales: Electronic Products, Aesthetic Experience and Critical Design* (London: Royal College of Art CRD Research Publications, 1999), 29.

9. Carl DiSalvo, "Spectacles and Tropes: Speculative Design and Contemporary Food Cultures," *Fibreculture Journal*, no. 20 (2012), http://twenty.fibreculturejournal.org/2012/06/19/fcj-142-spectacles-and-tropes-speculative-design-and-contemporary-food-cultures/.

10. A selection of pages from the catalog can be seen on our website: https://parsonscharlesworth.com/catalog-for-the-post-human/.

11. DiSalvo, "Spectacles and Tropes."

IV Materialities of Making

11 Some Things about Innovation

Jeffrey Bardzell, Shaowen Bardzell, and Silvia Lindtner

Introduction

As ethnographers collaborating on multisited ethnography in Shenzhen, China and Taipei, Taiwan, we have spent hundreds if not thousands of hours engaged in the field. As a result, we now have hundreds of hours of interview transcripts, thousands of photos, and countless notebooks filled with jottings, sketches, and diaries. We have seen machines in factories, played with interactive prototypes, and held in our hands various materials, parts, and accessories. Yet when we present our research, somehow the verbal triumphs over the visual; words beat out artifacts; quotes outnumber images. We began to reflect together on these visual data and insights that weren't making it into our papers. The field of science and technology studies (STS) has long practiced a study of artifacts to reveal otherwise concealed political and economic processes of technological and scientific production. Fields like human-computer interaction and recent experiments in design anthropology have explored in various forms how the making of things and design practice constitute a site and form of knowledge production that can complement other research methodologies (e.g., programs like critical making, research through design, and critical design). This chapter grows out of our various engagements with these scholarly traditions in STS and design research. Our approach was for each of us to begin with an artifact—rather than an interview or a theory—from our fieldwork, and to build a small conversation using the artifacts as central points. The approach was a kind of intellectual experiment in its collaborative mode of analysis, in the sense that none of us knew what the others would be focusing on or the kind of analytical lens that would unfold through our various object engagements.

Although our three thing-vignettes are diverse in their content and the rhetorical style of their presentation, they do have an underlying coherence. They arise from our multisited ethnographic fieldwork on histories as well as contemporary aspirations, practices, and politics of tech innovation in China and Taiwan. Over the last five years we have come together to study these sites collaboratively. They reflect the theoretical stances that each of us commonly works from as we bridge the disciplines of human-computer interaction, design research, and science and technology studies. And above all they reflect and rework themes that have come up throughout our research: who innovates, who is seen to innovate, what sorts of tools and artifacts are linked to innovation, how innovation is tied up in nation-building and policy discourses, and the complex relations between East Asia and the rest of the world in innovation discourses. The artifacts themselves tend to be evocative, perhaps seductive even, in what they promise—they are, after all, tied up in discourses about design, creativity, and innovation—but the stories behind them can be more complex.

The Hello Kitty Phone: Coming to Terms with the Consequences of Technological Promise

Silvia Lindtner

During research in the city of Shenzhen in Guangdong, China, in early 2013, I began collecting some of the phones that were offered for sale in the city's electronics markets, Huaqiangbei (华强北). At that time, the electronics markets of Shenzhen had just begun to garner attention by open source hardware and maker advocates. By 2015, Huaqiangbei was celebrated by Western media outlets, educators from American Ivy League universities, and even European politicians as key to Shenzhen's transformation into a rising hub of innovation.[1] The Shenzhen government had begun to incorporate the enthusiasm from abroad into their ongoing efforts to upgrade the city and its wider region of the Pearl River Delta into a high-tech innovation zone. In 2015, Huaqiangbei was declared by the mayor a "cradle for entrepreneurs/makers" that would fuel the transformation of Shenzhen into a "city of makers," as large screens throughout the city would have it. The electronics markets were upgraded in this effort, with many of their tiny stalls being remodeled into glossy showroom displays, interspersed with maker spaces, coworking spaces, and incubator spaces.

What had drawn open source hardware advocates to Huaqiangbei just a couple of years earlier was, however, not its ability to fashion the kind of maker spaces one can find nowadays in many cities across different parts of the world. Instead, the markets were celebrated by open source hardware and maker advocates because they were seen as providing firsthand access and allowing designers and engineers to embed themselves into the inner workings of the global supply chain of contemporary electronics production. Huaqiangbei promised the ability to hack not only hardware but markets.[2] Key to this promise was the region's history and continuous practice of *shanzhai* production, an informal manufacturing culture whose emergence is intertwined with China's history of economic experimentation. While long decried as copycat and fake and an exemplar of China's supposed inability to innovate, more recently *shanzhai* has experienced an image change. Crucial for this transformation, especially in the Western imaginary, were the end-consumer objects and artifacts offered for sale in Huaqiangbei.

One such artifact was what I have called the "Hello Kitty phone" (figure 11.1). This is a fully functioning phone, its shape mirroring the famous fictional character created by the Japanese designer Yuko Shimizu in the 1970s. Not only the exterior, however, but also the software, including sound features, interface design, and packaging, was designed through and through to match the Hello Kitty theme. In 2013, the markets of Huaqiangbei carried a myriad of similar phones, thrown on the market in small batches, each offering few alterations from the previous generation. Aside from the Hello Kitty phone, one could find phones that looked like a famous Chinese alcohol bottle, phones in the shape of a cigarette box and in the shapes of Chinese cartoon characters, phones that also functioned as flashlights and radios, phones the size of a brick and with golden exterior, phones the size of a credit card. In their wide variety, these phones make palpable the speed of production in Shenzhen, also often referred to as Shenzhen speed (深圳速度). This term originated during the 1980s, when Shenzhen was declared an experiment for China's transformation from socialist to capitalist modes of production.[3] Today, open source hardware advocates celebrate Shenzhen speed as an ultimate form of experimentation and tinkering that they believe is necessary in order to intervene into the entrenched structures of corporate monopoly and the loss of control due to automation and disruptive innovation.[4]

In a 2013 blogpost, the hacker Bunnie Huang, well known among open source hardware and maker advocates, stipulated the *shanzhai* phone to "feel like open source, but it's not: it's a different kind of open ecosystem."[5] Huang went on to describe how this form of *shanzhai* production was an open source approach to mass manufacturing that developed "independent from the West," comparable—as Huang argued—to the "Galapagos Islands." This approach of openness applied to manufacturing, concentrated in Shenzhen, Huang proposed, had much to offer the world of open source hardware. More specifically, it offered to recuperate open source hardware itself.

Around the time of Huang's writing, the Western open source hardware scene had gone through a series of controversies. For instance, the 3D printing company

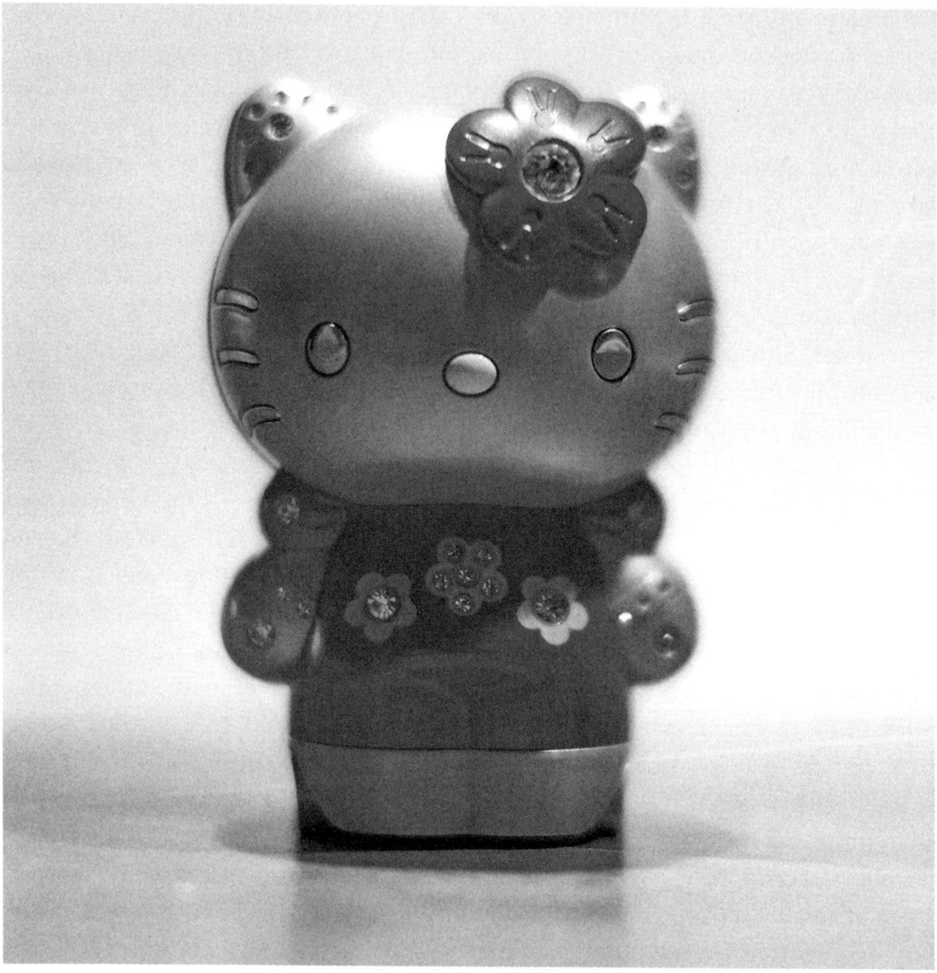

Figure 11.1
Hello Kitty phone. (Also plate 3.)

Makerbot, which had fueled the vision of a global maker movement rooted in the democratization of access to tools and techniques of technology production, had gone closed-source and was subsequently bought by Stratasys for US$600 million. The thousands of enthusiastic contributors to Makerbot had received zero compensation, making it painstakingly visible how much the promise of making fueled an economy of free labor[6] concealed by a seductive narrative of democratized production. That same year, the founders of the microcontroller platform Arduino, celebrated as the cornerstone platform that led to the proliferation of open source hardware in the first place, began what was often referred to as the "Arduino wars" as they were fighting over the ownership rights for the trademark "Arduino." It was at this very moment, as two Western companies that had been key to the visions of making and open source hardware were seemingly betraying their own promises, that some open source hardware advocates began turning toward *shanzhai* as a potential alternative not only to open source hardware but to the failed promises of modern technological progress more broadly. As I argue in greater detail elsewhere,[7] *shanzhai* production, embodied in devices like the Hello Kitty phone, was fueled by a widening distrust of technological promise. The speed and scale of *shanzhai* production simultaneously stoked fears of China's looming takeover and fueled desires for alternatives to a Silicon Valley model of hypermasculine and individualized technology innovation. What had earlier been decried as bad design, as lacking creativity, as low-quality production, and as mere fake was suddenly celebrated as constituting a hopeful alternative to the pitfalls of the promises of technological progress and modernity in the West.

There is no particular company, designer, or engineer who claims the Hello Kitty phone as their own, which was exactly why the phone was so intriguing to those who intended to remake design and engineering professions via an open source spirit. *Shanzhai* production as embodied in the Hello Kitty phone is so seductive because it offers an alternative both to modernist ideals of wholeness and individuated design and to Western-centric tendencies in postmodern critiques. As Fred Turner shows in detail, Bauhaus design was fundamentally a project of producing not only a new kind of design but also—and more importantly—a new kind of person, a model of individual human agency central to reformulating the nature of the democratic state faced with fascism. In Moholy-Nagy's thinking, for instance, "the practice of design became the link between the making of better selves and the making of a better America."[8] Bauhaus design, rooted in ideals of rationalist, modernist, and later machinic and industrial production, was positioned as enabling the creation of what Moholy-Nagy called "the whole man," capable of creating the built environment that would make possible democratic societies. *Shanzhai* production was articulated by open source hardware advocates as having emerged independently of both modern and postmodern paradigms. It is exactly because China and its modes of production have long been refused both a modern and a postmodern cachet that devices like the Hello Kitty phone have come to stand for a hopeful alternative, at the very moment when the Western promise of progress as well as its critiques have seemingly run out of steam.[9] Embedding oneself into the remainders of *shanzhai* culture promised to help one cultivate an engineer and designer self who not only reckons with the pitfalls of technological progress and modernist ideals but also prototypes concrete alternatives.

In the form and body of the childlike Hello Kitty, the phone conceals—perhaps better than an Apple iPhone can these days—its conditions of production. Stories about workers' suicides at the Taiwanese contract manufacturer Foxconn that produces for Apple have spread widely in Western mass media outlets. When the photo taken of a young female Foxconn worker during the test phase of an iPhone production run was left on the device, to be discovered by a British customer upon purchase in 2008, Western media began speculating about who this "cute iPhone girl" was, what her story was, and whether she got fired after the story became news (figure 11.2). The fetish—to invoke Marx—of the consumer product, i.e., the concealing of the conditions of labor, appeared temporarily disrupted.[10] The photo's depiction of a factory worker engaged in youthful play, however, did not fit the image of labor exploitation at Foxconn that had circulated in Western media previously.

The Hello Kitty phone presents a similar paradox. While Shenzhen is celebrated as a rising innovation hub, its history and continuous practices of *shanzhai* production have caused much debate in open source hardware circles. While some see *shanzhai* as a unique incarnation of open source (see Huang above), others decry it as the latest example of how Chinese care more about making money than about intervention in capitalist systems. Recent approaches in human-computer interaction design and beyond have sharply critiqued their fields' entanglements with capitalist market interests, from design's complicity in elevating efficiency and productivity over pleasure and play to the more recent commodification of user participation and play through digital labor.[11] The Hello Kitty phone appears to contradict such yearnings for a postcapitalist design, as it confronts the designer and engineer with their continuous complicity with neoliberal capitalism despite desires to break free. The controversy around *shanzhai* and the allure of phones like the Hello Kitty phone in the Western tech imaginary show a coming to terms with the broken promises of established traditions of design and engineering. Open source hardware and maker advocates envision an engagement with Shenzhen and *shanzhai* as not only tinkering with hardware but prototyping a renewed designer and engineer subjectivity, one that reckons with the consequences of both the modern promise of progress and a Western-centric metanarrative that continues in postmodern thought despite its skeptical stance toward Western rationalism and scientific objectivity.[12]

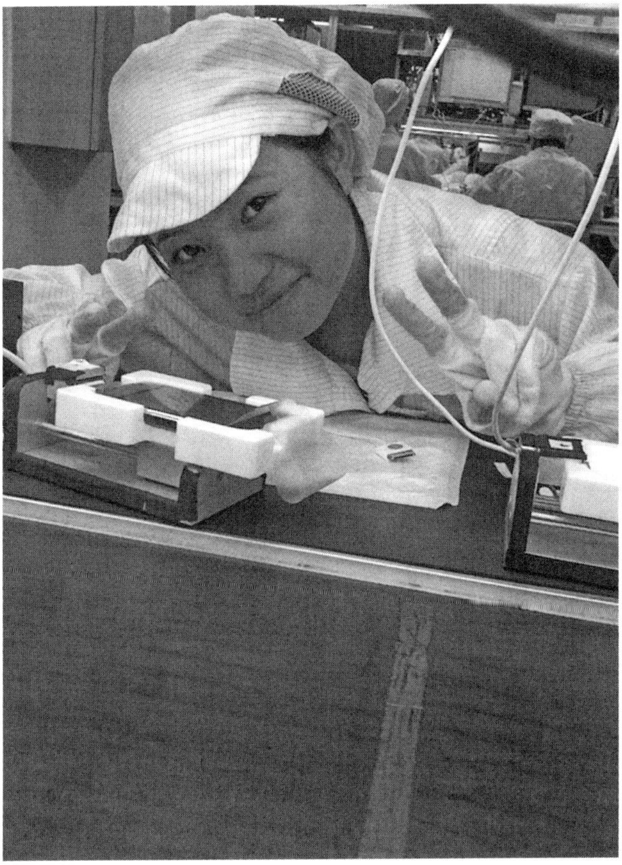

Figure 11.2
"iPhone girl."

Made in Borderlands

Shaowen Bardzell and Jeffrey Bardzell

We're all used to seeing Made in China, Made in Taiwan, Made in Mexico labels, which not only indicate the provenance of everyday products but also inscribe in them political connotations. Consider, for example, how "Made in America" became a political rallying cry, or how Shenzhen innovators tried to rebrand "Made in China" into "Innovate with China" to recast China's role in innovation,[13] or Volvo's "Made by Sweden" marketing campaign to assert the brand's Swedish identity, though the cars themselves are increasingly made in China. Thus the connotations of "Made in" labels often express global hierarchies and attitudes toward other countries. Yet as our fieldwork from Taiwan has shown, the denotative meanings of "Made in" labels might be as complex and slippery as their connotative ones. Take the case of the Japanese *shimenawa* (sacred straw rope), for example, which bears the label "Made in Taiwan," while the actual locations of its making are distributed across national borders. The *shimenawa*, a traditionally hand-crafted New Year's decoration, embodies the mobility of materials (dry rice straws) and actors (the workers who assembled and braided the straw ropes, day laborers, job supervisors, and even Western academics) in surprising ways.

In this section, we alternate between a descriptive characterization of our encounters with actors and a more analytical style, influenced by feminist geography and feminist border studies. The descriptions and analyses will show how materials, products, and actors move across different borders, including social and national ones.

Japanese New Year Decorations in a Taiwanese Rice Milling Factory

Our fieldwork took us to Shengou Village (深溝村) in the rural Yuanshan township of Taiwan's Yilan County on a chilly and rainy November day where rice paddies stretch the length of the village, making it a stunning landscape. In recent years, Yuanshan township has seen a surge of a new generation of farmers, many of whom are young (20s–40s), former city dwellers and professionals (e.g., lawyers, engineers, biologists, cultural anthropologists, media producers, designers, and architects) with advanced degrees. Shengou Village is especially known for 小農群聚 (small farmer collectives) that express a desire for a different kind of human-land relationship: They practice and experiment with alternative farming techniques and principles to address ever-increasing deleterious environmental impacts; they seek to create symbiotic (as opposed to competitive) communities to improve civic and communal farming life; and they proactively cultivate affective relationships with small animals and insects often found in farmlands for the betterment of a more resilient agricultural ecosystem.

We arrived at a rice milling factory in Shengou Village that November day as we waited to meet with the 30-year-old engineer-turned-farmer interviewee. His passion, and the intended topic of our interview, was his open-hack farm. The farm does not pay well, so he supplements that income with part-time jobs, that morning at a rice milling plant where he was helping load cargo. The rice milling plant belongs to a local farmer who returned to the village just a few years back to care for his ageing parents and take over the family farm lands as well as the rice milling plant. The plant sits adjacent to the owner's house on a narrow road in the village, facing the family rice paddies. As we got out of our car, we were greeted by its slender-built owner. He was in his black jacket operating a forklift made in Japan and directing a group of about 10 men wearing short-sleeve T-shirts and tank tops to load hundreds of boxes into the trailer of an eighteen-wheel semi. The boxes were marked with numbered stickers to indicate different sizes and weights of their content. The truck sat under the plant's awnings and was heading to Port of Keelung later that day, and the cargo was bound for Osaka, Japan.

Sensing our curiosity, the owner of the rice milling plant opened one of the boxes, and we were immediately drawn to the smell of dry rice straw as it wafted through the misty November air. All the Japan-bound boxes contained different sizes of braided ropes made with rice straw. The box shown in figure 11.3 housed two such rice straw ropes stacked snuggly one on top of the other, each about 60 centimeters long and 20 centimeters wide. No longer nourished by sun, water, and soil, and all the kernels having been threshed off, the once supple and willowy individual rice stalks were now hardened and brittle dry rice straw twisted into a new shared destiny: a braided rope with a rigid shape and distinctive pattern, harmonizing different shades of green. Along with other rice straw ropes the day laborers moved, these two would eventually arrive in Japan in time to take part in the traditional New Year celebration that commences immediately after Christmas.

Shimenawa (literally "enclosing rope") are lengths of laid rice straw ropes for ritual purification in the Shinto religion, important in Japan's celebration of the New Year. In modern Japan *shimenawa* are important. *Shimenawa* vary in size and are handmade and adorned with different objects for diverse purposes: some feature zigzag-shaped paper strips in the Shinto shrines; some are hung at the entrances of homes and decorated with auspicious items such as *daidai* (a variety of bitter orange) to keep misfortune away, or pine twigs for longevity and hope for health and growth from generation to generation, among others. The Izumo Taisha Grand Shrine in Izumo city is said to have the biggest *shimenawa* in Japan—it is 13.5 meters in length, 8 meters in diameter, and weighs 4.5 tons. It requires 3 hectares of rice straw and a total of 800 people for its assembly.[14] The *shimenawa* at the rice milling plant in Taiwan's Shengou Village would fulfill a much more modest purpose.

Movements in Borderlands and Hyperspaces

These Japan-bound *shimenawa* detail various kinds of movements across different networks and temporalities (e.g., a rice plant's life cycle and subsequent systems of food production, aggregation, and distribution). They also reveal different bordering processes and experiences at different social and spatial scales. As we argued elsewhere,[15] the notion of encounters refers to meetings where oppositions and distinctions are

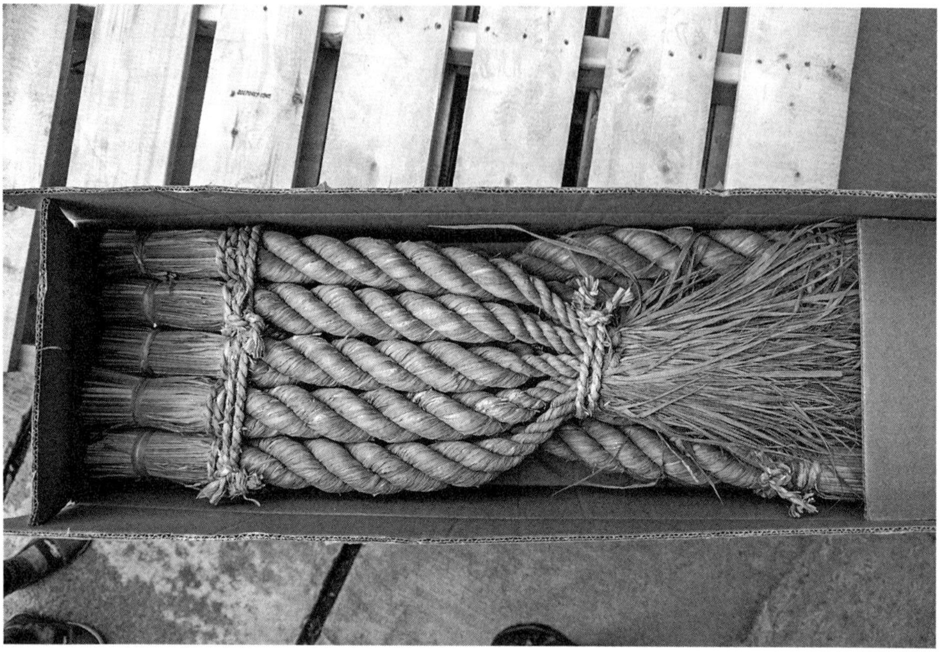

Figure 11.3
Japanese *shimenawa* for the New Year, handmade in ... well, that is the question.

active, enacted, imagined, asserted, and transgressed. In these meeting points, new possibilities are discovered, tried out, or shut down. In short, encounters represent a place/event where cultural labor—the creative work of producing culture—becomes manifest. We unpack these movements here through an analysis of a specific encounter.

As we admired the intricate rice straw ropes in the opened box and took in its distinctive smell, the owner of the rice milling plant related to us the context of the work. It is common for farmers in Shengou Village to take odd jobs here and there during the downtime in the rice-growing cycle. These jobs provide the necessary income and also opportunities for friends from the same village to get together. We also learned that while these *shimenawa* boxes all had stickers that read "Made in Taiwan" (figure 11.4), they were in reality made in Vietnam. "The Japanese only trust Taiwanese craft expertise and are reluctant to commission other countries in Asia for the work due to concern for quality control," said the owner of the rice milling plant. In other words, the "Made in Taiwan" label is part of the product. He continued: "Unfortunately we couldn't find any Taiwanese factories willing to engage in the laborious and time-consuming work of braiding dry rice straw following hundreds of Japanese patterns."

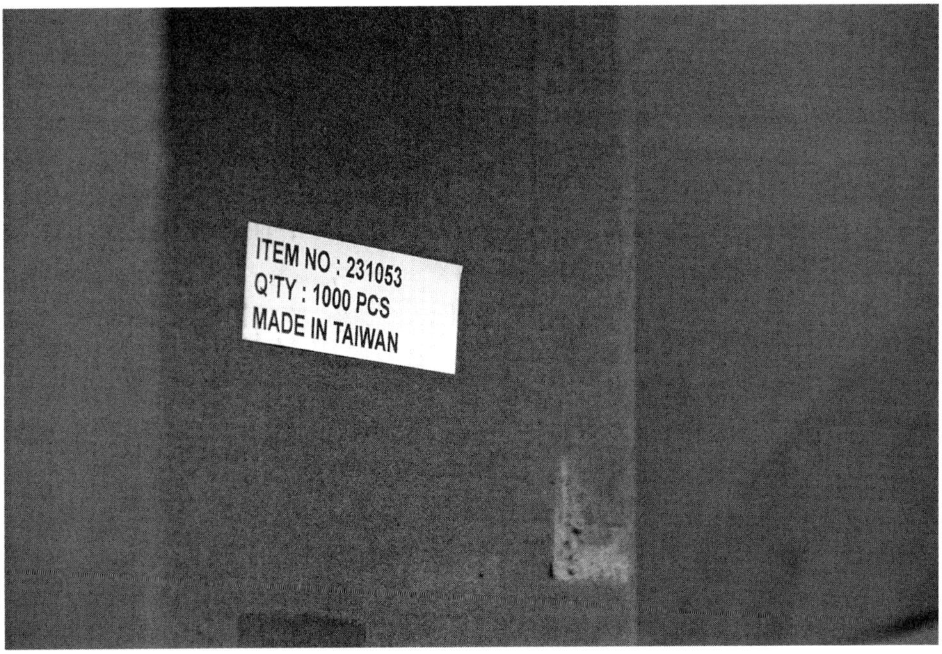

Figure 11.4
This sticker should not be understood to suggest that the box's contents were made in Taiwan.

He explained that they had developed a workaround where the Taiwanese company that got the order from Japan would take the work to Southeast Asia (in this case, Vietnam), where low-wage Vietnamese laborers would create the *shimenawa* under the watchful eyes of Taiwanese managers, who would guarantee its quality. Once made, the ropes were shipped in bulk to Taiwan, where they were put in individual packages, at which point the "Made in Taiwan" sticker was added, and then these were shipped to Japan—all of this with the full knowledge and consent of the Japanese buyers. We happened to show up on the day the individual boxes were being sent to Japan.

We return to border studies to unpack the significance. Rice straw used to make Japanese ceremonial *shimenawa* was assembled and reassembled in changing configurations, which hold different meanings and lose or retain their economic and ceremonial value as they move from place to place. Here, *shimenawa* makes contact possible across nations and production processes.[16] The material encounters, as manifested in rice straws-turned-*shimenawa*, contest labor markets and opportunity structures, and in so doing reimagine new forms of globalizing economics and regional interdependences. At the same time, they also reinforce the perpetuation of supposed nation/

group expertise, characteristics, and identity, thus leaving intact the commodity production paradigm of "Made in X, designed/engineered in Y, and packaged in Z" so often structured along the lines of racial and economic identities and inequalities.

Border Imaginaries

The case of the Japanese *shimenawa* in Shengou Village (深溝村) in rural Taiwan makes visible the hypercomplexity of production and geopolitical structure. Theoretical constructs from feminist geography and border studies enable us to attend to different kinds of movements of actors and materials—these movements engender a wide range of encounters in which some borders are asserted and maintained while some are contested, opened up, and reimagined. And just as the "Made in Taiwan" stamp allowed the Vietnamese product to enter the Japanese market, so in many ways do the stamps of Western research and science foundations allow the innovations of Vietnamese laborers to cross borders and enter the global scientific discourse on innovation. That innovation, at least, was made in Taiwan.

Culture's Industrial Aesthetics

Jeffrey Bardzell and Shaowen Bardzell

The relationship between fine art and industrialization has been a source of creative tension since the nineteenth century. William Morris's arts and crafts movement reacted to industrialization by valorizing craftsmanship in a way that continues to mark "good design" today. The arts and crafts movement set up a range of oppositions: handmade vs. machine-made, natural imperfections vs. machinic smoothness, tradition vs. modernity, nostalgia vs. looking forward. A generation later, the relationship between craft and industry would take a much more benevolent form in the Bauhaus of the 1920s. The legendary design school pursued a unity between art and technology, one in which craft expertise was a precursor to industrial design ability. The results were visible in the machine aesthetic common to much Bauhaus work. Since then, versions of the machine aesthetic would come in and out of style, e.g., in the streamline aesthetics of Raymond Loewy.

Today a new variation on these themes has emerged, only it is no longer a movement within design. It is rather a global approach to economic development, known as the "creative economy." The basic idea is expressed in a 2013 report by UNESCO and the United Nations Development Programme (UNDP):[17]

> The term "creative economy" [privileges] activities involving cultural creativity and/or innovation ... in order to uncover the increasingly symbiotic relationships between culture, economy and place. ... Cultural and creative industries not only drive growth through the creation of value, but have also become key elements of the innovation system of the entire economy. ... They stimulate the emergence of new ideas or technologies, and the processes of transformative change. ... In this view, the cultural and creative industries are trailblazers, nurturing overarching societal dispositions which stimulate creativity and innovation, working to the benefit of all.

Creative economy domains typically include tourism, heritage, arts and crafts, media production, design fields, and cultural assets (e.g., famous buildings or museum showpieces). The policy question is often framed as follows: How can culture and creativity be industrialized?

It is all but impossible to study Taiwan's IT innovation scene without encountering manifestations of the creative economy, into which Taiwan has invested hundreds of millions of US dollars. One area of investment has been the establishment of creative parks that are broadly analogous to the concept of industrial parks—that is, places where all the roles and materials needed for industrial production are collocated. Yet cultural creativity is a different sort of industry than traditional manufacturing, and so the places need to reflect those differences.

As we found ourselves frequently working in locations and domains supported by Taiwan's creative economy policies, we also began to notice visual and discursive patterns that collectively add up to an aesthetic: the aesthetic of industrialized culture.

This aesthetic is visible in many of Taiwan's culture and creative parks. Figure 11.5 shows two such parks in Taipei, in each case where a derelict former state-owned factory campus, with crumbling buildings and overgrown vegetation, was converted into a cultural park. In both cases, the original factory buildings were restored. At Huashan (figure 11.5, bottom), the original layout of the factory campus remains, with no new buildings and the previous buildings maintained, including the vestigial smokestack (not visible in the photo). At Songshan (figure 11.5, top), the original buildings at the left and rights sides of the image are nearly overwhelmed by the imposing modern Eslite bookstore, mall, and hotel complex. The older buildings could have been torn down but they were not; still standing, they are signifiers of creativity's "industrial" quality, and as historical buildings they are cultural objects in their own right.

Inside the buildings, cultural creativity also has different looks. Figure 11.6 shows two contrasting visions. At left is the interior of Huashan Culture and Creative Park. Set in a historic factory building, the walls and floors have been decorated with art, a mobile hangs from the ceiling, and the old walls still show the scars of age. At right is

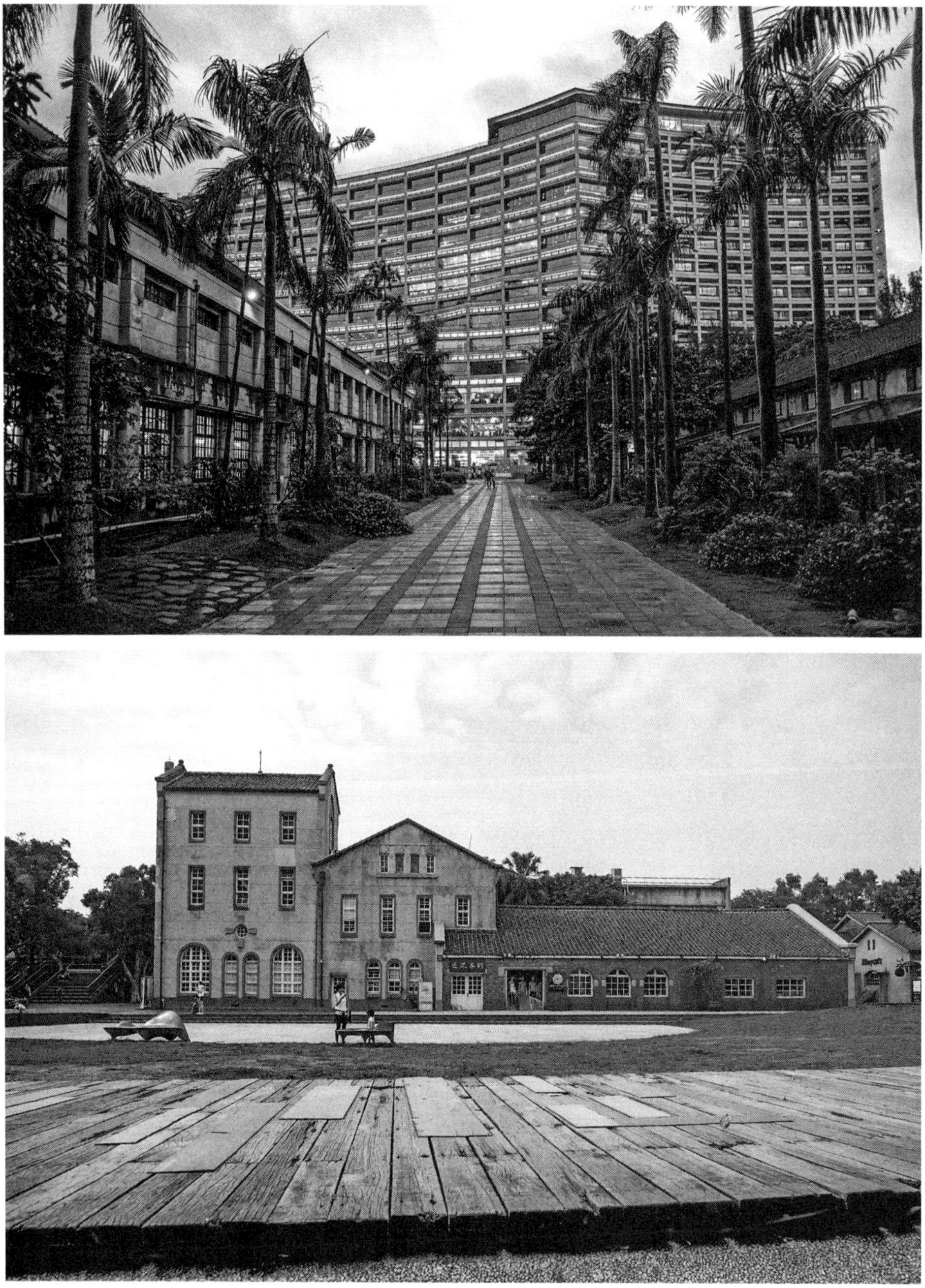

Figure 11.5
Songshan (top) and Huashan (bottom) culture and creative parks in Taipei, Taiwan.

the seventh floor of Syntrend Creative Park, a glorified shopping mall in many respects, whose interior is highly stylized and features elaborate product displays (see, e.g., the first photograph in figure 11.7). Its top floor features a startup and entrepreneurship support agency, which offers workshops and networking events.

Both inside and out, the cultural and creative centers offer spectacle. But for all of their use of old buildings and overt gestures to Taiwan's cultural past, the cultural centers are highly contemporary in their stylings: explosions of color often composed of contemporary Taiwanese IT products and their aesthetics. Yet those aesthetics, ironically, are not particularly Taiwanese. Consider figure 11.7. The Taipei 101 sculpture (shown in the first photograph) is a Taiwanese landmark (albeit a very recent one), yet it is made in a garish color out of a Danish product (LEGO). An architectural highlight—the high-peaked ceiling of the factory's central hall (second photograph)—showcases international movie posters. While themed cafes abound, many have nothing to do with Taiwan (third photograph), and even when they do (last photograph), the format of the display overwhelms its own content. The parks are not so much showcasing Taiwan's heritage or culture; they are trying to stimulate and showcase Taiwanese innovation, which has a different visual language than any traditional culture, including Taiwan's.

More traditional cultural products are also presented in industrial trappings. Liuli Gongfang crystal art company has been held up by Taiwan's Ministry of Economic Affairs as exemplary of the creative economy. Founded in 1987, Liuli uses a 2,000-year-old Chinese method of glass art production. The art itself features Chinese topics and stylings, including Buddhas, animals from the Chinese zodiac, and so forth. Yet Liuli is heavily marketed to foreigners; it is found in tourist attractions and can cost tens of thousands of US dollars. Liuli promises an authentic, even ancient, creative craft method, but the method is used for very contemporary purposes: to help market the quality of the work and to leverage its scarcity to drive up its economic value.

Outside of Taipei is the National Center for the Traditional Arts, also partly built from repurposed old buildings while also featuring new construction. But here the new building is no hotel and mall complex: it is instead the first temple ever built by Taiwan's central government, devoted to culture and scholarship (figure 11.8). This seeming contradiction—that a traditional Chinese temple dedicated to the gods of culture was designed and built as an economic development project by a government ministry—arguably symbolizes the central challenges of industrializing culture. It can be difficult to distinguish between decontextualized reality (e.g., a precious ceramic in a museum) and a carefully contextualized simulacrum. Another example at the Center is its festival parade, which uses local performers (figure 11.9). It seems like

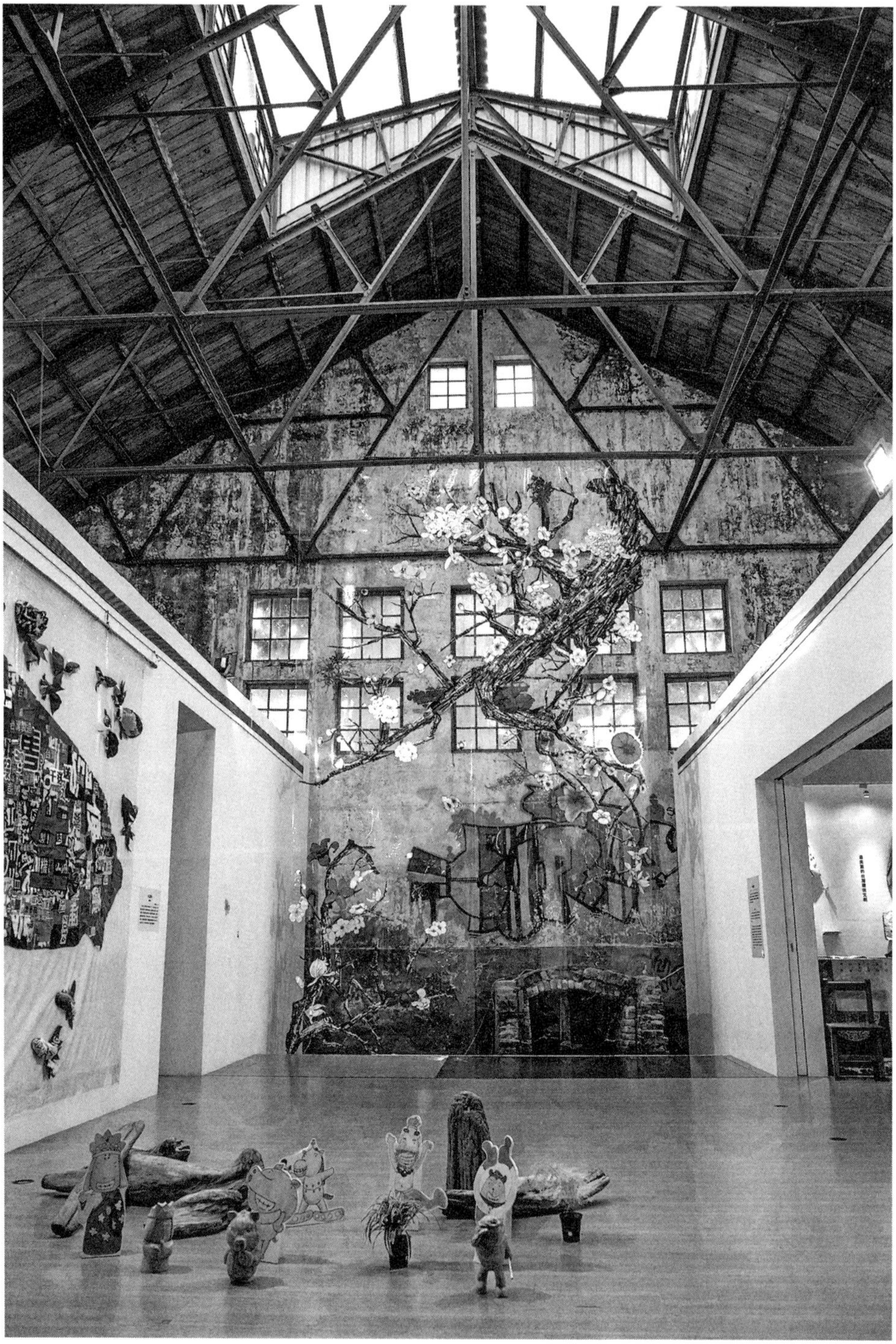

Figure 11.6
Interiors at Huashan Culture and Creative Park (this page) and Syntrend Creative Park (next page).

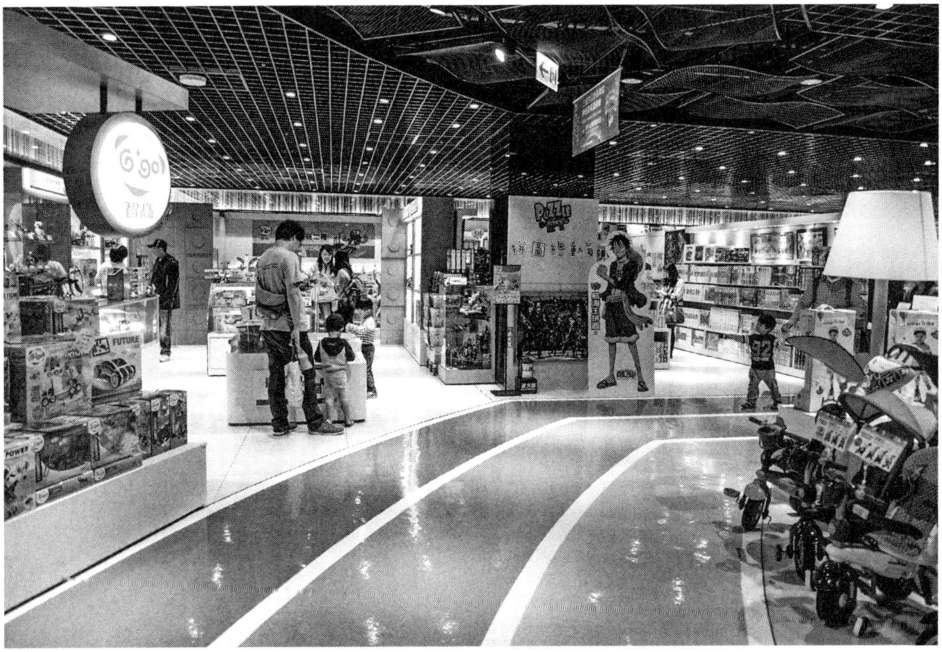

Figure 11.6 (continued)

a simulacrum, because it happens daily and no actual festival is going on. Its audience flits in and out of shops selling traditional craft souvenirs, while loudspeakers help energize the show. Performers stop and pose for pictures with tourists. But many of the performers have a sincere passion for traditional Taiwanese street performance and see their work as keeping those traditions alive by teaching new generations to appreciate them.

Nearby is Yilan Station, decorated using works of Taiwanese illustrator Jimmy Liao. The facade of the train station has been painted and modified to add animals' heads, and across the street is an open-air atrium-like structure featuring a suspended train that is about 40 meters in length (figure 11.10). While the park is relatively small, it also feels immersive, as if one is actually inside a Jimmy cartoon. Its colors are bright and it is populated with life-sized characters; items such as full-sized cartoon suitcase and handbag sculptures sit on the ground with their handles ready for grabbing. The park almost looks as if it had been designed for selfies and social snapshots.

Stepping back, we can begin to offer an account of the aesthetics of industrialized culture in Taiwan.

Collocated creatives. As policy documents show, the intention was to create spaces in which creatives not only would flourish themselves but also attract the public.

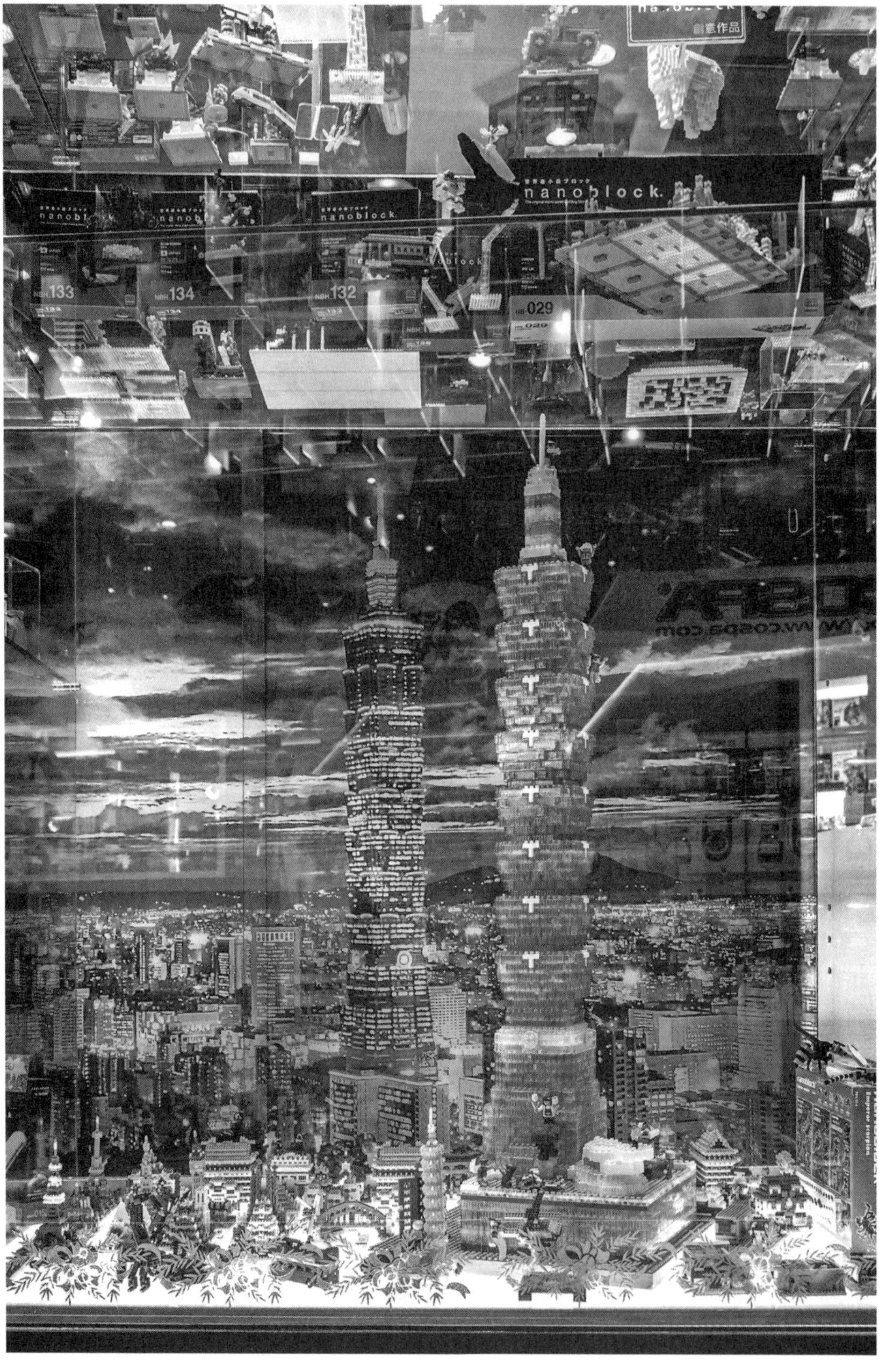

Figure 11.7

A LEGO reproduction of Taipei 101 at Syntrend (this page); a hallway of an old factory converted into a movie theater lobby at Huashan (next page, top); a themed cafe based on the work of Japanese artist Yayoi Kusama at Huashan (next page, bottom; also plate 4); and a themed cafe based on the work of Taiwanese illustrator Jimmy Liao at Huashan (page 152).

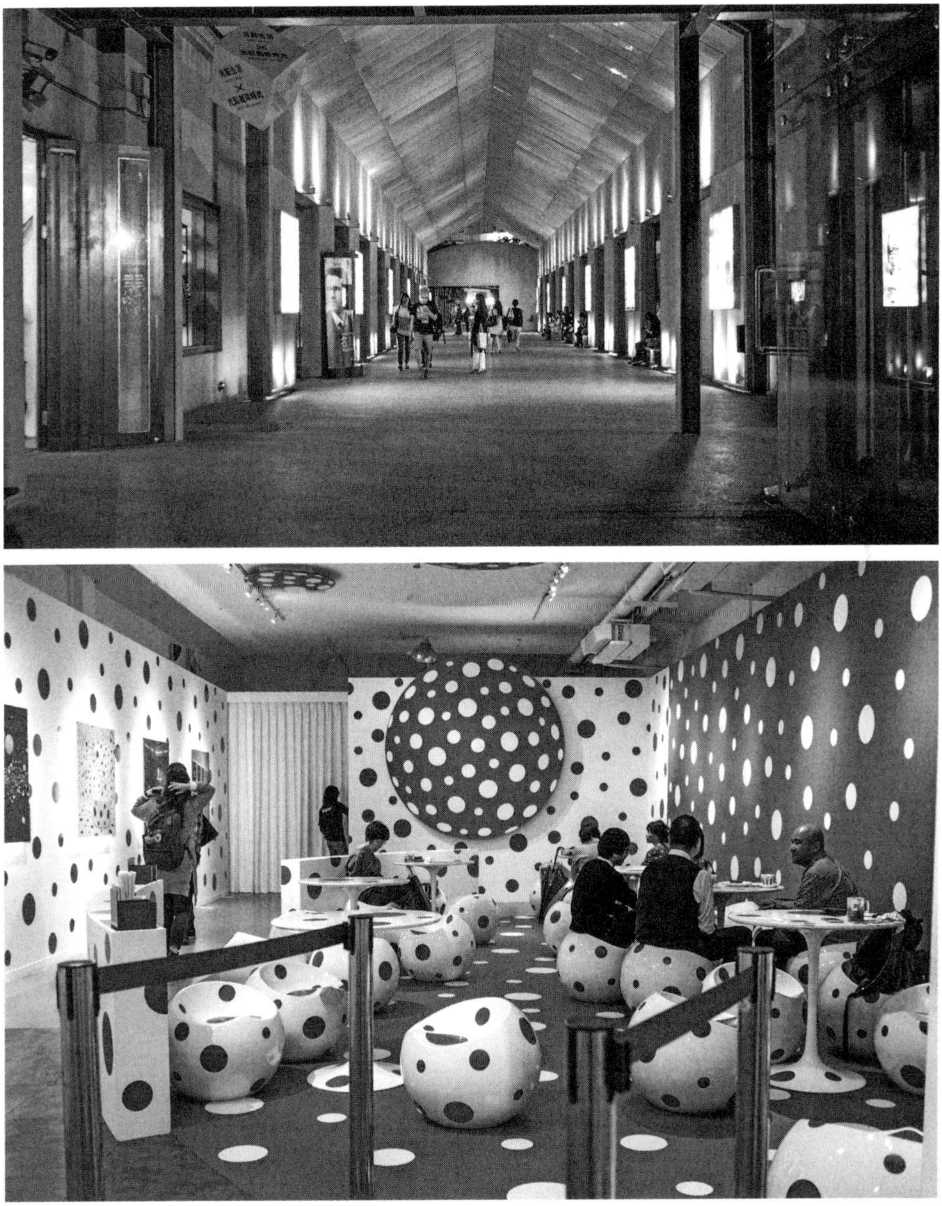

Figure 11.7 (continued)

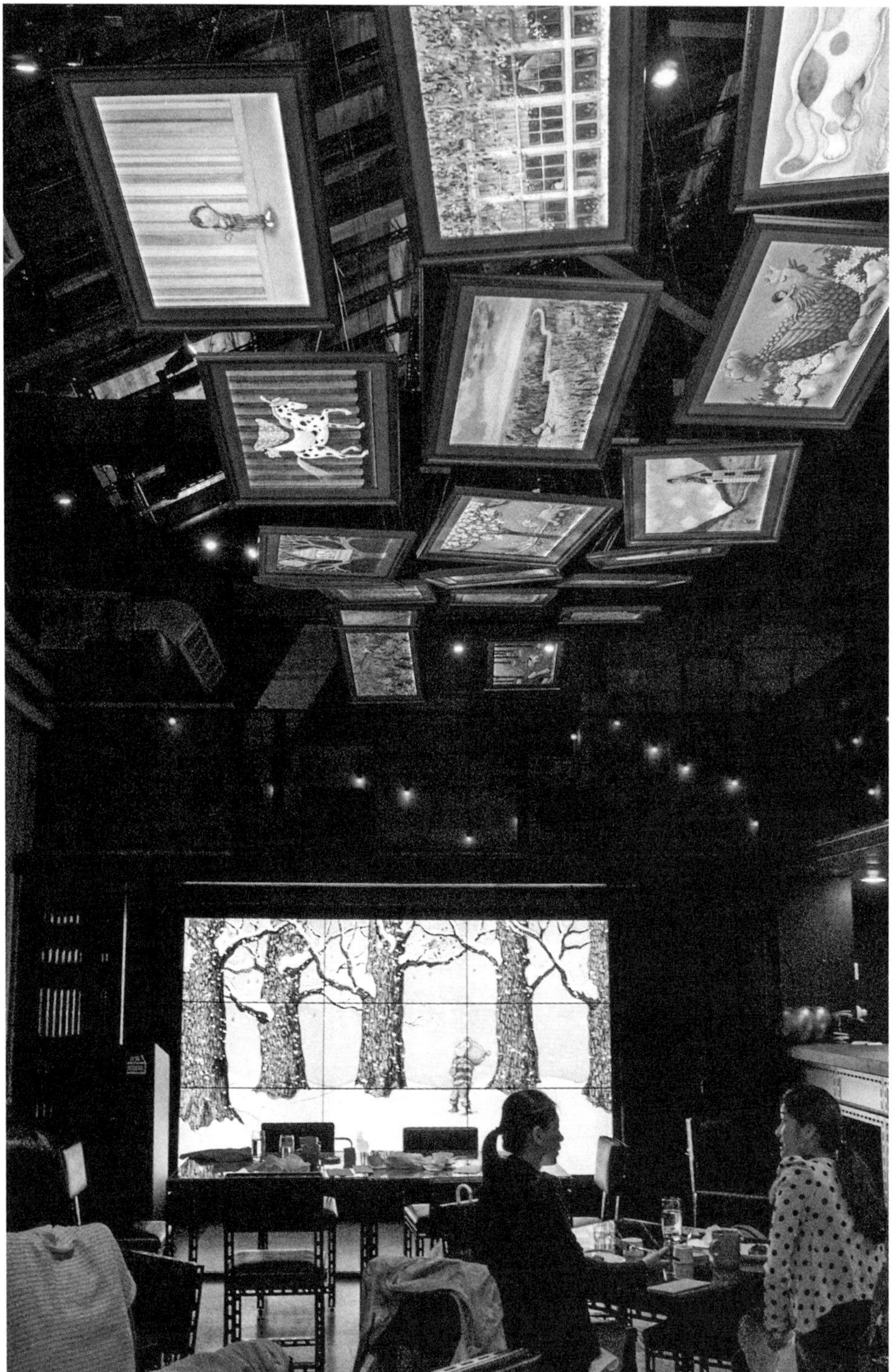

Figure 11.7 (continued)

"Creatives" is intentionally a broad term: it includes fine artists, designers, hackers and makers, performers, crafters, technologists, inventors, and entrepreneurs. The collocation of artists, technologists, and entrepreneurial individuals would create an innovation pipeline. At the same time, this innovation pipeline can be a cultural attraction in its own right, bringing families, tourists, and consumers to the site to witness it and consume its products. Shops selling creative lifestyle products and hip cafes can add to the attraction while helping to support it financially.

Retrofuturistic locations. This alchemy can only work if the sites function as real attractions. Quite a bit of architecture, urban planning, and interior design work has been done to make these sites look the part of culture and creativity parks, which simultaneously look to the past with nostalgia and to the already-arriving future with anticipation. Most have a campus-like atmosphere, with fields, water attractions, wooded areas, and winding paths throughout. These areas are punctuated by culturally interesting buildings, which include a combination of restored old buildings and architecturally ambitious new buildings. There are no strip malls or steel and concrete boxes, and

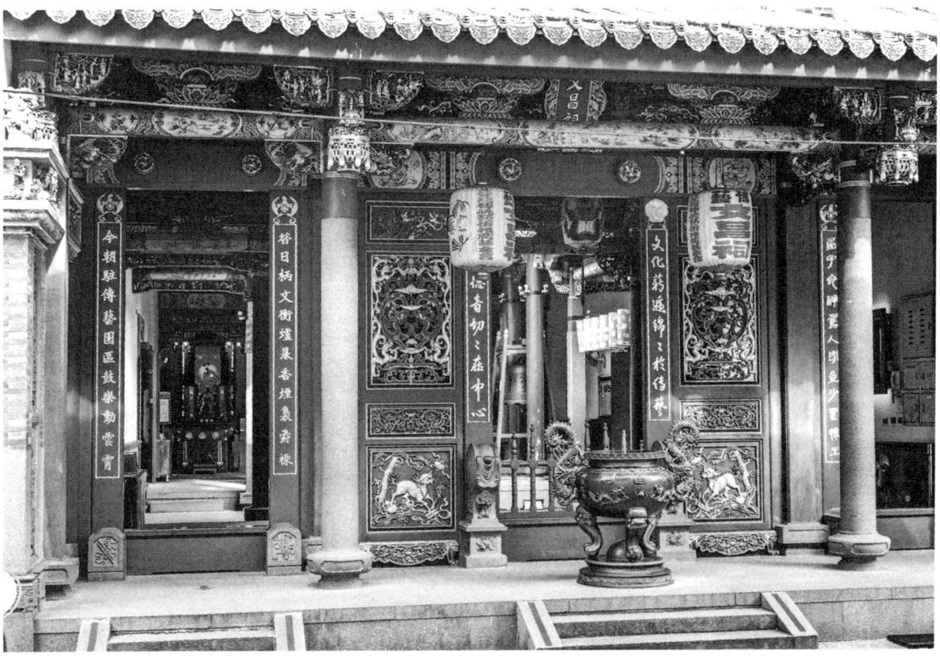

Figure 11.8
A temple designed and built by the Ministry of Culture, located at the National Center for the Traditional Arts. (Also plate 5.)

vestigial buildings and objects continue to dot the landscape. Interior design blends overtly contemporary choices, such as themed rooms, sophisticated LED lighting, and bold displays of cultural products, with nostalgic industrial touches, including room layouts that retain their original factory floorplans, surfaces, and fixtures from the post-war era, and ledgers and calculating machines from the factory era.

Cultural spectacle. The collocation of creative individuals in theme-park-style attractions creates spectacle, distinguished by at least three qualities. One is the international visual language of innovation, which today entails sleek consumer IT products, saturated bright colors that pop out from black or white backgrounds, and themed environments. Themes can be brands, popular artists, or cultural movements. This visual language is global and has few if any Taiwanese characteristics. Another is the visual language of the creative lifestyle: soaps, calligraphy brushes, handbags, teapots, needlework kits, science toys, or solid wood toys. Typically these products are of high quality and feature traditional materials (wood, leather, indigo), wholesome connotations, and high aesthetics. Some, but not all, will have Chinese and Taiwanese denotations and connotations. And the last is the appropriation of earlier cultural icons: old buildings,

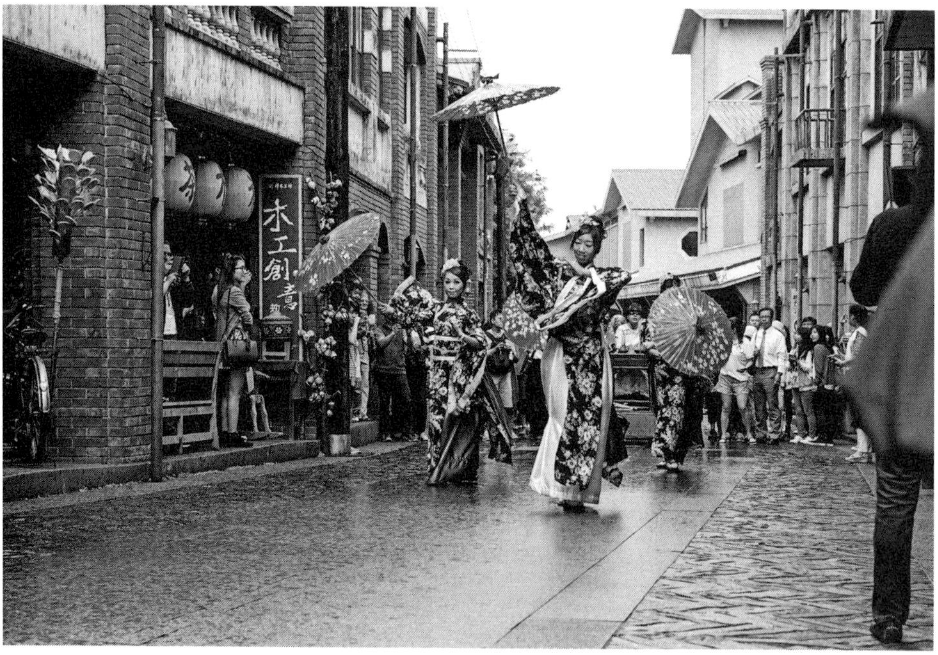

Figure 11.9
Daily festival parade, National Center for the Traditional Arts. (Also plate 6.)

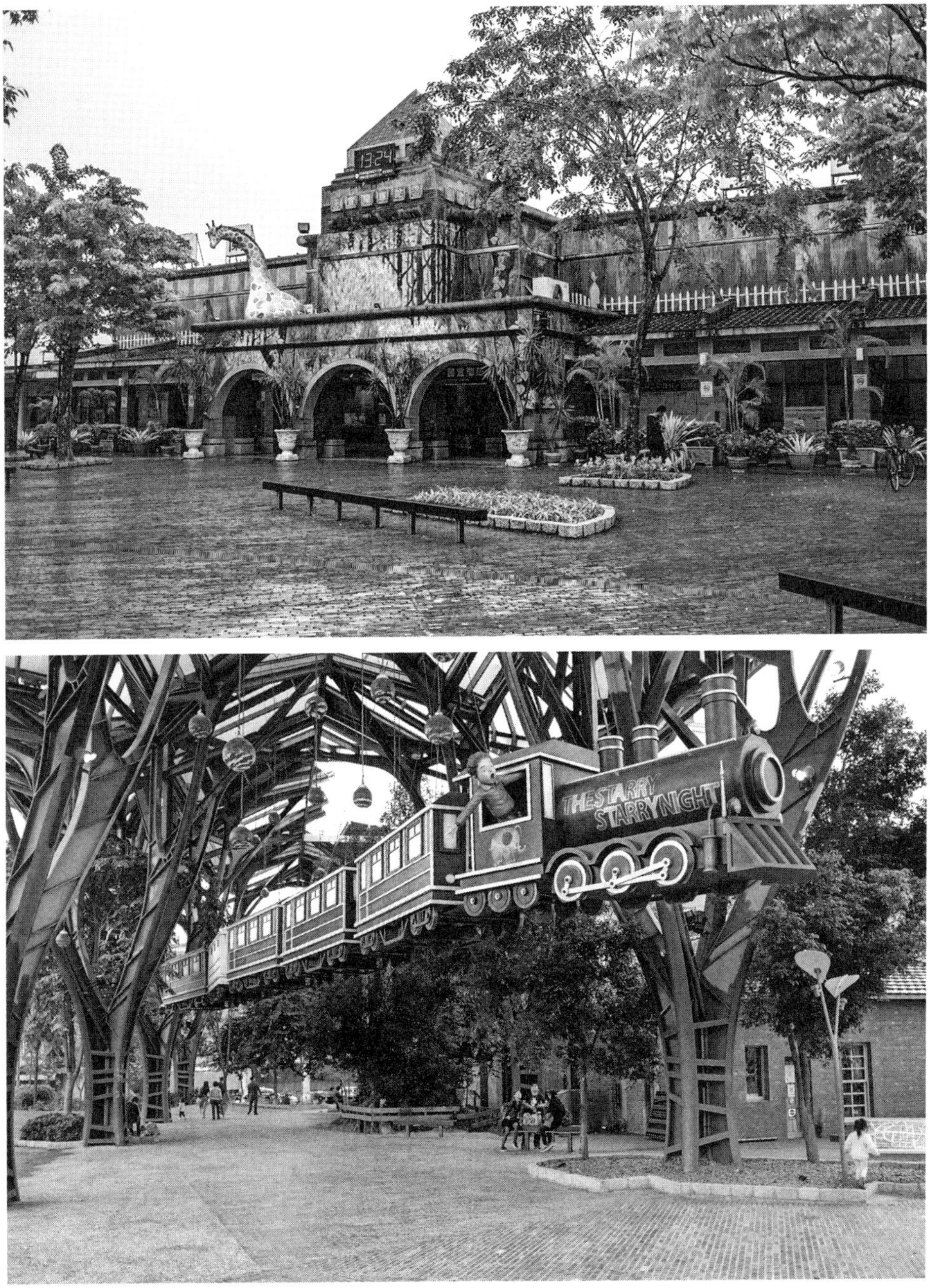

Figure 11.10
Yilan Station (top) and Jimmy Plaza (bottom).

train stations, two-thousand-year-old glassmaking practices, parades, street opera, and even temples. These icons ground the spectacle both in the past and in a highbrow sense of cultural heritage. They help guarantee a certain level of taste and seriousness. They also provide an atmosphere that transports one out of the mundane present and into a special place, a Taiwanese place that is somehow better than everyday Taiwan. In Taiwan's cultural parks, you can inhabit a nostalgic past and an optimistic future at the same time. You can immerse yourself in Taiwanese cultural heritage and be a frappe-drinking citizen of the globe at the same time. Your kids are entertained and Taiwan's economy surges forward.

When culture is industrialized, the museum shop is the museum.

The Things That Things Say

As mentioned at the beginning, our research investigates histories and politics of tech innovation in Taiwan and China. Though innovation and manufacturing were long imagined to be geographically separated, with innovation understood as happening in the West and manufacturing happening in the East, such binaries are increasingly contested by those labeled as belonging to the tech innovation periphery.[18] IT innovation has always been distributed across the globe but often unevenly, carrying on from previous modes of gendered and racial exploitation and exclusions. Some of the geopolitics visible in design and production in the tech industry have been shifting. Students originally from China and Taiwan do their graduate studies in the United States, work in American IT companies, and then return to their home countries and create their own IT startups.[19] Shenzhen is celebrated today by open source hardware advocates as a rising innovation hub exactly because it has long been denied the kind of cachet of modern progress and design reserved for Western design and IT innovation. Taiwanese precision manufacturers are pursuing the next generation of aeronautics, defense, and advanced graphics technologies. Meanwhile, recognizing the job-creating potential of IT innovation and entrepreneurship, governments are investing heavily in innovation, creating innovation parks, knowledge and networking resources for startups and entrepreneurs, and so on. We already know all of this, though, from our prior research.

This chapter addresses how these issues become manifest in the artifacts we encountered in our field work. Artifacts include, obviously, interactive products and a range of other consumer designs, such as the Hello Kitty phone and the *shimenawa* celebration ropes. But as we looked through our photos, we also noticed that we had many photos showing the contexts in which such products are first imagined, where they are produced, and how they become available to the public. Just as moral attitudes, artistic creativity, and conceptual explorations can be "read" from films, poems, and paintings, so attitudes toward innovation can be read from the artifacts that function as innovation's inputs and outcomes.

We saw themed environments, such as co-working spaces, hackerspaces, cultural and creative parks, and the upgrading of sites of industrial production and global electronics trade via a global language of DIY maker productivity as visible in the electronics markets of Shenzhen. In these environments, we also saw many (re-)appropriated cultural artifacts, such as the abandoned factory buildings now converted into culture and creative parks in Taiwan. The licensed cartoon character Hello Kitty is appropriated in *shanzhai* phones. Traditional farm plots are appropriated as citizen science-based agricultural hacking experiments. A government builds a traditional temple as part of a tourist attraction. The Made in Taiwan sticker becomes a commodity in its own right.

As we critically engaged these diverse artifacts, the question of labor and production, and more specifically of its visibility, became a regular theme for us. When open source hardware advocates celebrate Shenzhen speed and displace a techno-optimistic narrative onto China, old and continuous forms of labor exploitation are rendered a seeming nonissue, a thing soon to be of the past that will be overcome by people's self-transformation into empowered entrepreneurial actors. These contradictions manifest not because labor is concealed, but perhaps because there are too many images of it: photos of factory labor have been circulated widely by open source hardware advocates and media alike, from Foxconn factory suicides and the iPhone girl to photos of factory tours and assembly line work in maker blog posts and write-ups by startups and designers venturing into Shenzhen. In the *shimenawa* example, the labor of production is distributed in space and time: the labor of making the rope objects, of packaging them, and of shipping them, of supervising and guaranteeing the quality of all this labor, and of crafting a solution to the production/labor problem. Labor is concealed in the sense that Vietnamese labor is masked behind the "Made in Taiwan" label, but only to consumers; the Japanese import company is well aware of the arrangement. In the cultural and creative parks, a certain kind of labor—cultural creative labor as a specific form of "innovation"—is not only visible but is turned into a spectacle. Spaces are intended to blur the boundaries between innovation professions (e.g., product design, technologists, inventors, and entrepreneurs) and the public—e.g., in makerspaces and government-supported hackathons. Creative processes and outcomes are put on stage as key to the parks' attraction.

Our focus on artifacts helped bring certain aspects of all of the above into research focus. We attended to visual languages, for example, noting the ways that government-supported notions of innovation are packaged and in some cases literally marketed.

While we have attended to innovation ecologies—an abstract concept that operates on a system metaphor—we increasingly see such ecologies as tangible compositions: people and artifacts organized in space and time in ways that are not only productive but have aesthetic qualities. And one of the common forms of composition—something like a genre—is that of the theme park. By theme park we mean a location that has been set aside and in visible ways demarcated with borders. Inside the park, a theme—of innovation or a certain notion of innovation—serves as the organizing and sense-making principle. This is most visible in cultural and creative parks, but it is also present in Huaqiangbei (which a colleague once characterized as a "city-sized Radio Shack") and in the small-hold farm plots of Yilan.

That innovation ecologies have aesthetic and affective qualities, and not just organizational efficacy, is part of what makes them so seductive. Whether any of these examples is directly descended from the Bauhaus is beside the point (indeed it is in part what they themselves contest); the cases each simultaneously embody and also trouble, in their own ways, the core issues that helped shape the Bauhaus's take on design. This take comprises sometimes surprising interrelations between traditional craftsmanship and industrialized production; a yearning for design that would make people whole rather than alienated; and a taste for cultural products that are authentic, exquisite, and available to the masses. All three cases challenge any romantic engagement with technology and the design processes of the past. As postcolonial and feminist anthropology has long shown, Eurocentric ideals of modernist and rationalist future making have denied modernity to "others," who are rendered less modern, located in the past, and lacking both creativity and rationalistic thought. It is this very denial of modernity to others that haunts the Bauhaus and its Eurocentric legacies today.

Notes

1. Silvia Lindtner, "Laboratory of the Precarious: Prototyping Entrepreneurial Living in Shenzhen," *Women Studies Quarterly* 45, nos. 3–4 (2017), 287–305.

2. Silvia Lindtner, *Prototype Nation: China, the Maker movement and the Promise of Entrepreneurial Living* (Princeton, NJ: Princeton University Press, forthcoming).

3. Mary Ann O'Donnell, "Heroes of the Special Zone: Modeling Reform and Its Limits," in *Learning from Shenzhen: China's Post-Mao Experiment from Special Zone to Model City*, ed. Mary Ann O'Donnell, Winnie Wong, and Jonathan Bach (Chicago: University of Chicago Press, 2017).

4. Lindtner, *Prototype Nation.*

5. Bunnie Huang, "The $12 'Gongkai' Phone," https://www.bunniestudios.com/blog/?page_id=3107, last accessed August 15, 2018.

6. Tiziana Terranova, "Free Labor: Producing Culture for the Digital Economy," *Social Text* 18, no. 2 (2000).

7. Lindtner, *Prototype Nation.*

8. Fred Turner, *Democratic Surround: Multimedia and American Liberalism from World War II to the Psychedelic Sixties* (Chicago: University of Chicago Press, 2015), 95

9. Bruno Latour, "Has Critique Run out of Steam? From Matters of Fact to Matters of Concern," *Critical Inquiry* 30 (2004), 225.

10. Lisa Nakamura, "Economies of Digital Production in East Asia: iPhone Girls and the Transnational Circuits of Cool," *Media Fields Journal*, no. 2 (2011).

11. Silvia Lindtner and Seyram Avle, "Tinkering with Governance: Technopolitics and the Economization of Citizenship," *PACM of Human-Computer Interaction* 1, no. 2 (2017), article 20.

12. Shaowen Bardzell, "Utopias of Participation: Feminism, Design and the Futures," *ACM Transactions on Computer-Human Interaction* 25, no. 1 (2018), article 6.

13. Silvia Lindtner, Anna Greenspan, and David Li, "Designed in Shenzhen: Shanzhai Manufacturing and Maker Entrepreneurs," *Aarhus Series on Human Centered Computing* 1, no. 1 (2015), 12.

14. "Incomparable Dignity and the Craftman's Skill, the Largest Shimenawa (Shinto Straw Rope) in Japan," n.d., https://tinyurl.com/y8ddfxrb; "New Year Decorations in Japanese Homes," December 31, 2015, https://tinyurl.com/yar3xu2f.

15. Shaowen Bardzell, Jeffrey Bardzell, and Sarah Ng, "Supporting Cultures of Making: Technology, Policy, Visions, and Myths," *Proc. of CHI2017* (New York: ACM, 2017).

16. David Newman, "Contemporary Research Agendas in Border Studies: An Overview," in *The Routledge Research Companion to Border Studies*, ed. Doris Wastl-Walter (New York: Routledge, 2016).

17. "UNESCO 2013 Creative Economy Report," accessed April 2, 2016, http://www.unesco.org/culture/pdf/creative-economy-report-2013.pdf.

18. Anita Say Chan, *Networking Peripheries: Technological Futures and the Myth of Digital Universalism* (Cambridge, MA: MIT Press, 2014); Lindtner, Greenspan, and Li, "Designed in Shenzhen," 12.

19. AnnaLee Saxenian, *The New Argonauts: Regional Advantage in a Global Economy* (Cambridge, MA: Harvard University Press, 2006).

12 Prototypes, Products, and DIY Kits

From Bauhaus to IKEA and Maker Faire

Denisa Kera and Joanne Pouzenc

> "I do," Alice hastily replied; "at least—at least I mean what I say—that's the same thing, you know."
>
> "Not the same thing a bit!" said the Hatter. ... "You might just as well say," added the March Hare, "that 'I like what I get' is the same thing as 'I get what I like!'"
>
> —"A Mad Tea-Party," *Alice's Adventures in Wonderland*, 1865

The difference between "getting what you like" and "liking what you get" anticipates the cultural and social conditions leading to the Bauhaus movement. The legendary 1865 tea party conversation on politeness predicts our later obsessions with psychoanalysis, structuralism, and Marxism. It voices uncertainty over whether our desires will ever meet our needs, our words will ever match our meaning, and social institutions will meet our ideals of justice.

The Bauhaus was a design response to this uncertainty about desires and needs and the related discussions about words and meaning, ideology and practice, moral superego and its struggles with the impulses and instincts of the id. Bauhaus prototypes and buildings explored how improvements in the material conditions of life (what Marx called the "base" and "means of production")[1] could lead to improvements in the "superstructures" (social organization, culture). Since then, we have wondered how function relates to decoration, sustainability to disruptive innovation, and basic human needs to transgressive desires.

The essential challenges expressed in the tea party lesson remain: Should our designs and artworks serve private fantasies and desires and support idiosyncratic, single instances and the uses of some system (Alice's "paroles")? Should they fulfill community ideals, define some basic needs, and conform to the rules of some "langue"?[2] Is the ultimate purpose of language or any technology poetry and personal expression or efficient communication and organization of society? Who decides what the basic needs of the individual and the community are?

The Bauhaus responded to these challenges through prototyping, material explorations, and art.[3] Its methods, objects, and buildings[4] showed how to align the personal, idiosyncratic, and niche desires with the communal or even universal values, truths, and basic needs. The current practices and engagements with prototypes, products, and modular DIY (do-it-yourself) kits are heirs of this tradition of failing to reconcile the material conditions of life with various individual and collective aspirations. The ambiguities of the early Bauhaus prototypes can help us understand the current design fantasies of disruptive, niche, and/or sustainable products.

Marianne Brandt's Teapot

The Bauhaus's own "teapot party" started with one of Marianne Brandt's prototypes.[5] Her famous teapot[6] illustrates how design negotiates conflicting needs and desires and how it shares some of the characteristics of Carroll's riddles, as well as Freudian jokes and dreams. It is a literal, but also a tangible, expression of the "kettle logic," a name for another attempt to reconcile irreconcilable contradictions and paradoxes.

In his 1913 work *The Interpretation of Dreams*,[7] Sigmund Freud used a kettle joke to explain the paradoxical logic of dreams. A man accused of returning a damaged kettle responds by saying that he never actually borrowed the kettle, that he returned it unbroken, and that the kettle was already broken when he got it. Brandt's kettle is the ultimate Freudian dreamwork and a joke. It is an impossible object that embodies the fantasy of "having one's cake and eating it."

The silver-and-ebony teapot is a luxury product that is supposed to serve the needs of the masses. It is a handmade object with tiny hammer marks that paradoxically celebrates the metal-and-machine age of mass reproduction. It serves the business goals of the new industries while claiming to bring social justice with its disruptive materials and new ways of brewing tea. This teapot tries to reconcile the irreconcilable: the needs and desires for handmade and mechanical, luxury and mass-produced, disruptive and socially engaged design.

The Bauhaus embodies a similar kettle logic. It is a series of responses to the March Hare's famous riddle that started the whole discussion on needs and desires in Alice's adventures: "Why is a raven like a writing-desk?" Animate beings and inanimate objects in twentieth-century design share properties; they build unexpected and intricate relations, and the world of things and objects of common use are shamanistic probes into our deep-seated emotions, experiences, and fantasies. The whole riddle works as a user experience design challenge. It reveals that we prototype for the same reason that we lie down on the psychoanalytic couch or start a revolution. We are trying to understand, negotiate, and live with our conflicting needs, desires, and transgressions.

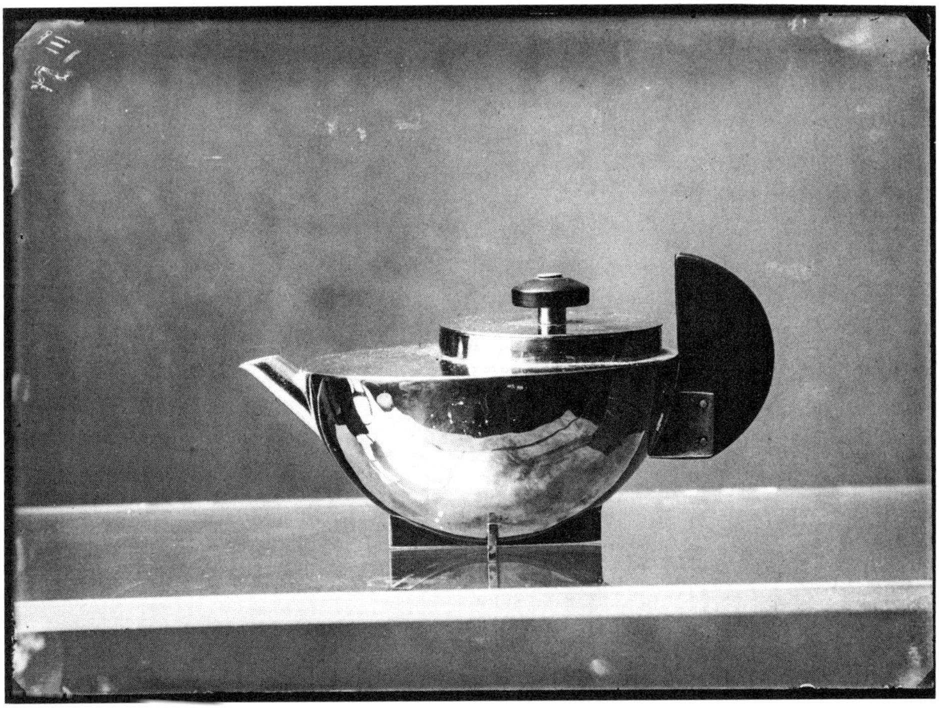

Figure 12.1
Marianne Brandt, teapot, 1924

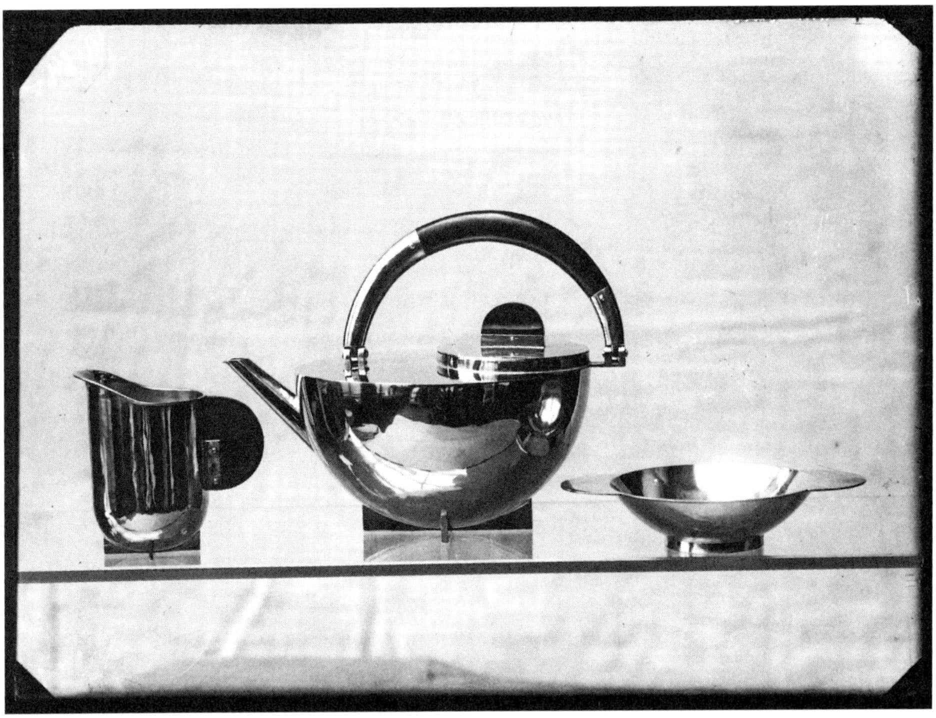

Figure 12.2
Marianne Brandt, teapot, creamer, and sugar bowl, 1924

The goal of the Bauhaus and design since then has been to balance various systems and technologies ("langue") with their single instances, (mis)uses, and appropriations (what structuralism calls "parole"). Our writing desk is a place of struggle with our personal "ravens" and their "nevermore" demands like Edgar Allan Poe's,[8] but it is also a mass product serving the basic needs of eating. The Bauhaus transformed us all into such wondering Alices in a mad design tea party that we are trying to respond to the same riddles and contradictions about ravens and tables, needs and desires, private and public goals and values. The mad tea party unleashed by Brandt's teapot explains all the later hopes and expectations about disruptive prototypes creating successful startups, the mass-consumed, cheap IKEA products, or the recent trend of DIY kits supporting niches.

Design, Politics, and Metaphysics of Teapots

The geometric shapes of Brandt's futuristic kitchenware and its luxurious materials (silver and ebony) embody the tensions between needs and desires, base and superstructures, system (langue) and use (parole). The shapes represent the minimalist and almost metaphysical search for universal and primary forms inspired by abstract art.[9] The final material is supposed to be a cheap metal to support the constructivist insistence on machine-based mass production for the new industries, but also the new wo/men (emancipated classes of workers).[10] This luxury teapot celebrates the machine age of the new industries and emancipates classes with its handmade work.

It is a teapot that interprets Gropius's 1923 slogan "Art and technology, a new unity!"[11] as a constant clash rather than unity of artistic (philosophical) experiments, industrial utility, and calls for social justice or revolution. All Bauhaus prototypes (or models, as Gropius preferred to call them) were supposed to be transitional phases transforming the handmade, crafted objects of the guilds (related to art) into mechanical/industrial (re)productions.[12] Rather than bringing any unity, the teapot and other Bauhaus prototypes revealed profound but also productive tensions.

For example, serving the needs of the new men clashed with the disruptive changes that new products and industries were supposed to bring to the masses. The Bauhaus functionalist revolt against decoration, tradition, and social conventions was always an attempt to transform rather than serve the masses and their needs. Like Le Corbusier, who famously accused the working classes of bad taste ("decorating is of a sensuous and primitive nature ... therefore, it suits the lower classes, peasants, and barbarians"),[13] the Bauhaus was also an attempt to reform the working classes. The teapot transformed the experience of brewing tea by offering extracts rather than tea leaves. Its material and

Rosetta Stone Memory Implants

Human memory is fickle at the best of times. Research shows that workplace forgetfulness contributes to a huge reduction in performance. No longer. Rosetta Stone presents tried and tested surgical memory implants that will transform your ability to recall workplace conversations. Remember names of new contacts, recall every fact you read or hear and most importantly out-memorize your competitors.

Drug Clock-In™

Ensure your employees are taking their enhancement meds by implementing the Drug Clock-InTM system.

Like conventional clocking-in devices, Drug Clock-InTM logs your employees entry and exit times, but the difference is that each clock-in card comes with an employee-specific daily dose of prescribed enhancement pharmaceuticals.

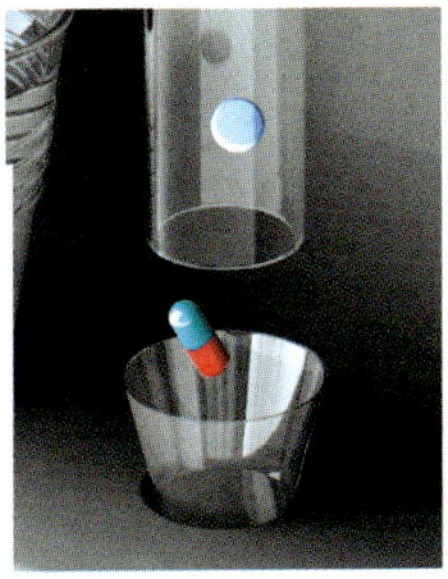

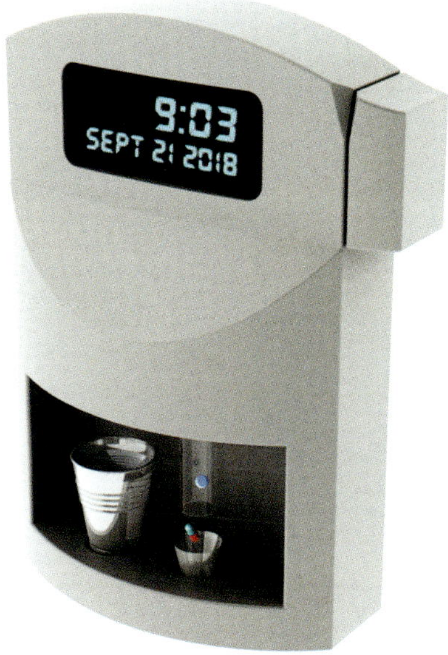

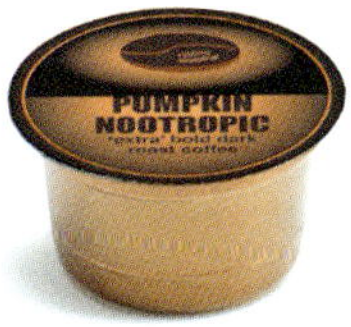

Feel assured knowing that your employees are always giving their best as soon as they walk into work.

Nootropic Extra Dark Roast Coffee

Take your daily "noots" in your morning cuppa with EnhancePharma's extra dark roast nootropic coffee. *A sublimely effective concoction rich in caffeine and subtly laced with the eugeroic Modafinil for ultimate memory recall and pattern recognition.*

GET 100 NUTRISYS ID CARDS WITH EVERY PURCHASE

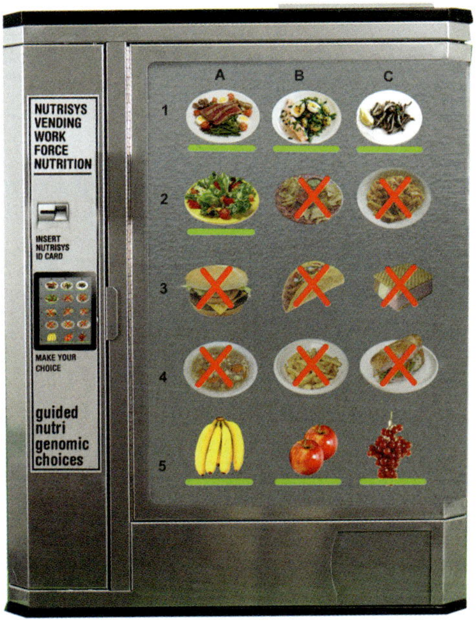

Keep your employees fit and healthy and ensure sick days become a thing of the past.

NutriSys Nutrigenomic Vending Machines

Tailor your employees' nutritional and pharmaceutical intake to their workplace needs and their genetic makeup with a NutriSys Nutrigenomic Vending Machine.

Nutrigenomics is the study of how foods affect our genes and how individual genetic differences can affect the way we respond to nutrients. NutriSys cross-references databases of your work-force's genetic makeup with their job descriptions and provide different functional foods to staff depending on their dietary and cognitive needs.

Plate 1

Page from Parsons & Charlesworth, "Catalog for the Post-Human," 2014.

Hed-Tek™ Transcranial Direct Current Stimulation

Transcranial direct current stimulation (tDCS) is a technology in which low electrical currents are applied to the skull through one or more electrodes, to modulate neuronal excitability in brain areas beneath the skull. It has proven results in increasing mental flow and the skillful operation of machinery. Hed-Tek™ offers an extensive range of tDCS products for personal and corporate use.

Hed-Tek™ tDCS Headsets

State-of-the-art anodal or cathodal stimulation of the prefrontal cortex using 2 x 2 focused electrode array. IOS and Android App controls current for a variety of operational modes.

Hed-Tek™ Mood Filters

Mood Filters is an amazing new app from Hed-Tek™ that allows users to plot and move through a series of preset cognitive states.

Team use of the app can transform meetings by focus attendees toward the proble at hand and foregrounding positive thinking.

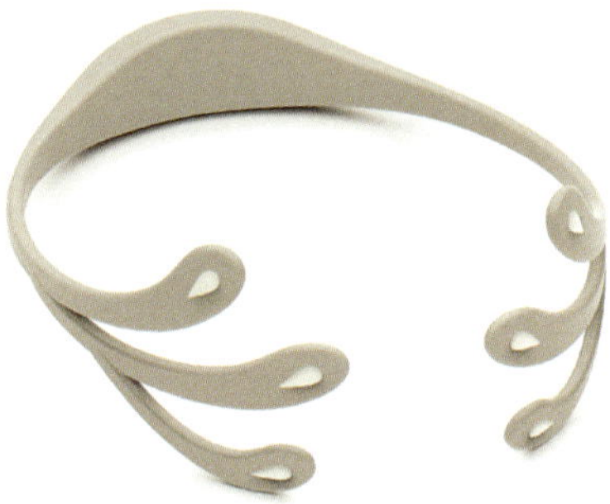

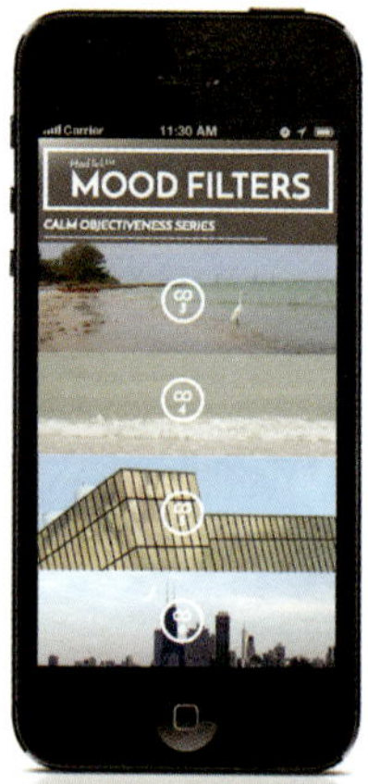

Hed-Tek™ Productivity Warning Software Plug-In

Are you a freelancer trying to hold down multiple jobs, yet frequently find yourself diverted by displacement activity such as social media? Used in conjunction with Hed-Tek's tDCS headset, Productivity Warning is an encephalographically controlled app, which monitors brain activity and alerts users when concentration wanes. Stay on top of your freelance workload or monitor the effectiveness of enhancement drugs with this efficiency alarm software. There is also a feature to automatically stimulate the brain with tDCS impulses in response to preset levels of brain activity.

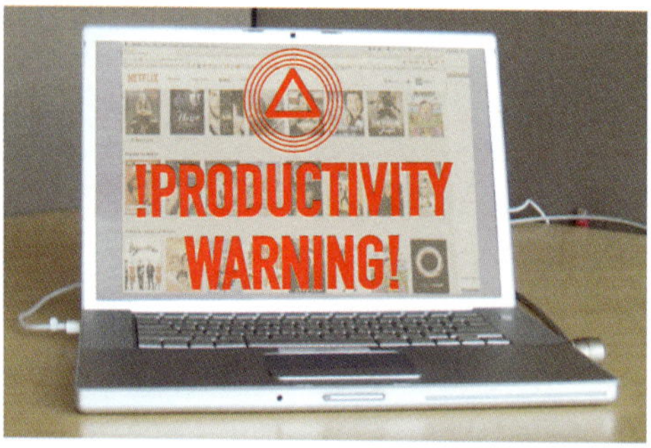

Monitor your concentration and avoid displacement activity

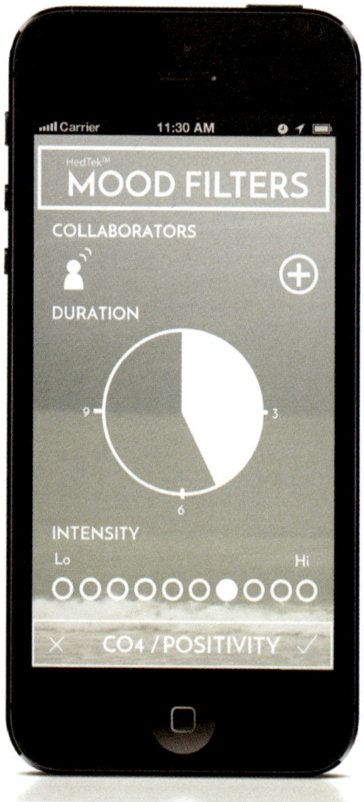

Plate 2

Page from Parsons & Charlesworth, "Catalog for the Post-Human," 2014.

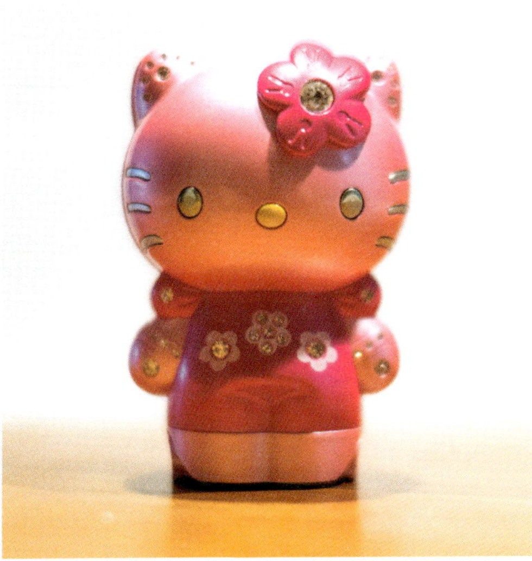

Plate 3
Hello Kitty phone.

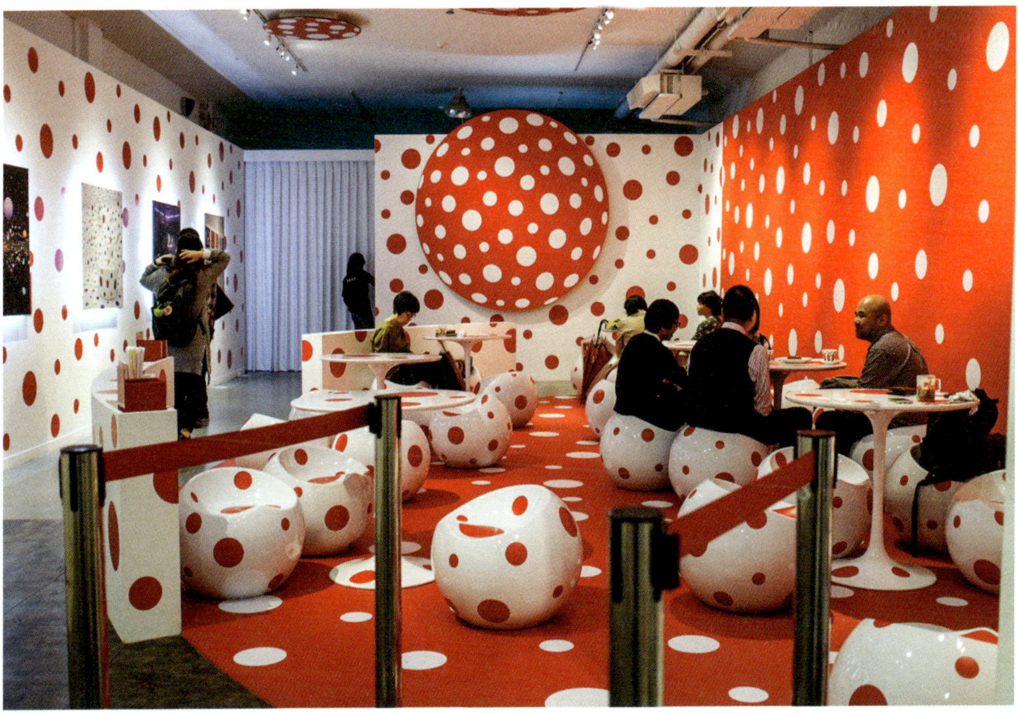

Plate 4
A themed cafe based on the work of Yayoi Kusama, Huashan, Taiwan.

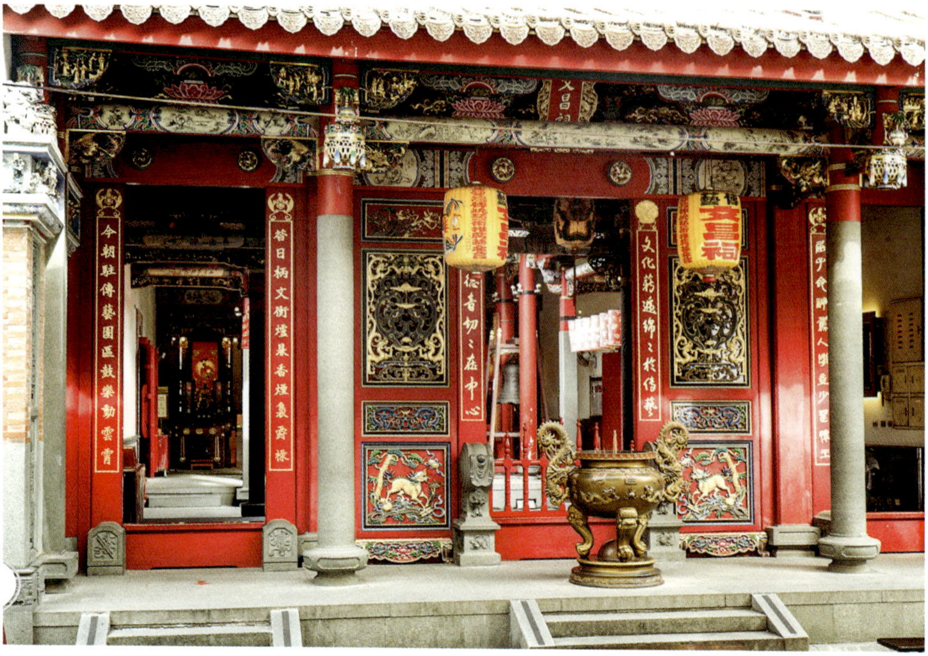

Plate 5
A temple designed and built by the Ministry of Culture, located at the National Center for the Traditional Arts, Taiwan.

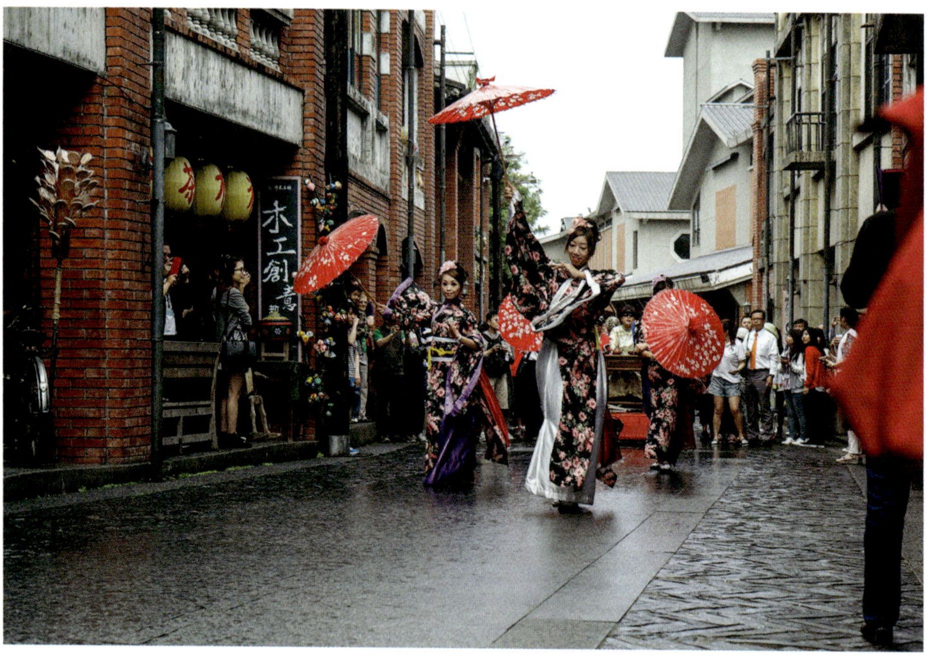

Plate 6
Daily festival parade, National Center for the Traditional Arts, Taiwan.

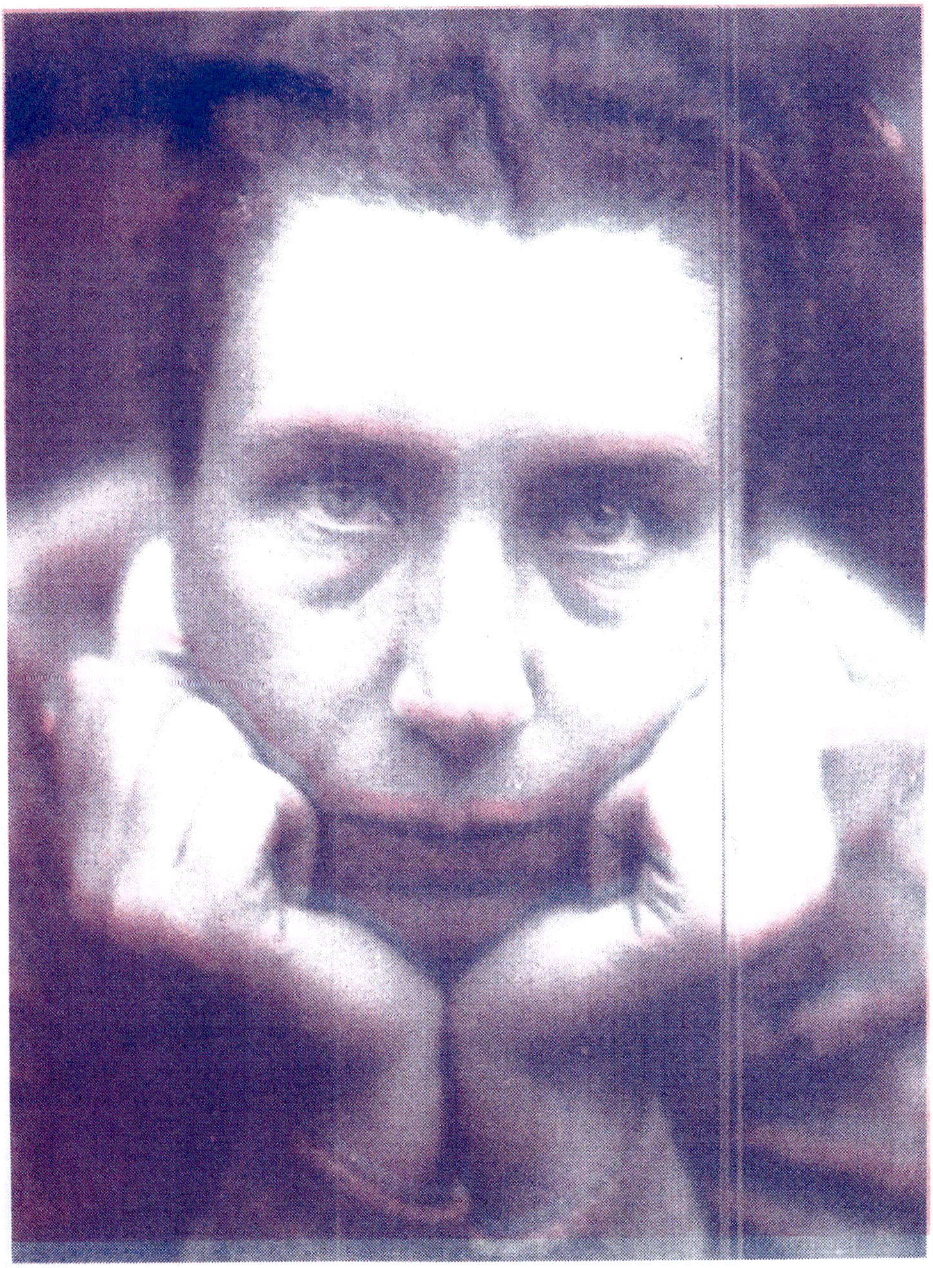

Plate 7
Risograph image remediating Lucia Moholy self-portrait.

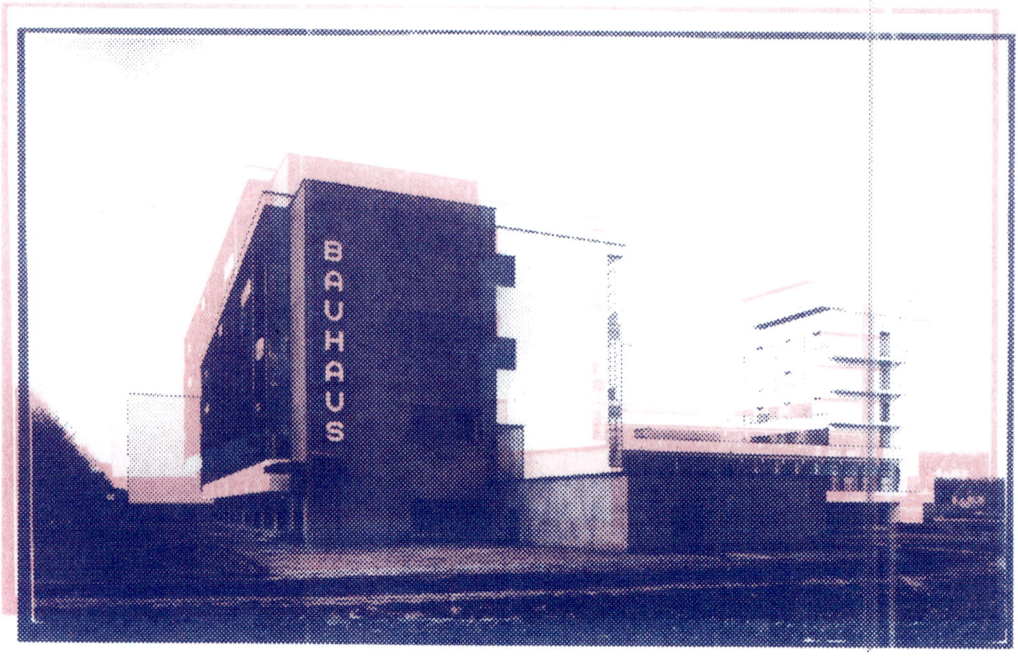

Plate 8

Risograph image remediating Lucia Moholy's photograph of the Dessau building

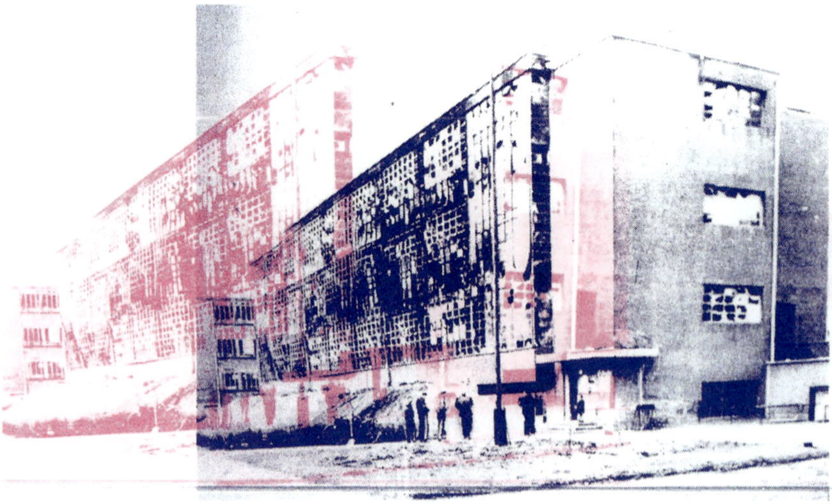

Plate 9

Risograph image remediating a photograph of the Dessau building in 1945. Adapted from "Conservation and Preservation of the Bauhaus Building in Dessau" by Monika Markgraf.

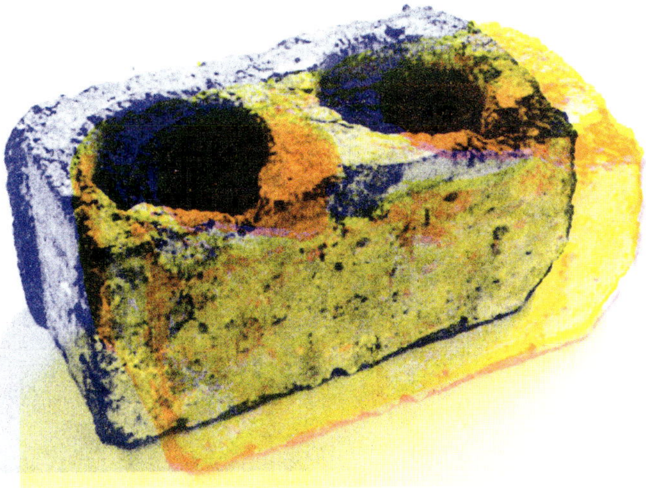

Plate 10

Risograph image remediating a hollow cinderblock. Adapted from "Conservation and Preservation of the Bauhaus Building in Dessau" by Monika Markgraf.

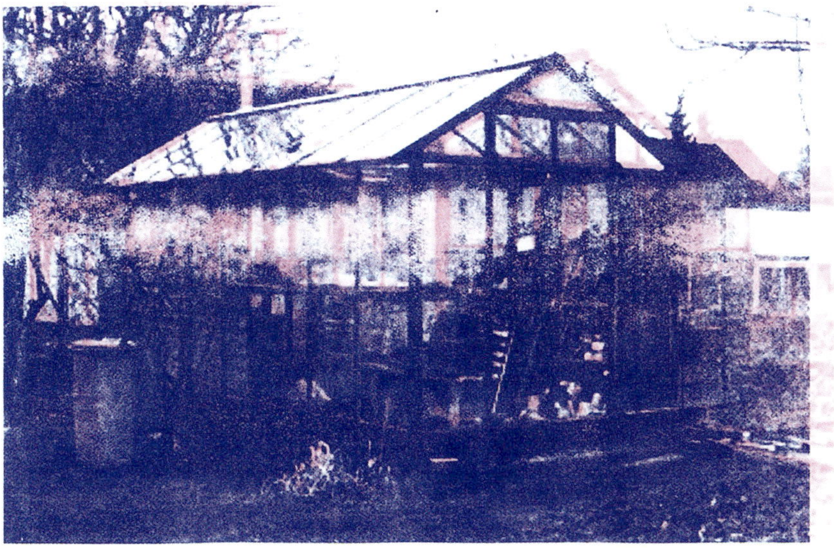

Plate 11

Risograph image remediating a photograph of the greenhouse at Dessau. Adapted from "Conservation and Preservation of the Bauhaus Building in Dessau" by Monika Markgraf.

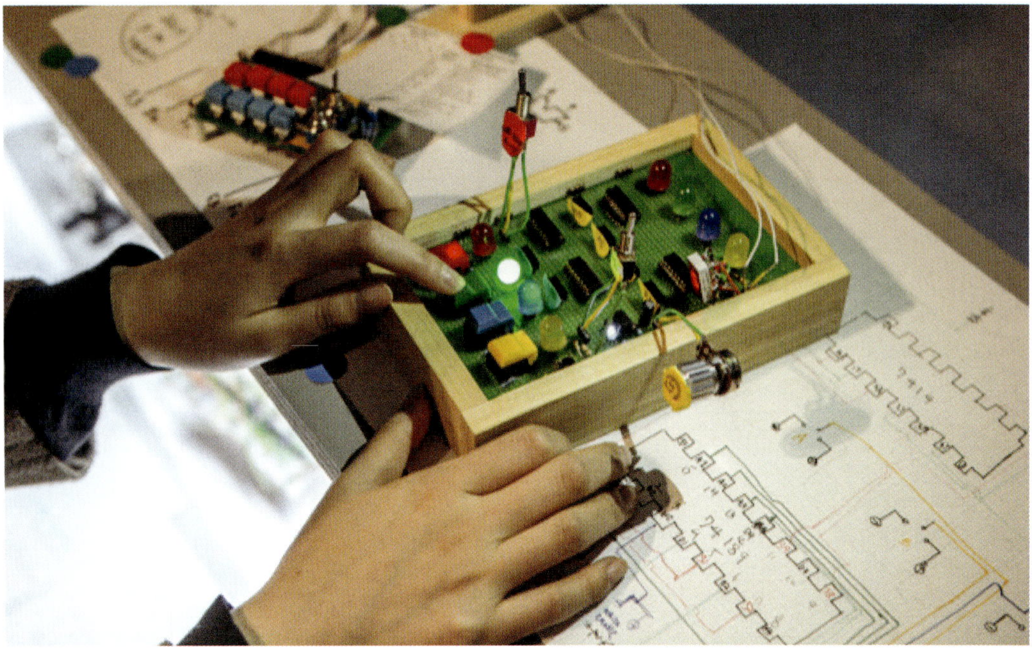

Plate 12
Taeyoon Choi, Handmade Computer, 2013–2017, custom electronics and drawings.

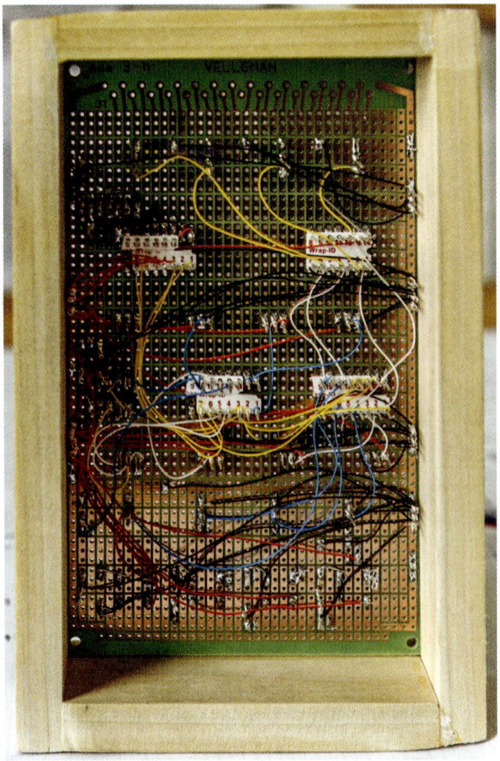

Plate 13
Taeyoon Choi, Handmade Computer, 2013–2017, custom electronics and drawings.

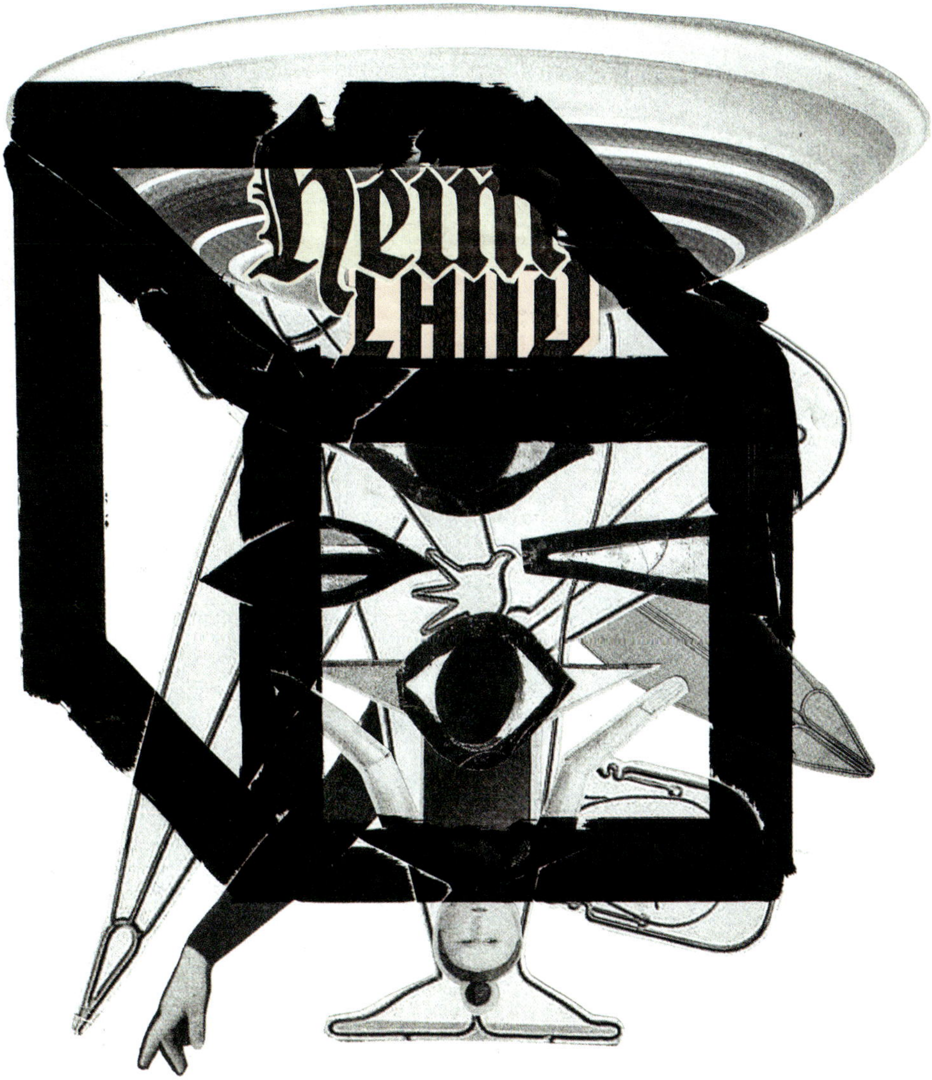

Plate 14
Luiza Prado, *Untitled 01*, 2018.

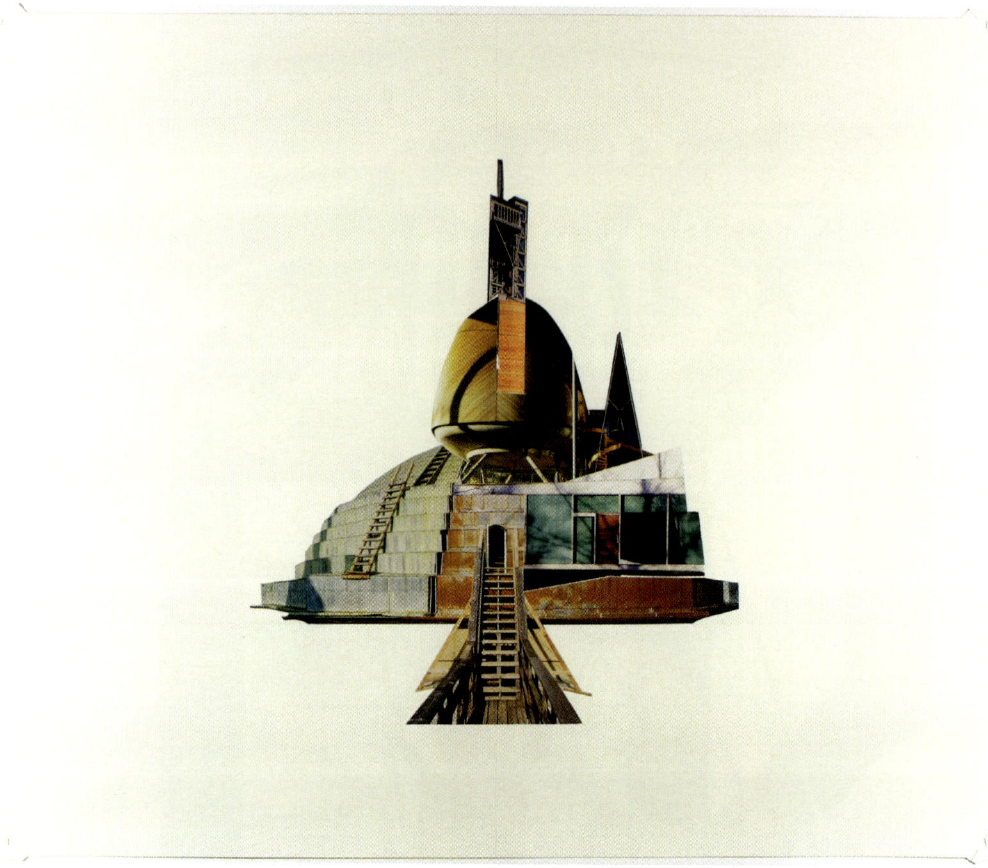

Plate 15
Marshall Brown, *Chimera*, 2014.

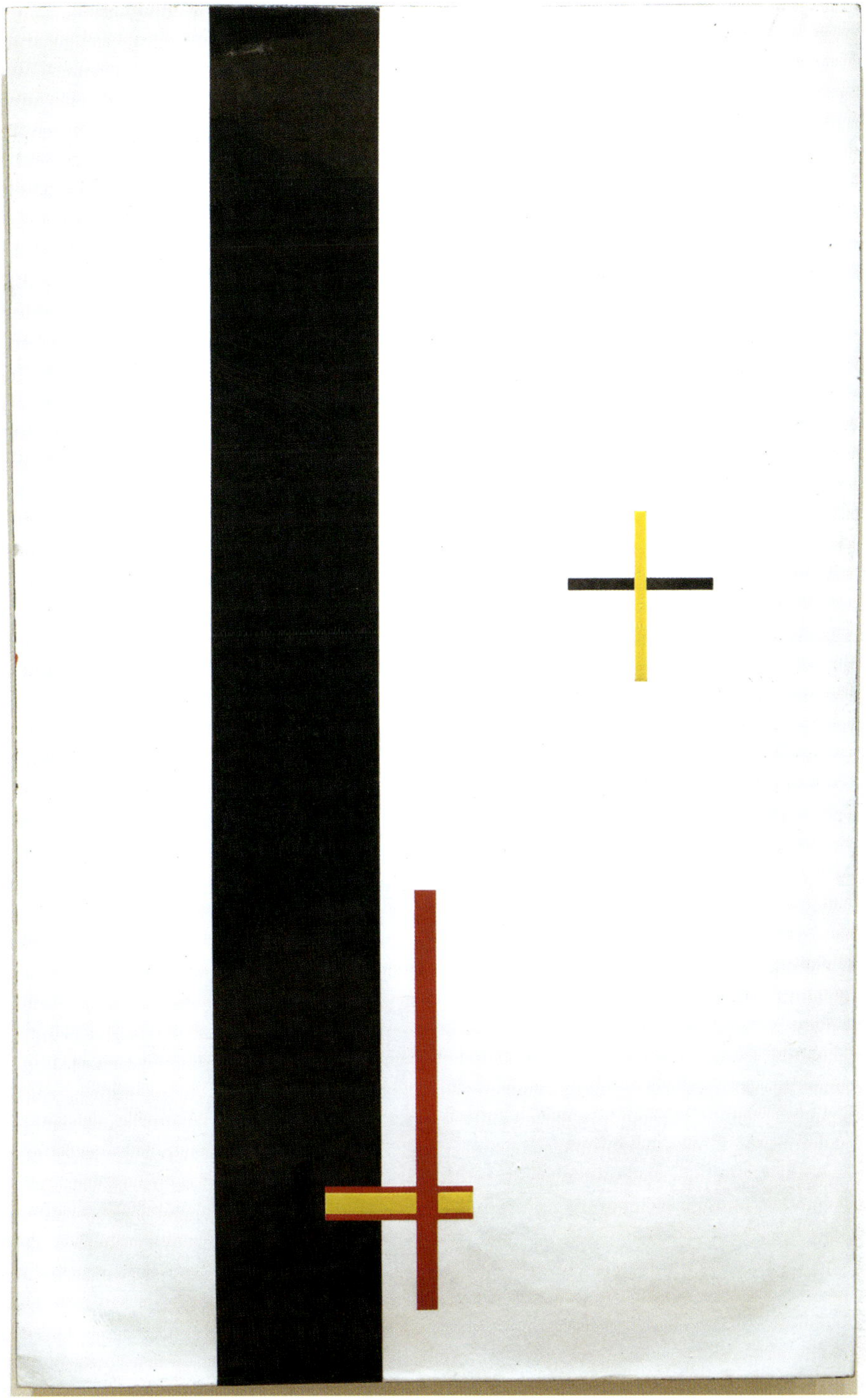

Plate 16

László Moholy-Nagy, *EM 1* (telephone picture), 1923. Porcelain enamel on steel. Credit: © The Museum of Modern Art/Licensed by SCALA/Art Resource, NY.

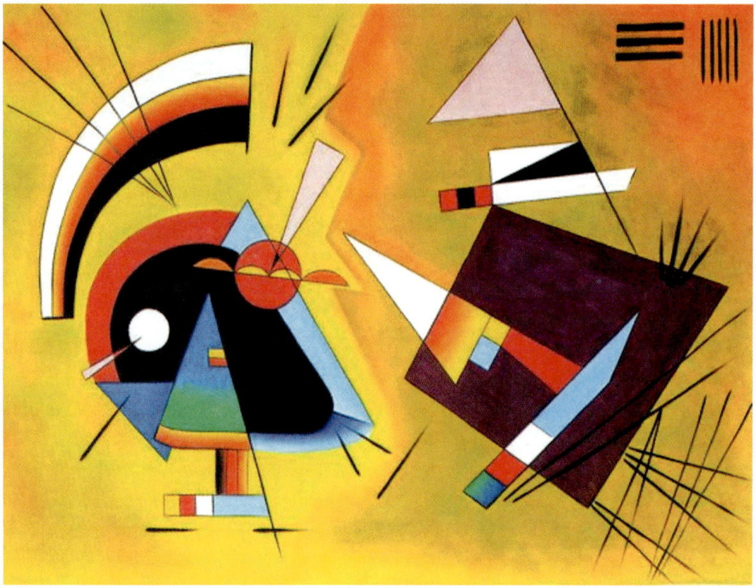

Plate 17
Wassily Kandinsky, *Black and Violet,* 1923.

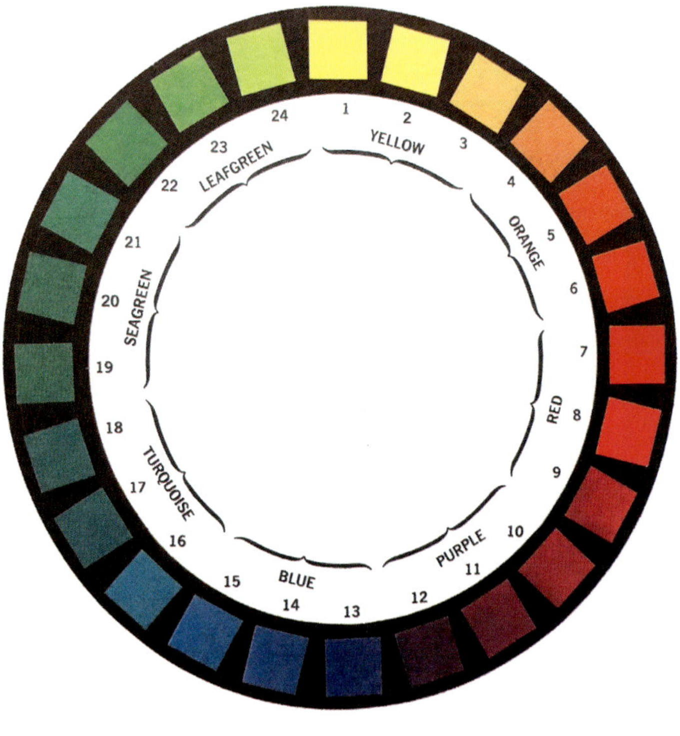

Plate 18
The Ostwald color system plates in *Die Farbenfibel* (The color primer), 1916–1917.

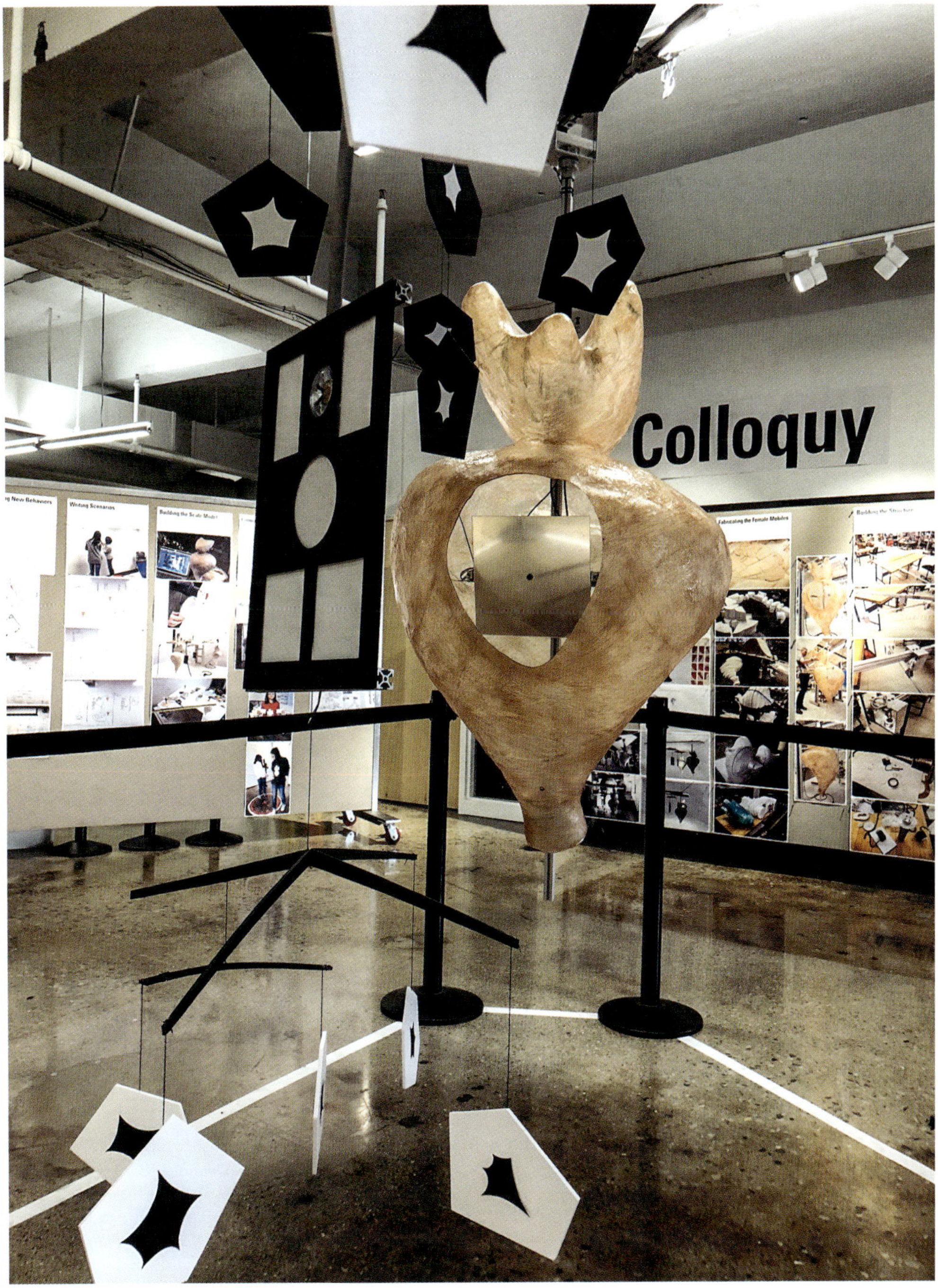

Plate 19

Colloquy of Mobiles installation, May 2018, Interaction Design Master's Program, College for Creative Studies, Detroit; full-scale replica of Gordon Pask's original design from 1968 by TJ McLeish, showing completed female mobiles and paper mock-ups of male mobiles, later replaced with finished forms. Photo by Paul Pangaro.

Plates 20–22

Color in the urban environment: Alice Arnold, *The Coca-Cola Sign at Two Times Square.*

Two Times Square sits on an irregular parcel of land on 47th Street between Broadway and Seventh Avenue. It is situated at the northern end of the x-crossing that makes up Times Square, as Broadway and 7th Avenue converge and then cross over at 45th Street.

Photographic research shows that since the 1920s the building on this site has been covered in large signs, turning the structure into an advertising scaffold. In the outdoor advertising industry these large-scale signs, often with effects such as motion, kinetic lights, and sculptural dimensions, are known as sign spectaculars. Times Square, the "Crossroads of the World," is famous for the sheer abundance and dazzling quality of its signs.

In the 1940s–1950s, Pepsi-Cola had a large sign on the Two Times Square building. Since the 1960s, however, this space has been the branded domain of Coca-Cola. About every decade the Coca-Cola company changes the sign's design, though in the 1970s and '80s the overall shape and content of the sign did not change. Perhaps this lack of investment in the sign reflected New York City's economic downturn in those decades. In the '90s, as urban renewal was under way on 42nd Street, the sign was redesigned, featuring a large sculptural Coke bottle. By the mid-2000s, with tourism soaring in Times Square, the sign was upgraded, becoming much larger and featuring video. In 2017, with the majority of the buildings in Times Square clad with digital signage, the sign was replaced by a newer version, showcasing LED lighting technology, 3D robotics, and motion technology.

Methodology and Analysis

Below each photograph of the sign on the Two Times Square facade is an image showing the component colors that are used in the sign.

To create the component image, the photograph was cropped to the dimensions of the sign; using Adobe Photoshop, a color palette was then generated of the colors that appear most frequently in the image. This Photoshop-derived color map of the sign was then recreated in Adobe Illustrator, to produce print-ready artwork.

The color palettes help us see the changing nature of color in the outdoor environment, because they remove the messaging from the sign. The Coca-Cola sign offers a unique opportunity to study the urban environment, because the sign has occupied the same space for over 50 years. What we see from these abstract color grids is that over the decades the Coca-Cola sign, which is predominantly red, the color associated with the brand, has become brighter and the reds more saturated. We also start to see the color palette expand after the mid-2000s, with the advent of video and LED lighting. These changes in the color palette reflect technological innovation, primarily in lighting and video technology, and show how color science has expanded visual culture, in terms of how color is used and also how and where it is experienced.

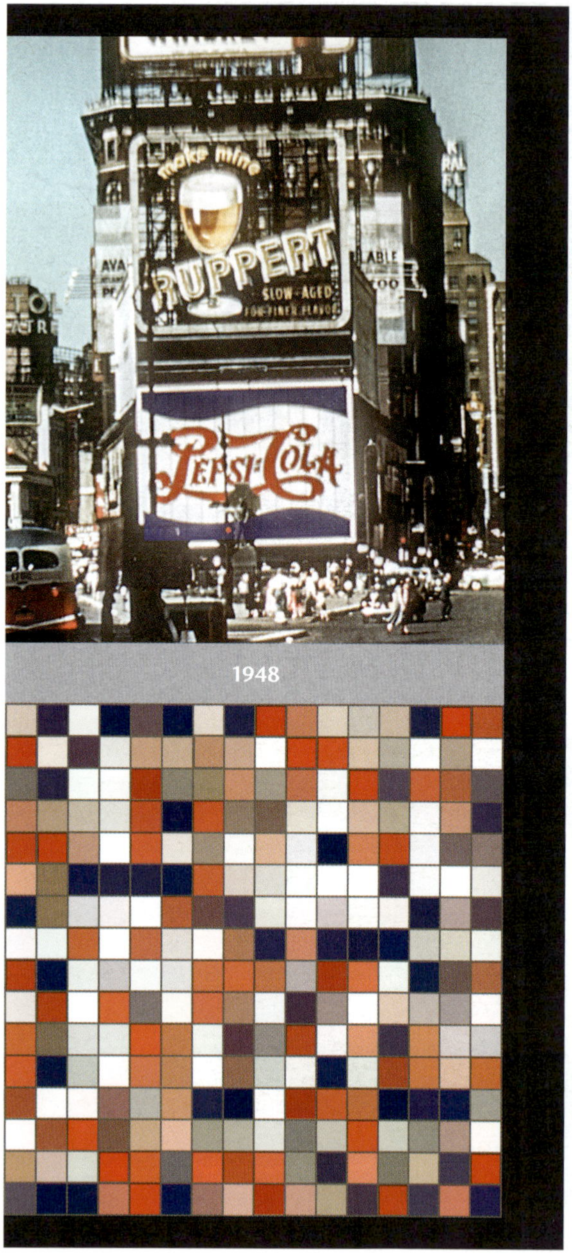

1948

Photo credits: Maurice Van Griffin (1948), Michael Jacobi, Gentle Giant (1969), Gerry Labrijn (1975), Mark Susina (1985), Alice Arnold (1999, 2010, 2018).

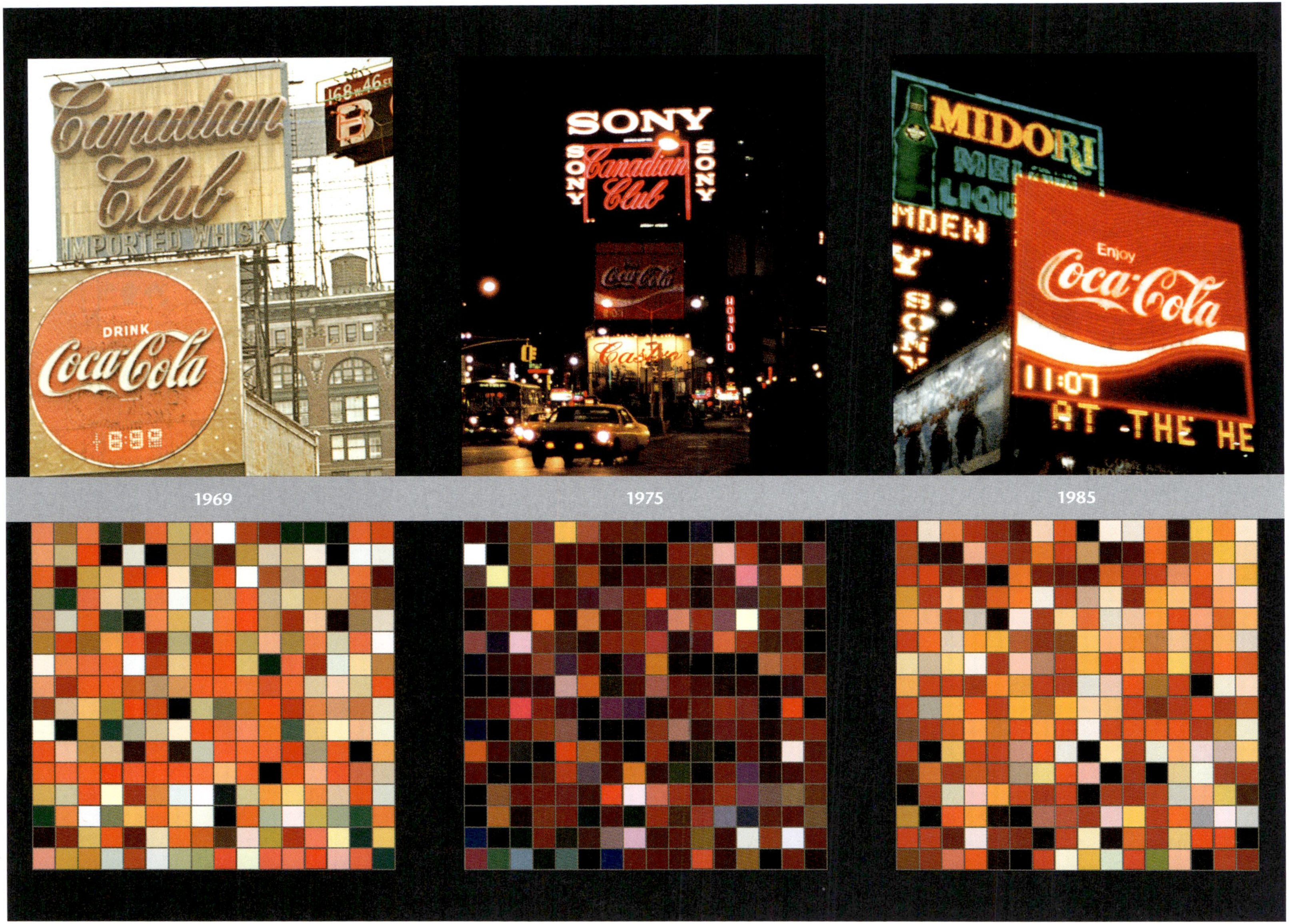
Canadian Club
IMPORTED WHISKY
DRINK
Coca-Cola
SONY
Canadian Club
Coca-Cola
MIDORI
Enjoy
Coca-Cola
11:07
AT THE HE
1969
1975
1985

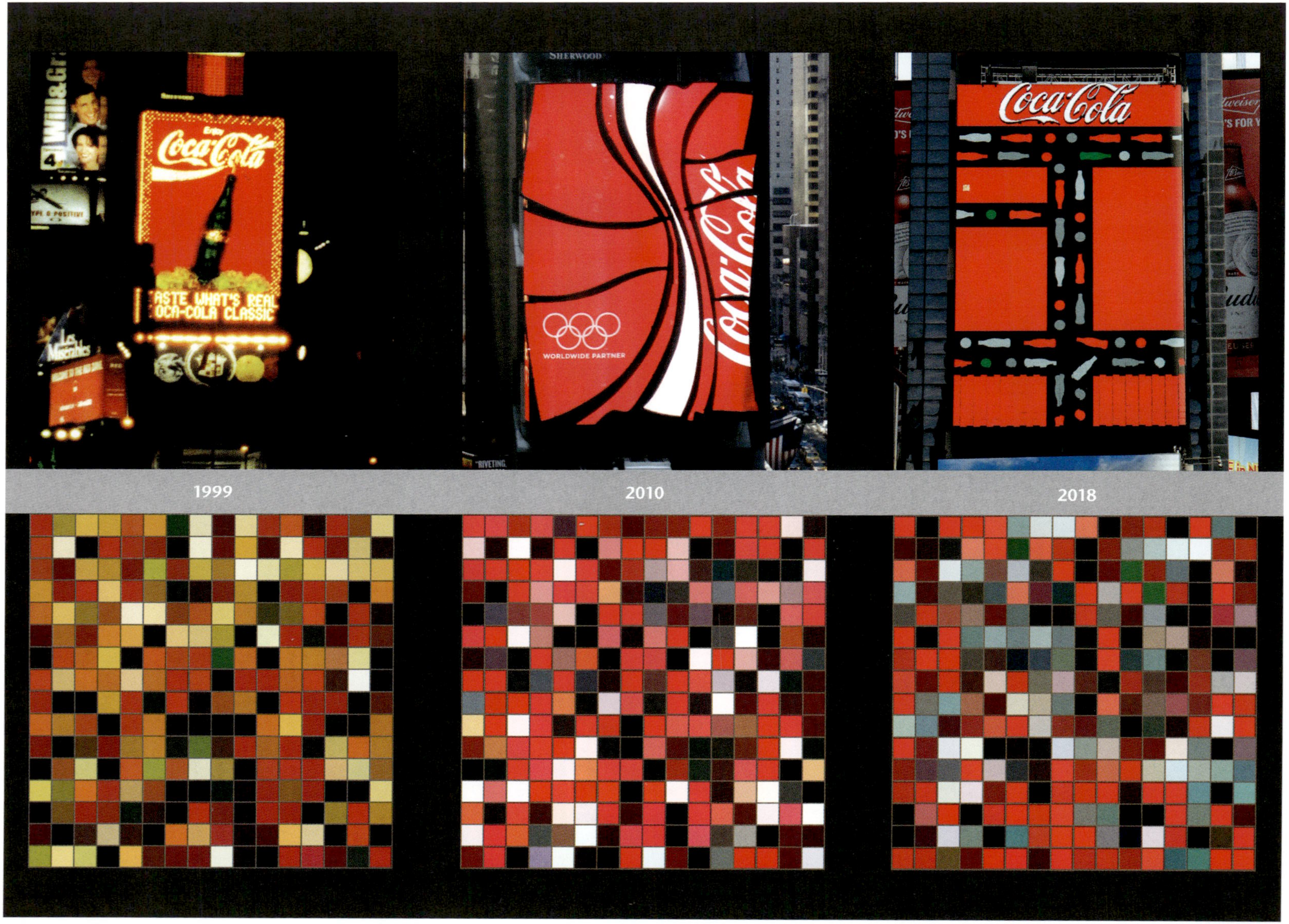
Coca-Cola
ASTE WHAT'S REAL
OCA-COLA CLASSIC
SHERWOOD
Coca-Cola
WORLDWIDE PARTNER
Coca-Cola
1999
2010
2018

shape also destroyed all references to traditional teapots and their homely feelings. The different habits and practices of tea-making sublimated into a more efficient form that will fit all. The decorative object of everyday use intimately connected to our private homes and lives became a tool for a social, industrial, and metaphysical revolution.

From Brandt's Teapot to Juicero and IoT Kettles on the Blockchain

Bauhaus design's kettle logic never dissolved the tensions between the common or basic needs and personal desires of tea drinkers, who were suddenly defined in terms of new classes. The tension between calls for social justice and support for new industries—between handmade and mass-produced objects—is why design plays such an important role and even defines our present condition.

The teapot's shape embodied the metaphysical search for primary, original forms that are purely aesthetic but suggestive of promising futures, revolutionary goals, and new classes and industries. It tried to transform the everyday habits and "false" needs of tea drinkers while claiming to bring social good to the working classes. The modernist way of drinking tea, which no longer involves sipping the tea, produces not only new industries but also more efficient, scientific, and socially inclusive societies. Metal as a material of choice then represents the possibility of mass production, which will serve the working classes while creating new businesses.

The paradoxes of Brandt's teapot anticipated the future excesses of Silicon Valley prototypes and gadgets, such as the infamous internet of things (IoT) $699 Juicero device[14] or the related Teforia,[15] the $1,000 internet-connected tea-brewing machine. Both these strange pots introduced rather expensive and unsustainable practices of making juice or tea that ended in disaster. Juicero closed operations in 2017 after losing $120 million in startup venture capital; Teforia shortly followed after burning $17 million. While everyone made fun of these machines, no one questioned the obsession with extracts common in the coffee espresso machines. There are still "disruptive" teapots—such as RAIN, described as "The World's Most Expensive Tea Machine" ($13,000),[16] a vacuum-based tool for extracting essences from the tea leaves—which are still in business.

The disruption of our ordinary practices of making tea by extracting the essences seems to extend Kandinsky's and Itten's search[17] for essential forms that guide product design. Making tea becomes a search for such "primary taste profiles." Rather than a private and everyday activity, it becomes a science experiment for beverage artisan elites that will form the new class of drinkers: "RAIN™ brewing technology allows beverage artisans to extract the entire flavor profile from any loose leaf tea, whole fruit pieces, and botanicals—enabling everyone to enjoy its rich complexity, wonderful depth, and full layers of flavor."[18]

The Bauhaus aspiration to merge art, technology, and life by making useful, affordable, and beautiful objects reached various extremes in our century. We witness, on one side, the bizarre attempts to define new classes of drinkers and users of disruptive teapots feeding the Silicon Valley modernist image, and on the other, the Bauhaus socialist utopia of mass production reaching its apex with the billions of cheap and metal IKEA teapots.

IKEA products paradoxically fulfilled the Bauhaus dream more than any other industry, design, or political movement. IKEA leveled all classes of citizens into Bauhaus workshop workers and worshipers of Kandinsky's and Itten's forms. The thousands of IKEA customers struggling somewhere around the world and assembling furniture unknowingly perform in a global Bauhaus theater. We all employ modular rectangles, circles, and other shapes to fulfill our basic needs for shelter.

The anarchistic kit makers and prototype adventurers from the Maker Faires offer some alternative to these IKEA mass-produced modular and standardized forms. The messy DIY prototypes of the maker movement revive the paradoxes between handmade and industrial production, technology and crafts. These "makers" use modular tools to build unique and often useless devices that embrace niche interests rather than minimalist design, mass production, or social utopia.

Hacking and communicating wirelessly with your messy DIY teapots[19] explores the anxieties, hopes, and fears about future IoTs[20] and blockchain[21] scenarios. The return of the repressed, handmade, messy, decorative objects of this new techno-folk culture represents a reactionary design movement. These DIY kits and prototypes seem to bring the revenge of the users against the industry and its designers, who are continually disrupting and transforming human lives with new products. Regaining control over your products and materials can end up in some extreme examples, such as the dysfunctional and inefficient but hand-picked and handmade Thomas Thwaites toaster,[22] that make the act of building your teapot or toaster a political and also a metaphysical meditation on the origins and geopolitics of all materials and ores.

Brandt's unique teapot paved the way for these radical strategies and reasons for prototyping. The Bauhaus paradoxes and tensions between technological experimentation and metaphysical reflection, along with social vision and industrial production, led directly to the present extremes of mass-produced IKEA products, disruptive Silicon Valley prototypes, and Maker Faire techno-shamanistic practices with DIY kits. Instead of form serving any function defined either by the users' (workers') needs or by the industry's business plans and profit, we are witnessing a full spectrum of uncanny and forbidden or at least excessive and carnivalesque qualities of the human relation to materials and objects. We no longer only passively consume the objects we use and abuse. The New(?) (Wo?)Man's increased desire for personal and social empowerment is constantly fulfilled and betrayed with every new prototype, product, and DIY kit.

What the Bauhaus discovered and explored in the early twentieth century was the impact of prototyping and design on defining our social identities, political goals, and worldviews. Design joined philosophy and politics as a tool for not just ontological and metaphysical but also social experiments. Prototypes probe not only our relation to the world of materials but also human needs and social biases of all kinds. The medium for defining and supporting our well-being or idiosyncrasies is also a political, social, and nowadays increasingly geopolitical tool, a possible battlefield. The recent calls for "designed (and not only made) in China"[23] and Shenzhen fantasies of DIY, open-hardware prototyping that dissolves geopolitical divisions already clash[24] with various plans to return 4.0 manufacturing to Europe and the United States.

Conclusions

The Bauhaus prototypes as artistic, metaphysical, and design explorations paradoxically serve future disruptive industries and lifestyles as much as a social(ist) utopia. They were a means of philosophical and artistic research into primary forms, laws of form and color, and essences of things in the preliminary courses by Itten, Kandinsky, and Klee.[25] They also embodied Gropius's 1926 principles and later László Moholy-Nagy's attempts to reform industry and explore new technologies and materials.[26] The resulting prototypes would create new factories and businesses based on the metaphysical insights into primary forms. The same prototypes also served the utopian dreams of Hannes Meyer and Oskar Schlemmer of meeting the needs of the workers and new classes.[27] The present democratization of the tools of production through DIY techniques, digital fabrication, and open hardware make these original Bauhaus tensions and paradoxes only more extreme and personal. Prototyping today never actually matures into something that offers resolution and insight. It devolves into DIY kits returning the value of handmade, customized, and unique products. It transgresses into mass-produced IKEA products and ridiculous Silicon Valley toys. While the mass-produced IKEA products turn consumers into Bauhaus slaves assembling Itten's perfect forms, the DIY kits transform all users into Mad Hatters and March Hares of the Maker Faires. Bauhaus is simply the original site of this interaction between the design workshop, society, and industry. The cathedrals, crafts workshop, and Bauhaus studios today may be called startup incubators, coworking spaces, or hackerspaces, but they still make prototyping the center of our private, social, and political lives and are a medium of exploring the unresolved conflicts between needs and desires, between "getting what you like" and "liking what you get."

Acknowledgment

The present essay is a report of the discussions initiated during the conference "Preliminary Course: From Bauhaus to Silicon Valley" in Berlin in December 2017 organized by *projekt bauhaus* (www.projekt-bauhaus.de) and ARCH+ Verein zur Förderung des Architektur- und Stadtdiskurses e.V.

Notes

1. Karl Marx, *A Contribution to the Critique of Political Economy* (1859; Moscow: Progress Publishers, 1993), https://www.marxists.org/archive/marx/works/1859/critique-pol-economy/index.htm.

2. Ferdinand De Saussure, *Course in General Linguistics* (1916), in *Literary Theory: An Anthology* (Malden, MA: Blackwell, 1998).

3. Barry Bergdoll and Leah Dickerman, eds., *Bauhaus 1919–1933: Workshops for Modernity* (New York: Museum of Modern Art, 2009).

4. Magdalena Droste and Peter Gössel, *The Bauhaus, 1919–1933: Reform and Avant-Garde* (Cologne: Taschen, 2006).

5. Ulrike Müller, Ingrid Radewaldt, and Sandra Kemker, *Bauhaus Women: Art, Handicraft, Design*, English-language ed. (Paris: Flammarion, 2009).

6. Alice Rawsthorn, "The Tale of a Teapot and Its Creator," *New York Times*, December 16, 2007, https://www.nytimes.com/2007/12/16/style/16iht-design17.1.8763227.html.

7. Sigmund Freud, *The Interpretation of Dreams*, trans. A. A. Brill, eBooks@Adelaide, 2014, https://ebooks.adelaide.edu.au/f/freud/sigmund/interpretation-of-dreams/.

8. Edgar Allan Poe, "The Raven," *Poetry Foundation*, accessed August 12, 2018, https://www.poetryfoundation.org/poems/48860/the-raven.

9. Ellen Lupton and J. Abbott Miller, eds., *The ABC's of* [triangle square circle]*: The Bauhaus and Design Theory* (New York: Herb Lubalin Study Center of Design and Typography, Cooper Union for the Advancement of Science and Art, 1991).

10. Michael Siebenbrodt and Lutz Schöbe, *Bauhaus 1919–1933: Weimar-Dessau-Berlin* (New York: Parkstone Press International, 2009).

11. Magdalena Droste, *Bauhaus, 1919–1933* (Cologne: B. Taschen, 1998).

12. Nicholas Fox Weber, *The Bauhaus Group: Six Masters of Modernism* (New York: Alfred A. Knopf, 2009).

13. Alena Vondravá, Alena Adlerová, and Jan Rous, *Český Funkcionalismus 1920–1940* (Prague: Umělecko-Průmyslové Museum, 1978).

14. "Juicero: Juicing Boss Defends $400 Machine," *BBC News*, April 2017, https://www.bbc.com/news/business-39664483.

15. "Teforia," accessed August 12, 2018, http://www.teforia.com/.

16. "Tea—TFG, LLC," accessed August 12, 2018, http://tfgroupllc.com/bkon/bkon-craft-brewer/tea/.

17. Johannes Itten, *Design and Form: The Basic Course at the Bauhaus and Later* (New York: Van Nostrand Reinhold, 1975).

18. "Tea—TFG, LLC," accessed August 12, 2018, http://tfgroupllc.com/bkon/bkon-craft-brewer/tea/.

19. "The Texting Tea Pot—Dan Saffer—Medium," accessed August 12, 2018, https://medium.com/@odannyboy/the-texting-tea-pot-5b33d2c9f726.

20. "WiPot WiFi Teapot—Connected Crib," accessed August 12, 2018, http://www.connectedcrib.com/wipot-wifi-teapot/.

21. "Slock.It on Twitter: 'The #blockchain Teapot. This Is the First Connected Object on Ethereum.' #iot #dao #devcon1 #smartcontract Https://T.Co/RwWfEkpeJY&quot," accessed August 12, 2018, https://twitter.com/slockitproject/status/664815326916407296.

22. "The Toaster Project: Thomas Thwaites," accessed August 12, 2018, http://www.thomasthwaites.com/the-toaster-project/.

23. Silvia Lindtner, Anna Greenspan, and David Li, "Designed in Shenzhen: *Shanzhai* Manufacturing and Maker Entrepreneurs," in *Proceedings of the Fifth Decennial Aarhus Conference on Critical Alternatives* (Aarhus: Aarhus University Press, 2015), 85–96.

24. Denisa Kera, "Maker Culture Liminality and Open Source (Science) Hardware: Instead of Making Anything Great Again, Keep Experimenting! | A liminaridade da cultura maker e o hardware de fonte (na ciência): Em vez de fazer algo ser grande de novo, continue experimentando," *Liinc Em Revista* 13, no. 1 (2017), doi:10.18617/LIINC.V13I1.3875.

25. Siebenbrodt and Schöbe, *Bauhaus: 1919–1933, Weimar-Dessau-Berlin.*

26. Ibid.

27. Ben Davis, "The Bauhaus and the Contradictions of Artistic Utopia," *Artnet Magazine*, accessed August 12, 2018, http://www.artnet.com/magazineus/reviews/davis/bauhaus1-28-10.asp.

13 Bauhaus Products for Our Time

Martin Thaler

Introduction

The approaching hundredth anniversary of the founding of the Bauhaus inspired the faculty and students at the Institute of Design at the Illinois Institute of Technology to reexamine the Bauhaus's and the Institute of Design's core ethos of teaching design and its application to the design of contemporary products. At the Institute of Design—the locus of the Bauhaus when it moved to America—we occupy a unique position from which to reevaluate these design values. As the Institute of Design's professor of the required preliminary course in product design for students entering the program without a design background, I wanted to assess how closely our institute's course upholds Bauhaus tenets found in the Bauhaus *Vorkurs*, in my Spring 2017 Bauhaus Futures Workshop. In this fifteen-week course, we sought to understand Bauhaus design values and use these values to inform the design of near-future product concepts in the areas of furniture, lighting, and housewares. The brief of the workshop was the design of three conceptual products for urban dwellers, a large and growing segment of the world's population.[1] More than simply applying the visual design language of the Bauhaus era, by combining foundational knowledge with current socioeconomic and technological issues, student teams used the longstanding Bauhaus *Vorkurs* values to create designs for today.

Grappling with Bauhaus Legacy: The *Vorkurs*

The direct lineage between the leadership and culture of the Bauhaus and the Institute of Design is a unique heritage, one to specifically consider in the history of the Bauhaus *Vorkurs*. The preliminary course, the *Vorkurs*, is core to the Bauhaus educational philosophy and training. The learning objectives, content, and methods of the training were defined by Walter Gropius, founder and director, and Johannes Itten, the first teacher of the course, who emphasized having the students develop their creative expression and intuition. Itten, a painter, believed that understanding color theory was foremost, after which form was considered.

Itten drew upon the teachings of Friedrich Froebel, Maria Montessori, and John Dewey,[2] educators who shared the philosophy of unleashing the student's imagination through play. They sought to create learning environments where students could physically interact with tactile materials to generate creative expression and have social experiences. Their experiential approach holds true today: design is taught by learning through doing and in an open, collective studio space.

Due to differences over the learning objectives of the preliminary course and the school itself, Gropius persuaded Itten to resign in 1922, after three years.[3] Itten's romantic approach was to train artists, not designers. László Moholy-Nagy with Josef Albers taught a very different version of the required *Vorkurs*. Their approach was to pursue new technologies within the realm of free experimentation, using craft techniques with the intention of moving products toward production. Moholy-Nagy favored logic over emotion. He was a notable practitioner of many art and design disciplines: product design, graphic design, sculpture, painting, photography, and cinema. Moholy-Nagy's broad abilities foreshadowed the idea of a multidisciplinary team and a kinetic and energized design process.

The Chicago chapter begins in 1937, when Moholy-Nagy created "The New Bauhaus." The school was renamed the Institute of Design in 1944, to highlight its stature as a college. Later, in 1949, it was incorporated into the Illinois Institute of Technology (IIT).[4] Contributing to this legacy was Ludwig Mies van der Rohe, the last director of the Bauhaus, who immigrated to America in 1938 to become head of the school of architecture at IIT.

At the Institute of Design, the preliminary program taught today is a yearlong immersion into many applied design disciplines: communication design, digital design, product design, and design theory and history. Students are required to gain knowledge about the field of design and develop necessary skills for the Master of Design degree program. Master of Design students may choose to tackle design challenges within industries such as healthcare, financial services, and education. As professor of the product foundation class based on Moholy-Nagy's approach, I teach graduate students how to design products and how this understanding of the design process spans and applies to many fields of design practice.

Product design education is continually evolving, although perhaps not fast enough for students who need to formulate a point of view for designing products for our time.

Today students need to be conversant with advances in 3D printing technologies as a new means of production, with artificial intelligence (AI) as a means to assist designers, and with virtual and augmented reality technology (VR and AR) as visualization tools. The internet has made possible new business models, and its content has provided quick access to data for problem-solving. Using low-cost digital tools, designers today can research and then model concepts with a high level of physical or visual resolution. Moreover, designers today can fund their ideas through crowdsourcing platforms, such as Kickstarter, and make and sell their designs locally as well as globally. It is now more common for designers to be entrepreneurs and intrapreneurs within large enterprises.

Our instinct tells us that we live in a much different world today and that the pace of change is much faster than in Germany between 1919 and 1933. But is this true? What can we learn from examining the historical, social, and design forces of the Bauhaus era? How best can we teach a product designer today?

Bauhaus Design Values and the Workshop Process

In the Bauhaus Futures Workshop, we followed a human-centered design (HCD) approach, a recognized design practice, to research Bauhaus values and conceptualize new products.[5] In particular, we used a method called "artifact analysis."[6] Student teams were assigned one of three archetypal Bauhaus products for seating, lighting, and housewares and then from these designed new products.

It was important for teams to have access to the physical object, and they examined artifacts in the European Decorative Arts collection of the Ryerson and Burnham Archives at the Art Institute of Chicago, as well as disassembling purchased products available on the market (figure 13.1). With firsthand knowledge of the object, they sought to answer: How do people experience these commonplace products? How were these products built? What are the properties of the materials used? What does it feel like to approach these objects and use them? Teams used written references and videos to further grasp the sociological context and the designer's intent.

This design process meant students would need to: (1) understand the Bauhaus legacy and be inspired by Bauhaus principles and practice and not be misled by "Bauhaus style"; (2) gather insights about past products and their context and understand and compare this with the present, then formulate their thinking to design a future product; and (3) delve into issues of design, such as proportion, scale, hierarchy, and composition, and use these to delineate potential future products. Our research of Bauhaus designers and their products led us to these five Bauhaus tenets.

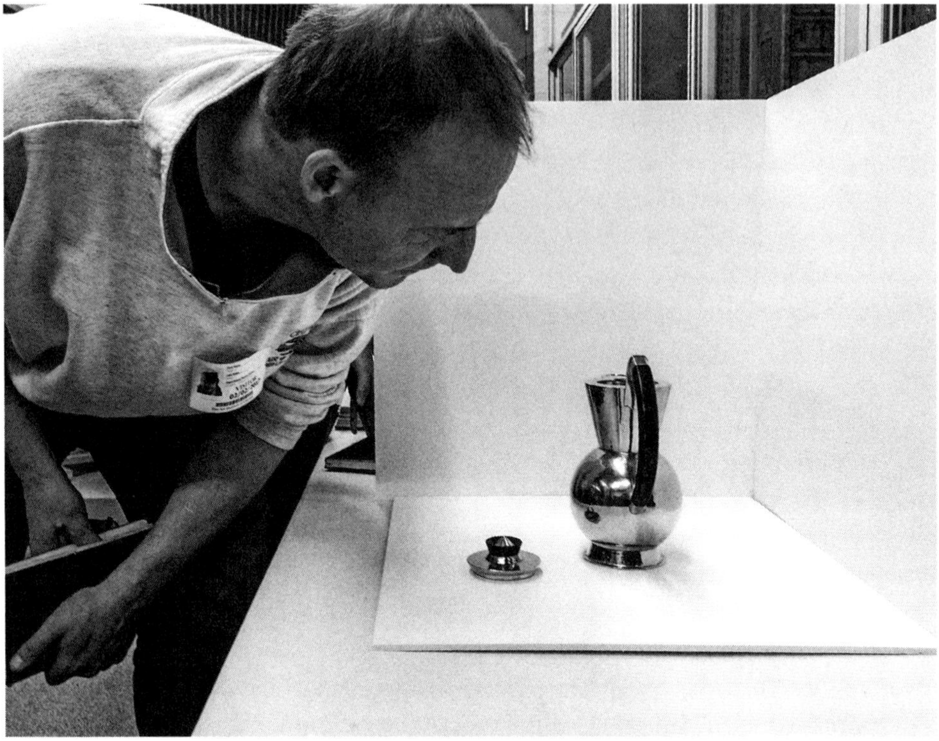

Figure 13.1
Andrew Bates inspects Dell Wine Jug of 1922 in 2017.

1. Simple objects. Products are intended for everyday use, with few parts and absent of complex function.
2. Strong compositions. Elements are arranged thoughtfully and convey a natural ease and inherent robustness.
3. Significant need. Products are not frivolous, but fill a gap in the market or improve upon an existing option.
4. Socially responsible. Designs follow the highest communal standards and are respectful of limited natural resources.
5. Truth to materials. Materials are used in their raw, unadulterated form and are left exposed.

In the workshop, student teams wrestled with the aims of modernism in contrast to objects in the contemporary maker movement. Conceptual directions ranged from technological products with digital interfaces using low-cost sensors and advancing energy technologies, to craft-based objects simply made from authentic materials and meant to last, to single-purpose objects with enhanced digital capabilities.[7]

Bauhaus Products for Our Time

Through a series of research reviews and concept critiques of their prototypes, student teams reimagined three iconic Bauhaus objects for the near-future market: the Cesca Chair of 1928 by Marcel Breuer (figure 13.2), the Wagenfeld Lamp of 1923–1924 by Wilhelm Wagenfeld (figure 13.5), and the Dell Wine Jug of 1922 by Christian Dell (figure 13.7). Here are the stories the teams wrote about the objects they designed and how each responds to the team's assigned reference object.

From Marcel Breuer's Cesca Chair (1928) to Basis (2017)

Andrew Bates and Isabel Dec (designers)

During the Bauhaus era, which concentrated on free experimentation with color, form, and material, Marcel Breuer wanted to explore the full potential of tubular steel, which, when combined with the technical innovations at that time, allowed him to develop a truly novel visual language of furniture. Breuer's Wassily Chair sought to celebrate the transparency of the form, and in an attempt to reduce visual noise even further, he created the Cesca Chair—a cantilevered seat supported by a continuous line of steel tubing. This was a progressive approach to the function of furniture.

Most contemporary designers aim to be visually original; aesthetics in furniture design are often valued above improved utility. However, the furniture designed at the Bauhaus was not predicated on style, but was an expression of our outward and constant, everyday needs. Or, according to the Breuer dictum, "Let our dwelling have no particular style."[8] Every piece should be as simple as possible, facilitating as much use in as many combinations and adaptations, and without controlling the environment. The work of the Bauhaus was intended to be a collaboration among the designer, user, and space, allowing for a redefinition of how we live and interact with our environment.

To this end, we designed a piece of furniture that addresses the needs of users in our near-future context. In most ways, our homes and how we live have not changed: seating is still as much a part of the modern home as it has ever been. However, some significant changes should be reflected in our designs. Specifically, contemporary society lives in less space, moves more often, and has begun to blend home and work lives

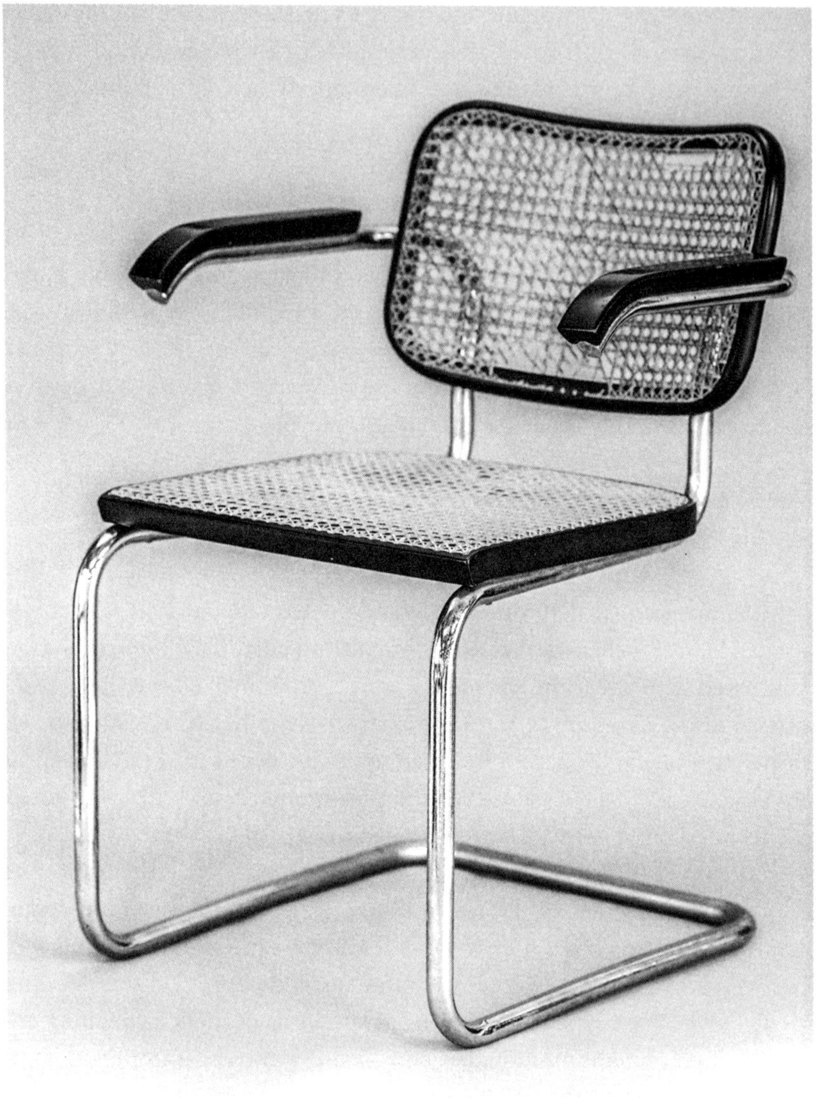

Figure 13.2
Marcel Breuer, Cesca Chair, reproduction of 1928 original by Knoll, 1980s.

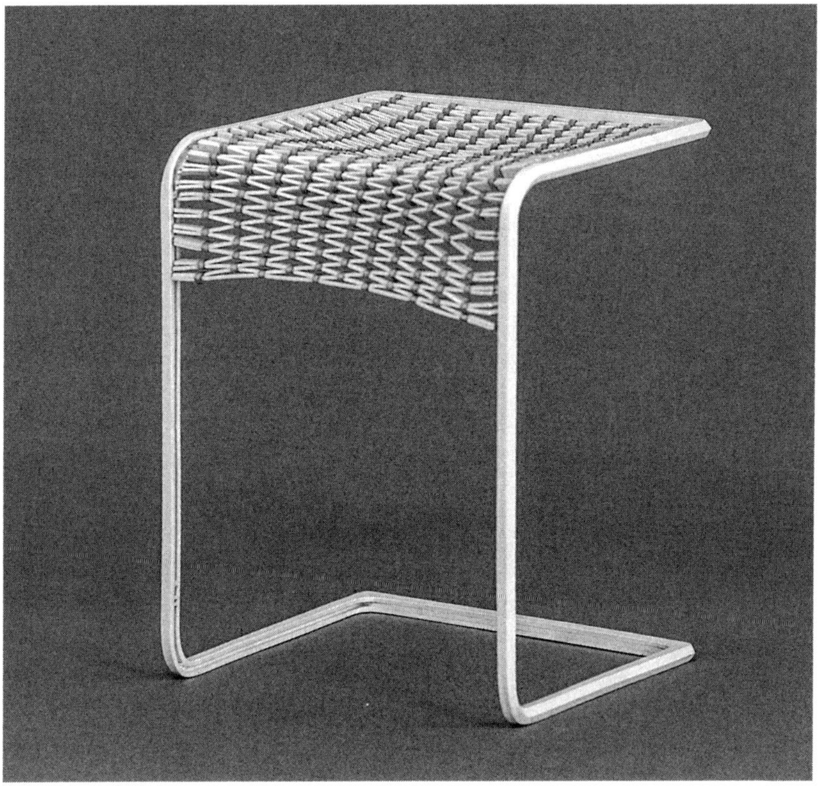

Figure 13.3
Andrew Bates and Isabel Dec, Basis, vertical orientation, half scale model of 2017, 11.25 × 9 × 8.8 in.

in ways made possible by digital technology and connectivity. Our position is that furniture with multiple functions is becoming more necessary.

Basis's components facilitate its function through a frame and a dynamic, shifting surface (figure 13.3). The individual configuration then can be changed from hard to soft, adapting to the user's needs. In this way, the dynamics of an almost fabric surface create a spectrum of use between task and comfort. The surface of Basis is woven, 3D printed metamaterial that becomes rigid when compressed and flexible when relaxed (figure 13.4). Stiffness is achieved through an interlocking, tongue-and-groove structural geometry.

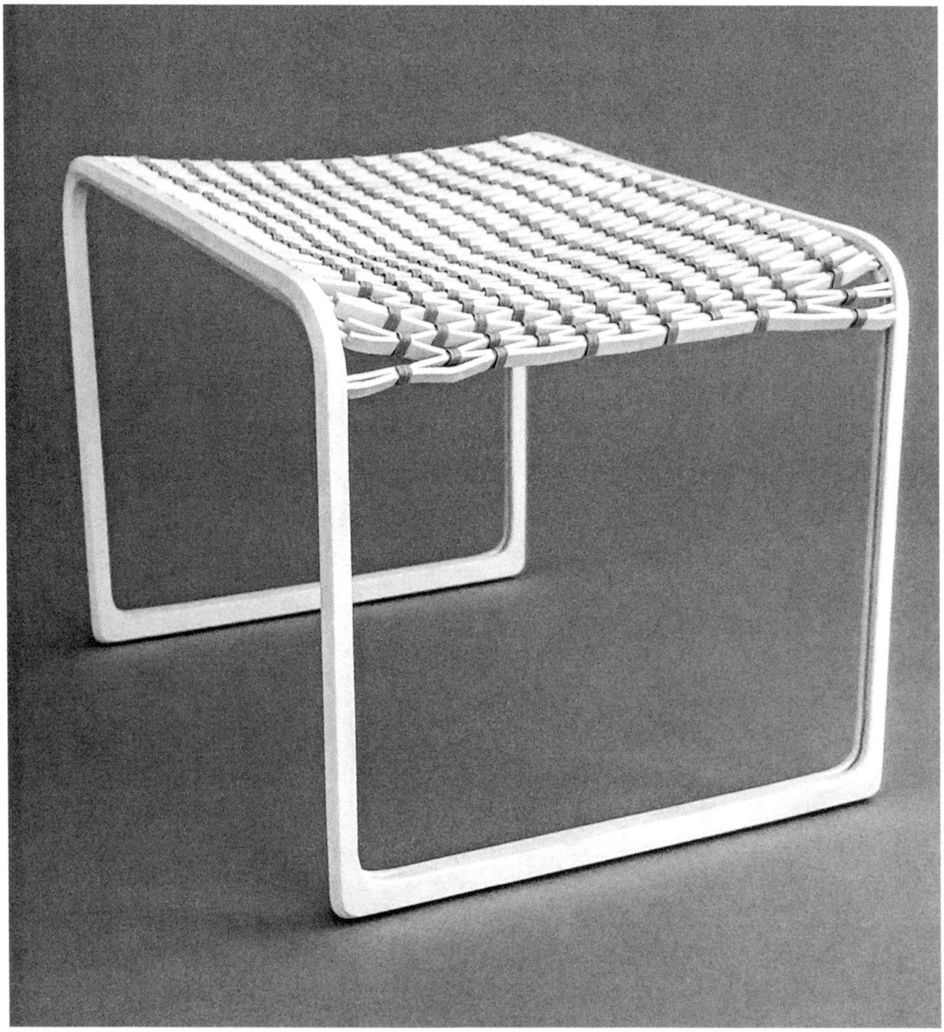

Figure 13.4
Andrew Bates and Isabel Dec, Basis, horizontal orientation, half-scale model of 2017, 11.25 × 9 × 8.8 in.

From Wagenfeld Lamp (1923–1924) to MaYu Light (2017)

Yu-Chieh Ho and Maho Kohga (designers)

Bauhaus design reflects the transition during the early 1900s, from craft-dominant products to mass manufactured products. Often, Bauhaus products adopted characteristics of both, such as in the Wagenfeld Lamp. The Wagenfeld Lamp combines geometric shapes—a circular base, cylindrical shaft, and spherical shade—and uses mass

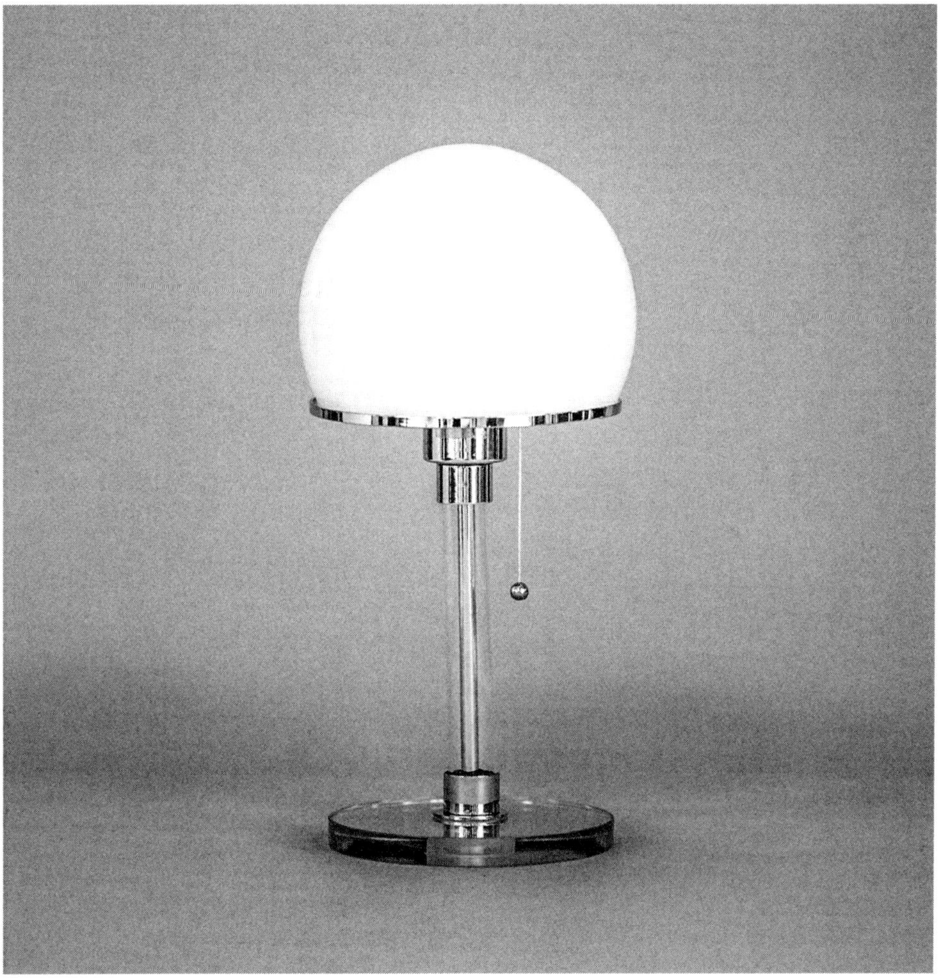

Figure 13.5
Wilhelm Wagenfeld, Wagenfeld Lamp, reproduction of 1923 original.

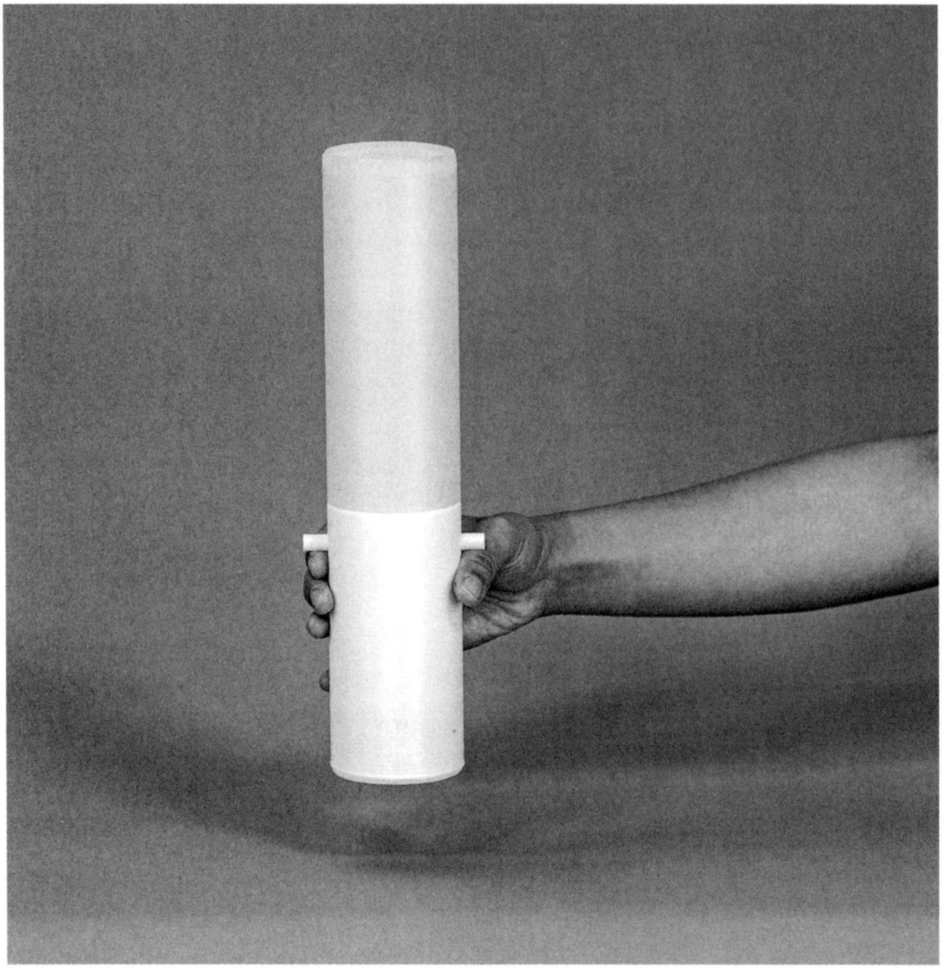

Figuere 13.6
Yu-Chieh Ho and Maho Kohga, MaYu Light of 2017, 12 × 2.5 in.

manufacturing processes. Its pull switch was a common solution for turning on and off hanging pendant fixtures in homes of the 1920s. The pull switch, glass globe, and a nickel-plated tube emphasized the aesthetics of handcraft. The core of Bauhaus design focused on function, materials, and the social trend of moving from craft to manufactured products. Honoring the design intent of the Bauhaus, we sought to balance a craft aesthetic with manufactured elements of our future product. The ways in which we use lamps has largely remained unchanged. People need light to perform their daily routines. Placing the lamp near an outlet constrains a person's ability to use the lamp.

With advanced technology, the cord may become obsolete. Low-energy-consuming LEDs and low-cost battery technology will make portable lamps possible and affordable. Furthermore, sensors and Wi-Fi modules enable the lamp to identify its surroundings and adjust its brightness according to its location in the room. Finally, 3D printing technology can combine and realize craft and mass production into an efficient process.

The MaYu Light is a simple, easy to pick up, lightweight tube (figure 13.6). Brightness is adjusted by turning the rod bisecting the tube. When carried, the rod also acts to transfer the weight of the light to the top of the user's hand.[9] We share the Bauhaus utopian ideal of providing people with a simple and pleasant life that values the craft movement. And we have made use of contextually aware sensing and 3D printing technologies to design this new lamp aligned with Bauhaus design tenets.

From Dell Wine Jug (1922) to Lynn Stand (2017)
Siyuan Ma and Jennifer Peterson (designers)

Humans have a basic need for connection and community. The Dell Wine Jug was created as an object for social gatherings. Handcrafted in the Bauhaus metals shop, its basic shapes and contrasting materials stood out as an exciting and modern piece in a mundane world.

In the Bauhaus ideal, everyone would have access to this modern style, and one's entire life would be led only with things that allow man to be free, think critically, and pursue his best life. And although few pieces made it to market before the school closed in 1933, those that did endure to this day as the epitome of exceptional design for people who support a modernist design aesthetic.

Today, the Bauhaus ideal of mass manufacturing for the common man has peaked, but ours is not a future that the Bauhaus would recognize or embrace. The Bauhaus utopian view was not about consumption, but aspired to make things for a better and more purposeful life. With new technology, we can now mass manufacture, often cheaply and quickly, just about anything that someone can design.[10] So unlike in the Bauhaus era, in the contemporary world the focus is on consuming the latest mass-produced thing.

In response, fueled by global social and environmental concerns, we are seeing a pushback against mass manufacturing and mass consumption. We have reached the point of market saturation and are confused by unlimited choice. Now, we want to be the ones in control, buying and consuming more consciously and with greater discretion and reflecting our values.[11]

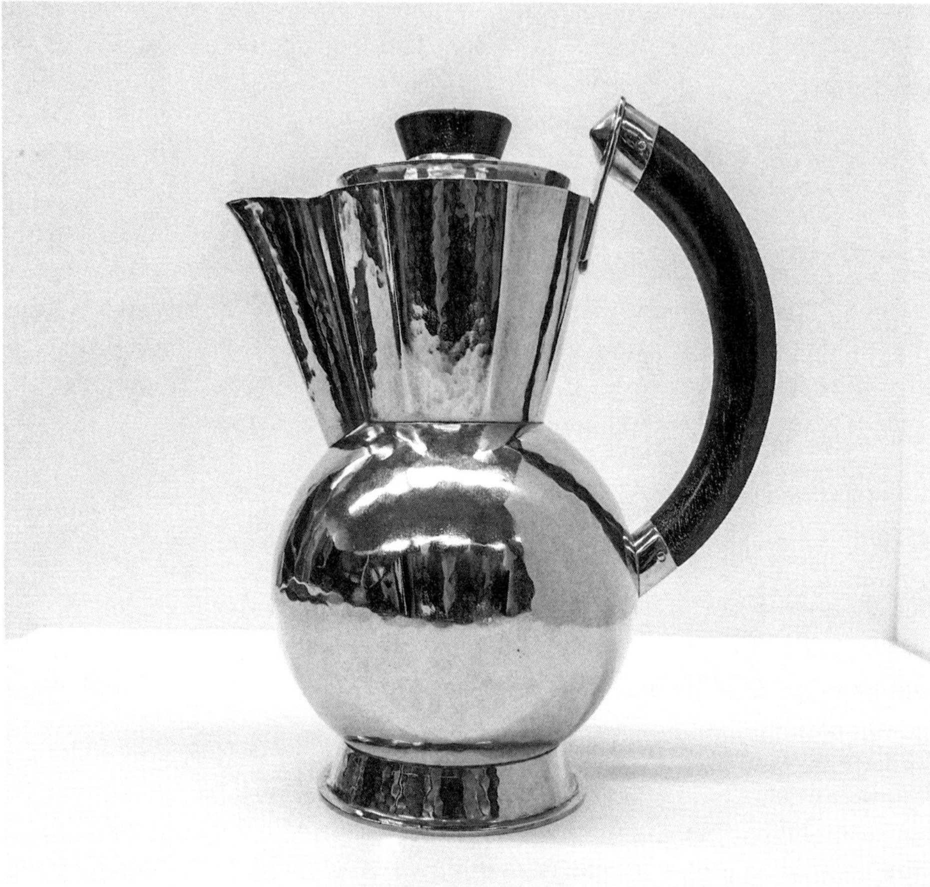

Figure 13.7
Christian Dell, Dell Wine Jug of 1922, 2017.

We seek experiences. We seek stories. We seek uniqueness. And most of all, we seek community. The objects we choose to bring into our lives can help realize these goals. Our team aimed to bring people together over the ritual of kombucha making. The kombucha community bonds over shared values, such as healthy living and the ritual of making through the stories and experiences they post online. The community also seeks to share their knowledge with family, friends, and the outside world. The Lynn Stand embodies the process of kombucha making as a personal and thoughtful journey, as well as a communal experience (figure 13.8).

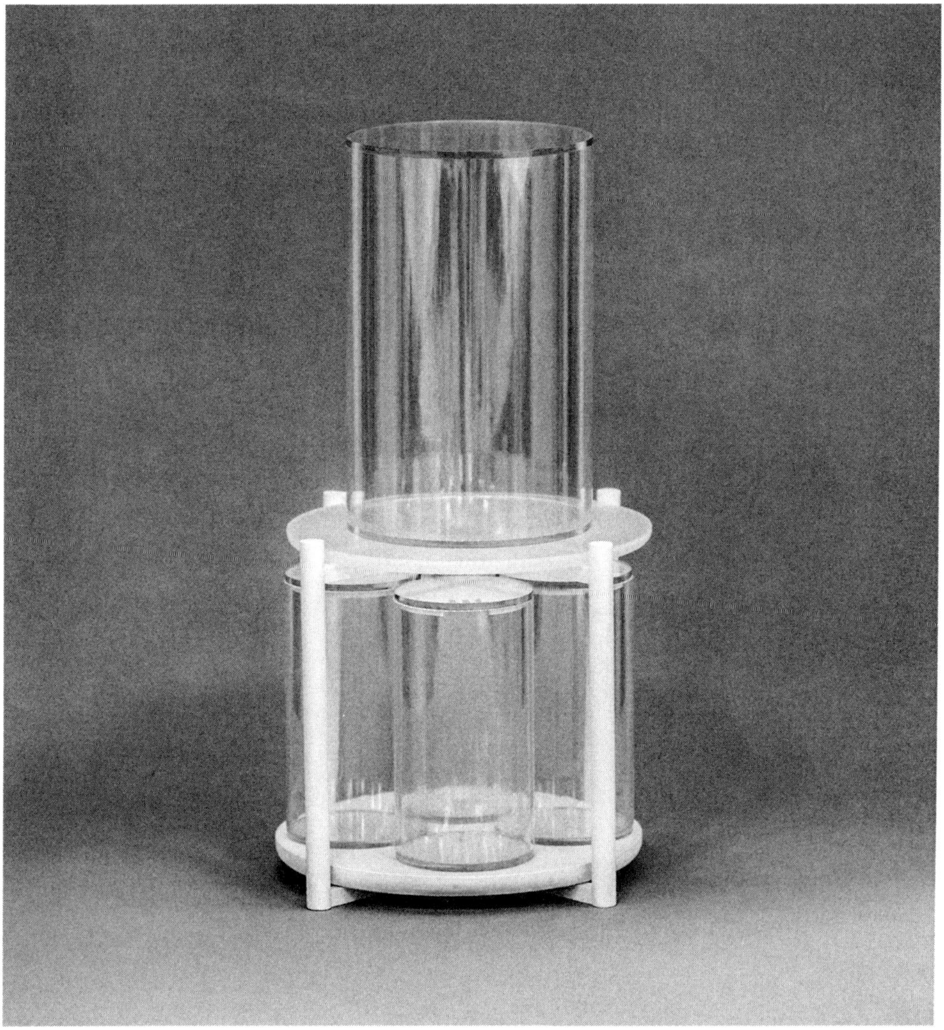

Figure 13.8
Siyuan Ma and Jennifer Peterson, Lynn Stand of 2017, 24 × 12 in.

The Way Forward

From our research, we defined five actionable, contemporary design principles. Each is a modern reworking of the five Bauhaus tenets framed in the course of our research. Each of the new principles maps to one or more of the original five tenets.

1. Effect. Select elements to form an intriguing yet familiar system.
2. Standards. Use discrete materials to simplify construction and recycling.
3. Subtraction. Reduce mass and incorporate only essential product attributes.
4. Utility. Use design details to support an elegant logic to portray its use.
5. Clarity. Be sincere and humanistic in your work.

In contemporary design, often too little attention is given to understanding and learning from what has come before and then applying these lessons to the design of a new product. With these newly defined design principles, we are building upon the tenets of Bauhaus masters, journeymen, and apprentices. They sought out possibilities to build a better, more unified world through art and technology. We strive to do the same.

Acknowledgments

I would like to acknowledge the written contributions to this chapter by my students at the Institute of Design: Andrew Bates, Isabel Dec, Yu-Chieh Ho, Maho Kohga, Siyuan Ma, and Jennifer Peterson. I greatly appreciate their research and design work in the Spring 2017 product workshop. For their contributions to the workshop, I thank Amanda Rosenberg, design researcher, for her research efforts; Dogan Sekercioglu, industrial designer, for concept guidance; and my teaching assistant Aktas Ahmet Burak for helping to ensure the workshop's success. I also thank Laura Forlano and Molly Wright Steenson for their guidance in developing this chapter; Lisa Thaler for making the ideas and thinking clear to the reader; and Junyoung Yang for his refinement of photography. All photos 2018 unless noted: Junyoung Yang and Martin Thaler.

Notes

1. See https://www.un.org/development/desa/en/news/population/2018-revision-of-world-urbanization-prospects.html, accessed July 23, 2018.

2. Kenneth Frampton, *Modern Architecture: A Critical History* (London: Thames and Hudson, 1992), 123–129.

3. Frank Whitford, *Bauhaus* (London: Thames and Hudson, 1984), 121.

4. Hans M. Wingler, *The Bauhaus: Weimar, Dessau, Berlin, Chicago* (Cambridge, MA: MIT Press, 1969), 193–206.

5. IDEO.org, "The Field Guide To Human-Centered Design," 2015.

6. Bella Martin and Bruce Hanington, *Universal Methods of Design: 100 Ways to Research Complex Problems, Develop Innovative Ideas, and Design Effective Solutions* (Beverly, MA: Rockport, 2012), 14–15.

7. David Rose, *Enchanted Objects: Innovation, Design, and the Future of Technology* (New York: Scribner, 2015), 91 and 109.

8. Jay Doblin, *One Hundred Great Product Designs* (New York: Van Nostrand Reinhold, 1970), 35.

9. Naoto Fukasawa and Jasper Morrison, *Super Normal: Sensations of the Ordinary* (Zurich: Lars Müller, 2007), 106.

10. Patrick Whitney, "Design and the Economy of Choice," *She Ji: The Journal of Design, Economics, and Innovation* 1, no. 1 (Autumn 2015), 58–80.

11. David Sax, introduction to *The Revenge of the Analog: Real Things and Why They Matter* (New York: PublicAffairs, 2016).

14 Anarchival Materiality

The Bauhaus Building in Dessau

Trudi Lynn Smith, Kate Hennessy, and Oliver Neumann

Introduction

In this essay we present a series of images remediating photographs of the Bauhaus building in Dessau, instances of its materiality, and of Lucia Moholy, who created iconic images of the building. Our process counters the assumed stability of photographic imagery and Bauhaus representations. Photographs of the Dessau building, which were later used by Walter Gropius to promote the Bauhaus design narrative,[1] are implicated here as precarious residents of the Bauhaus archive. Like the Dessau building itself, which has been repeatedly subject to destructive political and environmental forces, we explore these photographs as examples of what we call anarchival materiality, or the generative force of entropy and social relations in archives. The anarchival force of molecular transformation, violence, displacement, and other human and nonhuman interactions renders archival materials *fugitives*, both eluding and driving preservation.[2]

As a condition of all things, fugitivity foregrounds precarity over standardization, dynamism over stasis, and complexity over simplification. To this end, our photo-essay uses the risograph to experiment with the logics and migrations of photographic dye processes, which emerged as visual technologies concurrent with the establishment (and exile) of the Bauhaus in Weimar Germany. Color film and photographs—once imagined through the use of standardized chemical technologies as realistic representations of actualities—have not stood the test of time, with fugitive colors today transforming the archival past into monochromatic magenta hues. While representations of Bauhaus architecture were mainly based on black and white photography, color was central to the Bauhaus: color theories were explored as part of the school's curriculum; color painting manifested a significant part of the Bauhaus studies; and, Bauhaus book design used color prolifically.

Our experimental risomediations highlight fugitivity as integral to our image-making process. The risograph (figure 14.1) is an offset ink printing machine that was used by churches and schools as an inexpensive copier and is now used in art and activist worlds for prints, zines, and artist books. The risograph was invented by the Japanese company Riso Kagaku Corporation in 1986. Although *riso* means "ideal" in Japanese, the machines are notorious for unpredictability, variation, and imperfection, and produce nonarchival prints. Our misregistered *risomediations* therefore foreground the condition of anarchival materiality. Our experience and co-creation of misaligned cyan, magenta, and yellow layers with the risograph unbind the building and archive from a narrative of standardization and stability. In making and presenting a selection of five of these images in this essay, we argue that the Dessau building, envisioned by Walter Gropius as a manifesto of the Bauhaus idea, exists as an entropic material archive that is as precarious as it is iconic.

Anarchival materiality is a concept that two of us (Smith and Hennessy) began to explore after encountering intriguing material transformations in archives while doing research together. An imprint of a pastel drawing on a manila folder, an orphaned

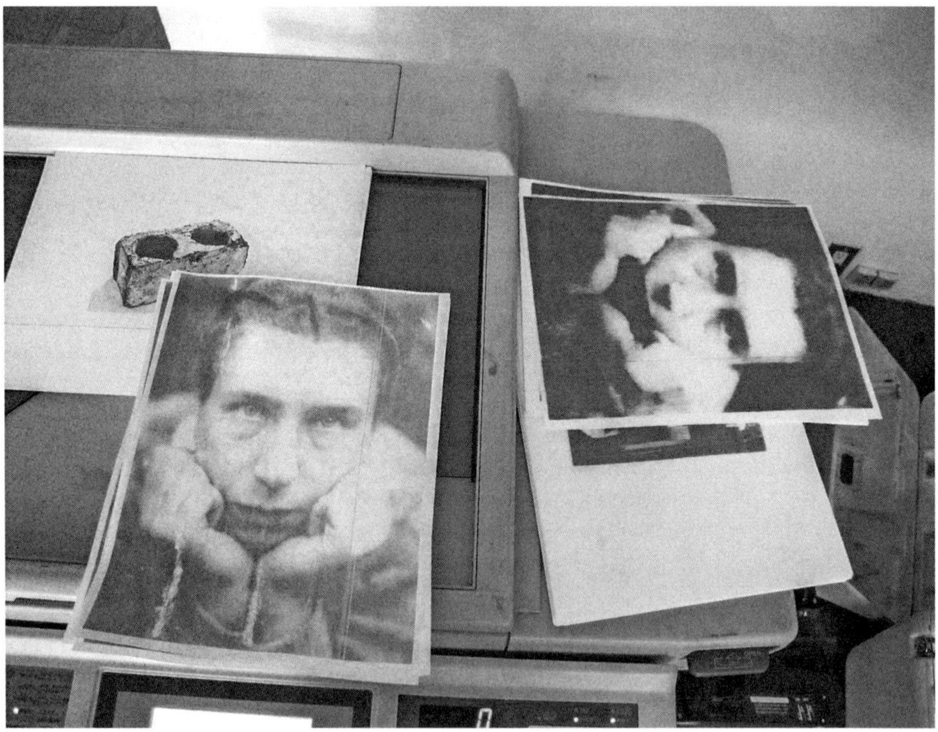

Figure 14.1
Risograph.

object that remains on a shelf in a bureaucratic archive, or a decomposing nitrate negative kept as a reminder of material deterioration[3]—all these things signal inevitable material transformations over time and the "thing-power" of what Jane Bennett calls vibrant matter, or the "active role of *nonhuman* materials in public life."[4] Our work sits in a space between anthropology and art practice,[5] and is inspired by ways in which artists both appropriate and disrupt the material formations of archives—photography, film, drawers, folders, naming conventions—to respond to the fetishization, objectification, and limits of institutions, objects, memory, and the past.[6] Contemporary artists, critics, and curators are disrupting representation through performances "in, with, and of the archive ... producing ontological change—from the archive as a repository of documents to the archive as a dynamic and generative production tool."[7]

The concept of fugitivity in our work first arose through oral history work with archivists and conservators at the British Columbia Provincial Archives. One of the archivists, Ann ten Cate, used the term *fugitivity* to signal a form of anarchival materiality that helps us to explore alternate organization within—and understandings of—archives. To be *fugitive* is to be apt or tending to flee, suggesting the slippery feeling of something escaping or eluding the grasp; and a fugitive is one who is driven out, banished, or exiled.[8] Fugitivity is a concept that we mobilize to better understand the agency of anarchival materiality in archives.

We also connect our use of fugitivity to the work of Maya J. Berry and her coauthors, who call for a feminist praxis of "fugitive anthropology, a rethinking of the contours of the political in co-creating spaces of liberation and transformation."[9] This important work further locates "a fugitive anthropology ... [that] cannot be tethered to preordained courses of predictable paths; it moves forward with an understanding that the path to reach spaces unknown is necessarily unpredictable."[10] As we will describe, materials become fugitive in multiple, unpredictable ways. Our risomediated images represent the fugitivity of the Dessau building and its photographic representations as (1) the product of historically situated social relations and gendered dynamics of power and representation; (2) inevitable material transformation (e.g., environmental and wartime deterioration); and (3) mutable regimes of value (materials and functions shifting across time). How does considering the Dessau building through a critical feminist ethos of anarchival materiality suggest an alternative reading of Bauhaus history and future?

Representing Anarchival Materiality

We came to our present experiments with the risomediation of photographs from within and outside of the Bauhaus archive in conversation with architect and coauthor

Oliver Neumann, who joined us to think though the potential of anarchival materiality to suggest an alternative reading of Bauhaus history, the Bauhaus future, and its inevitable and enduring embeddedness in the real as much as the ideal. As Bernard Tschumi has critiqued the "split between social reality and the utopian dream"[11] and "the dematerialization of architecture into the realm of concepts,"[12] we have selected images related to the documentation of the Bauhaus building in Dessau as a way to foreground the transformative potential of unpredictable encounters, and precarity, rather than stability, as a condition of our time.[13] We look to new tendencies such as Greg Lynn's[14] recent explorations that illustrate a shift toward the undetermined and unknown in architecture and other disciplines.

Our four-color risomediations (see plates 7–11) are a play on what we imagine as a shared historic impulse in Bauhaus architectural and graphic design—which emphasized free-plan structures, repetition and layering, experiments with color theory, and technologies of mass production—and in concurrent innovations in photographic reproduction technologies. The founding of the Bauhaus in 1919 coincides with a central development in photography made by Rudolph Fischer, a German chemist who filed a patent in 1912 for the process of chromogenic color photography.[15]

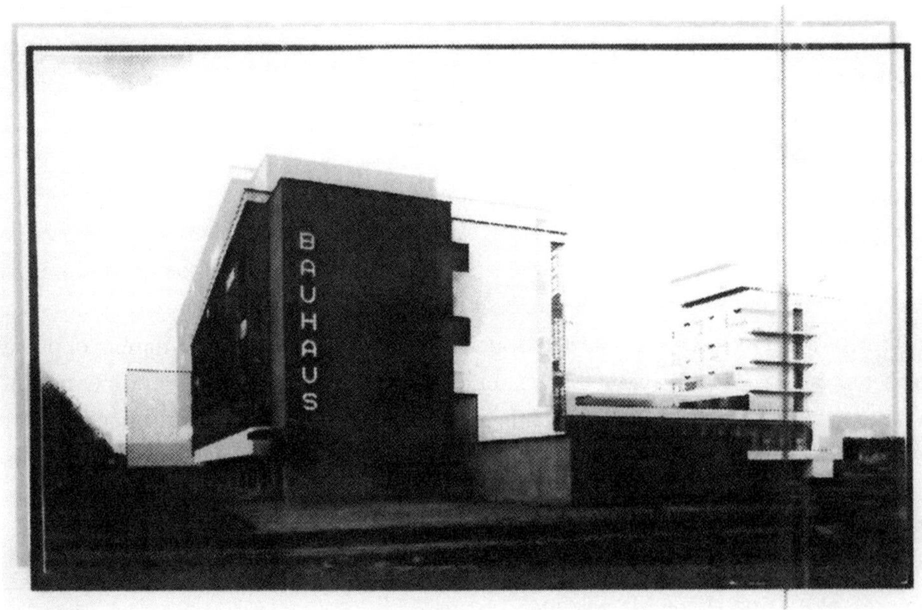

Figure 14.2
Risograph image remediating Lucia Moholy's photograph of the Dessau building. (Also plate 8.)

Chromogenic, meaning *giving birth to color,* is a dye-forming process that became the basis of color photography in the twentieth century. Rather than using separation negatives (e.g., processes of layering one after another, developed in the mid and late nineteenth century), chromogenic layered cyan, magenta, and yellow dyes together onto the cellulose acetate support to produce prints, negatives, and positive transparencies. While the Bauhaus attempted to "discover 'laws' in art that could be related to design and architecture, and its fundamental aim was to establish a universal language of form that would represent the elimination of social as well as national barriers,"[16] color photographic technologies that emerged during the time of the Bauhaus's original existence (1919–1933) have proven to be vulnerable, unstable, and subject to the variable forces of the world in which they exist.

Fugitives

Like color photographic negatives and our risomediations, the Bauhaus photographic archive and the materials that it documents are fugitive. Figure 14.2 is a risomediation of a photograph taken by Lucia Moholy of the Dessau building in 1927. Envisioned by Walter Gropius as a manifesto of the Bauhaus idea, the building exists as an entropic material archive that is as precarious as it is iconic. Like color migrations in film, the materiality of the building has been subject to the force of structural rearrangements caused by heat, moisture, pollution, human agency, and war. In a parallel argument, we draw attention to the multiple ways in which the Bauhaus archive, largely comprised of images from Moholy's photographic practice, is also fugitive.

To follow the lively forces of archives—whether the atomic vibrations causing color migrations or the tectonic vibrations causing brick deterioration—provides a view into underrecognized forces within archives. This is anarchival materiality—the principles of change, impermanence, displacement, violence, and other human and nonhuman interactions that render archival materials fugitives, both eluding and driving preservation.[17] To think about anarchival materiality and fugitivity in the Bauhaus Dessau archive is to consider the force of the building materials, the bulk and weight of photographic practice, the violences, anxieties, and displacements of war. Despite the commitment by the Bauhaus to repetition and uniformity, we are interested in how Lucia Moholy's lived experience of the Bauhaus archive is not one of modernist standardization and predictability but of precarity.[18]

While the Bauhaus practitioners were interested in technologies for mass production and innovations in color theory, representations of the Bauhaus photographic archive reveal a documentary vision: black and white images of people, performances, events, and design objects such as chairs and lamps. In his 1925 book *Painting Photography Film*, László Moholy-Nagy reaffirms the uncertain status of photography in art, and forwards that "our vision has only lately developed sufficiently" to grasp the potential of the medium.[19] Despite the importance of the photographic archive in maintaining the authority of the school, photography was a minor practice in the Bauhaus, and it is entirely absent from Walter Gropius's vision for Bauhaus training. There was apparently one camera at Dessau to document events, and it was rarely brought out and used; even with Lucia Moholy and László Moholy-Nagy's important individual and collective work with photography at Dessau, for the first 10 years of the Bauhaus photography was absent from the curriculum.[20] While an ambivalence about photography pervaded the Bauhaus, we draw attention to how Lucia Moholy's fugitive photographic images functioned over time to *become* the Bauhaus.[21] Attention to both the material conditions for the reproduction of the Bauhaus photographic archive and the materiality of the Bauhaus building in Dessau suggests an understanding of the Bauhaus as the product of historically situated social relations and gendered dynamics of power and representation.

Fugitive: Lucia Moholy's Photographic Archive

What is a work of art? How is it inseparable from its documentation? For most of the twentieth century, the Bauhaus Building in Dessau was not only a building but a photograph. Between 1924 and 1928 Lucia Moholy photographed the Bauhaus building as a *Gesamthkunstwerk*, the "working, learning and living" environment that created a structure for the Bauhaus.[22] As Robin Schuldenfrei has shown, Lucia Moholy's photographs form an essential part of the archive and functioned as significant and widely circulated proxies for the building itself.[23] When Moholy was forced to flee Berlin with the rise of the National Socialist party, the bulk and weight of her glass plate photography meant she had to abandon her extensive documentation of the Bauhaus, including the images from Dessau. The precarious plate photographs were later retrieved by Gropius from her apartment and exiled with him to the United States after pressure from the National Socialist party forced the closure of the Dessau building in 1932–1933. In their fugitive state, and without Moholy's knowledge or permission as rightful copyright holder, Gropius transformed Moholy's negatives from being part of her active work as a photographer and theorist into an archive that he would control and reproduce to reestablish the Bauhaus narrative from abroad. According to Schuldenfrei,

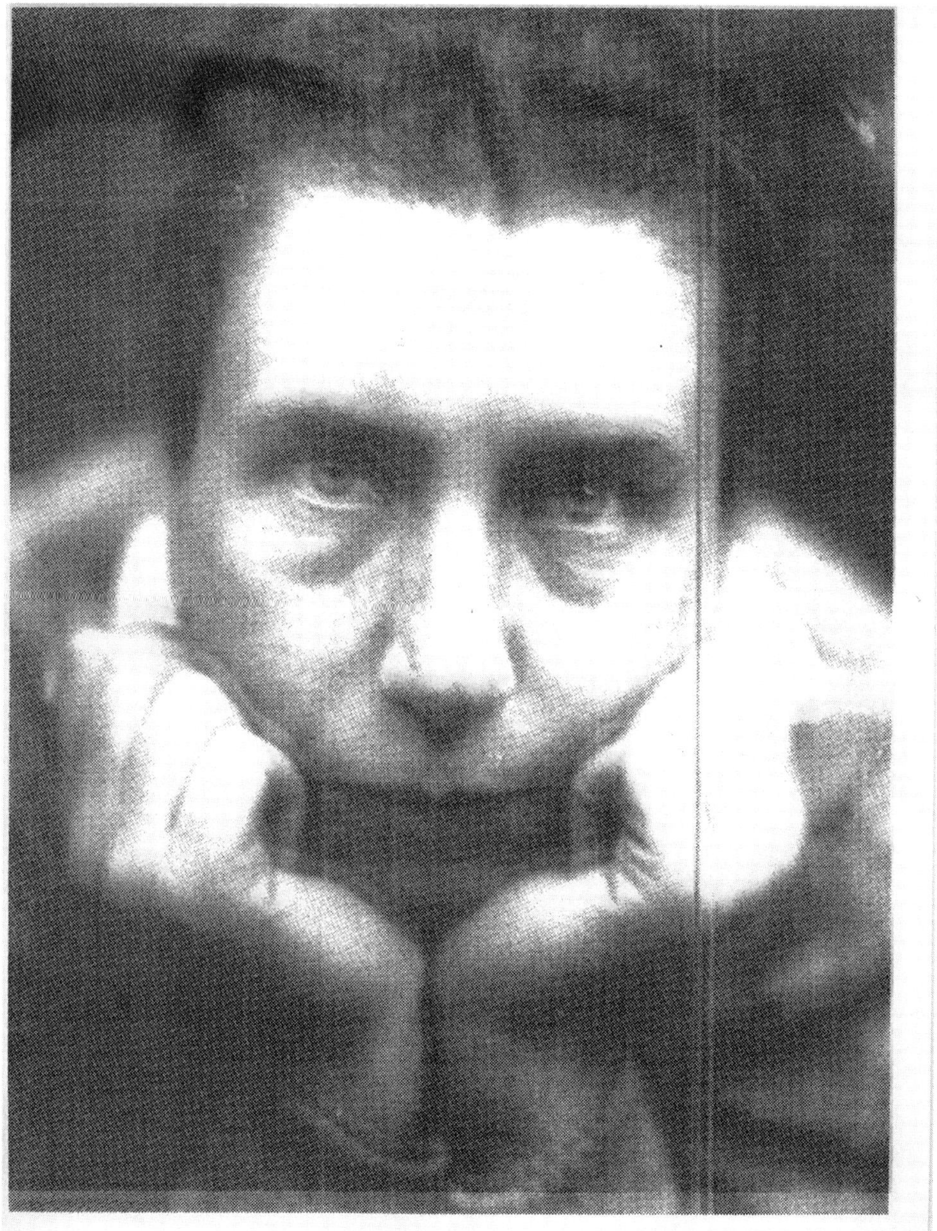

Figure 14.3
Risograph image remediating Lucia Moholy self-portrait. (Also plate 7.)

> The uneven power relation between Gropius, as former director of the Bauhaus, and Head of the Architecture Department at Harvard, and Moholy, with little wherewithal in London and rendered virtually anonymous without her negatives, was one that both were distinctly aware of. Gropius had, of course, long lost control of the Bauhaus buildings in Dessau, but he was to tighten control—to the point of usurping control—over its architectural image. Under the circumstances of exile and then the Cold War, not just the images themselves but the means of the reproduction became an oversized method of distribution and control, of power, of authorship, of ultimate signification.[24]

Fugitives: Being in and of the World

Although the force and structure of Moholy's photographic vision of the Dessau building constitutes the ongoing life of the building, the Dessau building has been repeatedly subject to destructive political and environmental forces. Our misaligned risomediation (figure 14.4) of the war-damaged Dessau building represents the lively specificity of enacting concepts in the world. In making three-color images, we line up the paper and press the "start" button, but this repetitive action does not connect to the outcome. In action, a part of the machine exerts more force than the last time, more stickiness or less spin, and the pink layer ends up fleeing to the edge of the page.

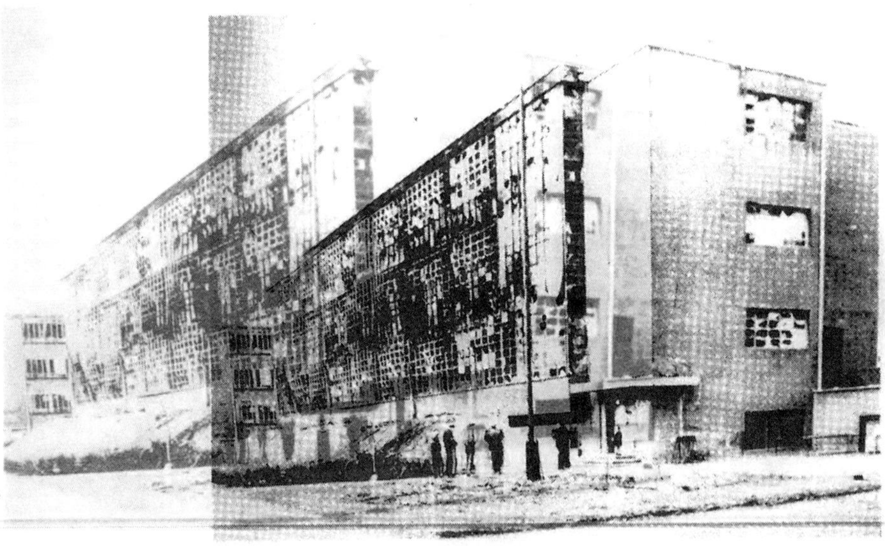

Figure 14.4
Risograph image remediating a photograph of the Dessau building in 1945. Adapted from "Conservation and Preservation of the Bauhaus Building in Dessau" by Monika Markgraf. (Also plate 9.)

The image shows significant building damage from bombing in 1945; the original glass curtain wall documented in Lucia Moholy's photography was destroyed and then changed in subsequent restorations.[25] Parts of the building that were destroyed were not reconstructed until 1976.[26] The wartime image amplifies the power of Moholy's original image as a persistent representation of a single moment of the early Bauhaus. Her photograph of the Dessau building (figure 14.2) shows its clean lines standing out against a white sky. The image stands in stark contrast to the rushed-feeling wartime photograph produced by lens distortions and curved lines that we make into figure 14.4. Moholy's original photograph, a powerful articulation of stability, permanence, and strength, makes the entropic wartime architecture seem impossible and unreal.

As the photograph becomes known, the Dessau building is enacted by the force of Moholy—a camera, f-stop, shutter speed, brightness, atmosphere, temperature, actinic rays of the sun, atomic vibrations of chemistry and substrate, the determinacy of making an exposure, her hands holding the shutter release or lens cap, storage in her apartment, and theft. This web of phenomena that constitute reality via *intra-activity* is a concept Karen Barad forwards to signal relational articulations of the world.[27] Thus there are two entangled ways the wartime photograph reveals what the Bauhaus obscures in its modernist vision of the world: a denial of the specific material arrangements that produce the world (Moholy's web) *and* the ways that the world is lively (the ongoing life of the building): "concepts are not ideations but specific material arrangements."[28] Moholy's photograph is the archival ideal, not the real. What the camera catches in that moment is the force of an agential cut[29] in the ongoing, entropic force of the world: anarchival materiality.

Fugitives as Mutable

Fugitives are mutable, in that their anarchival status can be reversed when changing regimes of value[30] make them archival once again. Figure 14.5 is a three-color risomediation of a hollow cinderblock, generated from a photograph from the construction research archive at the Bauhaus Dessau Foundation.[31] This ubiquitous building material, once unremarkable and anarchival, becomes significant and archival once again in the context of the building's world heritage status. As Monika Markgraf emphasizes, a lack of archival documentation of original materials used in the construction of the Dessau building means that this block is one of many materials that stand in as documents of the original building. The block is weathered, an imperfect form chipped away through the relational work of structure and insulation.

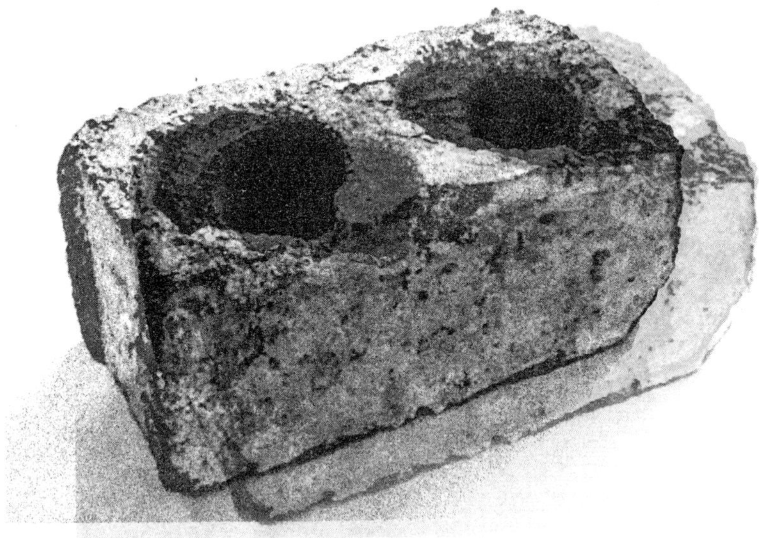

Figure 14.5
Risograph image remediating a hollow cinderblock. Adapted from "Conservation and Preservation of the Bauhaus Building in Dessau" by Monika Markgraf. (Also plate 10.)

Markgraf outlines archival practices of care that entangle past, present, and future worldings: "materials and building parts, data and documents on the Bauhaus buildings and the buildings of Modernism are ... stored."[32] Elements that were once invisible are identified and reclassified as heritage. The hollow cinderblock exists as part of the archive and as an archive itself, acting simultaneously as proof of the building technology and of its fugitivity away from the Bauhaus ideal via "tangible building problems."[33] Unlike Moholy's perpetually circulated photograph, the present-day construction archive foregrounds the agency of anarchival materiality and the mutable fugitive, in which entropic materials become integral to the designation of the building as a UNESCO World Heritage Site in 1996.

Figure 14.6 is a risomediation of a greenhouse documented by Monika Markgraf that was built on the grounds of the Bauhaus complex using original steel frame windows from the Dessau building. It is a phantom greenhouse, created and then dismantled during subsequent restorations as the original windows were deemed anarchival (garbage) and then became archival again.

The materiality of glass is central to the Bauhaus in Dessau. As we have drawn connections in this essay between the fugitivity of photographs of the Bauhaus and the materiality of the building itself, here glass is the substrate both for Moholy's photographic negatives and for the Dessau windows. The Dessau windows have architectural importance and are emblematic of the Bauhaus free plan. Comparing the Dessau glass with theater, Melissa Trimingham writes, "Glass walls hung like vast curtains, reflective from the outside, transparent from the inside, flooding the workshops with light."[34] Despite their centrality to the architecture, the Dessau windows are emblematic of fugitivity, an ongoing process of disassembly and reassembly in the building and its surrounds.

The large windows, made possible by structural innovation of materiality that allowed for larger spans, made for an architecture "defined by light."[35] This aspect remained important to the overall Bauhaus legacy, but it is one that moves in unexpected ways. The windows were circulated to make new and unintended architectural

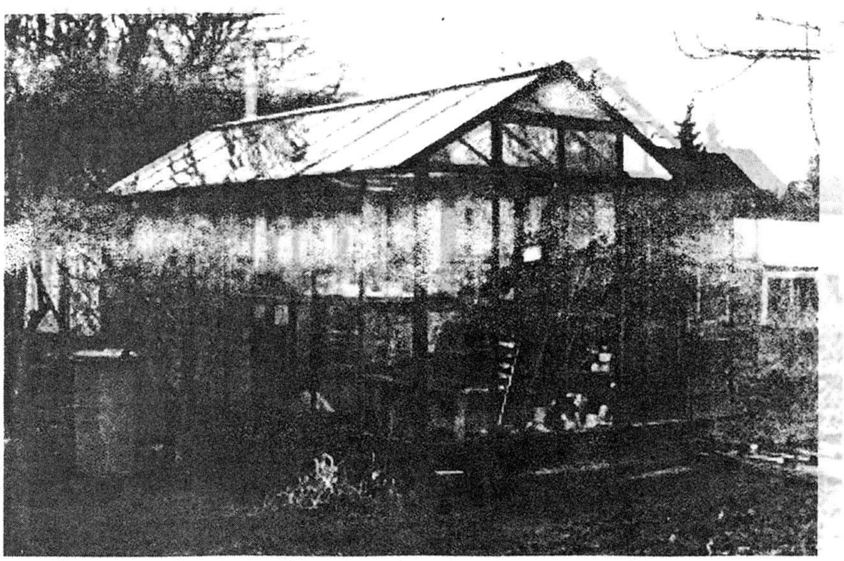

Figure 14.6
Risograph image remediating a photograph of the greenhouse at Dessau. Adapted from "Conservation and Preservation of the Bauhaus Building in Dessau" by Monika Markgraf. (Also plate 11.)

forms: removed from the Dessau building and considered waste in the 1976 restoration, they were salvaged by human caretakers for the construction of a greenhouse on the property. Cold winter temperatures likely meant that the large glass from the building was coveted for transformation into a greenhouse and garden to capture fugitive light. We can imagine the construction of the greenhouse addressing food insecurity in East German life: windows that allowed for a flood of light in the Dessau building workshops allow for a flood of light, warmth, and protection to nurture plant growth. Perhaps the greenhouse becomes an ideal form of Moholy-Nagy's *Lichtgestaltung* (light play) that sought to form light into new arrangements in photography?[36] In everyday life in late twentieth-century Dessau, the new architecture of the greenhouse arranges light to provide fresh produce: here, light play is life-giving, very much in and of the world.

Eventually, as Markgraf explains, the greenhouse windows were identified as the lost original Dessau building windows, and the greenhouse was dismantled. The windows were then "documented in drawings and photographs, carefully restored and finally reinstalled in the building."[37] In present-day Dessau, windows from three time periods are installed in the building: 1926, 1976, and 2000. In 2000, the process of restoration made the fugitive windows archival again, along with bricks and other original building materials that were viewed as integral to the archival material record of the Dessau design and construction. Anarchival materiality draws attention to ongoing transformations in use and meaning, like discarded windows transformed into greenhouses, and like destroyed places being reconstituted through the circulation of images and manifestation as heritage sites.

Conclusion

As we laid the image of the Dessau greenhouse on the risograph platen and hit the button, the dense intensity of the bottom half of the photograph made the paper sticky and the paper jammed on the drum. We opened up the machine, retrieved it, and ran it again; we were struck by its ghostly murkiness and inky illegibility, a manifestation of the changing boundaries of the Bauhaus in Dessau differently enacted and configured over time.

In the making of this essay, we worked through risomediations of images from the Dessau building and of Lucia Moholy to explore fugitivity of the Bauhaus material and photographic archive. Fugitivity provides a setting to understand the way that archives exceed their structures and to flesh out the way that materials have agency in the world. While archives are often considered stable repositories of memory and materials, the ideal of preservation is consistently undermined by human and nonhuman forces of the real. Looking through the lens of anarchival materiality, how will future transformations and mutability work through the materials left behind?

Acknowledgments

Special thanks to Open Space Arts Society, artist Kerri Flannigan, and the fledgling risograph collective. Thank you to Mike Ananny, Laura Forlano, and Molly Wright Steenson. This work is dedicated to the memory of Lucia Moholy.

Notes

1. Robin Schuldenfrei, "Images in Exile: Lucia Moholy's Bauhaus Negatives and the Construction of the Bauhaus Legacy," *History of Photography* 37, no. 2 (2013), 182–203.

2. Kate Hennessy and Trudi Lynn Smith, "Fugitives: Anarchival Materiality in Archives," *Public* 29, no. 57 (2018), 000.

3. Ibid., 000.

4. Jane Bennett, *Vibrant Matter* (Durham: Duke University Press, 2010).

5. Arnd Schneider and Chris Wright, eds., *Anthropology and Art Practice* (London: Bloomsbury, 2013).

6. Okwui Enwezor, *Archive Fever: Uses of the Document in Contemporary Art* (New York: International Center of Photography); Hal Foster, "An Archival Impulse," *October* 110 (Fall 2004), 3–22; Sven Spieker, *The Big Archive: Art from Bureaucracy* (Cambridge, MA: MIT Press, 2008).

7. Simone Osthoff, *Performing the Archive: The Transformation of the Archive in Contemporary Art from Repository of Documents to Art Medium* (New York and Dresden: Atropos Press, 2009).

8. Hennessy and Smith, "Fugitives," 000.

9. Maya Berry, Claudia Chávez Argüelles, Shanya Cordis, Sarah Ihmoud, and Elizabeth Velásquez Estrada, "Toward a Fugitive Anthropology: Gender, Race and Violence in the Field," *Cultural Anthropology* 32, no. 4 (2018), 538.

10. Ibid., 560.

11. Bernard Tschumi, *Architecture and Disjunction* (Cambridge, MA: MIT Press, 1999), 27.

12. Ibid., 35.

13. Anna Lowenhaupt Tsing, *The Mushroom at the End of the World* (Princeton, NJ: Princeton University Press, 2015).

14. Greg Lynn, *When Is the Digital in Architecture?* (Montreal: CCA and Sternberg Press, 2017).

15. James M. Reilly, *Storage Guide for Color Photographic Materials* (New York: Image Permanence Institute and University of the State of New York, n.d.), 5.

16. Gillian Naylor, *The Bauhaus Reassessed: Sources and Design Theory* (London: Herbert Press, 1985).

17. Hennessy and Smith, "Fugitives," 000.

18. Tsing, *The Mushroom at the End of the World.*

19. László Moholy-Nagy, *Painting Photography Film* (London: Lund Humphries, 1969), 7

20. Eugene J. Prakapas, foreword to *Bauhaus Photography* (Cambridge, MA: MIT Press, 1982), viii–xi.

21. Schuldenfrei, "Images in Exile," 182–203.

22. Ibid., 182.

23. Ibid., 182–203.

24. Ibid., 202.

25. Ibid., 182–203.

26. Monika Markgraf, "Conservation and Preservation of the Bauhaus Building in Dessau," in *World Heritage Sites of the 20th Century—German Case Studies—Heritage at Risk Special Edition: The Soviet Heritage and Europe Modernism,* ed. Jörg Haspel, Michael Petzet, Anke Zalivako, and John Ziesemer (Paris: ICOMOS, 2006), 108.

27. Karen Barad, *Meeting the Universe Half Way: Quantum Physics and the Entanglement of Matter and Meaning* (Durham: Duke University Press, 2007), 141.

28. Ibid., 144.

29. Ibid.

30. Arjun Appadurai, *The Social Life of Things: Commodities in Cultural Perspective* (Cambridge: Cambridge University Press, 1986).

31. Markgraf, "Conservation and Preservation of the Bauhaus Building."

32. Ibid., 111

33. Ibid.

34. Melissa Trimingham, "Bauhaus Lighthouse," in *Bauhaus Art as Life* (London: Koenig Books, Barbican Art Gallery, 2012), 200–211.

35. Ibid., 200.

36. Ibid.

37. Markgraf, "Conservation and Preservation of the Bauhaus Building," 110.

V Embodiment in Feminist Circuits and Cyborgs

15 Reading with Anni Albers

The Weave as a Lively Involution of Scale, Affect, and Feminist Precarity

Daniela K. Rosner and Alex S. Taylor

Introduction

This chapter examines the processes of scaling made visible within the words and work of the Weimar Bauhaus and, particularly, in Anni Albers's careful accounts of weaving.[1] We explore whether threading a feminist precarity into her writing helps illuminate new ways of examining tensions between what we scale up and what we scale down. Moving first over and across, we examine Albers's discussions of different scales of weaving, from the hand loom to industrial machinery. Traversing then downward and below, we consider her attention to the body, those fingers and hands interlacing threads along a pliable plane. Shifting around and through, we consider how an affect is present in Albers's reflections, and especially in how it pulls against the sturdy mechanistic logics visibly organizing her process. Across this writing, we hope to think with Albers, reading her prose somewhat against the grain[2] of conventional Bauhaus accounts by interweaving a feminist positioning.

For many, the Bauhaus conjures images of the sleek Wassily Chair or the sturdy Helvetica typeface—a minimal aesthetic that has had wide-reaching impacts on modernist design, making its way into all corners of contemporary life. On visiting the home Walter Gropius designed for himself in Massachusetts, for instance, one might be struck by how the aesthetics of the modern have not only persisted but have seeped into everyday surroundings over the last 100 years, even if unevenly.

In the chapters in this book—detailing architecture, furniture, ceramics, etc.—we continue to see this Bauhaus vision of a modernism for everyone.[3] With this vision, unsurprisingly, comes a tension between the arts and handwork, on the one hand, and the arts and mass production, on the other. The pioneers of the Bauhaus caught themselves having to reconcile the artistic integrity each associated with particular materials and processes with the requirements of large-scale production. Indeed, Albers

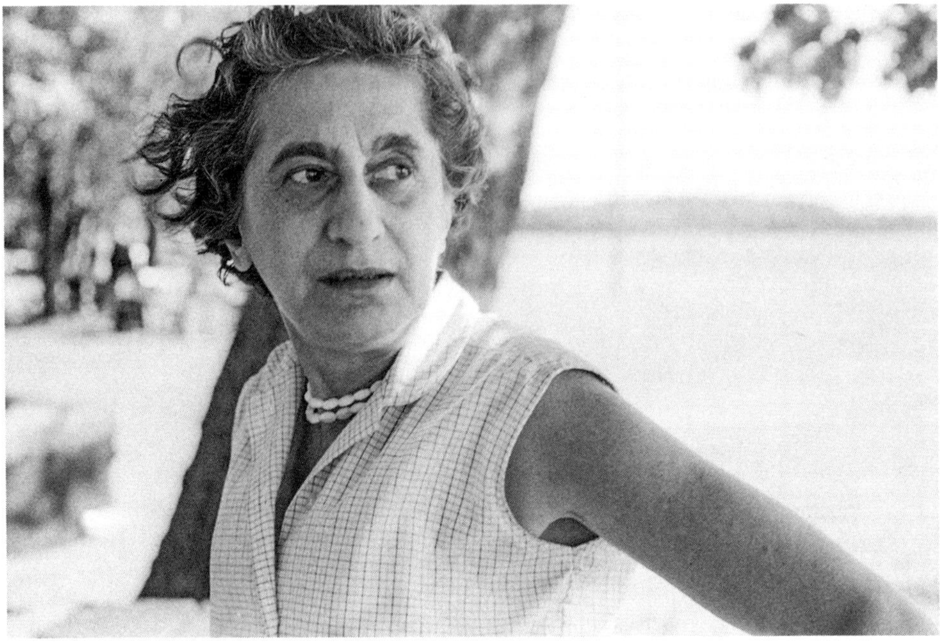

Figure 15.1
Anni Albers, ca. 1960. Photo: Josef Albers. © 2018 The Josef and Anni Albers Foundation/Artists Rights Society (ARS), New York.

herself writes of the shift in thinking demanded from her and her contemporaries at the Weimar Bauhaus. Citing Gropius's efforts to refashion the Marxist and expressionist proclivities that were instrumental for the school, she refers to "a new unity of art and technique"[4] and the need for new "norms" enabling "the development of prototypes for industry."[5] Her decrees speak to a prevailing narrative at the very center of conventional Bauhaus histories, one that has notably prioritized the project's scaling up, a narrative of shifting from small-scale artisanal practices to the processes and norms of mass production.

In this chapter, we explore work emerging from the Bauhaus through a prism of scaling—but not of scaling up, rather of scaling down and across. Perhaps because of the widespread prevalence of the modernist Bauhaus aesthetic (no matter how diluted), the bodily care invested in the work of design remains comparatively less visible (also see Knouf in this volume). With an understandable fascination for the expansion of the project, we find it too easy not to *look down*, so to speak, not to engage with the hands and materials and ask what might be learned from the details of this different direction of scaling, from a counterproject of making scale, in the anthropologist Anna Tsing's terms.[6]

Feminist philosophers have long dealt with such limits to the archive, the text-based documentation often stripped not just of bodies but of the kinds of questions, narratives, and arguments those bodies make matter. Saidiya Hartman, in her vivid retracing of the Atlantic slave route through Ghana, refers to such threading-together of absences.[7] Haunted by the untold and forgotten stories of her grandmother and other enslaved African women, stories missing from existing formal archives, Hartman visits present-day Ghana to recover aspects of this legacy. She scales down and across historical material, personal recollections, and contemporary bodies to weave something new in the unknown, "in the blank spaces of the story."[8]

Threading this feminist idea of scaling into our understandings of design, we want to draw out a story of the Bauhaus that places the entanglements between bodies and matter at center stage. We hope to show how the processes and attendant tensions of scaling up, so easily imagined as synonymous with the Bauhaus, weren't purely a matter of brute force—of scaling up by building bigger and more—but also something that stemmed from a sensitivity to bodies, materials, and machines, and how each made more of the other. In Albers's words, weaving comprises "a building up out of a single element, to building a whole out of single elements."[9] In thinking toward Bauhaus futures, we see this reflection to be a lesson in accounting from multiple scales, and scalings up and down at the same time. And by scaling, we draw attention to the shift not just of small to large, or one to many (or vice versa), but of flows and shifts of attitude, value, affect.

Across Scales

In her various accounts of weaving and textiles, Albers conveys a deep sensitivity to the relations between materials and practice. She writes of the "interaction between medium and process that results in form," and in turn of weaving's dependence on "the development of textile fibers, spinning and dyeing, each a part of the interplay resulting in a fabric."[10]

> The important fact implied is the influence of one upon the other, the modulation each undergoes through the agency of the other, the tuning up or down of some inherent qualities, or their alteration. For instance, the traits of linen, a somewhat hard and very sturdy fiber, will be underlined in a plain weave, which tends to produce a somewhat stiff and very firm fabric. In fact, the two correspond so well that the plain weave is also called the linen weave.[11]

By looking down to the body and hands, and what they do to weave, Albers captures the swirls and eddies of materials and processes and their connections to production. Her detailed descriptions of varying looms and the different configurations and manual interactions afforded by each show weaving to be a true assemblage of bodies, movements, threads, tools, weight, torque, machines, and so on. Critically, Albers's accounts not only romanticize the hand's role in making, they also recognize the back and forth, in her words the "interplay." Acknowledging the impact of "the modern age of power weaving," she writes of the profound effects new textiles and synthetic fibers have on weaving.[12]

In noticing these fibrous effects, we find an important intermingling of scales. With Albers's invitation, we cast our eyes in and down, but at the same time we take in the manual actions that resonate across other scales: across fibers, threads, and weaves; weaves, fabric, and cloth; fabrics with tapestries and looms; and across both manual and powered machines to production and circulation. We see a multiplicity of scales altogether. "The thoughts," Albers writes, "can, I believe, be traced back to the event of a thread."[13]

Interwoven Bodies

By describing the advantages weaving exhibited in the evolution of textiles and fabrics, Albers figures the body into and across the multiple scales. Although she aims to draw attention to the strengths and weaknesses of the woven fabric based on its early mode of production, we learn that the body matters in what it makes possible—in what it does and what it produces.

> The advantage of weaving becomes clear now. The weft, here a single thread, can be packed closely, resulting in a comparatively tight yet light fabric. On the other hand, it confines the resultant material to rectangularity; the width limited by the reach of the weaver's hands in inserting the weft, the length limited only by the amount of warp material that can be carried on the warp beam and of cloth that can be held by the cloth beam.[14]

The hands (and presumably the weaver's arms and body) reach across a loom's beams. This reaching is done to thread the weft through and across the tautly strung warps, but at the same time it places a constraint on the fabric or textile. The weaving, the reach, the supported weight of thread and cloth—altogether they give the fabric its shape and lightness.

The interweaving relations are made more explicit when Albers elaborates on an emerging correspondence between person and material. She speaks and writes in a number of different forums about the language one builds up with a material. Language, for her, quite literally refers to an exchange, a process of communication:

> "Accidentally." Something speaks to us, a sound, a touch, hardness or softness, it catches us and asks us to be formed. We are finding our language, and as we go along we learn to obey their rules and their limits. We have to obey, and adjust to those demands. Ideas flow from it to us and though we feel to be the creator we are involved in a dialogue with our medium. The more subtly we are tuned to our medium, the more inventive our actions will become. Not listening to it ends in failure.[15]

A tuning with the medium is a dialogue, an inventive becoming of actions. By tracing the history of the ways bodies entangle with the weave and with weaving machinery in this way, Albers is again shifting scales. Her accounts detail the technicalities and mechanics of various processes, but also draw us into other stories operating at very different registers of becoming. For instance, Albers describes a comblike instrument in writing about the process of compacting a weave, or weft, threaded through a loom's taught, perpendicular warp. This allows the weft to be "compactly beaten into place while at the same time the position of the warp threads is adjusted. ... The dents are pushed between the warp threads and pressed or beaten onto the wefts or the knots of a rug."[16] She goes on to describe the ubiquity of the instrument, writing: "It is found in many places, among them India, Persia, Africa, Asia Minor, Egypt in Roman times, and America before the Conquest. It is also found today among the Indians of the Southwest. Surely, it was also used in Europe in the weaving of the great medieval tapestries."[17] This account doesn't suggest so much a scaling up—an expansion from small to large—as a shifting, a torque of relations always already forming and tracing their way through longer spans of time and distributed across colonially marked geographies.

Such traces and shifts are evocative of Donna Haraway's *string figures*, those moving and merging images made by loops of string passed between fingers, a child's game of cat's cradle.[18] As with string figures, a downward-looking view, toward "twists and skeins that require passion and action, holding still and moving, anchoring and launching," illuminates stories in the making, a knotting of "diverse people, geographies, other critters, technologies, and knowledges, [that] shape practices of living and dying in rich worldings."[19]

Affect

Albers gives us much to reflect on in thinking about, as well as feeling, the embodied and material practices of weaving. As we've sought to foreground, her scalings—less familiar in typical accounts of the Bauhaus—invite us to attend to different qualities of scales. Still, tensions exist in her accounts. Though she speaks, writes, and, notably, *creates* evocatively as a form of affective noticing, she frequently resorts to a strikingly mechanistic language to describe weaving. Despite the potent exceptions we highlight above, she depicts the process of weaving in ways that more often than not elide the work of bodies and hands. Recognizing the historical moment Albers is writing in, we might read this as an effort to work through the challenges raised in (to use her analogy) the pendulum's swing "from art to industrial science."[20] Her descriptions, intentionally or not, amplify that scaling up of production that her work so carefully cuts across.

Our wish isn't to resolve this tension, but to approach it perhaps along a different woven thread. We might read, with Albers, a precarious experiment in rescaling, a move not merely up and down in scale but hesitantly across. That is, while keeping the tensions in play, we could read her work as an engagement with different registers of scaling, ones intersecting with care and affect, and thus quite different values.

Let us look in a little more detail at the way the tensions play out in Albers's text and what it is we might learn through them. With her notion of "tactile sensibility," she shifts our attention to just the sort of scaled-down focal point we have been discussing. She seems keen to acknowledge the tacit sensitivities at play in the processes of weaving.[21] Describing the tactile quality or *matière* of a textile, for example, she writes "it has to be approached, just like color, nonanalytically, receptively. It asks to be enjoyed and valued for no other reason than its intriguing performance of a play of surfaces."[22] Virtually in the same breath, however, Albers wants to keep this joy and different sense of value separate from production: "We are here revitalizing our tactile sense and are not dealing with *real* weaving."[23] "Our experiments in surface effects are therefore to be understood only as exercises to increase our awareness of surface activities, since the actual work of weaving is only in part concerned with the epidermis of the cloth."[24]

Albers leaves us with something curious to work with. She asks us to notice "those conditions that will make of our surfaces textile surfaces" and indeed harks back to a time when such "a faculty ... was so naturally ours."[25] At the same time, however, she wants us to understand this sensitivity as separate from the mechanics and machinery of manufacture. One might inform the other, but they are to be kept apart.

To stay with this trouble is to discover something prescient in Albers's conundrum. Her tensions capture the troubles also encountered in contemporaneous studies of the politics of science and knowledge, and specifically in feminist writings on the purification of science and technology executed through narrow registers and logics. Feminist scholars such as María Puig de la Bellacasa, Natasha Myers, and Vinciane Despret write vividly of technoscientific projects that "impoverish the range of explanations"[26] and that "cannot admit pleasure, play or improvisation."[27] Warning against reductionism and the overwriting of care, specifically, Puig de la Bellacasa reminds, "the picture on the ground is always more fuzzy, and contemporary engagements with care in new terrains continue to show this. Ethnographies of care show how absurd it is to disentangle care from its messy worldliness."[28] In her terms, such reduction comes down to the question of what makes an entity, whether a hand, body, thread, or world.[29]

Hustak and Myers take up this question of affect and reduction by rereading Charles Darwin's "affectively charged" work with orchids and asking how such stories might speak more broadly to the ecological sciences.[30] Set against Darwin's writings, contemporary ecology is seen to constrain—to "stultify"—theories of evolution and interspecies relations, reducing the processes to highly deterministic models.[31] What Hustak and Myers recommend instead is "reading with our senses attuned to stories told in otherwise muted registers."[32] Working, as they say, "athwart the reductive" frameworks that order such scientific worlds, they complement the evolutionary with the *involutionary*—a process of "turning inwards" so that new and fleeting possibilities might form. Through them, we find Darwin to be far less of the asymmetrically dominant, but still passive, objective observer, a perspective enforced by the methods of neo-Darwinism. Instead, Darwin reads as a considerable and lively part of biology today. He "participated actively with his experimental subjects, to such an extent that he *moved with and was moved* by them."[33]

By finding inspiration in this generative mode, and by reading Albers's work in a similar vein, we come to see her turning down and inward as a way to draw the muted back into the presumed and dominant registers. We begin to hear a voice that discovers different logics of value and seeks not to conquer but rather to participate in and care for worlds that have a greater symmetry. Here it is not the industrial science overcoming art, but the "affectively charged" moments where one becomes attuned to other things, speaks to them, and learns from them.[34] We find these logics, though hard to reconcile, come nonetheless together, already intertwined.

> In my case it was threads that caught me, really against my will. To work with threads seemed sissy to me. I wanted something to be conquered. But circumstances held me to threads and they won me over. I learned to listen to them and to speak their language. I learned the process of handling them.[35]

Counterhistory

With these involutions of bodies and thread in mind, how might we understand the modes of scaling we mentioned at the start? What of the scaling up and scaling down that produce different emphases between manual and mass production, and between the hand and the machine? How might rescaling design, what Hustak and Myers call "turning inwards," reveal different and perhaps uneven histories of material practice around the Bauhaus?[36]

Returning to Hartman's historical elisions, the "blank spaces," and drawing out what Stephen Monteiro has recently described as an "alternative narrative" of computing, we follow Albers's threads to imagine a counterhistory amid the Bauhaus.[37] For Monteiro, the textile origins of computing interfaces reveals how meanings and metaphors always entwine with otherwise hidden legacies of practice. When computers retrieve an image file from their server, for example, they use the microprocessor's algorithms to convert binary code into a grid of pixels observable on a diode mesh that we call a display screen. From the Jacquard loom to modern day touch screens, Monteiro traces computerized imagery like this eight-bit display to needlecraft histories such as the patterns produced by a threaded shuttle traveling over and under an eight-threaded warp. Two hundred and fifty-six color combinations result from the mesh of overlapping thread.[38] "The imaginary of computing," he writes, "is fashioned from the processes surrounding the making and assembling of cloth."[39]

Within the Weimar Bauhaus, such counterhistories reflect a greater impulse to notice shifts in affect around design. Albers opines, "The more subtly we are tuned to our medium, the more inventive our actions will become. Not listening to it ends in failure."[40] Refashioned by the work of knotting, netting, and looping, of the spinning of thread around the hand, design exists as a process of listening, one of tuning in and turning in that produces new ways of living in the present.

We have begun to read Bauhaus design imaginaries as processes of weaving that comprise scaling up and scaling down, but also across. "Increasingly," Albers wrote in 1975, "industry is turning to hand weavers for new design ideas, worked out on hand looms, to be taken over for machine production."[41] When the Weimar Bauhaus confronted the wider uptake of power-driven machines with renewed attention to weaving and its material histories, few expected the development of a pervasive modernist aesthetic. And yet the entanglement of hand and machine continued. Our counterhistory conjures Albers's prints titled *Enmeshed I* and *II* (1963) as such opportunities for intermingling. Both pieces display a knotted imagery that Albers created by dripping acid on a gray background, emphasizing the possibilities of interlacing an old medium with a new. History becomes enmeshed in the very workings of the substances Albers put to use and the methods she used to assemble them. Across threads and knots, through this scaling and rescaling, moving the thread from hand to industrial production and back again, the Bauhaus history flows, shifts, moves. "Weaving is a particular method,

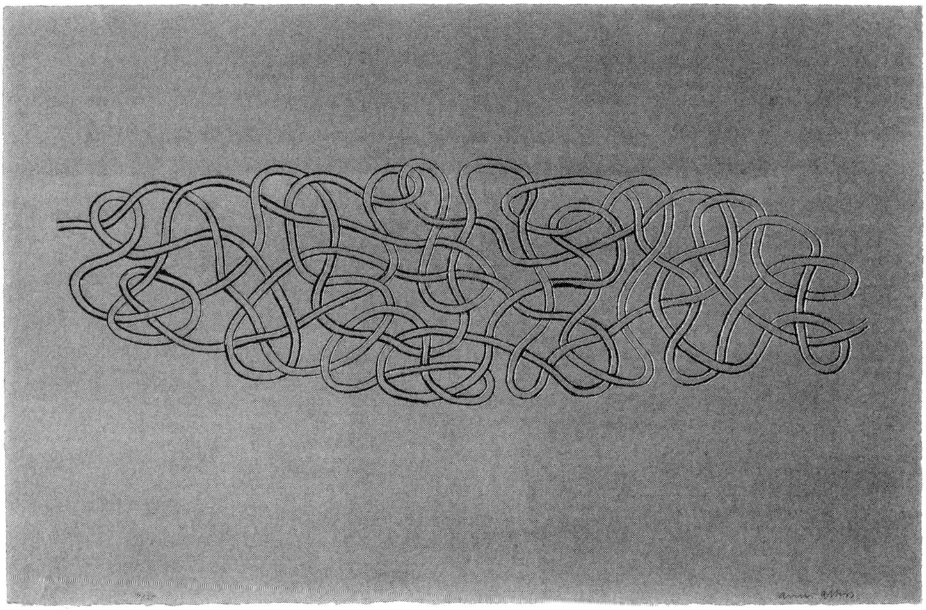

Figure 15.2
Anni Albers, *Enmeshed II*, 1963, lithograph, The Josef and Anni Albers Foundation, 1994.11.2, © 2018 The Josef and Anni Albers Foundation/Artists Rights Society (ARS), New York. Photo: Tim Nighswander/Imaging4Art.

like writing, that binds or connects historical movement," writes T'ai Smith of Albers's work in the newly released edition of her *On Weaving*.[42] It is this movement, this rescaling, we seek again.

Notes

1. To a large extent, we use Albers's book, *On Weaving*, first published in 1965, as a source for her words and thinking. However, we also use a number of other short articles and documented conversations both in print and available online.

2. We find inspiration for this reading "against the grain" from the wonderful paper by Carla Hustak and Natasha Myers in which they use Darwin's evocative writings on orchids to *read against the grain* of the dominant paradigm of neo-Darwinism in ecology. We come to this work later in the chapter. See Carla Hustak and Natasha Myers, "Involutionary Momentum: Affective Ecologies and the Sciences of Plant/Insect Encounters," *differences* 23, no. 3 (2012), 74–118.

3. This universal vision for design was later taken up by cyberneticists like Buckminster Fuller as a form of comprehensive design. See Fred Turner, "R. Buckminster Fuller," in *New Views on R. Buckminster Fuller*, ed. Hsiao-Yun Chu and Roberto G. Trujillo (Palo Alto, CA: Stanford University Press, 2009), 146–159; and Daniela K. Rosner and Fred Turner, "Theaters of Alternative Industry: Hobbyist Repair Collectives and the Legacy of the 1960s American Counterculture," in *Design Thinking Research*, ed. Hasso Plattner, Christoph Meinel, and Larry Leifer (Berlin: Springer International, 2015), 59–69. See also Daniela K. Rosner, *Critical Fabulations: Reworking the Methods and Margins of Design* (Cambridge, MA: MIT Press, 2018).

4. Anni Albers, *On Weaving* (1965; Princeton, NJ: Princeton University Press, 2017), 216.

5. Ibid.

6. Anna Lowenhaupt Tsing, *The Mushroom at the End of the World: On the Possibility of Life in Capitalist Ruins* (Princeton, NJ: Princeton University Press, 2015), 120.

7. Saidiya Hartman, "Venus in Two Acts," *Small Axe: A Caribbean Journal of Criticism* 12, no. 2 (2008), 1–14.

8. Saidiya Hartman, *Lose Your Mother: A Journey along the Atlantic Slave Route* (New York: Farrar, Straus and Giroux, 2008), 12. For connections between Hartman and design practice see Rosner, *Critical Fabulations*.

9. Sevim Fesci, oral history interview with Anni Albers, July 5, 1968, Archives of American Art, Smithsonian Institution.

10. Albers, *On Weaving*, 3.

11. Ibid., 49.

12. Ibid., 17.

13. Ibid., xi.

14. Ibid., 38.

15. Anni Albers, "Material as Metaphor" (1982), available at https://albersfoundation.org/artists/selected-writings/anni-albers/#tab4.

16. Albers, *On Weaving*, 11.

17. Ibid.

18. Donna J. Haraway, *Staying with the Trouble: Making Kin in the Chthulucene* (Durham: Duke University Press, 2016), 9.

19. Ibid., 10.

20. Albers, *On Weaving*, 45.

21. Ibid., 44.

22. Ibid., 45.

23. Ibid., 44 (emphasis added).

24. Ibid., 47.

25. Ibid., 45–46.

26. Vinciane Despret, "The Body We Care For: Figures of Anthropo-zoo-genesis," *Body and Society* 10, nos. 2–3 (2014), 117.

27. Hustak and Myers, "Involutionary Momentum," 77.

28. María Puig de la Bellacasa, *Matters of Care: Speculative Ethics in More than Human Worlds* (Minneapolis: University of Minnesota Press, 2017), 10.

29. Ibid.

30. Hustak and Myers, "Involutionary Momentum."

31. Ibid., 79.

32. Ibid.

33. Ibid., 85 (emphasis in the original).

34. Ibid.

35. Albers, "Material as Metaphor."

36. Hustak and Myers, "Involutionary Momentum," 96.

37. Stephen Monteiro, *The Fabric of Interface: Mobile Media, Design, and Gender* (Cambridge, MA: MIT Press, 2017).

38. Ibid., 59.

39. Ibid., 5.

40. Albers, "Material as Metaphor."

41. Albers, *On Weaving*, 3.

42. Ibid., 242.

16 Woven Circuits

An Interview with Taeyoon Choi

Shannon Mattern and Taeyoon Choi

The Jacquard loom, programmable by punched cards when it appeared in the early nineteenth century, weaves together the histories of textiles and computation. Entangled in those two histories are a number of shared concerns, including the tensions between craft and automation, between formula and experimentation, between technique and expression; the influence of new tools and industry demands; and the knotting together of manual and intellectual labor. These were also among the central preoccupations of the Bauhaus and its weaving workshop, where the institution's few women used a variety of contraptions, including Jacquard looms, to fashion rugs, wall hangings, and other textiles—as well as a new feminist theory of design, art historian T'ai Smith argues.[1]

The work of these weavers, and particularly that of Anni Albers, who went on to lead the weaving department at Black Mountain College from 1933 to 1949, has been threaded through the work in another present-day workshop: the acclaimed School for Poetic Computation (SFPC), where collaborators explore the intersections of code, design, hardware, and theory. Drawing intellectual and pedagogical inspiration from Albers, SFPC fashions itself as "a space where logic meets electricity, math meets language, and analytical thinking meets creative expression." In this interview with SFPC cofounder Taeyoon Choi—humbly self-described artist, educator, and activist—we study those seams linking SFPC to Albers's workshops. In the process, we examine how programming is (and isn't) like weaving, how an awareness of history enhances our engagement with new tools and demystifies technology, why "teaching and learning to code" should emphasize poetry as much as pattern, why poetic computation demands a sensitivity to machinic materiality, and how logical systems can facilitate poetic expression.

Shannon Mattern: As we trace the hundred-year-long thread that ties the Bauhaus to today's design and craft, I wonder what pedagogical value you see in infusing our contemporary practice—particularly computational practices—with historical awareness. Historical and intercultural exploration were key to Anni Albers's work. In *On Weaving*, she wrote, "I find it intriguing to look at early attempts in history, not for the sake of historical interest, that is, of looking back, but for the sake of looking forward from a point way back in time in order to experience vicariously the exhilaration of accomplishment reached step by step."[2] And in a 1968 interview she discusses her own speculative historical pedagogy, one based on imagined fundamentals and first principles. She states: "I tried to put my students at the point of zero. I tried to have them imagine, let's say, that they are in a desert in Peru, no clothing, no nothing, no pottery. ... So what do you do? ... How do you gradually come to realize what a textile can be?" When we consider traditional technologies like the Peruvian backstrap loom, she says, we see that it "has embedded in it everything that a high power machine loom today has. And they understand it in a completely different sense than walking into a factory and seeing these things operate because they know what is necessary and what kind of inventions have occurred in the course of history."[3] How can such historical consciousness, and an understanding of basic principles (mechanical, electrical, communicative, etc.), help us to learn computation? And why is Albers's work one of the touchstones—one of those past places from which we can look forward—for your work at SFPC?

Taeyoon Choi: SFPC is an artist-run school based in New York City within the Westbeth Artists Community, which, from 1898 to 1966, was the headquarters of Bell Telephone Laboratories. Our main program is a ten-week immersive session for adult students to learn coding, electronics, critical theory, and poetry. We also offer a variety of public programs, such as our "Learning to Teach" conference for educators teaching computation in creative fields. Our motto is: more poetry, less demo. As an artist and educator, I've been teaching and working in administration at SFPC for six years from school's beginning.

The idea of computing long predates the development of transistors and, similarly, extends far beyond a strictly Western narrative. Approaching computing with a historical and global consciousness allows us to appreciate the generativity of other traditions. Various cultures, for example the medieval Islamic world, had mechanical forms of computers. Knowing the variety of past inspiration helps us understand how present technologies can inspire the future we want to see.

In her work at Black Mountain College, Albers also considered the dynamic between fundamental concepts and technique—how the evolution of form is driven in large part by the material properties of the medium. She writes: "Creating means ... reacting to material rather than the execution of a dream, as the layman conceives it. The first vision of something to be done gives more the mood of the work than its final form. The form emerges as the work progresses."[4]

Thinking more about the evolution of forms: The words "text" and "texture" share a common lineage, stemming from the Latin *texere*, meaning to weave. At SFPC, we want our students to engage deeply in the materials and the fundamental logic of computation. We ask them to have a conversation with the material, iterate with it and progress the concepts through it. Similar to how Albers envisions weaving, it is our hope that thinking *materially* through computation will evolve into forms that might have initially been inconceivable.

SM: I'd like to talk a bit more about the threads connecting weaving and computation. T'ai Smith draws a distinction between weaving and painting. "Unlike painting, where the formal idea is laid on top of the canvas support," she says, "weaving's design is embedded in the material and process of its making." The weaver "develops the design in tandem with the fabrication of the surface."[5] Computation has its own distinctive materialities—its own ways of relating figure and ground, design and support surface. Could you describe how weaving is like computation, and how it's not?

TC: To begin on a granular level, weaving and coding share the logic and action of 0's and 1's, stitch and pass. Both activities depend upon information, instruction, and repetition; they share a logic that is transmitted through language, and that language can either be a line of code or a weaving design. They share a powerful transformative quality: turning information that is two-dimensional into an object or experience or interaction that is three-dimensional.

It gets a bit more interesting when we think about their differences. With coding, that dimensional transformation is usually not seen. Its execution occurs in the background, which means it happens invisibly for most users. Weaving makes that execution tangible and highly visible. The next difference is in regard to iteration. Software runs and changes; it transforms the data fluidly. But if you want to iterate on a woven piece, you have to either start a new one from scratch or unweave to where you want to change your pattern. In that way, code forgives more easily, as iterations and changes can be done quickly and without leaving any trace history. The act of undoing with physical materials leaves a mark: the yarn might feel looser than it was before, for example.

SM: Let's talk a bit more about how we can help our students appreciate the materiality of their tools—including code. How can we practice a materialist pedagogy? Albers proposed that "tangible material can teach that it has demands of its own and suggestions of its own for its forming."[6] Can we say the same for the material of code? It's

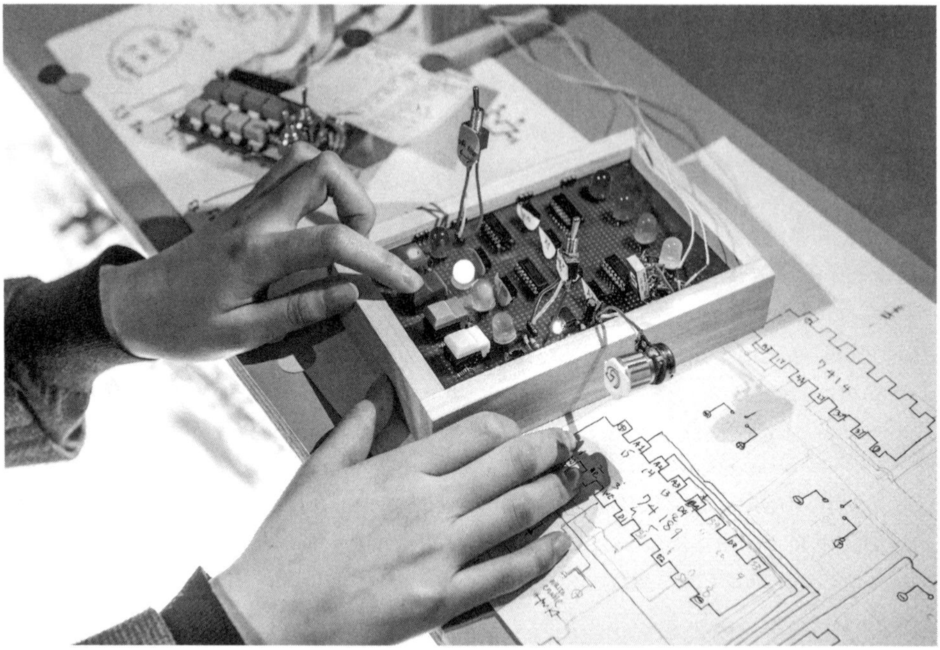

Figure 16.1
Taeyoon Choi, Handmade Computer, 2013–2017, custom electronics and drawings. Image credit (left image): National Museum of Modern and Contemporary Art, Korea. (Also plates 12–13.)

also worth noting that Albers's teacher, Gunta Stölzl, the only female master at the Bauhaus, thought that weaving's material affordances—"play with form and color, ... the ability to feel and adapt strongly, more rhythmic than logical thinking"—made it a distinctively feminine field.[7] I imagine you'd strongly disagree. How does SFPC frame materiality—epistemologically, ideologically, and so forth? How, through your pedagogy, do you reinforce the *integration* of logic and rhythm and poetry?

TC: Something that's great about being in the same room together at SFPC is that we can try things out in real life, with each other. There are a number of activities we do to help students appreciate that computing is a series of instructions, which can be performed materially. We play "becoming pixels," where each student functions within an array of pixels, transforming themselves into an embodiment of data. Another activity is enacting a sorting algorithm. When I explain binary logic, I ask a student to become a logic gate—AND, XOR, or other gates—by responding to a two-hand gesture that they take as input. More complex computing paradigms and systems can be explored by making illustrations, writing stories, or designing playful games. In enacting and

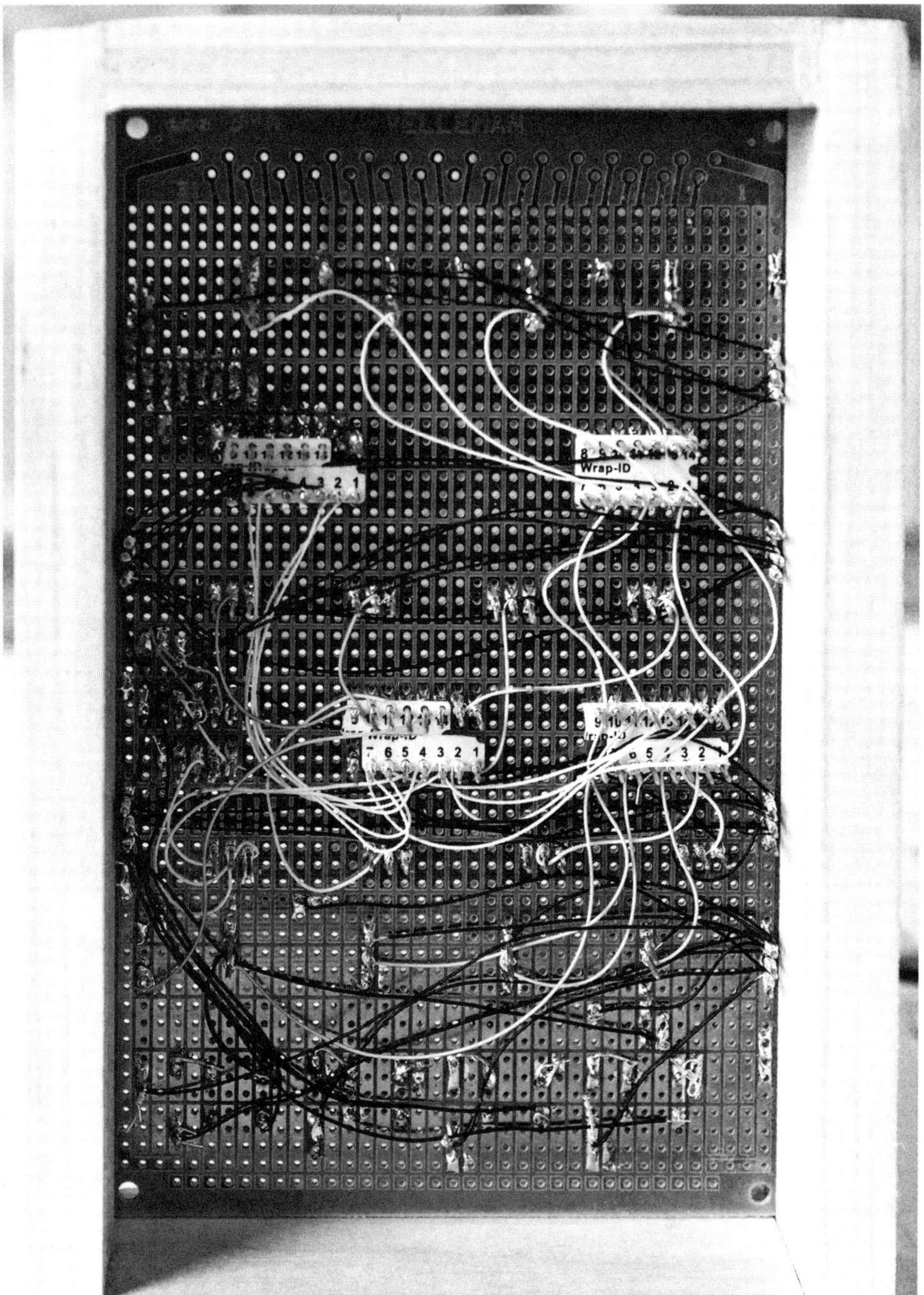

Figure 16.1 (continued)

performing instructions, by physically *feeling* computing, a poetics of computation emerges. This focus on mechanics often reveals the poetics and play inherent in code. This can mean finding poetics in the failures, glitches, and misinformation of computation as well. Embracing the intentional and accidental process of expression one can create with code leads to poetic computation.

Practitioners who experiment with the materiality of computing and weaving tend to employ two different approaches. Some people explore these connections by building tools, reinventing through crafting and new technologies. This approach prioritizes the tool as the poetic work, as in the work of Pam Liou, who created Doti: Desktop Jacquard Loom.[8] The other approach focuses on poetic outputs—for example, creating something, such as custom textiles, with ancient or contemporary tools. The emphasis here is more on the output than the enabling constructs. Although tools may not be their initial concern, their work often requires the creation or customization of tools to make something unique. Here I am thinking of the work of Mariko Kosaka, who creates computationally designed, handcrafted knitting projects, and who also talks about Knitting for Javascripters.[9] And of course some practitioners are interested in both, in storytelling through both the tool itself and its output. An example of this hybrid approach is the work of KOBAKANT, a collective that works on electronic textiles and wearable technology (http://www.kobakant.at/). All three names I've mentioned are artists I respect, who've taught at SFPC or continue to inspire how we think about poetic computation.

To your point on the gendered labor of weaving: weaving is certainly not limited to women; there is plenty of historical and contemporary cultural evidence that defies this stereotype. However, reclaiming the preconceived notion of feminine craft can offer something new, as my former student from NYU ITP, Francesca Rodriguez Sawaya, explained to me. She writes: "something I've seen [in] presenting my work about weaving stories is that women naturally feel attracted to it. And in societies where technology and engineering are really separated from arts and crafting, it's a good way to start connecting these two worlds and to involve more women in tech. [And] in the same way weaving has historically empowered female identity, it could also be a great tool to use today to empower females and get them more involved in the tech sector."

If weaving and coding can be equally appreciated in early education, I think we may cultivate a generation of creative individuals whose interests are as fluid as their identities. In other words, we should celebrate boys who are into weaving, as much as girls who are into coding.

SM: In "Handweaving Today," Albers argued that "teaching should be the development of structures, from the elementary weaves to more complicated derivations rather than the passing on of patterns for weaving."[10] In other words, teaching a craft is not merely a matter of instilling formulas and scripts. Instead, by "return[ing] to fundamentals" and general structures, the teacher can help to "clear the way for new forming." Yet in an age in which "code camps" are filled with both ambitious grade-schoolers and adults seeking a career change, in which the value of education is measured in terms of starting salaries, in which code and data seem to be ends in themselves, how has SFPC managed to balance practical application with experimentation, pattern with poetry? What have we learned from the Bauhaus, and what have you learned in your own work, about why poetry and code are best thought and practiced together?

TC: Returning to fundamentals is central to my practice. My Handmade Computer project began in order to change my relationship with the computer, fundamentally.[11] I wanted to become less of a consumer by demystifying the computer. Processes of technical demystification lead to "new ways of forming," as Albers says, but perhaps we can also say that demystification leads to new ways of giving form to an idea—whether that be through production, fabrication, or by some other means. Technology is a means of effecting power—that is, force or energy; but it's also a tool for manifesting power in a political sense. By demystifying these technologies we can feel less scared, less exploited, and more able to offer creative alternatives. There is so much potential once we see the CPU as a series of sequential and combinational logic systems. As we begin to understand the technologies around us, we change our perception and understanding of the world.

If we look at the trajectories of students at SFPC after graduating, we see some going into corporate industries and others working as artists, making work with computation. The fact that these students coexist, the spectrum of artists that we support, is our way of balancing practical applications with experimentation. This diversity is reflected not only in our students but also in our teachers and founders. We come from a variety of backgrounds, and for me, the most important thing is that we can sit in the same room and discuss the art, engineering, the industry, and the myriad facets of the field altogether. SFPC is not a demilitarized zone apart from the larger tech industry, nor are we an isolated utopia; rather, we act as a fair-trade zone of sorts. We offer alternative, safe places for people who are transitioning or exploring tech to find themselves.

At SFPC we prioritize students finding themselves rather than finding or innovating technologies. Learning through technical boot camps has its value, but boot camps as the sole narrative for computational education is problematic. It's important to establish a critical and explanatory engagement with computers, and that happens by taking things apart, putting them back together, finding the poetics and the glitches in the code. These experiences become sources of empowerment. And this type of learning enables coding as expression, coding for joy. We're helping artists and technologists find their voice through the poetics and materiality of code. That is the outcome we hope for, and in some ways the formation of the school is a denial of this pervasive binary between experimentation and application. Coding and weaving can be a work of self-discovery, which I think is fundamental to human creativity.

Today, the teachers of critical coding—along with their affiliates in media and information literacy, critical algorithm studies, and related fields—are going through their own processes of self-discovery. In this new age of data leaks and privacy breaches and media manipulation, of inscrutable algorithms and deep fakes, the old pedagogical protocols are proving insufficient. Fundamental logics, like reason and mechanical functionalism, are unraveling. Will counting likes and links—one-time indices of credibility—help us explain the popularity of an extremist ideology? Can studying a backstrap loom help us understand a neural net? Will modeling a graphics processing unit help us discern how proprietary intelligence systems target immigrants for deportation? Perhaps to some degree, but what more must we know about the tangle of technologies, ideologies, and state and corporate interests that enmesh our new algorithmic everyday?

The Bauhaus sought to serve as a bridge between art and industry. Today, countless coders and engineers serve as bridges between governments and corporations, on the one hand, and some of our most vulnerable communities, on the other. In order to understand the tight weave of operational codes behind a Facebook newsfeed or a predictive policing algorithm—to appreciate their potential for both illumination and mystification, liberation and exploitation—we have a lot more ciphering and unraveling to do.

Notes

1. T'ai Smith, *Bauhaus Design Theory: From Feminine Craft to Mode of Design* (Minneapolis: University of Minnesota Press, 2014).

2. Anni Albers, *On Weaving* (1965; Princeton, NJ: Princeton University Press, 2017), 34.

3. Sevim Fesci, oral history interview with Anni Albers, July 5, 1968, Archives of American Art, Smithsonian Institution, https://www.aaa.si.edu/collections/interviews/oral-history-interview-anni-albers-12134.

4. Anni Albers, "Handweaving Today: Textile Work at Black Mountain College," Albers Foundation, http://www.albersfoundation.org/teaching/anni-albers/texts/.

5. T'ai Smith, "'Pictures Made of Wool': The Gender of Labor at the Bauhaus Weaving Workshop (1919–23)," *Invisible Culture* 4 (2002), https://ivc.lib.rochester.edu/pictures-made-of-wool-the-gender-of-labor-at-the-bauhaus-weaving-workshop-1919-23/.

6. Albers, "Handweaving Today."

7. Gunta Stölzl, "Weaving at the Bauhaus," in *Gunta Stölzl: Bauhaus Master* (New York: Museum of Modern Art, 2009), 87.

8. Pamela Liou, "Doti: The Desktop Jacquard Loom," accessed August 6, 2018, http://pamelaliou.com/doti.html.

9. Mariko Kosaka, "Knitting for Javascripters," JSConf US (2015), https://www.youtube.com/watch?v=X1Cc1vrvjdY.

10. Anni Albers, "Handweaving Today: Textile Work at Black Mountain College," *The Weaver* 6, no. 1 (January-February 1941), 4.

11. Taeyoon Choi, "Handmade Computer," *Avant.org* (n.d.), http://avant.org/thread/handmade-computer/.

17 The Decolonial Cyborg and the Bauhaus Automaton

A Play

Luiza Prado de O. Martins

[A Stage. The set is painted a dark hue, not exactly black; it's difficult to tell its real color. Two figures walk onto the stage, each coming from one side.

The figure on the right moves stiffly, deliberately. Its pale limbs are like stuffed pillows, cumbersome and pliable; they are surrounded by what looks like a rigid exoskeleton, lending a vaguely menacing look to an otherwise soft form. In spite of its strangeness, the figure is undeniably anthropomorphic: two legs, two arms, a trunk, hands, feet, a head. Its features seem to have been painted from a vague description of a human face, motionless against the glossy, flat surface of a bald head; if a machine were to design a human, perhaps this is what it would look like. The figure moves toward the center of the stage, each calculated step feeling almost ceremonial. It has the elegance and the uncanniness of an automaton, as if it were hiding something incomprehensible beyond its surface. It finally stops moving right under the center stage lights and bows to the empty theater.

The figure on the left moves less predictably. Instead of moving toward the center of the stage, it wanders restlessly from left to right, from back to front. Its steps, unlike those of the first figure, are uneven, irregular; it seems unsure of where it is going, and how. It's difficult to discern its features: perhaps due to the sharp shadows of directional stage lighting, their shape seems to be constantly changing. When not faced directly, the figure seems to melt into the shadows of the stage—as if it were able to erase itself from the onlooker's mind, or as if it were able to temporarily cease to exist; yet it remains there, restless and unpredictable. Every so often, the figure reappears under one of the bright stage lights in an abrupt, violent burst of movement. It is in these moments that one can see a fleeting shimmer of sinuous limbs; a Cyborg being of flesh and metal. It finally comes to a halt in the far left side of the stage with a tired sigh.]

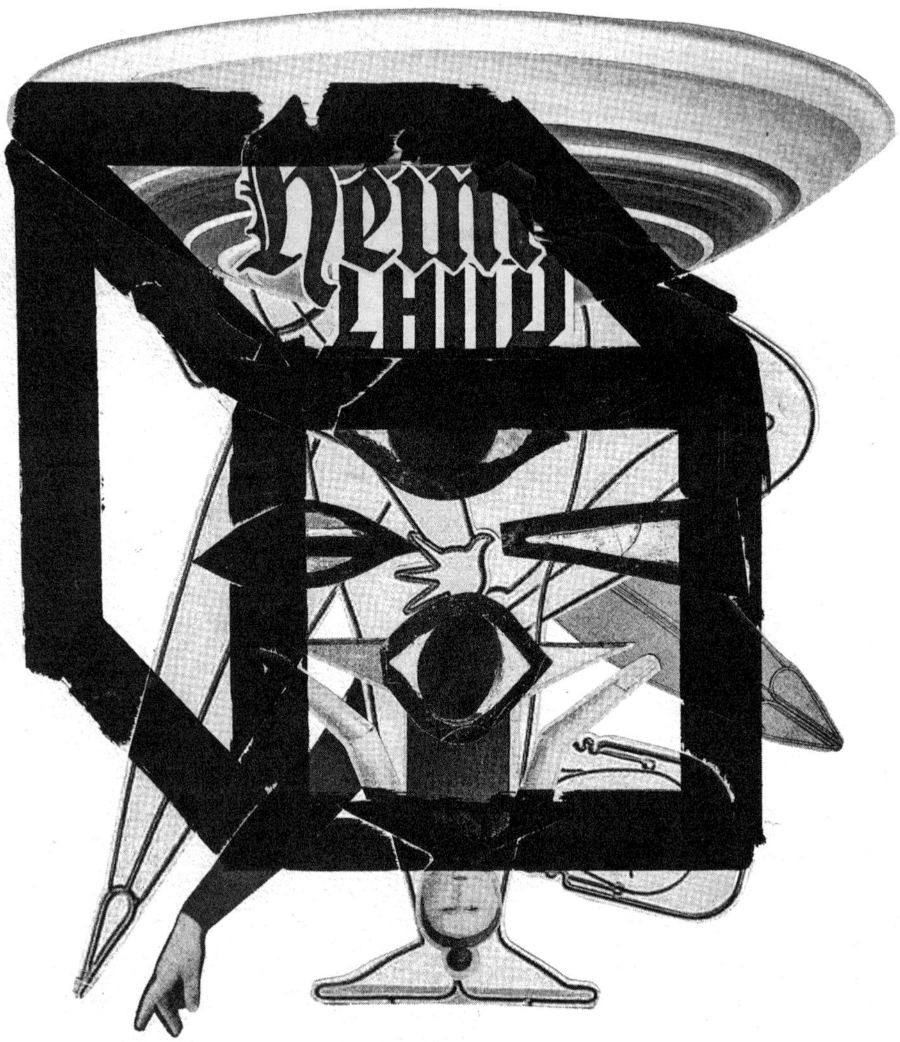

Figure 17.1
Luiza Prado, *Untitled 01*, 2018. (Also plate 14.)

Automaton: I am not sure if you are supposed to be here.

[There is a brief moment of hesitation. The other figure shifts uncomfortably before replying.]

Cyborg: I am, but not officially. This stage isn't exclusively yours, you know.

A: I was told I was going to be the only one performing. I've put together a wonderful play about my own trajectory ... but you could help—I need someone to do the lighting, now that I think about it.

C: I'm on the stage. I didn't come here to be in the background. I've done that for way too long.

[The Cyborg moves a few steps toward the center of the stage. The Automaton takes a deep breath.]

A: I am the harbinger of a new era. I was born amongst war, violence, and turmoil; a time of dissolution. Everything was in flux. I saw the need to remake Man into a new form, a new Being floating toward a new order of things—even if I didn't yet understand what that new order was, or what it meant.[1]

I've gone through many phases in the process of remaking myself. In my youth I shaved my hair, learned to control my breathing and my food intake. I punctured my skin and rubbed it with oil, in an attempt to get rid of impurities. I wore clothing as austere as the grueling routine of physical exercises I imposed on myself. I believed in self-denial and strict discipline; the sense of power and belonging I obtained from this was inebriating. I was certain that I—and those like me—represented the pinnacle of evolution, of civilization. We were superior to all others. The future belonged to me, to us; the chosen ones, the most evolved oh humans. The site of the future—modern, rational, functional—would be the House of the White Man.[2]

C: The beliefs you espoused ... these were the same beliefs of those who ultimately destroyed you. You thought of yourself as extraordinarily gifted. You assumed your values, your model of modernity, your ambitions to be universal, and the ability to fulfill those parameters to be the measurement of a culture's success. Yet you never questioned the fact that you, yourself, set the parameters that defined your own success. You looked at yourself, and saw your yearnings as everyone's.

A: I wanted to find a universal language for things, one that could speak to all. This was a necessary endeavor; you need to understand that it was sorely needed, at the time.

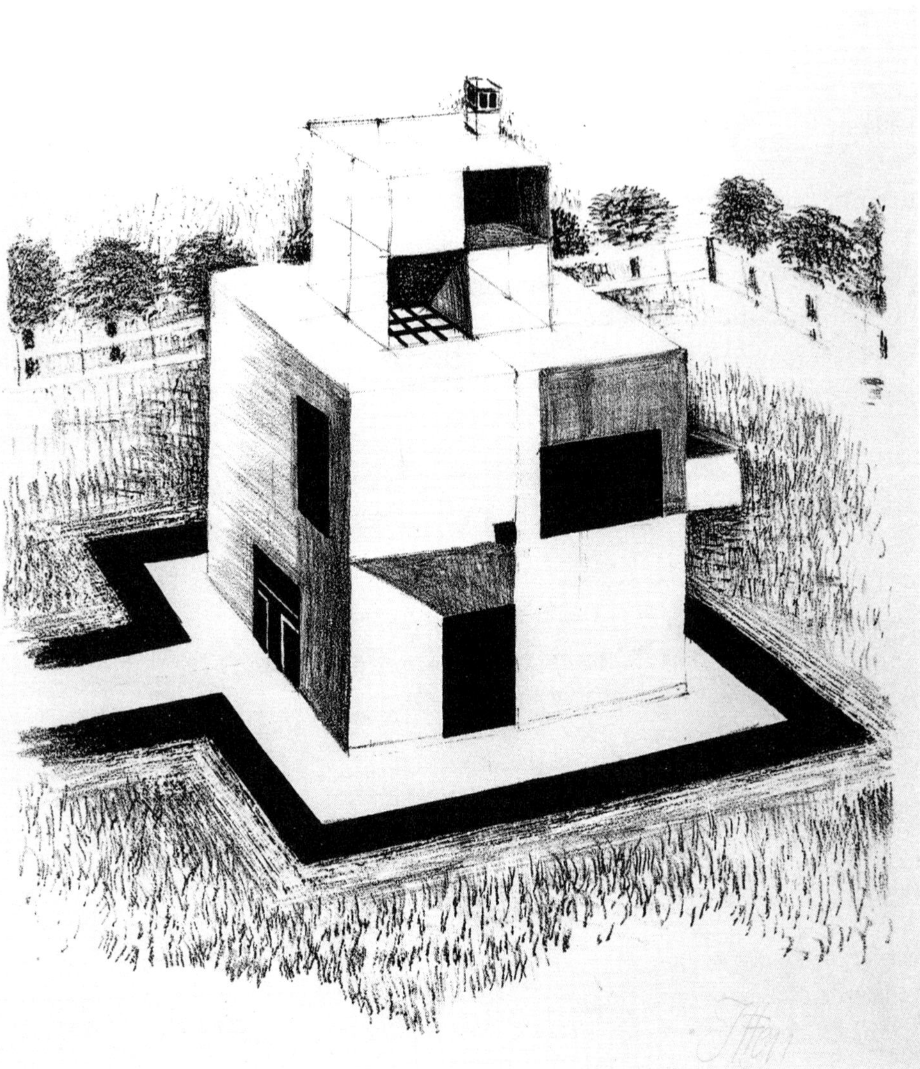

Figure 17.2
Johannes Itten, *The House of the White Man*, 1921. © 2018 Artists Rights Society (ARS), New York / ProLitteris, Zurich. Harvard Art Museums/Busch-Reisinger Museum, Gift of Curt Valentin. © President and Fellows of Harvard College.

C: I'm not so sure. Your model of civilization doesn't fit me, it never has. I am one, and yet I am many; my world is not comprised within a universe, like the one you imagine. I exist in a world where many other worlds fit,[3] and where we live in relation to one another. We do not yearn for a hegemony of thought, nor do we settle for mere tolerance of each Other's differences within a hegemonic framework.[4] We do not strive for pluralism; we reject your birthplace—the project of Modernity. I've been bleeding since 1500,[5] and it is time to stop. I refuse to bend my tongue to your language.

[There is a pause as the Automaton's features, in spite of their immobility, seem to grow harsher. As it pronounced these last sentences, the Cyborg's voice seemed to be growing louder, coming not just from the figure on the stage but from all over the theater: upstage, downstage, wings, offstage, house. From each direction, the voices seemed to have a different pitch, a different rhythm, a different accent.]

A: Why are you blaming me for things I had no control over? Why are you berating me for a history I had no choice in? I went through my fair share of hardship, too. I was scorned, disbanded, persecuted. Some of my children died; others were labeled as degenerate. All I did, I did because I believed in it, and I still do.

C: I know. Yet you have to understand that the insistence on a hegemonic universality of Whiteness created the conditions for this to take place. Hegemony feasts on subalternity. Of course your fascination with universality wasn't meant to contribute to the persecution that would, ultimately, be your undoing; yet it is also undeniable that the push for universality hides, at its core, a desire for domination. You said it yourself earlier—you thought you were the pinnacle of civilization, superior to all others.

[The Automaton remains silent. After a moment of hesitation, the Cyborg continues to speak.]

C: The history of your persecution is not singular, either; its impact is just felt more widely because it took place within the confines of your birthplace. My peoples, those you considered to be intrinsically inferior to you, have been sacrificial offerings to an awaking monster, hungry for our flesh and blood. And Modernity, this unfathomable beast, cast its curses on us. It cursed us so that we would forever see ourselves only through your eyes and never our own; so that our bodies would forever be too queer; so that our hands would forever be the vectors for someone else's wealth; so that our languages would forever be unintelligible. These curses were attempts to obliterate our knowledges, our identities, our civilizational and material histories. Yet we persist. We are still present because we have learned to wield our own magic; we have learned to wear many faces in order to navigate the world. And so we became *nepantleras*,[6] shape-shifters, tricksters. I am not here for you to grasp. I am one, and I am many. I am one, and I am many.

A: I'm not like that anymore. It was just a small part of me who actually believed and practiced this; I moved on, I changed.

C: But what does it mean that this interest was there in the first place? Why were these ideas so seductive; why were they embraced so enthusiastically by so many of your children?

A: These ideas were a product of their time. Of their context. I admit that, looking back, I was constrained by some of the patterns of thought I had set out to break. I was born in an era where things were in motion, when the world was shifting. I had seen war, and been marked by its brutality. Emerging from conflict, I realized that I had to make myself anew. I had to construct a new notion of man, a universal life-form of the people. The culture I engendered was harsh because it had been conceived by scarred men, amongst fire and blood.

C: You use the word "man" as a placeholder for a universal human form.

A: I know. I tried at first to be neither man nor woman; later I tried to be both at once. None of this worked; femininity felt uncomfortable and alien in my world. I thought it would make me look weak and incapable. So I constrained it to as few activities as possible—weaving, pottery, bookbinding,—while I allowed masculinity to become the driving life-force of all that I was. In the theater—so important to how I came to see and understand myself—I was interested in exploring the idea of the *Gesamtkunstwerk*; the human body itself was a project I concerned myself with.[7] Actors and dancers were quasi-mechanical beings, vessels of my all-encompassing idea of design. These were much more pressing concerns of mine; I did not think about my relation to gender very much at that point. It wasn't a categorization I was particularly interested in, so I defaulted to gender neutrality.

C: Yet this supposed gender neutrality ultimately meant masculinity. Your femininity was kept hidden and marginalized; even when you discuss your many achievements, you gloss over those associated with it. Not thinking or talking about gender does not mean that it ceases to exist; on the contrary, it provides fertile ground for an unaddressed patriarchal culture to thrive. You legitimized and nurtured your sons' artistic abilities, whilst dismissively classifying the work of your daughters as "crafts."[8] This gender neutrality that you claim was a way of allowing an Other to be present, but only at the margins.

[The Cyborg pauses at this point. The Automaton stands, steely, in the center of the stage.]

C: Some parts of me feel that I need to be eternally grateful for what you taught me. They feel like I should be paying homage, acting like you did; after all, this is what I was taught, to look up to you. Yet other parts of me know that you are not universal.[9] We come from such different times and places. Believing in what I know to be true, when I was taught that truth belongs to others, is an effort.

A: This is exactly what I was worried about; you don't believe in me anymore. I've always been concerned with the needs of all; I wanted to explore the essence of things, their true nature, so that I could construct a world where things do exactly what they should. I wanted to bring order to a disordered world. To a broken world.

C: I see. But you need to understand that the notion of order itself is not universal, and that our yearning for order is not universal. There is beauty in disorder, too. Chaos is a condition of the world; your impulse to make chaos into order is an impulse of systematization, of classification, of translation—ultimately, an impulse of domination. And in these processes, inevitably, things are left behind; a translation can never fully account for the richness of the world that is being translated. Once, someone asked me why shouldn't I revel in opacity, instead of trying to make myself (and others) transparent. He encouraged me to resist the impulse of translating and systematizing the world. To translate, he insisted, is to measure the other with one's own scale, in order to judge and, inevitably, reduce. Ditch the scale, he told me. Instead of using myself, and my own scale, as a tool for grasping (or appropriating) the world, he told me to recognize and embrace that which is opaque. He told me to gaze at it, and recognize it. Opacity, he said, is "not the obscure, though it is possible for it to be so and be accepted as such. It is that which cannot be reduced."[10] Opacity doesn't imply individualism; rather, it allows us to position ourselves in relation to one another, as part of a whole of relations.

A: I don't believe in that. I believe in what I told you, deeply. I tried to live by these ideas: it was my way of trying to understand the world, and to understand myself. I saw everything around me changing so fast; I saw flesh meeting metal, metal becoming machine, machine going back to flesh. I am the result of that, a creature of my time. I wanted to project myself into the future, to design myself anew. And I did: by naming

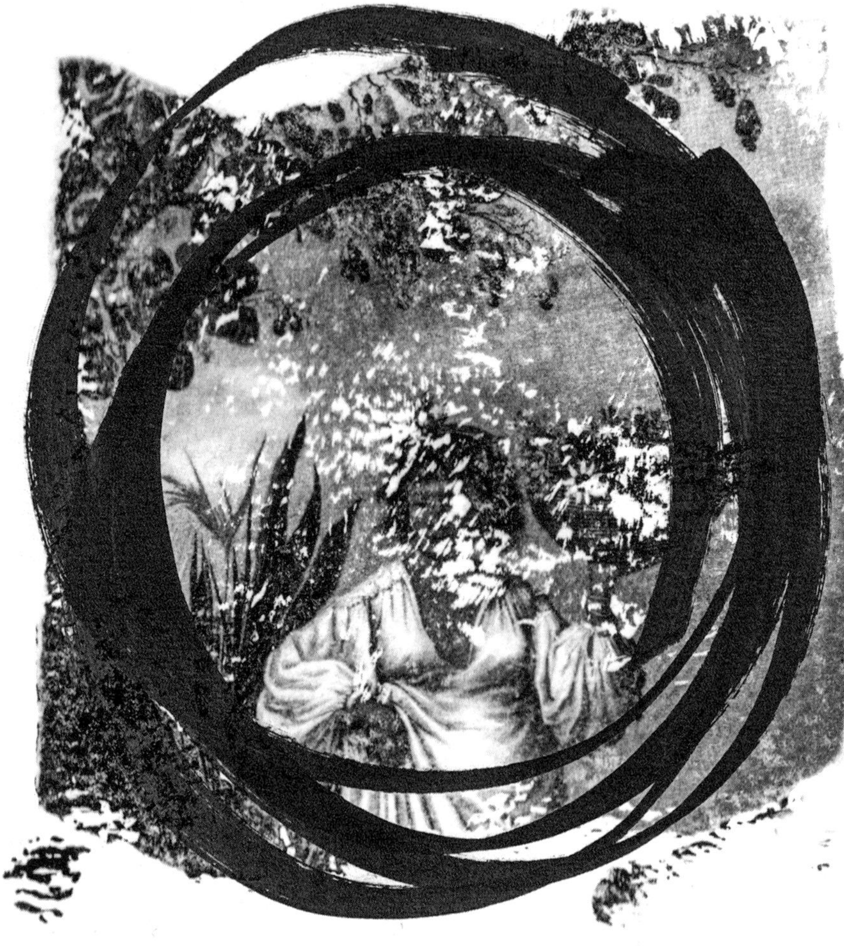

Figure 17.3
Luiza Prado, *Untitled 02*, 2018.

the future as such, by envisioning what would populate this future, I made it happen. The future is here because I created it; because I said that it would be here. It's a singular power to have.

C: It is also a dangerous power to have. Many of your children still live by this idea, without realizing that, by naming their futures, they are cursing those of others. Mine, too.

[The lights on the Stage slowly dim until it is engulfed by complete darkness. It is impossible to know whether either of the figures has left; one is left to wonder.]

Notes

1. See Walter Gropius, "Ja! Stimmen des Arbeitsrates für Künst," Bauhaus Archive, 1919: File 69, cited in Katerina Rüedi Ray, "Bauhaus Hausfraus: Gender Formation in Design Education," *Journal of Architectural Education* 55, no. 2 (November 1, 2001), 73–80, doi:10.1162/104648801753199491.

2. Ulrich Linse, "Die Mazdaznan-Pädagogik des Bauhaus-Meisters Johannes Itten," in *Bauhaus-vorträge: Gastredner am Weimarer Bauhaus 1919–1925*, ed. Peter Bernhard (Berlin: Mann, 2016).

3. Ejército Zapatista de Liberación Nacional (Mexico), *EZLN: 2 de octubre de 1995–24 de enero de 1997* (Ediciones Era, 1994).

4. Édouard Glissant, *Poetics of Relation*, trans. Betsy Wing (Ann Arbor: University of Michigan Press, 1997).

5. Moor Mother, *Creation Myth* (official audio), Don Giovanni Records, n.d., https://www.youtube.com/watch?v=fm93dYZIVIo.

6. Gloria Anzaldúa, *Borderlands / La Frontera: The New Mestiza*, 4th ed. (San Francisco: Aunt Lute Books, 2012).

7. Éva Forgács, *The Bauhaus Idea and Bauhaus Politics* (Budapest: Central European University Press, 1995).

8. Ray, "Bauhaus Hausfraus."

9. Rafael Cardoso, *Uma introdução à história do design* (São Paulo: Ed. Blucher, 1999).

10. Glissant, *Poetics of Relation*.

18 Electronic Inclusions in Handmade Paper, or How to Finesse Material Incongruities in the Spirit of the Bauhaus

N. Adriana Knouf

Let's begin with plant fibers, the cellulose that is the material substrate of paper as well as the cotton, hemp, or linen thread of some textiles. This cellulose can be spun together to form threads, which can be knit or crocheted or woven into fabric. Weaving: a simple thing, it would seem, simply shuttling weft threads across the taught warp. But nothing could be further from the truth, for the complexity of the loom is not to be underestimated, and is in fact vital to our thinking about programmable computers. In the early days of cyber studies Sadie Plant, drawing on Ada Lovelace's commentary about the Jacquard loom and its importance to her own thinking about Charles Babbage's Analytical Engine, argued that weaving and cybernetics were fundamentally interrelated. Consequently, the developing web of information technology, according to Plant, would allow women to move beyond masculine mimicry. Plant writes: "The computer was always a simulation of weaving; threads of ones and zeros riding the carpets and simulating silk screens in the perpetual motions of cyberspace."[1] Plant's approach was indebted to strands of second-wave feminist thought that held strong assumptions about the category of "woman." It is hard to overstate, however, the importance of Plant's research in reactivating the work of Lovelace, as well as beginning cyberculture's love affair with the Jacquard loom and the metaphor of weaving more broadly.

As with Ada, so with Gunta and Anni. Scholars in recent decades have also reactivated the power of the Bauhaus weaving workshop, in light of the ways in which the purported gender-neutral pedagogical environment of the Bauahus was anything but.[2] Gunta Stölzl, the only female master at the Bauhaus, ran the weaving workshop from 1927 to 1931 and encouraged the students to experiment not only with technical proficiency on the hand loom but also with alternative materials for weaving such as cellophane. In describing the Bauhaus, Walter Gropius wrote, "I insisted on manual instruction, not as an end in itself, or with any idea of turning to incidental account by actually producing handicrafts, but as providing a good all-round training for hand

and eye, and being a practical first step in mastering industrial processes."[3] Thus for Gropius the purpose of handicraft was in *service* of the resulting mass-produced object. Stölzl saw things a bit differently:

> Since mechanical weaving today is not far enough advanced to provide all the possibilities offered by hand weaving, and because these possibilities are necessary for people to develop their creativity, we deal in particular with hand weaving. It is only by working on a handloom that one has enough room to play, to develop an idea from one experiment to the next, until there is enough clarity and specification about the model for it to be handed over to industry for mechanical reproduction.[4]

Here, experience on the hand loom allows for a particular kind of "creativity" that is not possible with then-contemporary forms of machine weaving. There needs to be a space for "play," not only with the loom as apparatus but also with the fibers themselves. Anni Albers, a student of Stölzl's at the Bauhaus, would dedicate an entire chapter of her text *On Weaving* to a discussion of "Tactile Sensibility," writing:

> Surface quality of material—that is, *matière*—being mainly a quality of appearance, is an aesthetic quality and therefore a medium of the artist; while quality of inner structure is, above all, a matter of function and therefore the concern of the scientist and the engineer. Sometimes material surface together with material structure are the main components of a work—in textile works, for instance, specifically in weavings or, on another scale, in works of architecture. Parallel to this overlapping of outer and inner characteristics in a work is the overlapping of artistic, scientific, and technological interests on the part of the weaver or the architect. The pendulum of their work swings, from art to industrial science.[5]

Here is a restatement of the desired unity between art, craft, science, and technology that Gropius wrote about in the Bauhaus manifesto with respect to architecture.[6] This textual representation of weaving's complexity existed alongside, and with the same status as, the textiles. T'ai Smith has argued that the writing of Bauhaus weavers like Stölzl and Albers were just as important as the woven works themselves, as they "had to secure their status at the school by way of text."[7] Thinking, making, writing: a web of practices that fed off and reinforced each other.

This introduction is meant to illustrate the importance of the Bauhaus in general, and the writings on materiality in particular, to my own practice-based work. The legacy of the Bauhaus—its often problematic gender dynamics notwithstanding—cannot be overestimated. In recent years, I have been exploring the integration of handmade paper, electronics, and writing as a way to put into practice my belief about the speciousness of the analog/digital distinction, as well as to think through possible ways of engaging differently with digitality. What would it mean if we were to foreground the sensual qualities of our technologies, not just in finished form but during production as well? If we were to argue, through material production, for a twining of the natural and the unnatural, the analog and the digital, the organic and the inorganic, without valorizing one over the other? If we were to think about how to incorporate the ancient technology of papermaking with more "modern" technologies?

I've turned to the Bauhaus weavers in particular because of their connection to the specific qualities of plant or animal fibers, but also because there was no papermaking at the Bauhaus. While the Bauhaus of course had strong typography, graphics, and wallpaper workshops, they did not focus on paper per se, but rather saw the paper as a substrate for the production of visual works.[8] There was indeed a short-lived *bookbinding workshop*, run by Otto Dorfner, a master craftsman who had worked at one of the predecessors of the Bauhaus. After Dorfner left in 1922, Anna Wottitz ran a small bookbinding workshop until the Weimar Bauhaus closed in 1925.[9] Interestingly, there were no further bookbinding workshops, either in Dessau or in Berlin, as, according to a contemporary commentator, "this purely craft-based skill offered no scope for modernization."[10] However, photographic documentation of student works from 1920 belie this comment, showing covers made of wood and "woven fabric," an interesting potential connection with the weaving workshop that I have not seen explored in any depth.[11]

It is not surprising, however, that papermaking was not a part of the curriculum at the Bauhaus, even though works on paper, such as typographical experiments, were so valued. Prior to the early nineteenth century, all paper in the West was made by hand, by workers who used raw materials like cotton and linen rags that were then processed in a machine called a Hollander beater that broke the rags down into individual fibers that could then be used in papermaking. In the early nineteenth century, with the development of the continuous web papermaking machine, hand papermaking nearly died out as a craft, and paper began to be made from the cheaper, although lower-quality, wood pulp.[12] So it could be said that, "Of the 1043 vats [for papermaking] that existed in Germany in 1846, only two or three remained in 1938."[13] Papermaking as a craft diminished in the Austro-Hungarian Empire as well: "The last of the mills for hand-made paper in the former Austrian Empire ceased to work at the end of the 19th century; they either went out of production entirely because there was no demand for hand-made paper, or because this product was ousted by the cheaper machine-made papers."[14] In the Western world the tacit material knowledge of hand papermaking nearly died out by the mid-1930s. For contemporary papermakers in the West, it was the work of the American researcher and craftsman Dard Hunter that saved hand papermaking from disappearing entirely.[15] He traveled widely throughout the world in the early decades of the twentieth century, collecting histories, hands-on techniques, and samples of handmade paper that allowed papermaking to continue as an underappreciated craft until a revival began in the 1970s, especially through the Twinrocker mill started by Kathryn and Howard Clark in 1971. Today papermaking is a regular part of numerous college and university as well as summer craft school curricula. At the Haystack Mountain School of Crafts on Deer Isle, Maine, papermaking takes place in the "graphics" studio right next to "fibers," where weaving and mixed-media courses are taught.

Works *with* paper were not entirely absent from the Bauhaus, however. Josef Albers, in the preliminary course, asked students to work with all manner of everyday materials, such as newspaper, wire, cellophane, rubber, and wood. Albers described the use of paper thus:

> One example: outside, i.e., in industry and craft, paper is most frequently utilized horizontally (laying), flat and glued. One side of the paper in this way usually loses its expression. The edge is almost never utilized. This leads us to use paper standing, not flat, plastically, involving both sides and stressing the edges. Instead of gluing it we shall bind it, arrange it, sew it, button it, rivet it, that is to say we shall fasten it differently. We shall investigate its performance under tensile and compressive stress. In this way "Works (of Art)" do not always originate, but rather experiments.[16]

A student's account of one of these exercises is illuminating. Albers had asked the students to take a newspaper and make something *more* out of it. The only work that passed Albers's muster was one that folded the newspaper along the edge so that it could stand up like a folding screen: "Josef Albers explained to us how well the material was understood and utilized—how the folding process was natural to paper, because it resulted in making a pliable material stiff. ... He further pointed out to us that a newspaper lying on the table would be hidden. Now that the paper was standing up, both sides had become visually active."[17]

In light of the Bauhaus's lacunae regarding handmade paper, but drawing upon their impulse toward material exploration and the integration of art, craft, technology, and engineering, I offer my own recent explorations in the incorporation of electronics in handmade paper. I do this through an account of the papermaking process, given that this arcane craft is not well understood today. An attention to the material and chemical processes at work illustrates how being in tune with the specific affordances of handmade paper can offer new potentials to contemporary technologists and designers.[18]

On the Sensual and Technical Qualities of Incipient Paper

December 24, 2017: I draw my hand through the pulp, the fibers suspended in the water. Four hours of beating in a Hollander has fibrillated and macerated the cellulose strands into something ready for sheet-pulling. The fibers arrived a few weeks ago as "half-stuff," a 3-to-5-mm-thick sheet of preprocessed material accordion-folded for shipment. Before their arrival in the United States, the fibers were a living part of the *Musa textilis* plant from the Philippines, also known as "Manila hemp." I'm not sure what day and time these fibers died, when exactly the leaf stems were taken from the *Musa textilis* tree, which tree it was in which grove, the names of the workers who processed the leaves to extract the desired cellulose fibers and discard the undesirable lignin. I don't know when these fibers started their journey toward the United States. I know that only about 1 to 3 kg of fiber is harvestable from 100 kg of leaves.[19] I know that abaca exports contribute around $79 million to the Philippine economy.[20] I know that the rhizomatous tendrils of global commerce allowed me to order this half-stuff online and to receive, yesterday, a unique mass of thousands upon thousands of cellulose fibers for my own processing this evening.

Because for what I want to make I need *these* cellulose fibers, and not other ones. Cotton won't work. Linen neither. Wood pulp most definitely not. Kozo, or "paper mulberry," while stronger than abaca, won't give me the translucency that I desire. For with abaca, and abaca alone, something happens between hour three and a half and four and a half in the beater, an inflection point, so that the sheets I will soon pull will be beautifully translucent rather than flecked with masses of flocculated fibers.

In the vat with the pulp, there is incipient paper. Cellulose fiber and water are all that one needs for paper, fundamentally. Yet there are many further steps before the chemical reaction happens. First, the pulling of a sheet, where the papermaker—tonight, me—takes the mould and deckle, draws pulp onto its meshlike surface, shakes it in the x and y directions, lets the water drain, and puts the mould and deckle aside. If I were using cotton as my fiber, I could immediately transfer, or *couch* (from French, pronounced "cooch"), the newly formed sheet onto wool felts. But the abaca is resistant. It *demands* more time from me, more time for the water to drain from the mould. So I put the mould and deckle aside and wait. I can pull another sheet while waiting for the first to drain. Finally enough water has drip-dripped to the floor (cleanup is itself an arduous process), and I can couch the sheet. I build a *post*, interleaving wet couched sheets with felts (ideally wool, but the needed wool is now rare and expensive, so perhaps the wool is not wool but polyester instead) which then goes into a hydraulic press. Five thousand pounds per square inch is what I want, slowly accumulated starting from atmospheric pressure. I don't want a blow-out. Water again drip-drips onto the floor. I release the pressure, the decreasing intensity of the hissing letting me know I can finally transfer the somewhat drier sheets of still-wet paper to blotter paper. Onto the blotters the sheets go, interleaved again, this time with corrugated cardboard.

Then, into a box with a fan at its rear, the sheets now being dried "under restraint" and checked for dryness every day for two to three days.

It is throughout this process—from the formation of the sheet on the mold and deckle, to the dripping of water onto the floor of the studio, to the pressing of water out of the fragile sheet, to the evaporation of water while the sheet dries in the dry box—that the chemical reactions occur that turn pulp into paper. Water evaporates, enters into its own suspension in the air, and the cellulose fibers bind together through hydrogen bonding.[21] A chemical reaction that requires only the chemicals of water and cellulose. We might brand this process "natural" and "without added chemicals."

This is but one way of making paper.

At various steps of this process I can embed different things into the sheets of paper, adding what papermakers call *inclusions*. Flower petals, bits of thread—these are the kinds of inclusions beginners are first taught to incorporate. Tonight, however, my inclusions are decidedly not natural. From a different strand of the global supply chain, I've procured piezoelectric disks. I know less about how these disks were formed. In between two thin, circular blanks of metal (silver on top and a nickel alloy on the bottom) sits a crystal with the amazing property that it outputs an electric voltage when compressed. Alternatively, it can vibrate if one applies a changing electric voltage. And the electronic representation of sound is one such changing voltage, and thus the piezoelectric disk becomes a *speaker*. This "unnatural" component can be used as an inclusion within our sheet. I couch one sheet of abaca on the felt. I take the "piezo"—modified by me with two sets of 3-foot-long wires that I earlier soldered to the disks—and place it upside down on top of the couched sheet. Another sheet of abaca goes on top, *double couching*. I take tweezers and carefully pull the two wires through the newly couched sheet so that they'll be where I need them once the sheets are pressed. Into the hydraulic press they go. But these sheets don't go into the dry box. On another table are tens of disposable plastic water bottles. I take this paper-piezo-wire mongrel, place it on top of a bottle, and caress the sheet onto the curves of the bottle, as if I were trying to create a gramophone horn. This is, of course, not incidental. Because another remarkable property of abaca fibers, once they've gone through all of this arduous processing, is that the sheets containing them shrink *dramatically* if left to dry in open air. The surface constricts in unpredictable ways with a strength that can bend metal wires. So bypassing the dry box, and letting the sheet dry around the form of the plastic water bottle, creates a speaker horn that, surrounding the piezo, possesses "organic" qualities of form that result from the precise distribution of fibers in the sheet, the particular rate at which the water evaporates, the vicissitudes of how I laid the sheet on the bottle. Things that are out of my control.

But let's return to the sheets dried under restraint. I take them to a different building. It's no longer Christmas Eve, but another late night a couple of weeks later. These sheets are see-through, solid flexible planes of cellulose that possess incredible strength but also appear fragile because of their translucency. I stand in front of our laser cutter, a machine more used to cutting through plywood or acrylic, or engraving drawings in the surfaces of materials. I update the settings to what I think will work: 14% power, 95% speed, 1,000 points per square inch. I tape down my 12-by-18-inch sheet onto a substrate, now prepared for its 45 minutes in the machine. The exhaust fan comes on, I hit the green arrow for "play," and the laser does its work. The laser heats the surface of the abaca sheet 1,000 times in a square inch, yet the sheet doesn't burn. It isn't cut. Rather, some currently unexplainable chemical process takes place by which the translucency becomes opaque, the milky clarity of the sheet turning to solid white where the laser has entangled with the surface. Again the choice of abaca is important. Other fibers just burn; their textured surfaces become charred and black-brown. Abaca doesn't experience this. Unlike in printmaking, where the pigment transferred to the sheet merely *binds* with the substrate (the paper), here the *paper itself* is being transformed. It's like carving into rock, but not, as this paper is decidedly more pliable, flexible, and fragile. This is a new discovery, unexpected, presently inexplicable: why is the text white and not charred? Others remain perplexed by this. The text that I etch takes shape on a translucent background.

The shrinking of abaca over a form, the chemical transformation of the surface under laser light: aren't these examples of what we mean when we talk about the "organic" in design? The relinquishing of some control in order to make spacetime for other processes to come to the fore, processes that have their own temporal unfoldings and vicissitudes and potentials. This is that knife edge we balance upon, an acutely uncomfortable place to be, indeed, but a place whose unknowability allows for the production of precisely what we desire. Where the materiality of our material is allowed to express itself within the constraints we have constructed. And where surprise, chance, and discovery come to the fore.

Ripples of Spacetime, or the Linkage between Waves of Influence and Electromagnetic Waves

To the works themselves: material condensates of our relationships with extraterrestrial entities such as satellites, rockets, space probes, and extraterrestrial beings. Papermaking and electronic manufacturing technologies allow me to enfold art and science, craft and the digital, the old and the new within a set of objects. This work valorizes the assemblage, not any individual component.

In the series *PIECES FOR PERFORMER(S) AND EXTRATERRESTRIAL ENTITIES* (2017–present), I laser-etch event scores into handmade abaca paper, drawing from the work of Yoko Ono, Pauline Oliveros, and Hannah Weiner.[22] "PEACE FOR QUEER ROCKETS" (figure 18.1) from this series is a reimagining of our aging nuclear arsenal and its assorted infrastructure as a site for radical transformations of subjectivity. From a distance the pieces look like they have been carved in stone, but closer inspection highlights the fragility and suppleness of the paper.

they transmitted continuously / but our times rarely aligned / and their signals dissipated in the æther (2018) is a 20-channel sound installation that re-presents recordings of satellite signals I have collected using custom-built antennas. To track the satellites and convert the radio frequency transmissions to sound I use software from the open-source SatNOGS project, written by a group of satellite enthusiasts around the globe who are interested in opening up access to space.[23] The speakers are the aforementioned piezoelectric transducers embedded in handmade abaca sheets and let to dry over forms (figure 18.2). Within the gallery space one is enveloped by the beeps, blips, and noises of the transmissions. These faint nonhuman signals foreground that this is communication by machines and for machines; we eavesdrop, perhaps searching for the interstitial space where our signals intermix with the machinic, transforming both in the process.

Karen Barad's work is helpful in further understanding these projects and their relationship to the Bauhaus: "*Phenomena are specific material relations of the ongoing differentiating of the world, where 'material' needs to be understood as iteratively constituted through force relations. Phenomena are not located in space and time; rather, phenomena are material entanglements enfolded and threaded through the spacetimemattering of the universe.*"[24] As we consider the legacy of the Bauhaus, we cannot understand it as a linear linkage to the past, but rather a set of "entanglements" that enfold moments and matter together. This is the spacetimemattering of Barad, where the ripples of the Bauhaus constructively interfere with my own activities today. Those activities enfold ancient craft techniques with modern technology, resonating with the work of Albers and Stölzl at the Bauhaus by looking beyond the imperative of industry.

The utopian impulse embedded within Gropius's initial dream for the Bauhaus needs to be reimagined for our present moment. The fact that its influence is still felt today indicates the potential of its professed unity between art, craft, and technology. Rather than the teleology of progress, the Bauhaus indexes a more complex spatial-temporal enfolding of ancient and modern, hand and machine, concept and material.

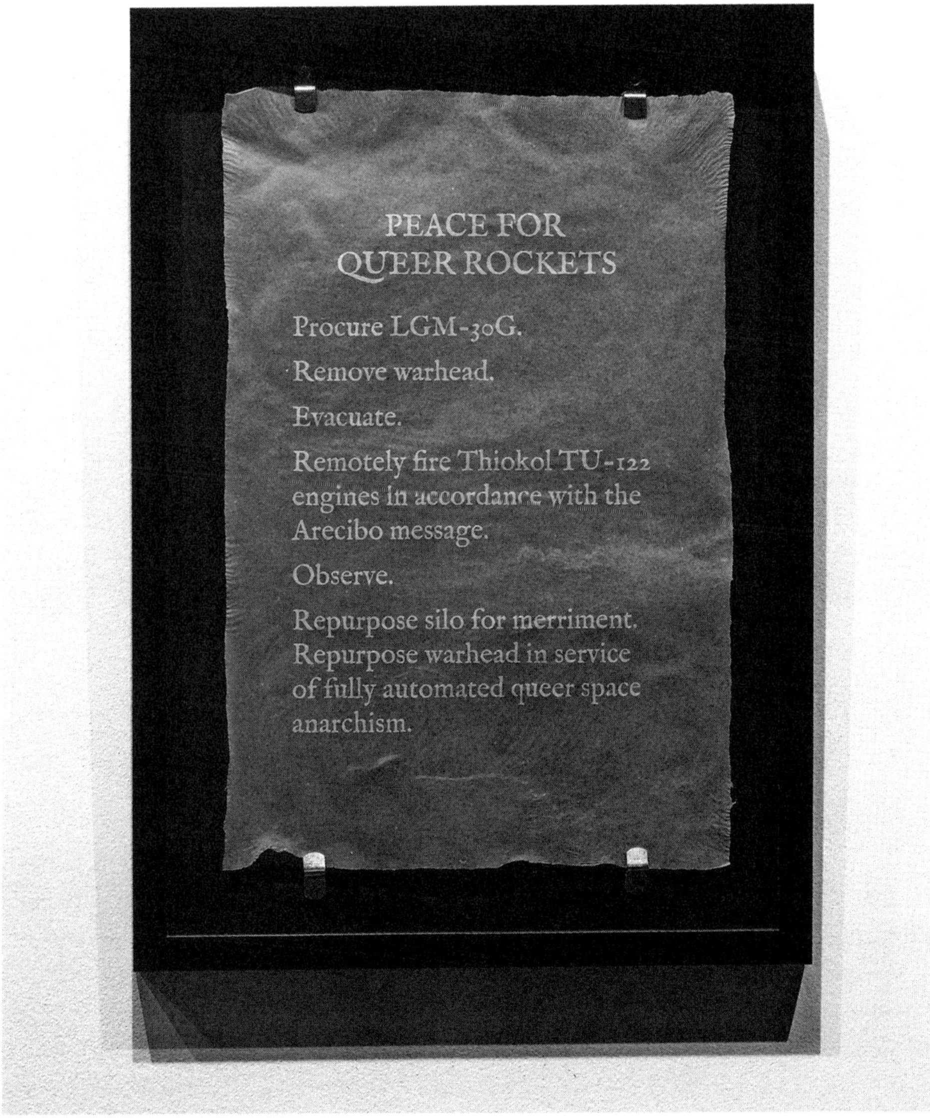

Figure 18.1
N. Adriana Knouf, *PIECES FOR PERFORMER(S) AND EXTRATERRESTRIAL ENTITIES* (2017–present), "PEACE FOR QUEER ROCKETS." 12 × 18 in. Laser-etched text in handmade abaca paper. Photo by author.

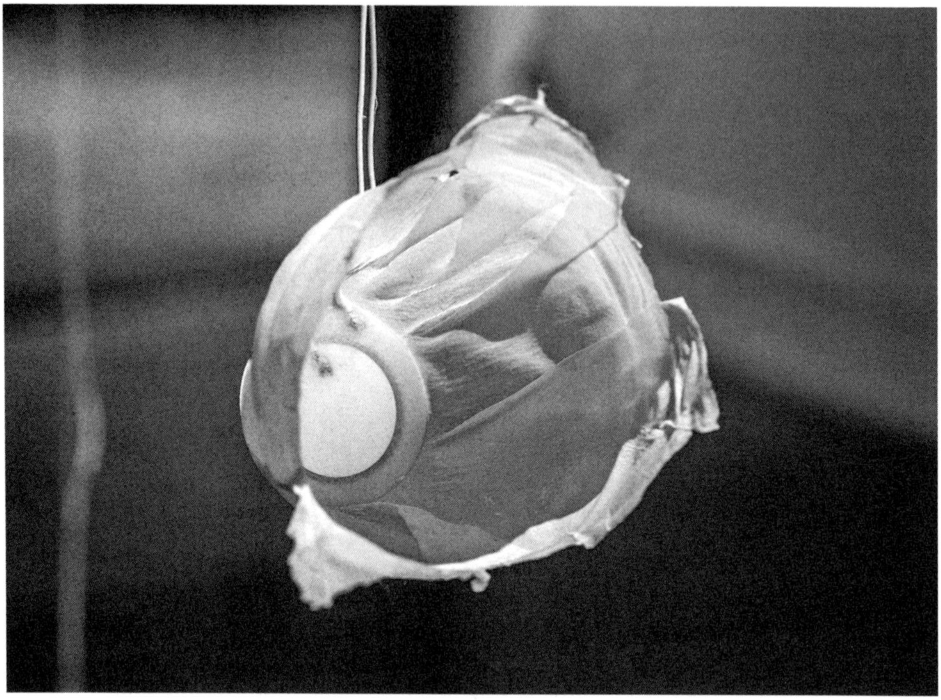

Figure 18.2
N. Adriana Knouf, *they transmitted continuously / but our times rarely aligned / and their signals dissipated in the æther* (2018). Dimensions variable. Handmade abaca paper, piezoelectric speakers, custom antennas, and software. Photo by author.

With Thanks to ...

Fio Russo for her papermaking assistance, Claudia Pederson for her editorial comments, Kristen Beal and the Clayton Staples Gallery at Wichita State University for allowing me to exhibit my work, the various *Musa textilis* plants for their fibers, and the following satellites for their transmissions: KKS-1, LUSAT, LILACSAT 2, CUBESAT, AAUSAT, BEEAGLESAT, CUBESAT XI 5, CUTE-1, VZLUSAT, PRISM, AALTO, LISHUI 1, JAS-2, ITUPSAT, CAS-4A, CAS-4B, UKUBE-1, XW-2F, XW-2B, MAX VALIER SAT, SUCHAI, ROBUSTA-1B, SOMP, NOAA19, NO-84, PCSAT, RADFXSAT, FOX-1A, SAUDISAT 1C, FOX-1D, NJUST, LINK, NANOSATC, FUNCUBE-1, DELFI-C3, NAYIF-1, PICSAT.

Notes

1. Sadie Plant, "The Future Looms: Weaving Women and Cybernetics," *Body and Society* 1, nos. 3–4 (1995), 63.

2. Sigrid Wortmann Weltge, *Women's Work: Textile Art from the Bauhaus* (San Francisco: Chronicle Books, 1993); Anja Baumhoff, *The Gendered World of the Bauhaus: The Politics of Power at the Weimar Republic's Premier Art Institute, 1919–1932* (Frankfurt am Main: Peter Lang, 2001); T'ai Smith, *Bauhaus Weaving Theory: From Feminine Craft to Mode of Design* (Minneapolis: University of Minnesota Press, 2014).

3. Walter Gropius, *The New Architecture and the Bauhaus*, trans. P. Morton Shand (Cambridge, MA: MIT Press, 1965), 52–53.

4. Gunta Stölzl, "Weaving at the Bauhaus" (1926), quoted in Smith, *Bauhaus Weaving Theory*, 66.

5. Anni Albers, *On Weaving* (1965; Princeton, NJ: Princeton University Press, 2017), 45.

6. Carpenter Center for the Visual Arts, *Bauhaus—a Teaching Idea* (Cambridge, MA: Harvard University, 1966), 12–13.

7. Smith, *Bauhaus Weaving Theory*, xxxii.

8. See, for example, Michael Siebenbrodt, ed., *Bauhaus Weimar: Designs for the Future*, trans. Michael Robinson and John Southard (Ostfildern-Ruit: Hatje Cantz, 2000), 210–255; and Hans M. Wingler, *The Bauhaus: Weimar Dessau Berlin Chicago* (Cambridge, MA: MIT Press, 1978), 518.

9. Siebenbrodt, *Bauhaus Weimar*, 205.

10. Ibid.

11. Wingler, *The Bauhaus*, 342–343.

12. Dard Hunter, *Papermaking: The History and Technique of an Ancient Craft* (1947; New York: Dover, 1978), 341–399.

13. Ibid., 255.

14. Georg Eineder, *The Ancient Paper Mills of the Former Austro-Hungarian Empire and Their Watermarks* (Hilversum: Paper Publications Society, 1960), 21.

15. It's important to note that there are distinct kinds of papermaking often lumped under the categories of "Eastern" and "Western," with significant differences in the kinds of fibers used, fiber preparation, sheet formation, and drying. During the time of Dard Hunter's research, "Eastern" papermaking was similarly in decline, but not at as precipitous a rate. See, for example, Timothy Barrett, *Japanese Papermaking: Traditions, Tools, and Techniques* (1983; Easthampton, MA: Floating World Editions, 2005).

16. Carpenter Center for the Visual Arts, *Bauhaus—a Teaching Idea*, 16.

17. Hannes Beckmann, quoted in Rainer K. Wick, *Teaching at the Bauhaus*, trans. Stephen Mason and Simon Lèbe (Ostfildern-Ruit: Hatje Cantz, 2000), 181.

18. I have also written about a different technique involving handmade paper called "joomchi" that allows one to "felt" multiple sheets made from paper mulberry trees together into a single sheet, thereby allowing one to embed electronic components inside the sheet. See N. A. Knouf, "Felted Paper Circuits Using Joomchi," in *Proceedings of the Eleventh International Conference on Tangible, Embedded, and Embodied Interaction*, TEI '17 (New York: ACM, 2017), 443–450, https://doi.org/10.1145/3024969.3025071.

19. E. R. Palmer, "The Use of Abaca for Pulp and Papermaking," *Tropical Science* 24 (1982), 1–16.

20. Antonio G. Lalusin and Maria Lea H. Villavicencio, "Abaca (*Musa Textilis* Nee) Breeding in the Philippines," in *Industrial Crops: Breeding for Bioenergy and Bioproducts*, ed. Von Mark V. Cruz and David A. Dierig (New York: Springer New York, 2015), 265–289, https://doi.org/10.1007/978-1-4939-1447-0_12.

21. J. C. Roberts, *The Chemistry of Paper* (Cambridge: Royal Society of Chemistry, 1996), 56–59.

22. Yoko Ono, *Grapefruit: A Book of Instruction and Drawings* (1964; New York: Simon and Schuster, 1998); Pauline Oliveros, *Anthology of Text Scores*, ed. Samuel Golter and Lawton Hall (Kingston, NY: Deep Listening Publications, 2013); Hannah Weiner, *Hannah Weiner's Open House*, ed. Patrick F. Durgin (Berkeley: Kenning Editions, 2007).

23. For more information see https://satnogs.org/.

24. Karen Barad, "No Small Matter: Mushroom Clouds, Ecologies of Nothingness, and Strange Topologies of Spacetimemattering," in *Arts of Living on a Damaged Planet*, ed. Anna Tsing et al. (Minneapolis: University of Minnesota Press, 2017), G111 (italics in the original).

VI Emerging Technologies, Techno-utopian Aesthetics, and Interactions

19 From Bauhaus Color to LED Color

Alice Arnold

Introduction

What is color? It is "supercalifragilisticexpialidocious," something so extraordinary that, as Mary Poppins sang, we need a special word to describe how wonderful it is. The quest to understand color and how to use it (across different mediums and technologies) has been asked and reasked by scientists, philosophers, and artists for thousands of years. At the beginning of the twentieth century new insights into the perception of color and new color technologies made it a topic of experimentation and exploration among Bauhaus masters and students. This dialogue with color continued in the postwar era as the Bauhaus pedagogy gained influence in the United States and in other places where the Bauhaus cohort established roots. Two of the Bauhaus masters, Johannes Itten and Josef Albers, both wrote highly influential books on color in the 1960s. Itten's *The Art of Color* (1961) and Albers's *Interaction of Color* (1963) have had a major impact on art and design education and on how color is studied, used, and applied by designers, artists, scientists, and advertisers, among others utilizing color.

In the twenty-first century color continues to be a catalyst for discussion and experimentation regarding the role of technology and art in society. This chapter outlines color studies and usage from the Bauhaus era to today's digital color era, when LED (light-emitting diode) lighting technology and computer algorithms play a role in shaping how color is produced, perceived, and consumed. As a photographer, documentary filmmaker, and designer, my own color work spans analog and digital processes, from film to print to screens. In the Bauhaus spirit, this essay is extended into the visual realm with a project, *The Coca-Cola Sign at Two Times Square*, which explores the use of digital color and color in the urban environment (see plates 20–22).

What Is Color, Part 2

Color is emotional and scientific, sensual and technical, abstract and concrete. From a scientific perspective, color is defined as a wavelength of light, the visible light spectrum that Isaac Newton discerned in a darkened room with the aid of two prisms in the seventeenth century. For psychologists and cognitive scientists (and for other disciplines that study how the mind works), understanding how we see color sheds light on understanding the process of perception. This is because of a disparity between the physiology of how the eye perceives color and the psychology of how people experience color. The human eye only sees colors in variants of red, green, and blue (RGB) at the retinal level. However, the brain interprets and synthesizes this information from the retina based on prior knowledge and experience. It is in this further processing of the visual information from the retina that we are enabled to see and feel a much richer palette of colors.[1]

A Brief Note on Color Terminology

One of the main ways that artists and designers organize color is through a color wheel, which is a progression of hues in a circular arrangement. This arrangement helps show the relationship between, for example, primary, secondary, and tertiary colors. There are three main color models, each with its own set of primary colors. For painters, red, yellow, and blue (RYB) are considered the primary colors. Printing presses utilize cyan, magenta, and yellow (CMY, known as the subtractive primary colors), and those working with light, such as photographers, filmmakers, and web designers, use red, green, and blue (RGB), the additive primary model, which is based on the visible light spectrum (they are called the additive primaries because adding red light, green light, and blue light results in white light). All colors produced for screen output, from our mobile phones to digital billboards, use the RGB color model. The secondary colors are formed by mixing two primary colors. In the RGB model the secondary colors are cyan, magenta, and yellow, which are also the subtractive primary colors. The tertiary colors are formed from mixing one primary and one secondary. A more complex way to model color is to describe it in three dimensions (like a sphere instead of a circle): hue (the color), saturation (brightness or dullness), and value (light-dark). Digital design software like Adobe Photoshop uses this model to organize color. There are also several different organizations and businesses that are involved with color management, such as CIE (International Commission on Illumination), ICC (International Color Consortium), Pantone, and Munsell. Each of these organizations sets standards that are important for accurate color definitions and usage.

Artists and designers harness color to express emotions, indicate depth, create emphasis, signal importance, sharpen perceptual awareness, and catch the eye and create attraction. Color also plays a very important supporting role in the economy. It is exploited as a style element to encourage consumption, from fashion to furnishings, electronics, and cars. In short, color provides immense meaning, depth, beauty, and stimulation for people. Without color, to paraphrase Johannes Itten, the world appears dead.[2]

Color Studies at the Bauhaus

The Bauhaus opened its doors in Weimar in 1919, two years after the end of World War I, upon a wave of hope and ambition. 150 students enrolled, attracted by Walter Gropius's message of educating artists and craftsmen to "build the building of the future"[3] and "hoping to make a fresh start and give meaning to their lives."[4]

Itten was one of the first teachers appointed by Gropius. He was an experienced art teacher and his ideas helped shape the first iteration of the Bauhaus, known as its expressionist phase, from 1919 to 1923. Itten had initially studied to be a kindergarten teacher, absorbing pedagogical methods such as Friedrich Froebel's ideas on learning through experimentation and play.[5] Later he studied art with Adolf Hölzel, who taught a theory of color, influenced by Goethe's work,[6] that was rooted in complementary contrast.[7]

In 1919 Adolf Hölzel was involved in a debate about color harmony with the Nobel Prize-winning chemist Wilhelm Ostwald,[8] who created a color system that organized colors based on (tonal) value.[9] This debate underlies issues in color and technology that remain relevant to the use and study of color, which currently is largely driven by digital processes that convert colors to numerical values. For Hölzel, Itten, and most artists of the time, color harmony was grounded in the interaction of the various hues, as perceived by the artist's eye,[10] not by a system that organized color based on mathematically derived relationships, as Ostwald's method did. Paul Klee, a Bauhaus master and a masterful painter, critiqued Ostwald's method because, he wrote, "the psychological aspect of color is neglected."[11] But for others thinking about industrial manufacturing, including Gropius, who invited Ostwald to speak at the Bauhaus, Ostwald's systematic way of ordering color by value enabled a standardized range of colors to be produced and used in mass-produced products and mass media.[12]

Itten was a powerful teacher and personality at the Bauhaus, but his mysticism (he was a follower of the Mazdaznan cult) and focus on artistic self-expression increasingly clashed with Gropius's vision for the Bauhaus, which by 1922 had changed from a new unity of art and craft to one of art and technology. Itten, with his monklike robes, shaved head, and spiritual ethos, was replaced by László Moholy-Nagy, who sartorially signaled his functional, design-oriented focus by wearing construction worker's overalls.[13] Moholy-Nagy was assisted by Bauhaus graduate Josef Albers, who then taught the preliminary course on his own from 1928 to 1933 (Gropius and Moholy-Nagy left the Bauhaus in 1928).

Moholy-Nagy's and Albers's version of the preliminary course marks the second phase of the Bauhaus, which emphasized the use of materials, product development, and mass manufacturing. In terms of color studies, they shifted Itten's emphasis on the subjective and expressionistic use of color to the use of color as a material, a component part of a larger design. Students experimented with the perceptual aspects of color, how it can shape space and emotions; they investigated the use of color with different materials, such as wood, metal, and textiles; and they observed the effect of light on materials and colors.[14] Moholy-Nagy and Gropius espoused the use of primary colors, because they promoted utilitarian values. Primary forms and colors, Gropius wrote, were "readily accessible to everyone,"[15] and they also helped in establishing standards for mass production. At the Bauhaus, keeping colors simple was an expression and articulation of modernity. The industrial production of well-designed and affordable spaces and products was a means to a more equitable society.

With the move to Dessau in 1925, the Bauhaus was able to test its architecture, design, and planning ideas. The Dessau building, designed by Gropius and furnished and decorated by Bauhaus students and teachers, was largely pristine white on the outside, but used color in interesting ways in the interior. For example, in one of the stairways, the ceilings were painted yellow, the handrails red, the walls white, and the edges of the stairs black. Color was used on walls, ceilings, beams, and trim elements to communicate wayfinding information, indicate spatial use, and for its psychological effects. Psychologically, the use of color in three-dimensional space can alter people's spatial perception and influence their mood.[16] Warm tone colors, such as red and yellow, have a stimulating affect, while blues and greens, cool-temperature colors, are considered calming.

Optical Trickery

Another branch of color studies in the early decades of the twentieth century was led by the Gestalt psychologists, whose work influenced many people at the Bauhaus, including Albers.[17] Largely based in Germany, Gestalt psychologists carried out experimental work on human perception. They were particularly interested in how people make sense of the visual field.[18] How do they perceive and understand forms, shapes, and colors? How do they interpret the new sources of media, such as cinema and radio, which extend people's ability to see and hear? One way these psychologists tested their ideas was through visual illusions, low-representational images that could be interpreted in different ways. "Edgar's Vase" (1915) is an illusion that contains within it two different images: (1) a white vase on a black background and (2) two profile faces silhouetted on a white ground. When looking at this image, most people will immediately see either the white vase as the figure or the black profile faces as the figure. As one looks at the image longer, it is possible to shift figure-ground perception (either the white is the ground or the black is) so as to see both of the images. This trick highlights the psychological and perceptual aspects of vision, ideas that were explored in Bauhaus design and photography.

Color can also create optical illusions. Albers wrote that "if one says 'Red' and there are 50 people listening, it can be expected that there will be 50 reds in their minds." And even if the red is well known to people, "such as the red of the Coca-Cola signs, which is the same red all over the country—they will still think of many different reds."[19] Color perception is based on several factors, such as how a color is perceived in relation to other colors, the lighting and environmental conditions, and cultural and contextual knowledge. The Gestalt psychologists were exploring how people see and how they create visual meaning from complex visual stimuli. These ideas are useful to artists and designers because they model the psychological process of seeing and interpreting visual stimuli, and thus offer a framework for constructing visual compositions.

Industrial Color

Several new technologies developed during the second industrial revolution expanded people's experience of color and increased the volume of imagery available to them. Innovations in printing press technology led to more printed materials and more photographic reproduction, from newspapers to magazines, advertisements, and packaging. Chemically produced paints, dyes, and inks rendered color cheaper and easier to use and created a wider palette of colors, all of which contributed to the mass reproduction of printed color images. And as already noted, advancements in color science, like Ostwald's system and also Albert Munsell's,[20] created objective standards of color measurement, which supported color use and reproduction on an industrial scale.

The use of neon lighting in advertising signs was another new form of media and color in the early twentieth century. Neon lighting creates colored light by heating up noble gases (e.g., neon, argon, and xenon) sealed in a glass tube. This electrochemical process creates a unique color palette, one that is not otherwise seen in the natural environment. Neon lights are also distinctive because of their unusual combination of bright illumination with a soft glow. Neon lights were used to create sign spectaculars in the 1920s and '30s—large, extravagant signs that combined electric light, text, images, and color to create a powerful message in the night sky.[21] Writing in Berlin in the 1920s, Walter Benjamin grasped the seductive power of neon signs. "What, in the end," he asks in "These Spaces for Rent," "makes advertisements so superior to criticism? Not what the moving red neon sign says—but the fiery pool reflecting it in the asphalt."[22] Today neon signs are beloved but have been largely replaced by digital lighting technologies that offer new ways to display commercial messaging. The spirit of neon, though, lives on in these new digital signs, which also create a palette of fantasy colors and spectacular viewing experiences.

From 1919 to the close of the Bauhaus in 1933 by the Nazi government, color played a vital role in intellectual and artistic experimentation in the school. And it became a more visible force in society, from its use in newly manufactured products to new media, such as neon signs, movie posters, and advertisements. After 1933, many of the Bauhaus teachers and students found refuge and jobs in the United States, and the color studies that began at the Bauhaus continued and expanded with the advent of new technologies and new ideas, arising from shifting social, political, and economic conditions.

New Worlds, New Colors

The Bauhaus educational philosophy and design culture were brought to the United States primarily by László Moholy-Nagy (he founded the New Bauhaus in Chicago in 1937, which later became the Institute of Design), Walter Gropius (he joined the faculty at Harvard University's Graduate School of Design in 1937), and Josef Albers (at Black Mountain College, 1933–1949, and Yale University, 1950–1958). Through his teaching and his artistic practice, Albers had a significant impact on art, design, and visual culture in the United States. He mentored and/or inspired many influential twentieth-century artists, such as Robert Rauschenberg, Robert Irwin, Eva Hesse, and Cy Twombly, and his work contributed to several art movements, including geometric abstraction, op art, and minimalism.

Upon his arrival at Black Mountain College, Albers famously stated that he wanted to "open eyes."[23] He adapted the *Vorkurs*, begun by Itten at the Bauhaus, to fit the context of a liberal arts school and oriented the curriculum to focus on visual perception.[24] Perception for Albers involved understanding how to see form and its underlying structure and learning to see with the eye and the mind, so as "to see in the widest sense."[25]

This in turn encouraged experimentation. And studying color was an integral way into that process. His color studies classes involved direct experimentation with pieces of colored paper to learn how to see color, understand color relationships, and perceive the difference between optical seeing and perception.[26]

Color studies became a significant aspect of Albers's teaching and painting in the United States. His book *Interaction of Color* (1963), still widely used by students, artists, and teachers, codifies his ideas about perception and color. "In visual perception," Albers wrote, "a color is almost never seen as it really is—as it physically is. That fact makes color the most relative medium in art."[27] For example, an ochre square on a blue background looks like a different color than the exact same ochre square on an orange background. On the blue background the ochre square looks like a bright orange, whereas on the orange field it appears to be a darker and duller orange.[28] Albers's color studies built on the work of Gestalt psychology, playing with the difference between optical seeing, what our eyes see, and perceptual seeing, how our brains interpret the visual information from the retina. In *Interaction of Color* Albers posits that if a color can change its appearance due to the background it is seen on (its environment and context), this opens up a space to see the world not just in the realm of facts but with vision, with imagination.[29]

Johannes Itten continued teaching after he left the Bauhaus, and he also published an influential book on color, around the same time as Albers, *The Art of Color* (1961; a more economical edition, *The Elements of Color*, was published in 1970). In both Itten's and Albers's color books, a central theme is the relativity of color perception. Itten shows how color appearance changes through his theory of contrast. He delineates seven kinds of contrast in which to characterize color effects: contrast of hue, contrast of value, cold-warm contrast, complementarity contrast, contrast of saturation, contrast of extension, and simultaneous contrast.[30] Itten's color philosophy was grounded in the idea that color is the "chief vehicle of expression."[31] He favored color over line,[32] believing that a "composition must begin with color areas, and these will determine the lines."[33] In order to use color "to express the ineffable,"[34] he developed a mathematical system to arrange and show color and value (or tonal) relationships. For Itten, understanding these relationships is key to mastering the use of color for artistic self-expression. His mature color philosophy thus manages to integrate the color harmony ideas of Hölzel, his teacher, and of Ostwald, the chemist, whose ideas had clashed in the early days of the Bauhaus.

Style Industries

In the 1960s, when Albers's and Itten's color books were published, modernism, which had been revolutionary at the Bauhaus, had become part of the status quo in US corporate culture. At the Bauhaus modernism was a critical stance. The school sought to create "new men," designers educated in arts, crafts, science, and technology who would work together to improve society. These ideals were transported to the United States by Bauhaus professors and students, who took on active roles as teachers and design professionals. But what took hold in the US educational system was primarily the idea of the preliminary course.[35] The school's political and utopian message was not able to establish strong roots in the US educational environment. Moholy-Nagy's New Bauhaus in Chicago was sponsored by Chicago businessmen who had a more narrow educational focus: a vocational school that trained professional designers for industry.[36] Hal Foster writes, "For good and for bad, this squaring of the circle—of techno-science with human biology, of capitalist divisions in labour and knowledge with a 'universal outlook'—became the American version of his Bauhaus idea."[37] Corporate America "embraced the aesthetic and economic benefits of modern design ... [but not] the modernists' metaphysics."[38] For American business leaders of this era, modernity implied youthfulness, mobility, and optimism, and advertising men were modernity's "town criers."[39]

Color is one of the main visual elements deployed in products and in advertising to encourage people to consume more. It is used for its psychological capacity to create emotion, stir desire, and influence mood. It can endow utilitarian products, such as telephones, with fashion appeal;[40] add a gloss of product differentiation, such as the choice offered to consumers in the 1920s between a black Ford Model T car and the blue lacquer General Motors model;[41] and provide a sense of self-expression and identity in one's consumer choices (do the red sneakers or the purple ones convey a sense of who you are?). From the car industry to the fashion industry, a range of color experts, from designers to scientists, chemists, stylists, and forecasters, are now employed to create new pigments, to design novel color combinations, to package color trends, and to market these ideas to the public.

From Pigment to Light

A significant change that parallels the rise of the consumer society after World War II is the shift from pigment-based color to electronic color, from the printing press to television and video, and also the rise of digital color. Some of these changes were imagined by László Moholy-Nagy, who was experimenting with photography, film, and light machines in the 1920s.

Moholy-Nagy, who considered light to be an artistic medium like paint, envisioned an "architecture of light."[42] His *Light-Space Modulator* (1922–1930) combines a motor, gears, light bulbs, and rotating reflective surfaces to create an environmental experience of light and shadows. He also saw the potential of light as a design or communications tool and imagined a future cityscape with light displays "with ever changing planes and angles," light frescos on buildings and projections onto clouds.[43]

Several of these futurist ideas are possible now with LED lighting technology that can display moving images on building facades. This form of light is unique because it is programmable and individual red, green, and blue LEDs can be grouped together to create full-spectrum lighting (the visible light spectrum). However, this new light economy is not a benign gloss of light and color up in the clouds; it is a powerful media instrument designed to catch and focus our attention in a targeted way. This is a very different conception of imagery from Moholy-Nagy's, whose work encouraged viewers to expand their sense of perception and vision in society.[44]

Color in the Public Realm

Color became ubiquitous in the urban environment in the United States in the second half of the twentieth century. Typically, the built environment has a muted color palette, arising from a preponderance of gray concrete, black asphalt, neutral stone, metallic steel and aluminum surfaces, and reflective glass. Outdoor advertising, in the form of billboards and signs, injects large-scale color images (along with their marketing messages) into the commercial areas of cities and along freeways. In *Learning from Las Vegas*, Robert Venturi, Denise Scott Brown, and Steven Izenour reassessed modernist architectural ideas and celebrated the vernacular nature of signs inserted into the urban environment: "there is no reason why the methods of commercial persuasion and the skyline of signs analyzed here should not serve the purpose of civic and cultural enhancement. But this is not entirely up to the architect."[45]

Historically, the outdoor advertising industry has been lightly regulated in the United States, and today billboards are an important revenue source for many cities. In the early 2000s two new forms of outdoor advertising had a tremendous impact on visual culture in cities, a subject explored in my film *Electric Signs*. One development was very large signs printed on a flexible vinyl material. These signs, known as super-graphics, were wrapped around buildings. Giant faces and colorful graphics looking down on pedestrians and motorists from their glass tower perches inspired an advertising backlash in Los Angeles and other cities. The second development, digital billboards, vastly increases the amount of advertising messages in public space. Instead of one fixed image, several images are seen on a loop in one space, vying for the public's attention. This also affects the nature and quality of public space, because when the visual environment is overpopulated with commercial messaging, the public aspect of the public domain is weakened.

The postmodern city celebrated in *Learning from Las Vegas* has perhaps become too pumped up—like a balloon ready to pop—by digital color. The illuminated electronic surfaces of these signs, and of the screens we carry around with us, visually seduce us, bursting with bright, shiny, crisp colors not normally seen in the natural environment.

Electronic Color

Television was a new technology when Moholy-Nagy was imagining structures of light and color in space, but it has since become a powerful cultural, political, and economic force. The television image, which used to be contained in a box but now floats on screens of various sizes, commands a great deal of space in society. With its unstoppable, kaleidoscopic flow of images, it shapes the dreams, ideas, behavior, and tastes of millions of people. It yields power through its ability to command and sell people's attention, which affects the contours of the consumer landscape and influences political decisions and cultural values.

For all its ease of use—just click a button and start channel surfing—television is a very technical and abstract system. A video image is formed by converting light (from the visible light spectrum, which is RGB color) into an electronic signal. Television is the result of broadcasting the electronic signal (as recorded by the video camera) from the TV station to a TV set. During the first couple of decades of commercial television, the TV image had a very low resolution, prompting Marshall McLuhan's analysis that it was a "cool medium," because the image received on the TV set is "comprised of pixels that the audience must first decode back into shapes again in an active and almost tactile way."[46] Color television became a reality for the majority of US households by the mid-1960s. Color TV brought bright colors with a fuzzy glow into people's living rooms, but the color range people saw was actually less than what the human eye can perceive. The color information in the video signal was compressed into a smaller bandwidth for broadcast transmission. In 2009, television in the United States switched from standard-definition (an analog broadcast signal) to a digital signal, featuring high-definition video. There is a lot more color information in digital video (the color is sharper, more vibrant, and there is better transition from one hue to another), so the digital signal is still compressed for broadcast. Another factor is the screen itself. Standard-definition screens (the old CRT screens with the boxy back) show a smaller gamut of color than what the human eye can perceive. Newer, high-definition screens (this includes most tablets and mobile phones today) display better color tonality, but still do not match the sensitivity of the eye.

Digital Color

Digital color, generated by computer software and algorithmic code and reproduced on screens, is having a robust impact on the art and science of color. In the computer environment colors are defined as numbers. Pure red, for example, is 255/0/0 and black is 0/0/0 (as defined in the RGB system). This reduction of color to numbers is an evolution of the dispute in the early years of the Bauhaus over how to define color harmony. Clearly Ostwald and Gropius's argument for standardization has won the debate, but Paul Klee's point that mathematical equations can never capture the emotional and psychological complexity inherent in color is important to hold onto in a systems-driven world.

Digital color for consumer use starts in the 1980s, with the introduction of personal computers, continues in the '90s with the advent of the World Wide Web (where there is no cost to using color), and consolidates its hegemony further with digital camera sensors, social media, and streaming services in the 1990s–2000s. Prior to digital color, color use, in paintings, textiles, and printed materials, was expensive, as it still is. Digital color makes color accessible, easy to use, and cheap. But this story doesn't end happily somewhere over the rainbow, because the colors we choose on our computers, see on our screens, and record with our cameras are largely controlled by algorithms that limit our color palette and influence our color decisions.[47] For example, high-definition camera sensors can record a wider gamut[48] of color than what the software application and monitor used for display will show. Also, compression software used to output photos and videos for online use (such as jpg and mp4 files) reduce the color information in images (to make the file smaller).

Interestingly, "the more user friendly the interface, the more computational obfuscation and complexity is hidden from the end-user."[49] Instagram is a perfect example of this. The app allows users to tweak color and tonal values with the swipe of a finger. But in fact the code has already defined the parameters and choices that are available, and our control over how the algorithms work is also limited. The quick and easy changes that digital apps foster is having an impact on color and visual culture in other ways too. Instead of creating the image in the viewfinder (looking at the image through the lens), as one does in analog photography, many images today are crafted in postproduction by manipulating color values, lighting temperature, and exposure, resulting in very high-contrast, overly saturated or vibrant images. This changes the actuality of what was seen in the lens, one of the elements that has made photography such a unique form of image-making since the nineteenth century.

The results of this digital processing are unreal colors and unnatural-looking environments. Jean Baudrillard coined the term "hyperreality" in the 1980s to describe how media technologies (films, TV, news, amusement parks) provide a more intense experience for people than what is experienced in everyday life. Digital color manipulation of images is also contributing to this hyperreal world, in which media simulations of reality are perceived as more real than real.[50]

Conclusion

During the Bauhaus era the role of color in society and in people's lives started to change. It became a mass-manufactured product, a component in an industrial process, and a resource for abstract self-expression. These changes were connected to Bauhaus pedagogy, research, and practice, as we have seen in the work of Itten, Albers, Gropius, and Moholy-Nagy. After World War II, color science expanded through television, video, and color film. And now, 100 years after the close of the Bauhaus, digital technology and algorithmic computations are recalibrating the contours of color use.

Whether color is generated through light, as in the RGB systems used in video, photography, and digital screens, or through pigments (e.g., paint on canvas or ink on paper), the colors we see are created through a unique blending of technology, biology (from the interaction of the eye and the brain), social constructs, and the natural environment (the physics of light). Color, as Josef Albers observed, is deceptive, because "there is a discrepancy between physical fact and psychic effect."[51] And with digital color the deception thickens, because, paradoxically, color choice is abundant and restricted at the same time. Understanding and exploring these color tricks, however, shows us how to see more deeply, how to think more creatively, and how to understand visual and spatial relationships better, which was at the heart of the Bauhaus mission.

Notes

1. R. L. Gregory, *Eye and Brain: The Psychology of Seeing* (New York: McGraw-Hill, 1966), 117–125.

2. "Color is life; for a world without color appears to us as dead." Johannes Itten, *The Elements of Color* (New York: Van Nostrand Reinhold, 1970), 8.

3. Magdalena Droste, *Bauhaus, 1919–1933* (Cologne: B. Taschen, 1998), 18.

4. Ibid., 22.

5. Kai-Uwe Hemken, "Clash of the Natural and the Mechanical Human: Theo van Doesburg vs Johannes Itten, 1922," in *Bauhaus Conflicts, 1919–2009: Controversies and Counterparts*, ed. Philipp Oswalt (Ostfildern: Hatje Cantz, 2009), 36.

6. John Gage, "Colour at the Bauhaus," *Architectural Association School of Architecture*, no. 2 (July 1982), 50.

7. Complementary colors are colors that are opposite each other on the color wheel. These colors contrast, or complement, each other, such as red and green (in the RYB color model). When mixed together, complementary colors create a neutral dark gray, in effect canceling each other out.

8. Gage, "Colour at the Bauhaus," 50.

9. Value refers to a contrast range of light to dark shades of a given hue.

10. Gage, "Colour at the Bauhaus," 50.

11. Ibid., 52.

12. Ibid., 50–51.

13. Droste, *Bauhaus, 1919–1933*, 60.

14. Clark Vandersall Poling Jr., "Color Theories of the Bauhaus Artists" (PhD diss., Columbia University, 1973), 6.

15. Cited in ibid., 49.

16. Ibid., 86–87, 100–102.

17. John Gage, *Color and Meaning: Art, Science, and Symbolism* (Berkeley: University of California Press, 1999), 16.

18. Gregory, *Eye and Brain*, 8.

19. Josef Albers, *Interaction of Color* (1963; New Haven: Yale University Press, 2006), 3.

20. Munsell was working on a color system in the United States around the same time as Oswald. His system is based on a three-dimensional model, defining colors with a numerical system based on their hue, value, and saturation. Munsell's system was adopted internationally and is still in use today.

21. Alice Arnold, *Electric Signs: Signs, Screen and Public Spaces* (film, 2013).

22. Walter Benjamin, *One Way Street* (Cambridge, MA: Belknap Press of Harvard University Press, 2016), 77.

23. Eva Díaz, *The Experimenters: Chance and Design at Black Mountain College* (Chicago: University of Chicago Press, 2015), 15.

24. Ibid., 5–6.

25. Ibid., 30.

26. Ibid., 24.

27. Albers, *Interaction of Color*, 1.

28. French chemist and color expert Michel-Eugene Chevreul described this effect as simultaneous contrast in 1839.

29. Albers, *Interaction of Color*, 2. Also see the color plate on p. 77.

30. Itten, *The Elements of Color*, 32.

31. Ibid., 18.

32. There has been a long-standing debate, since Renaissance times, between the merits of *disegno* (drawing, line, analytical) and *colore* (color, decoration, emotional) in painting. This debate surfaced again in the baroque period between the followers of Poussin (line, *disegno*) and Rubens (color) and in the nineteenth century between Ingres (line) and Delacroix (color).

33. Itten, *The Elements of Color*, 18.

34. Ibid.

35. Gabriele Diana Grawe, "Continuity and Transformation: Bauhaus Pedagogy in North America," in Rainer K. Wick, *Teaching at the Bauhaus* (Ostfildern-Ruit: Hatje Cantz, 2000), 361.

36. Ibid., 357–358.

37. Hal Foster, "The Bauhaus in America," in *Albers and Moholy-Nagy: From the Bauhaus to the New World*, ed. Achim Borchardt-Hume (New Haven: Yale University Press, 2006), 97.

38. Grawe, "Continuity and Transformation," 359.

39. Roland Marchand, *Advertising the American Dream: Making Way for Modernity, 1920–1940* (Berkeley: University of California Press, 1985), 1.

40. Ibid., 121–122.

41. Regina Lee Blaszczyk, *The Color Revolution* (Cambridge, MA: MIT Press, 2012), 115–116.

42. Richard Kostelanetz, ed., *Moholy-Nagy* (New York: Praeger, 1970), 37.

43. Ibid., 38.

44. See László Moholy-Nagy, *The New Vision: Fundamentals of Design, Painting, Sculpture, Architecture*, trans. Daphne M. Hoffmann (1938; Mineola, NY: Dover, 2005), 10–15; and Kostelanetz, *Moholy-Nagy*, 40–41, 51–54.

45. Robert Venturi, Denise Scott Brown, and Steven Izenour, *Learning from Las Vegas: The Forgotten Symbolism of Architectural Form* (Cambridge, MA: MIT Press, 1977), 6.

46. Friedrich Kittler, *Optical Media* (Cambridge: Polity Press, 2010), 222.

47. Carolyn Kane, *Chromatic Algorithms: Synthetic Color, Computer Art, and Aesthetics after Code* (Chicago: University of Chicago Press, 2014), 170–171.

48. A color gamut helps standardize color use across a multitude of devices, from different screens to scanners, printers and sensors. The most commonly used color gamut is sRGB, which portrays a narrow color range, compared to what the human eye can detect.

49. Kane, *Chromatic Algorithms*, 170.

50. Jean Baudrillard, *Simulacra and Simulation*, trans. Sheila Faria Glaser (Ann Arbor: University of Michigan Press, 1994).

51. Albers, *Interaction of Color*, 2.

20 The Dematerialization of Complexity, Dynamic Iconography, and Iconic (Past) Futures[1]

Michael J. Golec

Our contemporary world is one of relentless pressure to keep pace with the dynamism of virtual space, primarily in the case of social media, but not exclusively so.[2] This isn't a claim for technological determinism. Rather, there exists a pervasive anxiety regarding a perceived lack of homeostasis when it comes to the abstract functions of digital technologies. The anxiety arises where there is a sense that abstract functionality aspires to make the individual desire what the system needs in order to optimize its own performance. And yet these concerns may themselves result from an overriding principle of homeostasis.[3] As so often discussed, the systems that support data visualization, social media, the internet of things, and their digital interfaces internalize complexity, withdrawing their inner workings from immediate view and material access. The politics of transparency are especially pressing where facts are mystified and direct actions are thwarted by deceptive modes of visualization, as Bratton and Jermijenko discuss, and where there are calls to more mindfully engage the "material realities of digital technologies," as Forlano advises.[4] Such concerns are driven by the speed of development and the unfathomable abundance of sophisticated systems that provide the digital framework for virtual space, which are matched by their retreat into the ever-expanding opacities of black boxes.

Histories of the evolution of complicated technologies may suggest that such withdrawals are inevitable. For example, the Bauhaus-affiliated cultural historian Sigfried Giedion observed this very development. In *Mechanization Takes Command* Giedion described the historical development of ever more secure locks, from the "artistically wrought iron work" of the Gothic locksmith (figure 20.1) to the compact lock mechanism of Linus Yale Jr.'s cylinder lock. In his account, Giedion charted the necessary internalization of complexity to better facilitate the function of security.[5] Of course, the more pervasive the Yale cylinder lock, the less one was concerned with its inner workings, and thus the misleading thought that such a result is unavoidable. At the

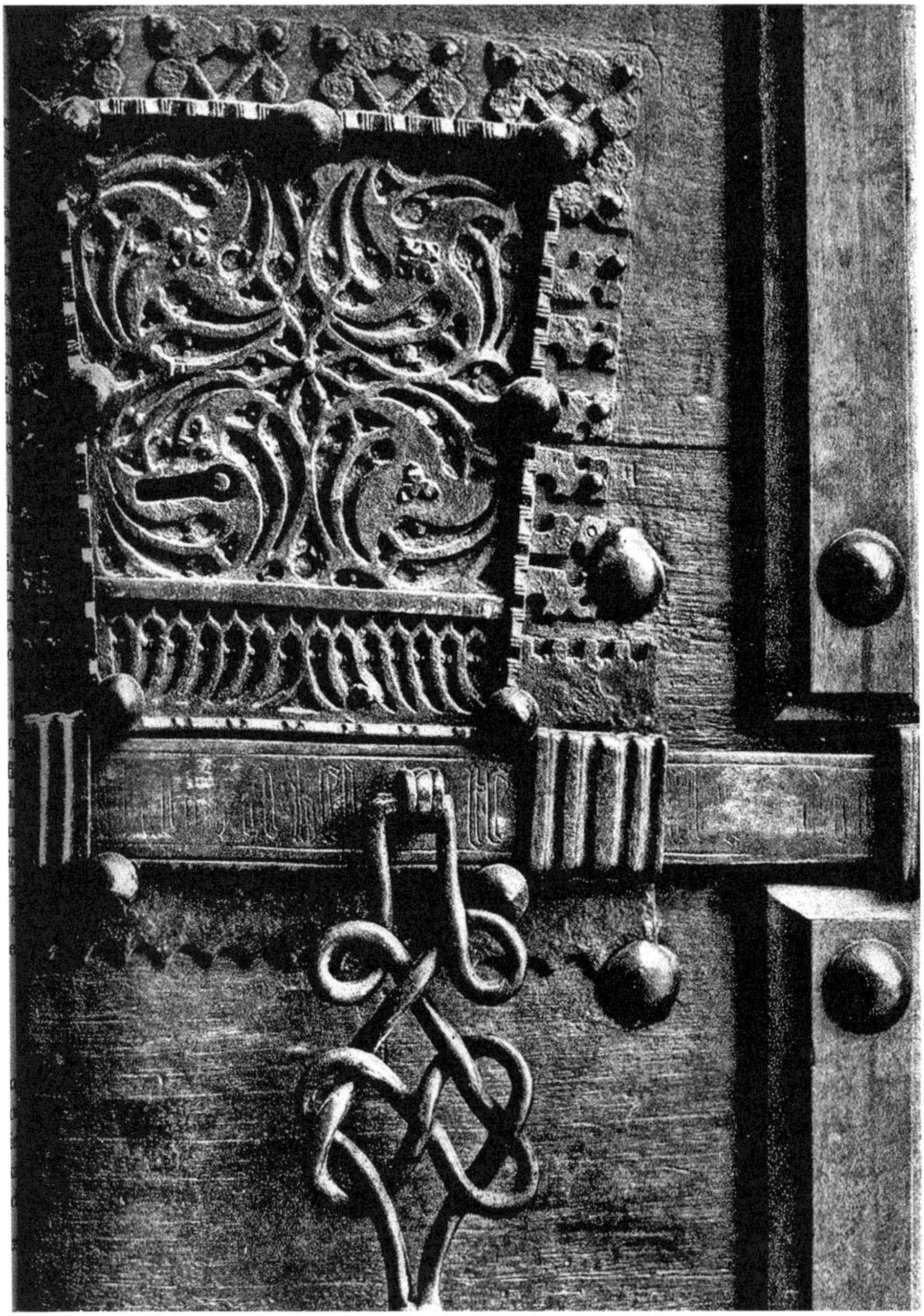

Figure 20.1
"Late Gothic Lock of a House at Visp, Switzerland" (Giedion, *Mechanization Takes Command*, 53).

same time that the technology of the cylinder lock was adopted everywhere, its mechanism became invisible to public scrutiny. Thus, the complexity of the lock was, as it is today, transparent only to specialists who possessed the skills of a locksmith. Giedion's is much the same story as that told by Weiser, who, along with his colleagues at Xerox PARC, studied the second nature of the backgrounding of technology as related to ubiquitous computing.[6] In our contemporary moment, the introduction of networked "smart" locks engenders more fluid interactions with everyday technologies, while at the same time it further widens what Kuniavsky refers to as "information shadows" that undergird our internet of things (figure 20.2).[7] Indeed, the simultaneous emergent agency of smart technologies and increasing withdrawal of their structural systems challenges us to consider, as Forlano encourages, the "politics at play" in the design of invisibility.[8]

Giedion's observation on the development of the modern deadbolt lock from its premodern "illuminated" predecessor was a lamentation of sorts. His mournful critique of the loss of affirmative and positive complexities of surfaces resonates with our contemporary concerns about hidden algorithms and control. I'll return to Giedion below, but first I will introduce a mid-twentieth-century confrontation with the dematerialization of complexity in what, in Giedion's day, was referred to as a theory of "dynamic iconography." In his book *Language of Vision* (1944), the then New Bauhaus instructor György Kepes defined dynamic iconography as the ability of design to integrate—to make visual so as to make perceivable—the intensities and complexities of the modern world. He claimed that design, through constructions of sophisticated optical and visual interfaces, could (and should) respond to and influence the "dynamic field of social existence."[9] For Kepes, the virtual space of visual display responded to social spaces and practices. In this sense, he argued that design should make visible what too often passed unnoticed in ever-changing modern environments. I take up dynamic iconography in order to propose its relevance to contemporary concerns about the politics of withdrawal and invisibility and how they intersect with discussions of visuality and iconicity as modes of engaging, or interfacing with, the material realities of digital technologies.

Kepes's concept of dynamic iconography—social space responsive to virtual space—reverses the logic of the dematerialization of complexity, suggesting that the modernist designer's proposal remains in dialogue with contemporary design discourses. Reviewing the concept of dynamic iconography, I briefly discuss iconicity and the cognitive and perceptual intricacies of surfaces integrating the flow of communication and information into everyday life.[10] Kepes was invested in a data-based positive science that revealed both cause and effect. His positive theory of dynamic iconography attempted

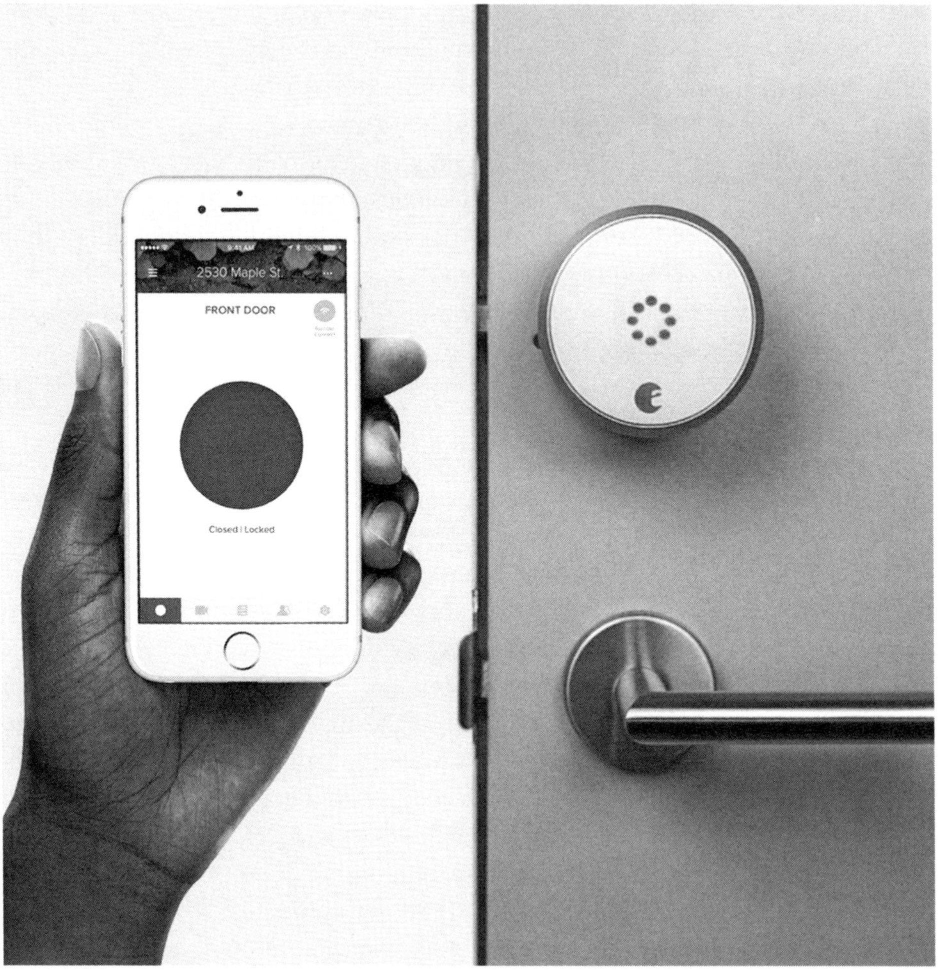

Figure 20.2
August Smart Lock Pro-Locked (© August Home 2018).

to construct a reality, and to alter the social world in doing so. Finally, for Kepes, surface and facticity were identical, since the goal of design was, for him, to bring complexity out into the open.[11]

During the mid-twentieth century, as is often the case today, the goal of designing for seamless interaction was to enhance function. Function was at the heart of Kepes's theorization of dynamic iconography, but, in highlighting function, he considered its social implications beyond the usual "form follows function" routine. In "Function in

Modern Design" he took an admonishing tone, stating that the meaning of the term "function" had migrated too far from its life source; the term too often referred to everything and nothing in design. Every pronouncement of the word "function," according to Kepes, revealed a perverse attachment to an illusion. This was, as he unambiguously proposed, design's self-delusion at midcentury (and perhaps remains to this day). His response to this error: the function of design is for humans to "function better, that is, [to] live fuller and freer."[12] Therefore, for Kepes, function was not a source for design to draw on or a reference to inform the process of design. Rather, as he proposed, function should be *in* design as an expression of its attentiveness to human social life.

Kepes's claims for function were in keeping with his concept of dynamic iconography, first articulated in his *Language of Vision.* As I mention above, Kepes theorized dynamic iconography to address the manner in which design integrated the dynamism of the modern world. "Thinking and seeing, in terms of static, isolated things identical only with themselves," he wrote, "have an initial inertia which cannot keep pace with the stride of life, thus cannot suggest values—plastic order—intrinsic in this dynamic field of social existence."[13] If design ceased to be dynamic (if it turned sclerotic), it would not inspire "positive social action," he held. Design can achieve the goal of dynamism through "plastic integration," or the formation and shaping of "unified, organic wholes."[14] Through such a plastic formation, as Kepes explained, the iconic becomes a "living form of human experience."[15]

In this characterization of function and dynamic iconography, Kepes maintained that design should be responsive; that is, it should reflect the vitality of a modern world made up of advanced technologies of communication and of industrial objects. There was a circular logic to his proposal. In this sense, the meaning of design—its function—was derived from its capacity to mimic its modern surroundings, and thereby expose the social and political intricacies of modern life. Social space innervated the virtual spaces of all manner of design. "Positive social action," therefore, was only possible by way of the visual presencing of dynamic iconography. As Kepes put the case in terms of function, "The living fiber of our unconscious responses is given by the concrete images of the surrounding environment."[16] The goal that he set for design, its functional capacity to direct humans to "live fuller and freer," was to turn unconscious responses into conscious actions. The failure of design—that is, its inability to properly activate function—would result in a disconnect between human cognitive and psychological capacities and the world at hand. As Kepes advised, design should provide "new equipment with which we must function if we are to maintain our equilibrium in a dynamic world."[17]

In his introduction to *Language of Vision*, entitled "Art Means Reality," Giedion wrote approvingly of Kepes's theory of dynamic iconography's "liberation of plastic elements." Visual plasticity involved a material approach to reality that, according to Giedion, culminated in a "new spatial conception." Crucial to an understanding of Kepes's theory of dynamic iconicity—as a matter of functionality—was Giedion's observation that Kepes showed "the contact of modern art [and design] with reality."[18] The "illuminated" keyhole of the Gothic lock that Giedion examined in *Mechanization Takes Command* acknowledged its situatedness between the iconic potential of the technical device and the world beyond the door by visually demarking a threshold that faced out to the social world. Like examples reproduced throughout Kepes's book, the dynamic iconicity of the Gothic lock—an example of contact between art and reality—iconically communicated its function of keeping out those without a key. As in Giedion's account of the outward-facing appearance of Gothic locks, Kepes's dynamic iconography placed design within the realm of the iconic, and more specifically within the realm of the visual communicative disclosure. The iconicity of Kepes's dynamic iconography is, for us today, what Sybille Krämer has acknowledged as the "cognitive power" of the graphic, diagrammatic, and/or notational systems.[19] While these systems are integral to human interaction with smart devices, the challenge remains of how to divulge the intrinsic logic of smart technologies through their outward-facing iconic presence. Dynamic iconography elicits (or affords) a cognitive power in us, a power that, as Kepes argued, could bring about such an *illumination*.

Considered today, dynamic iconography is relevant to contemporary discourses that focus on the so called "iconic turn." For example, there are echoes of Kepes in Boehm's understanding of the meaning-generating process of the image as distinct from language, and his distinguishing of iconic research from art history's reliance on external sources in iconographical research to derive meaning;[20] in Alloa's observation of the non-domain-specificity of the image in its pervasiveness;[21] in Hoel's analysis of iconic differential and how images are not "things to be seen but ... differential matrices that *make visible*";[22] and, finally, in Renner's caution that "images based on digital technology might be considered a potential threat to any democratic process."[23] The legacy of Kepes's dynamic iconography is not merely the inheritance of tacit and/or explicit knowledge of theories of the iconic. When inherited conventions of design are critically scrutinized, the challenge to designers and design is to reinterpret conventions through a process of improvisation, rather than mindlessly reapplying already existing forms. The dynamism that Kepes regarded as essential to proper social function was derived from the relationship between the image *of* social space and image *in* virtual space. Considered in terms of inheritance or legacy, design has long adopted

Kepes's world-changing attitude.[24] Yet his greatest frustration was that, in his lifetime, the world never did change in the direction he thought that it should.

What is most crucial to our contemporary circumstances is that in following Kepes we can explore how the image in its iconic virtuality unlocks the world's stock of imaginary possibilities. Dynamic iconography was, and continues to be, always pitched toward some speculative future in social space. The iconic character of design is, following Kepes, a premise or an exploratory assertion that indicates, in its organization of elements, some future outcome. In this sense, dynamic iconography resembles the social in that, as iconic, designed objects are not pictures of things (e.g., symbolic in the postmodern sense) but are materializations of interconnections and comparisons that permit observations of what *should* be the case. The age of speculative design, smart technology, and ambient intelligence, therefore, requires that a recognizable image in design bring to light what is obscured in the information shadows cast by contemporary technologies.

Notes

1. My thanks to Laura Forlano for her thoughtful comments on a first draft of this essay. Her insights pushed me to consider the vexing problems presented here.

2. By "virtual space" I mean to indicate modes of imaging and communicating without direct presence. In the case of contemporary digital technologies, facts are determined by the relationship of virtual space and social space. On these points, I borrow from David Summers's definition of the virtual as a "substitution and representation in two dimensions." See David Summers, *Real Spaces: World Art History and the Rise of Western Modernism* (London: Phaidon, 2002), 26.

3. For an overlooked account of this double-bind, see Jean-François Lyotard, *The Postmodern Condition: A Report on Knowledge* (Minneapolis: University of Minnesota Press, 1984), 60–67. On a more recent examination of the crisis of technological determinism and pacing, see Judy Wajcman, "High-Speed Society: Is the Pace of Life Accelerating?," in *Pressed for Time: The Acceleration of Life in Digital Capitalism* (Chicago: University of Chicago Press), 13–36.

4. Benjamin H. Bratton and Natalie Jermijenko, *Suspicious Images, Latent Interfaces* (New York: Architectural League of New York, 2009); and Laura Forlano, "Invisible Algorithms, Invisible Politics" (review essay), *Public Books*, February 12, 2018, http://www.publicbooks.org/invisible-algorithms-invisible-politics/.

5. Sigfried Giedion, *Mechanization Takes Command: A Contribution to Anonymous History* (Oxford: Oxford University Press, 1948), 51–66.

6. Mark Weiser, "The Computer for the 21st Century," *Scientific American* 265, no. 3 (1991), 94–105. Referring to Weiser's article on the backgrounding of technology, the philosopher and

design theorist Betti Marenko remarks, "The more that technology is woven seamlessly into the fabric of everyday life, the more it goes unnoticed. Users are particularly incognizant when they use ordinary objects whose technological operations are 'below the radar.'" For Marenko, the backgrounding of technological operations enhances the "emergent agency" of the internet of things. Betti Marenko, "Neo-Animism and Design," *Design and Culture* 6, no. 2 (July 2014), 230–231.

7. Mike Kuniavsky, *Smart Things: Ubiquitous Computing User Experience Design* (Amsterdam: Morgan Kaufmann, 2010), 79.

8. Forlano, "Invisible Algorithms, Invisible Politics."

9. György Kepes, *Language of Vision: Painting, Photography, Advertising-Design* (Chicago: Paul Theobald, 1944), 202.

10. The literature on iconicity is extensive. For an application of iconic theory closely related to the topic of this essay, see Inge Hinterwaldner, *The Systemic Image: A New Theory of Interactive Real-Time Simulations* (Cambridge, MA: MIT Press, 2017). Hinterwaldner argues that the iconic, or the material facticity of image effects, dominates computer simulations and impacts the rapidity of calculation for simulation. For a broader sample of key texts, see Gottfried Boehm, "Die Wiederkehr der Bilder," in *Was ist ein Bild?*, ed. Gottfried Boehm (Munich: Wilhelm Fink Verlag, 1994), 11–38; W. J. T. Mitchell, "The Pictorial Turn," in *Picture Theory* (Chicago: University of Chicago Press, 1995), 11–34; Horst Bredekamp, "A Neglected Tradition? Art History as *Bildenwissenschaft*," *Critical Inquiry* 29, no. 3 (Spring 2003), 418–428; Hans Belting, "Image, Medium, Body: A New Approach to Iconology," *Critical Inquiry* 31, no. 2 (Winter 2005), 302–319; and Whitney Davis, *A General Theory of Visual Culture* (Princeton, NJ: Princeton University Press, 2011).

11. While completing a rewrite of *Language of Vision*, Kepes was already at work on an exhibition and his next book *The New Landscape in Art and Science* (1956). In *The New Landscape*, according to Halpern, Kepes argues for an embrace of advanced forms of visualization that would cease to operate "at the levels of the human sensorium." Kepes refers to "self-referential technologies of perception," and writes that new sensory technologies "have made a new order of objectivity possible when looking at the world" (Kepes quoted in Halpern). As I understand the "new order of objectivity" that Kepes refers to, self-referential technologies of perception—optical scanning devices or disembodied eyes—perceive worlds that do not appear to humans. Kepes's "new order of objectivity" is very much like what Zylinska refers to as "nonhuman photography." It may be that Kepes acknowledges the possibility that nonhuman virtual spaces do not necessarily have to correlate to human social spaces. Therefore, the shift from "vision" to "landscape" may indicate a shift from humanism to posthuman in Kepes's theories of visualization. See Orit Halpern, *Beautiful Data: A History of Vision and Reason since 1945* (Durham: Duke University Press, 2014), 94; and Joanna Zylinska, *Nonhuman Photography* (Cambridge, MA: MIT Press, 2017).

12. György Kepes, "Function in Modern Design," in Kepes et al., *Graphic Forms: The Arts as Related to the Book* (Cambridge, MA: Harvard University Press, 1949), 3–5.

13. Kepes, *Language of Vision*, 202

14. Ibid., 15. On Kepes and Gestalt theories of wholeness see Michael J. Golec, "A Natural History of a Disembodied Eye: The Structure of György Kepes's *Language of Vision*," *Design Issues* 18, no. 2 (Spring 2002), 3–16; Reinhold Martin, *The Organizational Complex: Architecture, Media, and Corporate Space* (Cambridge, MA: MIT Press, 2003), 42–79; and Julia Moszkowicz, "Gestalt and Graphic Design: An Exploration of the Humanistic and Therapeutic Effects of Visual Organization," *Design Issues* 27, no. 4 (Autumn 2011), 56–67.

15. Kepes, *Language of Vision*, 30.

16. Ibid., 209.

17. Ibid., 12.

18. Sigfried Giedion, "Art Means Reality," in Kepes, *Language of Vision*, 7.

19. Sybille Krämer, "Graphism and Flatness: The Line as Mediator between Time and Space, Intuition and Concept," in *The Power of Line*, ed. Marzia Faietti and Gerhard Wolf (Munich: Hirmer, 2013), 13.

20. Gottfried Boehm and W. J. T. Mitchell, "Pictorial versus Iconic Turn: Two Letters," in *The Pictorial Turn*, ed. Neal Curtis (London: Routledge, 2010), 10–12, 14.

21. Emmanuel Alloa, "Intensive, Not Extensive," in *What Is an Image?*, ed. James Elkins and Maja Neaf (University Park: Pennsylvania State University Press, 2011), 150.

22. Aud Sissel Hoel, "Differential Images," in Elkins and Neaf, *What Is an Image?*, 154.

23. Michael Renner, "Practice-Led Iconic Research: Towards a Research Methodology for Visual Communications," *Visible Language* 51, no. 3–52, no. 1 (December 2017–April 2018), 14.

24. One example is Kevin Lynch's *The Image of the City* (1960) and its methodological claims for a "two-way process between the observer and his [or her] environment." Lynch's idea that there exists a directly "perceptual form of the city" was first formulated in his work with Kepes on a Rockefeller Foundation research project on the "Perceptual Form of the City." Later, with the quasi-cinematic layout of *The View from the Road* (1964), Lynch and his coauthors took up questions of imageability and mobility posed in Kepes's "Notes on Expression and Communication in the Cityscape" (1961). Recent work by ScanLAB Projects suggests otherwise (https://scanlabprojects.co.uk/). Using light field sensors and/or Lidar, ScanLAB Projects has revealed that there exist virtual spaces apart from the human perceptual form of the city. ScanLAB Projects and its emphasis on what Merleau-Ponty might call the "anonymous visibility" of the city realize Kepes's "new order of objectivity" in ways that he and his followers may not have intended. See Maurice Merleau-Ponty, *The Visible and the Invisible* (Evanston: Northwestern University Press, 1968), 142.

21 Telephone, Color Chart, Napkin

Logistical Legacies of the Bauhaus

Matthew Hockenberry

From the moment it was established, the Bauhaus was a site of investigation into not only art and design but the possibilities of a new means of creation—one founded on experiments into distribution, mobility, and assembly. From Walter Gropius's adaptation of architecture for the age of machines to László Moholy-Nagy's "telephone pictures," the Bauhaus provided insights into the nature of operation in the modern world. In the formation of his school, Gropius spoke of the "universal unity" that would replace the dualistic conception of the creative and creation. But, as I will suggest, one of the legacies of this unity was the radical distribution of productive practice through the instruments of modernity.[1] In its wholehearted embrace of modernity's constraints, and the new infrastructures of design and distribution it employed, the logistical legacy of the Bauhaus leaves behind a form of production that is, if not suspect (in the case of Moholy-Nagy's *Telephonbild*), at the very least obfuscating and instrumental. This chapter reflects on the logistical legacies of the Bauhaus and their implications for the future of making, not only in artistic practice but in industrial manufacture. This is evident not only in the practice of later artists like Andy Warhol, Sol LeWitt, Tony Smith, and Donald Judd, but in contemporary productions ranging from Atelier Van Lieshout's Almost Perfect Chair—designed on a cocktail napkin and sent, without instruction, for production in China—to the idea of digital assembly itself.

Toward a Universal Unity

While its beginning was perceived, by the Weimar establishment, as radical, the early years of the Bauhaus followed from Gropius's desire not to abandon the legacy of artistic practice but rather to infuse it with the rigor of craft—to dispense with "art for art's sake" and its arrogant snobbery. It would also bring an orientation toward the more mechanical ends of modern production. In the earliest days such an outcome may have seemed surprising. After all, Gropius wrote, "mechanized work is lifeless, proper only to the lifeless machine." So long as the machine "remains an end in itself rather than a means of freeing the intellect from the burden of mechanical labor, the individual will remain enslaved and society will remain disordered." This was reflected, at least initially, in the appointment of the expressionist Johannes Itten to teach the *Vorkurs*, the preliminary instruction from which all Bauhaus students would begin.[2] And while this arrangement seemed to place the Bauhaus as a bridge between the romantic legacy of expressionism and the rational rigor that would come to define the New Objectivity, Itten and Gropius came into conflict over the direction of the course. When Itten left in late 1922 it created the opportunity for Josef Albers to be appointed, a responsibility he shared with the Hungarian artist László Moholy-Nagy.

Albers eliminated the expressionistic tendencies that had characterized Itten's teaching in favor of experimentation and objectivity. It was an instrumental approach to the productive process, where no single method (or material) stood as the answer to any particular problem. "Ours is an economically oriented age," he wrote, where "economic form arises out of function and material." It is only natural, he suggested, that the study of material—the attempt to come to terms with form—would proceed from an understanding of function.[3] Albers challenged students with materials as varied as paper, wire mesh, corrugated cardboard, glass, tin foil, and plastic, and he encouraged them to plan with an "economy of form measured in relation to the anticipated expenditure of material and labor."[4] It reaffirmed the commitment to "economy, speed and efficiency" that had not only led Gropius to the idea of the "factory-made building" but had produced this new school in its image.[5]

Telephone Pictures, Telephone Programs

One of the questions for the Bauhaus was how to respond to the rationalism that had increasingly come to define industrial practice. The 1920 *Dada Almanac* derided this seemingly absurd reality, suggesting that through technologies like telecommunication, any painter who suffered from an "aversion to manual labor" could just as well *order* pictures and have them fashioned by a carpenter.[6] In response, Moholy-Nagy would write an account claiming to have done exactly that, presenting the results of a 1922 experiment in "telephonic reproduction" at the Der Sturm gallery in Berlin. In place of a carpenter he brought in a sign factory, ordering, by telephone, five paintings on porcelain. At one end of the line sat Moholy-Nagy, with, he wrote, the factory's color chart before him as he sketched paintings on graph paper. At the other sat the factory supervisor, who "took down the dictated shapes in the correct position." As

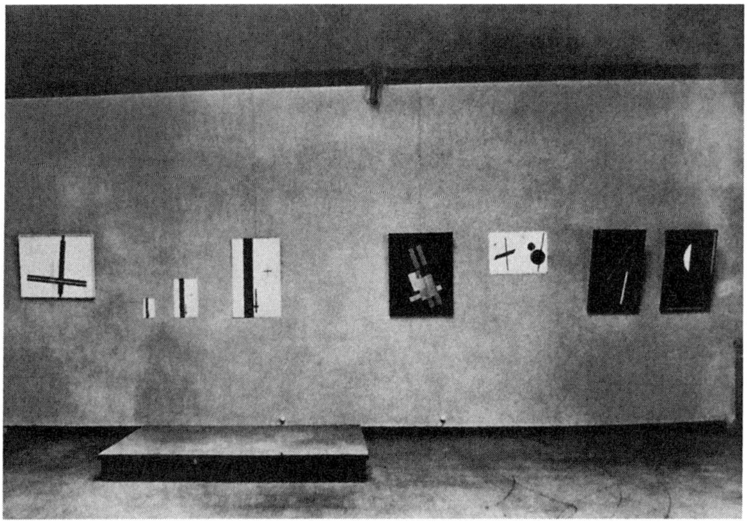

Emaille im Februar 1924

In dieser Zeit der fabrikmäßigen Produktion und der technischen Exaktheit streben wir auch danach, Werke der bildenden Kunst mit vollkommener Präzision auszuführen. Unter den neuen Arbeiten, die ich im Februar im Sturm ausstelle, zeige ich eine Reihe von Emaillebildern, die auf maschinellem Wege hergestellt worden sind. Diese Art der Bildherstellung kommt allerdings nur für Arbeiten in Betracht, die mit dem Willen zur präzisen und unpersönlichen Technik geschaffen wurden. Werke dieser Art kann man auf der Grundlage der Ostwaldschen Farbentafeln und eines Maßnetzes jederzeit in der Fabrik herstellen lassen. Man kann sie also sogar telefonisch bestellen.

Meine Ausstellung zeigt auch die Partitur-Skizze einer mechanischen Exzentrik, die durch die Synthese von Form, Bewegung, Licht (Farbe) und Ton an die Stelle des heutigen Theaters treten will. Da die heutigen Film-, Variété- und Theaterdirektoren ihr Publikum gewiß nicht falsch einschätzen, kann dieser Entwurf zunächst nur Ausstellungs- statt Ausführungsobjekt sein.

L. Moholy-Nagy

Figure 21.1
Exhibition view of Moholy-Nagy's *Emaille* series, 1922, and his notice in *Der Sturm*, 1924.

a pattern of production and means for artistic endeavor, it was, the artist would celebrate, "like playing chess by correspondence."[7]

This is striking given contemporary conditions, in which the very structures of digital assembly depend entirely on these sorts of programmatic fabrications. But technologies like the telephone do not become the foundation of a new kind of productive practice all on their own. Just as one cannot (reasonably) play chess without common knowledge of the board and all the pieces, so Moholy-Nagy's work required an understanding of the ensemble necessary for its coordination. It required, as John Durham Peters might put it, its own complement of *logistical media*—the sort of standards defined not by content but their ability to orient and index in space and time.[8] Despite Moholy-Nagy's comparison, there was nothing quite as recognizable as a chessboard here. Of all the material mediators sprawling out of his account, the most prominent seemed to be the otherwise mundane color chart. But in spite of its unremarkable appearance, it was not only a more *contemporary* creation than the telephone; it was a necessary condition for the entire enterprise. Indeed, while the telephone provided the infrastructure through which logistical signals could be sent, the color chart offered a manifest representation of the sort of systems necessary for decoding them. On its own, the chart would prove a significant instrument for Bauhaus artists (see also Arnold, this volume). Coupled with the capabilities of contemporary industrial practice, and the sort of standardization of form required of them, it was emblematic of the logistical legacy that would come to *define* Bauhaus instruction, from Itten to Albers to Moholy-Nagy himself.[9]

As Bruno Latour has noted, "by telephone," and by telephone alone, "you and a salesperson *cannot* match samples of wallpaper." Without standards, systems, and fixed references—here those that array the color spectrum and number it accordingly—rational coordination would be impossible. For any device to operate remotely, to increase the effective range of productive operation beyond the immediate scale of conventional human assembly, it must be compiled with a particular structure of system in mind. So while one cannot match colors by telephone, one *can* "based on a color chart the salesperson has given ... select a reference number." In Moholy-Nagy's account, Wilhelm Ostwald's chart becomes the first of many Latourian immutables, marvelously mobilized in a "comprehensive system" of control.[10] Here is Gropius's "universal unity," not as some abstraction, but in the potential of these protocols to carry with them representations accessible to the new programming of creation.

It was the grid of graph paper that served to constitute the site of study for this work, as it did for other Bauhaus artists. As Bernhard Siegert explains, the grid orders a space, making it addressable. Constituting a new world of objects imagined by a subject, it is "a medium that operationalizes deixis."[11] Rosalind Krauss contends that it was the grid that announced the "will to silence" of modern art—its "hostility" to literature, narrative, and discourse. But while for her it maps "the surface of the painting," the space it coordinates for Moholy-Nagy is composed by the disjoint geographies of production. As Louis Kaplan has suggested, it is through this that Moholy can sketch the network *itself*.[12] While Krauss argues that the grid walls the visual arts "against the intrusion of speech," the effect it has here is to open them up, ruling them for transmission *by* speech—a development with profound implications for artists like Warhol and LeWitt.[13] As Walter Gropius put it, "we must know both vocabulary and grammar in order to speak a language; only then can we communicate our thoughts."[14] As the "universal" connection of the grid separated screen from reality, the language of assembly becomes fixed with form. It does more than merely "resemble the world"—it now reencodes and reassembles it.[15]

It is *this* realization, of a *system* of code and structures that necessarily includes, here, the color chart as *catalog*, graph paper as *order form*, and the telephone as *interface*, that positions Moholy-Nagy's productive arrangement as the programming language of contemporary assembly. This reconfiguration was not without consequence. With the originary "place where it happens to be" now removed, the "presence in time and space" that had bound means and maker to their otherwise "unique existence" ceased

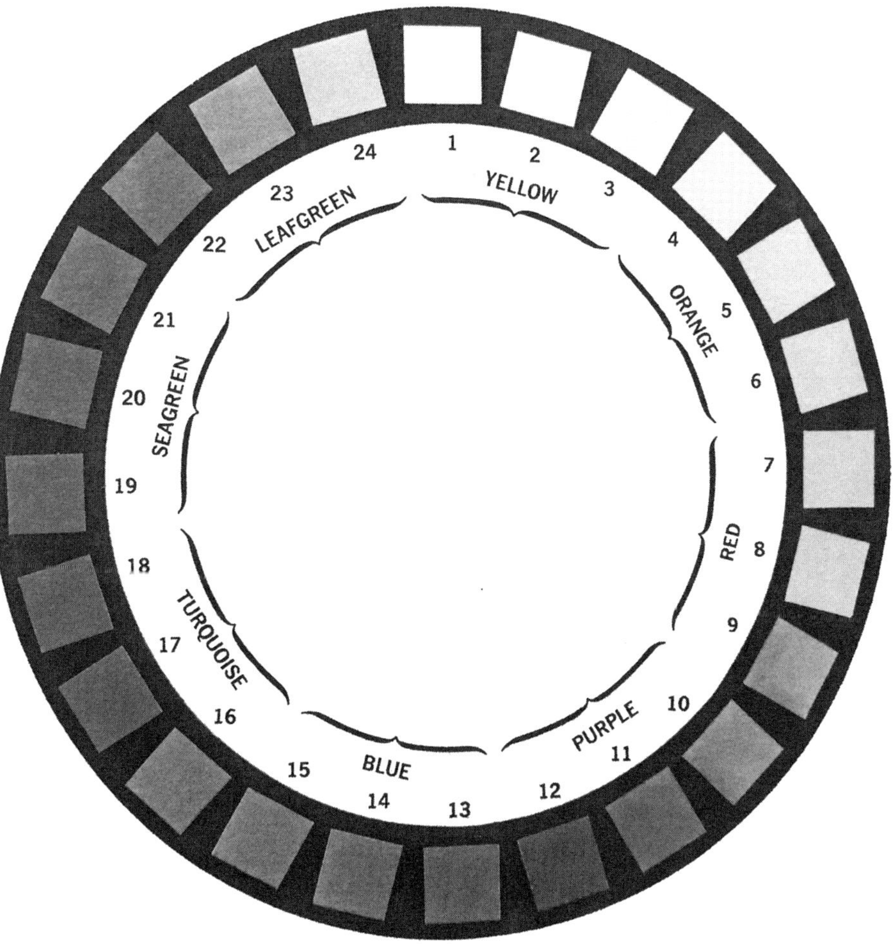

Figure 21.2
The Ostwald color system plates in *Die Farbenfibel* (The color primer), 1916–1917. (Also plate 18.)

to be.[16] The process of analog production had been marked, literally, by this singular situation, the creation of an original from which descendent copies were produced. Even if printing and pressing brought the idea that there could be "multiple originals," even if Duchamp's readymades had questioned the "originality" of the "original," they'd still rested on the same fundamental conception of process. From the hand of the artist comes the original. From the original there can come only copies. And while Moholy-Nagy's work may not absent him entirely from this process, it does seem to remove him from its past articulation. Instead of carving and casting, he has only to determine, "precisely," the position of his form within the "minute squares" of the graph paper's grid. The result is a "process of pixelation" that anticipates the mediation of computation, both on the screen that will display its results and on the punched cards that will carefully encode its content. In order to explain the composition over the phone, Moholy-Nagy had to convert "the art work from a physical entity to a description," producing a new "relationship of semiotic equivalence." The effect was that the art object would no longer stand as the "result of the hand or the craft of the artist." Indeed, it is Moholy-Nagy's decision to call a sign factory—a "fabricator," "capable of providing industrial finishing and scientific precision," instead of, say, "an amateur painter"—that attests to this transformation.[17]

Each of Moholy-Nagy's paintings is numbered (*EM 1, 2, 3*) from largest to smallest, otherwise identified only by the material on which the bonded surfaces were made. In this regard each *Emaille* is the same—identical in composition but variable in size. But quite unlike Monet's sequential paintings, Eduardo Kac points out, these pictures are "not a series." They were not constituted in sequence or succession, preceding or proceeding from some "original." They represent the singular result of the same productive act. This "multiplication of the final object in three variations," Kac suggests, is what is responsible for finally destroying "the notion of the 'original' work." As a signal for the promiscuous potential of mechanical reproduction, this act of assembly has produced objects that stand outside the conventions of the prior productive practice. They are constituted by codes, inscribed by information, and mediated by machines in a way that gestures to the understanding that they were not transmitted, and indeed *could not have been transmitted*, in "the form of an image made by the human hand."[18] As a consequence, they become "copies without an original," each a new version with the same proliferative potential as the last.[19] Like Warhol's silkscreens, they are "'original' reproductions," *programmed* rather than painted.[20] Readied as a new sort of ready-made, they are born without aura. And as such they can be produced (or reproduced) entirely at will—and nothing will seem to have been lost. For Moholy-Nagy, this was the pinnacle of the Bauhaus ideal—that the "constructivist concept," the "objectivity" of visual production and value, could be "independent of the artist's inspiration."[21] "In this age of industrial production and technical exactness," he wrote, one must strive to produce work with "total precision." His series at Der Sturm offered nothing less than a new "manner of manufacturing," one possible *only* for "works created with a will to precise and impersonal technique."[22] But this, the undeniable realization of the Bauhaus's experiments in distribution, mobility, and assembly, seems all but overshadowed by its startling implications for questions of authenticity, originality, and authorship.

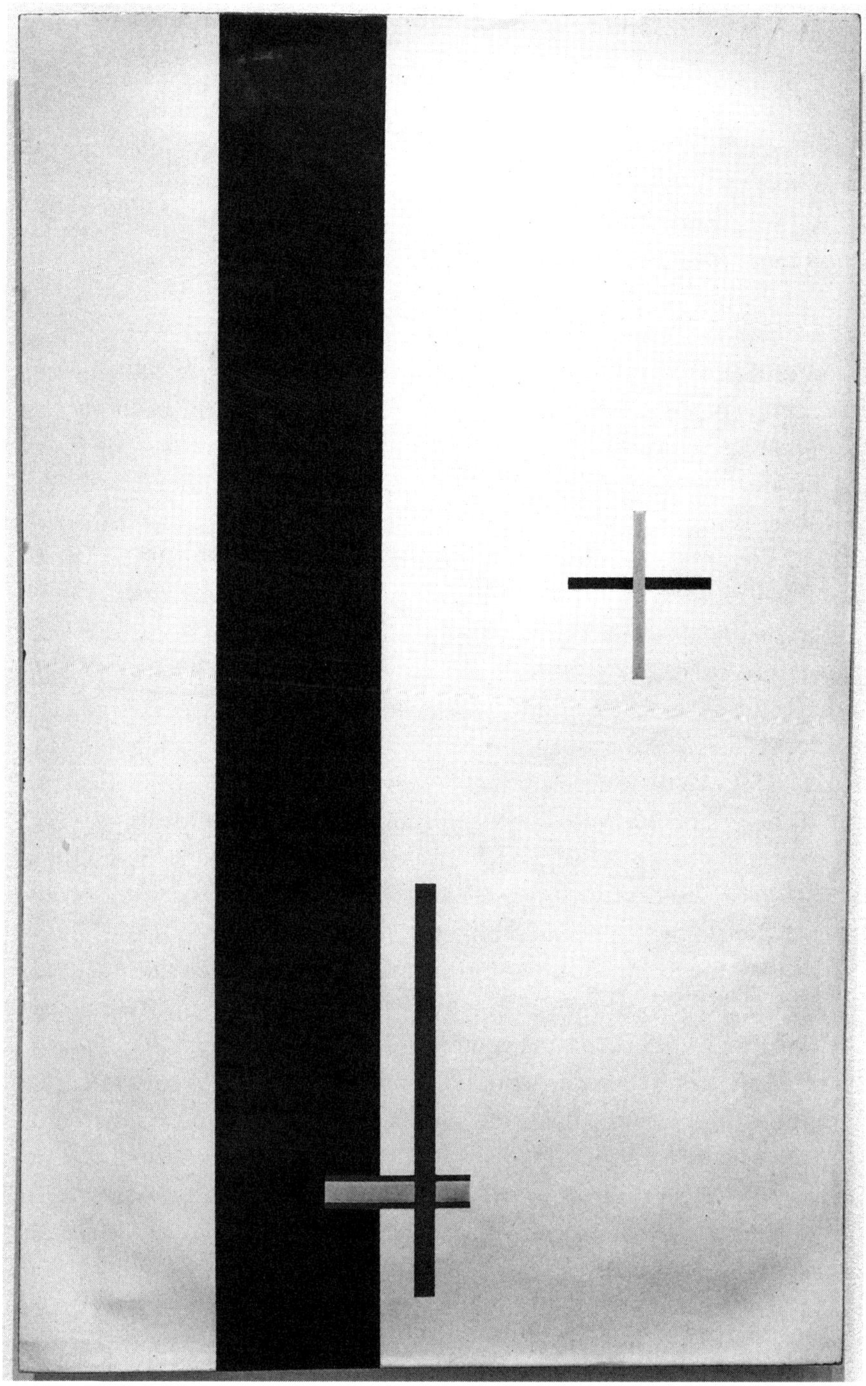

Figure 21.3

László Moholy-Nagy, *EM 1* (telephone picture), 1923. Porcelain enamel on steel. © The Museum of Modern Art/Licensed by SCALA/Art Resource, NY. (Also plate 16.)

In answering *this* call to the unity of the creative and creation, we find that neither remains intact. Originals are now reproductions. "Impersonal techniques" are entirely removed from the person.

Logistical Legacies of the Bauhaus

The legacy of these logistical experiments, particularly in their orientation toward the protocols of rational assembly, can clearly be seen in the work of later artists. Andy Warhol would often call himself by the same name he gave to the building where he worked—each, he explained, was a "factory." By the 1970s it was such a well-ordered one that Warhol needn't be involved at all. He was so removed from the details of his designs that, as his printer Rupert Smith claimed, anyone could make them. "Even Augusto [the security man] was doing the painting"; they actually called it "art by telephone."[23] Indeed, in the winter of 1969 the newly established Museum of Contemporary Art in Chicago had announced plans for an exhibition with that very name, with thirty-six artists from the United States and Europe instructed to "relay by telephone" work that could be "executed by an intermediary." By graph paper and landline, artists like Sol LeWitt plumbed the productive potential of logistical communication. LeWitt's variation on his wall drawings, for example, gave instructions for a 3,600-square "program." "Like a composer who writes notes for the pianist," he explained, his work would be interpreted, compiled, and constructed by a remote draftsman. The museum's director, Jan van der Marck, avowed a formal realization of the aesthetic possibilities of objective assembly. With an exhibition gathering the work of artists who sought "anonymous or indirect production" by, for example, "sending orders in to factories," the functional and rationalized design of the Bauhaus was taken up as a product of an artistic practice that was coded, not crafted.[24]

But the most lasting consequence of the Bauhaus's experiments seems to be in demonstrating the capability of modern media to radically alter the distribution of all sorts of productive practice. As John Brooks writes, the effect of the telephone was not just to produce speech, but to direct it toward an other in "constant demand for immediate readiness."[25] After all, what had been the first telephone call if not such a demand? "Mr. Watson—come here—I want to see you." The result, Alexander Graham Bell recorded to his "delight," had been a ready response to his request. Moholy-Nagy's contribution tethered this demand to its own assembling force, as the constituent connection for an entire "network of potential relationships among apparatuses"—"activating," as Brigid Doherty wrote, "from a distance, the factory's machinery."[26] This transformation is what connects Moholy-Nagy's sign factory to contemporary configurations, to

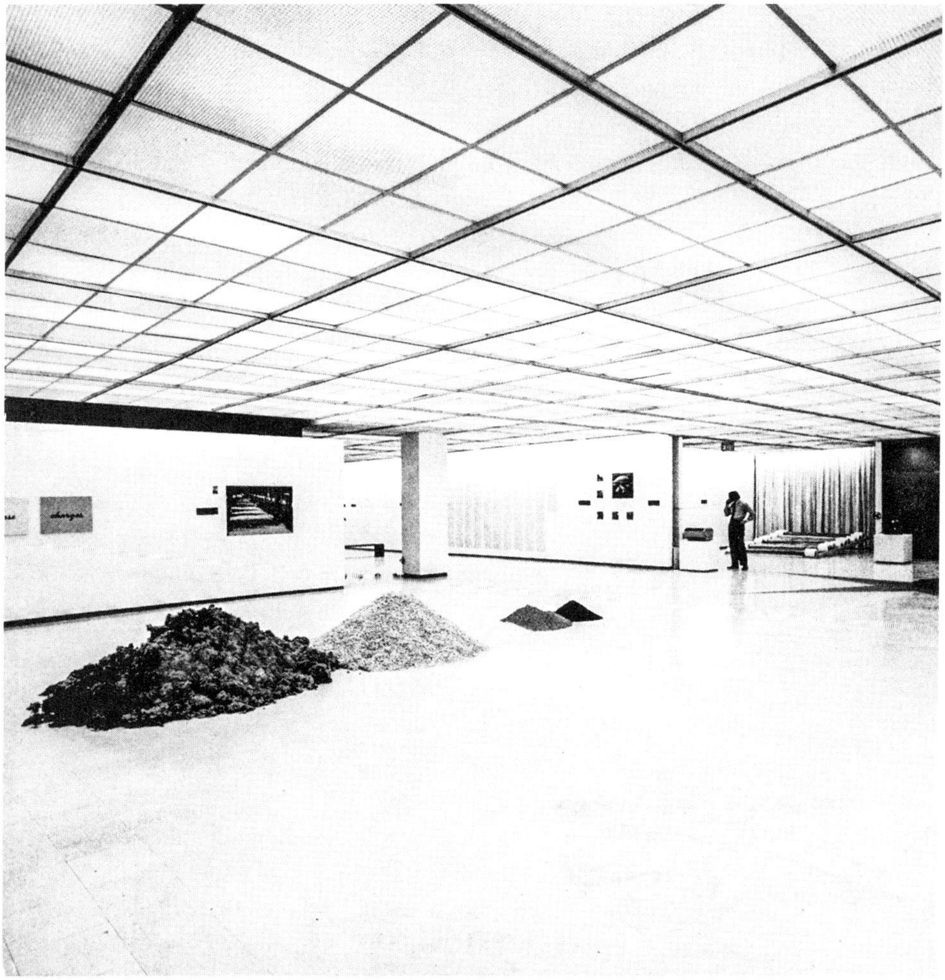

Figure 21.4

Back cover of exhibition catalog for "Art by Telephone" (album sleeve for a 33 rpm, 12-inch vinyl record), Museum of Contemporary Art Chicago, 1969.

the aesthetic of global bricolage, the endless versions and varieties that define much of modern assembly. If the transition to the digital is marked by the moment when the model and mold became one, then digital designs seem indebted to this new "manner of manufacture." After all, how could it matter *where* a specific series of ones and zeros was first assembled, or indeed what they might have been prior to their emanation on the screen?

Perhaps it is no surprise, then, that "art by telephone" has given way to *everything* by telephone. In the assembly of the remote factories that define contemporary production, designers find themselves tied to a network as functionally present as it is materially and socially removed. The logistical legacies of the Bauhaus not only animate "lifeless machines" but—with disturbing frequency—the human forces that underlie their undead appearance. It is a power of production that was previously unimaginable, now programmed into protocols that support all manner of anonymous exchange. The first generation of modern "makers" marveled at the unexpected impact of their design decisions. Demands for innovation coupled with the now-familiar refrain of "economy, speed and efficiency" brought to bear supply chains terminating in workers tasked with stitching cases in six seconds or less, or hand-placing connectors for a nickel apiece—with "words, colors, and letters," all drawn by hand.[27]

But perhaps the most compelling example of this legacy is still to be found in the world of design, with the Almost Perfect (King Kong) chair that was designed by Dutch firm Atelier Van Lieshout in 2005. Its suggestion of a completely turnkey telecommunicative operation begins, not on a grid of graph paper, not in the margins of the global apparatus of production, but within the margins of a cocktail napkin. To achieve the unique aesthetic of the chair's design, AVL sent a sketch across the network to "an anonymous Chinese company" for final production.[28] An operation that would have previously produced a complex array of processes for a designer to direct (the selection of material, identification of sources, production of detailed technical drawings, models, and prototypes) came here with no such information. The realization of this work suggests that the consequences of production have been themselves redirected. Far from precisely placed pixels, careful details of manufacture are capable of being replaced by a careless slip of the pen, and by factories that must sort out these scribbles. Still, as Michelle Kuo reminds us, even this legacy may not be everything it seems. Like the suspicion that surrounds the veracity of Moholy-Nagy's experiment with the telephone pictures, the "mythical accounts" of firms like AVL and of artists like Donald Judd employing industrial manufacturing "at arm's length" are never as aloof as they might appear.[29] The Almost Perfect chair's unnamed "Chinese company" was not so distant after all—housed in a factory the firm's partner had established.

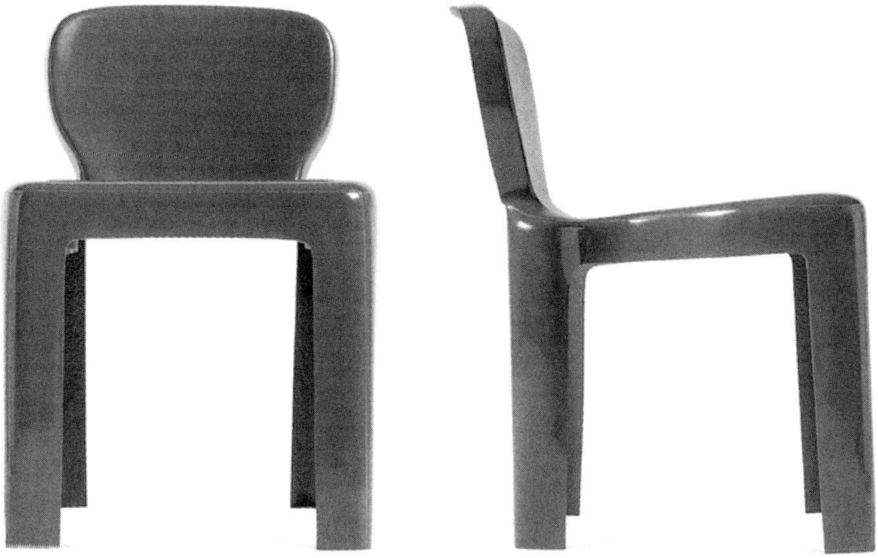

Figure 21.5
Atelier Van Lieshout, Almost Perfect (King Kong) chair, 2005. Image courtesy of Atelier van Lieshout.

Acknowledgments

My thanks to Ella Klik, Kate Crawford, and Patrick Davison, to Bernhard Siegert, Lorenz Engell, and the IKKM, and to this book's editors—especially Mike Ananny—for their generous comments and critique.

Notes

1. Walter Gropius, "The Theory and Organization of the Bauhaus," in Herbert Bayer, Walter Gropius, and Ise Gropius, *Bauhaus, 1919–1928* (New York: Museum of Modern Art, 1938), 20–29.

2. Walter Gropius, "Manifest und Programm des Staatlichen Bauhauses, April 1919," in *Das Bauhaus*, ed. Hans M. Wingler (Cologne: DuMont, 1962), 39–41.

3. Josef Albers, "Werklicher Formunterricht," *Bauhaus* 2, no. 3 (1928), 3–7.

4. Oliver Barker, "Experimentation, Not Replication: Josef Albers and the Vorkurs," *Bauhaus Magazine* 1 (March 2011).

5. Éva Forgács, *The Bauhaus Idea and Bauhaus Politics* (Budapest: Central European University Press, 1995).

6. "In principle no difference was made between painting and ironing handkerchiefs. Painting was treated as a functional task and the good painter was recognized, for instance, by the fact that he ordered his works from a carpenter, giving his specifications on the phone." Alexander Partens (a pseudonym for Tristan Tzara, Hans Arp, and Walter Semer), "Dada Art," in *The Dada Almanac*, ed. Richard Huelsenbeck (1920; London: Atlas Press, 1993), 95.

7. László Moholy-Nagy, "Abstract of an Artist" (1944), in *The New Vision and Abstract of an Artist* (New York: Wittenborn, 1947), 79. See also László Moholy-Nagy, "Emaille im Februar 1924," *Der Sturm* 15 (February 1924).

8. Carolyn L. Kane and John Durham Peters, "Speaking into the iPhone: An Interview with John Durham Peters, or, Ghostly Cessation for the Digital Age," *Journal of Communication Inquiry* 34, no. 2 (2010), 123.

9. Wilhelm Ostwald's *Die Farbenfibel* having been published in 1916.

10. Exchanging, here, the Ostwald color chart for Munsell's. See Latour's description in *Science in Action: How to Follow Scientists and Engineers through Society* (Cambridge, MA: Harvard University Press, 1987), 227.

11. Bernhard Siegert, *Cultural Techniques: Grids, Filters, Doors, and Other Articulations of the Real* (New York: Fordham University Press, 2014), 98.

12. Louis Kaplan, "The Telephone Paintings: Hanging Up Moholy," *Leonardo* 26, no. 2 (1993), 166.

13. Rosalind Krauss, "Grids," *October* 9 (Summer 1979), 50–64.

14. Gropius, "The Theory and Organization of the Bauhaus."

15. Bruno Latour, *Pandora's Hope: Essays on the Reality of Science Studies* (Cambridge, MA: Harvard University Press, 1999), 58–59.

16. Walter Benjamin, "The Work of Art in the Age of Mechanical Reproduction," in *Illuminations*, ed. Hannah Arendt (London: Fontana, 1968), 217–221.

17. Eduardo Kac, *Telepresence and Bio Art: Networking Humans, Rabbits, and Robots* (Ann Arbor: University of Michigan Press, 2005).

18. Brigid Doherty, "Constructions in Enamel," in *Bauhaus 1919–1933: Workshops for Modernity*, ed. Barry Bergdoll and Leah Dickerman (New York: Museum of Modern Art, 2009), 130–133.

19. Kac, *Telepresence and Bio Art.*

20. The descriptive given by the collection entry for Andy Warhol's *Pepper Pot* (1968) in the Whitney Museum of American Art.

21. Sybil Moholy-Nagy, *Moholy-Nagy: Experiment in Totality* (Cambridge, MA: MIT Press, 1969), xv.

22. Moholy-Nagy, "Emaille im Februar 1924."

23. Bob Colacello, *Holy Terror: Andy Warhol Close Up* (New York: Cooper Square Press, 1990), 478.

24. Press release, Museum of Contemporary Art, Chicago, September 30, 1969.

25. John Brooks, "The First and Only Century of Telephone Literature," in *The Social Impact of the Telephone*, ed. Ithiel de Sola Pool (Cambridge, MA: MIT Press, 1977); and Kac, *Telepresence and Bio Art*, 33.

26. Doherty, "Constructions in Enamel."

27. See, for example, Andrew "Bunnie" Huang, "Adventures in Manufacturing," in *The Hardware Hacker: Adventures in Making and Breaking Hardware* (San Francisco: No Starch Press, 2017), where Huang reprints a series of blog posts from 2007 detailing his early experiences in mass manufacture.

28. Jennifer Allen, Aaron Betsky, Rudi Laermans, and Wouter Vanstiphout, *Atelier Van Lieshout* (Rotterdam: NAi, 2007), 287, catalog description for the Almost Perfect (King Kong) chair: "Instead of the designer, random and external factors in the production process decided the chair's final appearance. Far from a slick product fresh from the factory, the chair has irregularities, a non-geometrical shape and a handmade look—features that make for a better product."

29. Michelle Kuo, "Industrial Revolution: The History of Fabrication," *Artforum* 46, no. 2 (October 2007), 306–315.

22 Bauhaus Generative

Avant-Garde to Algorithmic Aesthetics in Three Chairs

B. Coleman

Generative Bauhaus

In 1926, the Bauhaus designer Marcel Breuer created an advertisement for a film that did not exist, entitled "A Bauhaus Movie Lasting Five Years." The movie poster showed a filmstrip of six images cut together, spanning several years of Breuer chair designs. It began with the 1921 wood and textile African Chair, moved through other increasingly minimalist wooden chairs to land on the 1925 tubular-steel B3 lounge chair, and ended with an image of a prototypically modernist Bauhaus woman floating on a chair made of air, with the date of "19??."[1] At first glance, Breuer's poster shows a linear development from the romantic ethos of the early *völkisch* years of the Bauhaus to the city-scale industrial design of its iconic fame, crescendoing with a disappearance of materiality altogether. The sequence posits Breuer's own future; over his 50 years of architecture and design practice he moved toward a horizon line of "heavy lightness" that progressively stripped away materiality for light and structured space.[2]

And yet, in thinking of the ongoing impact of the Bauhaus—100 years with incalculable half-life decay—there is an opportunity to see this poster with its sequence as also illuminating the recursive. In other words, what if Breuer's speculative exercise is a film *loop* that picks up at the end—the moment of pure air structures—to return to the spirit of the symbolic and hand-carved? The Bauhaus "future" we continue to live in is a profoundly generative modernity: a legacy of infrastructure and aesthetics that frame how we know a smooth, executable first world and the traces of other worlds that harbor more fugitive logics of the subaltern and the surround. I use the pronoun "we" in this case and not "one" as it is hard to discern who, if anyone, has escaped the touch of this ontological and aesthetic empire, whether they are located at center or periphery.

Despite the grandeur of its legacy, an effect both desired and resisted by the Bauhaus members themselves, I address a more humble scale of object: the generative relationship (how they are culturally productive and formally produced in relation to each other) between three chairs. The first two, by Breuer, are the African Chair and the B3 club chair. I compare their histories with that of a newly minted model, the 2017 computationally produced Elbo chair coming out of the Autodesk generative studio. Speaking to a Bauhaus genealogy, I argue for an aesthetic shift that recursively imagines futures of design as both strong repositionings but also profound reinscriptions of the markers of a long modernism. My reading moves from the valuation of the handcrafted to that of machinic production toward computational process in which the human designer is more collaborator than creator. In tracing a relationship between the Bauhaus and an algorithmic architecture, I focus on questions of materiality and production in concert with the generation of aesthetic and ideological modalities. I argue that the Bauhaus modernist ethos of "form equals function" is extended toward an algorithmic production of the auratic. Toward the construction of this genealogy, I reference the work of Luciana Parisi and others in the fields of architecture, philosophy, and critical theory of computational objects to develop an argument regarding the "autopoiesis of architecture."[3] Based on this materialist analysis, what may look like baroque folds in a generative architecture—an excess that the digital facilitates—we might also understand as a somewhat ruthless logic of machinic functionalism.

Generative Aesthetic

In the language of computationally modeled objects, generative design describes the algorithmic production of unique variation in forms such as sound, 3D models, etc. To this effect, I argue that twenty-first-century computational design is *generative* in the sense that it not only synthesizes the informational but also enacts a mode of *poiesis*; like poetry or architecture, it produces a thing that has not existed before.[4] Where the ethos of industrial production had been perfect replication and scale, a hard smoothness of the identical, we can identify a generativity of code-based material production that speaks to a computational aesthetic. It is a design ontology that describes a condition—malleable, algorithmically unique (as opposed to the uniqueness of hand tooling) unique, and often bordering on the physically impossible. And this condition of production—function in this case dictates form—renders an aesthetics of a *folded* modernism. The straight steel and glass of modernist towers (apologies to Wright's Guggenheim Museum) and radiant avenues metamorphose into belled, fat-bottomed beasts, moving from ethos to *Geist* (spirit). These are uncommon forms that move distinctly away from an industrial production of *Baukasten im Grossen* (large-scale modular building blocks).

This makes for an increasingly strange context in which to think about the Bauhaus 100 years later as avatar of an industrial high modernist aesthetic. To a certain extent, the conception of "good design" has stayed constant, representing, decades later, the minimalist, planar spaces that the Bauhaus minted. And yet we are in a present moment (with no cessation in sight) of a computational hegemony. In relating the two, the historic form of the Bauhaus and the generative function of algorithmic architecture, we locate a Bauhaus generative that reimagines *function* along lines of formal process. The argument is that computation is not tautological. Rather it relies on a reflexivity that is *not merely repetition*. Like an organic thing, the branching trees of code produce an *algorithmic* emergence, which brings us back to wooden objects in a roundabout way. At a time marked distinctly by artificial intelligence and the increasing ubiquity of computing across the built landscape, it is ironic—and apt—that we are compelled to think about the mythic of an "African Chair." But in this case, the relationship between the magic of mythology and the magic of technology meets in a recursive relation.

A Brief History of a Famous Chair

The B3 club chair has become an iconic object of intrigue presenting its own form of imitation game in advance of computational procedures. The figure sits in repose, one arm resting nonchalantly on the chair arm, the other at ease by her side, legs crossed at knees (not ankles) to further project the image of the modern woman signified by her simple metallic shift dress and shiny hood of a mask. But it is the armature in which she is suspended—the minimal rolled aluminum rods with strips of treated black cotton—that places her in a particular scene, a domain of design that invokes part industrial machine and part bondage sex play. In the photograph that captures this moment, titled *Untitled (Woman in B3 Club Chair ...)*, she is named as either Lis Beyer (the creator of the dress textile) or Ise Gropius (the wife of Bauhaus founder Walter Gropius). She could be either. It does not much matter for the purpose of the photo, as the punctum of the image is not the lady but the chair.

The story of this object, the B3 club chair by Bauhaus apprentice and then master Breuer, built first in 1925 in the context of the Dessau Bauhaus, illuminates a path from the craftwork of the first phase of the Bauhaus through its high modernist industrial production to the continued aftershock of class and cultural markers. (I sit in a coffee shop writing this chapter with a fatigued steel shelf with leather straps—a brutalist magazine rack—facing me down as a reminder of where the B3 comes from and the aesthetic that has rendered the design of building and location "modern.")

In looking at that chair, what has become known as the Wassily chair after Kandinsky, one of Breuer's masters in the atelier model of the Bauhaus, I encounter its past and its future at a glance: it evidences the material history of three chairs, the past, the modernist present, and the computational postmodern. To speak of the Bauhaus as a

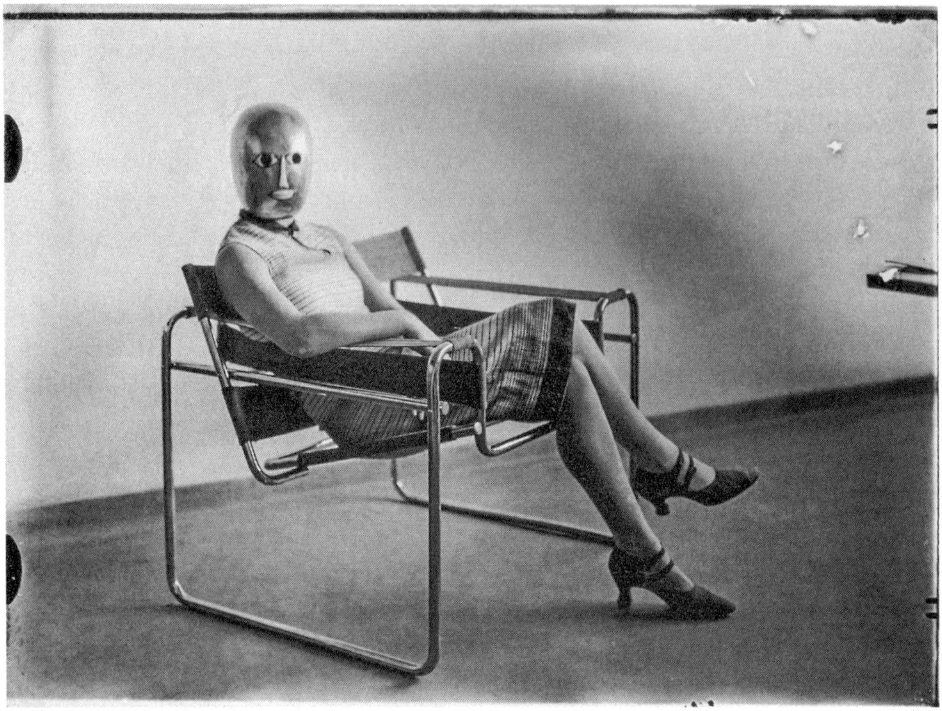

Figure 22.1
Untitled (Woman [Lis Beyer or Ise Gropius] in B3 Club Chair by Marcel Breuer Wearing a Mask by Oskar Schlemmer and a Dress in Fabric Designed by Beyer), c. 1926, photo by Erich Consemüller.

generative program, I move from an avant-garde to an algorithmic aesthetics. But I also cite the ongoing Bauhaus effect that continues to infuse the state of *good design*. It is a design ethos with the specific history of a European avant-garde between the two world wars that both allows for a greater inclusion of women artists and the continued exclusion of woman as interchangeable object (thus the passive sexual figure of Beyer or Gropius) and the fantasy of exotic others that seduces the modernist gaze.

Along with Le Corbusier's LC2 Armchair and the Eameses' DSR chair, the B3 club chair is easily one of the most recognizable images of a functionalist modernist aesthetic that has been identified over time with the established chic of good design. No frills, all hard lines. Breuer's B3 began with a modest inquiry into new materials: the lightweight rolled aluminum taken directly from the new generation of bikes the Bauhaus enjoyed. He understood the B3 as awkward and ugly even as it became the awkward and ugly of high modernism, a building block within a larger self-referential

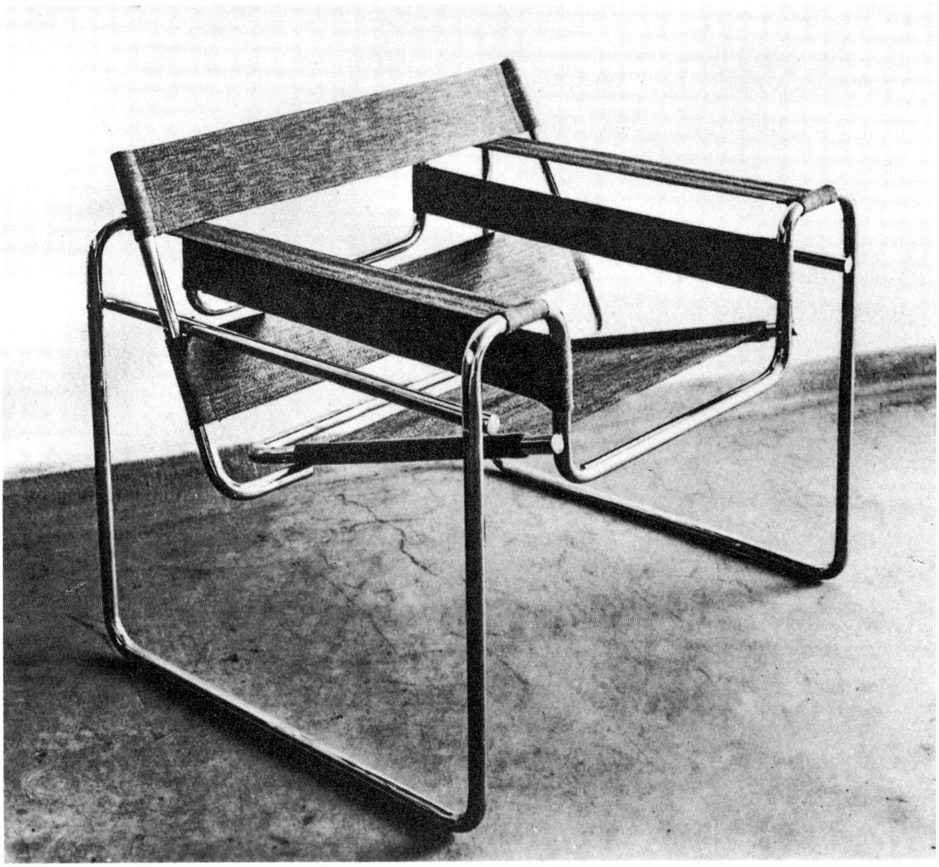

Figure 22.2
Marcel Breuer, Stahlrohr-Armlehnsessel (Club Chair B3), Bauhaus-Fotopostkarte, 1925.

set.[5] It is a taste that says, "a house is a machine for living in," which of course is the articulation of the modernist master Le Corbusier from his 1927 manifesto *Vers une architecture* (Toward an architecture).

The Bauhaus, in which Breuer had first been a student, had framed its own system of design along similar values that spoke to an integration of the artistic, pedagogic, and social.[6] Gropius spoke literally and conceptually of scalable, modular building blocks. This concept of integration across a flexibility of form directed an aesthetic of functionality. In this sense, by 1926 the conceptual design framework within which Breuer produced his B3 prototype called for a move away from handcraft to the factory production of a replicable, comfortable, and inexpensive chair that would fit into a household of the same values.

The B3 was conceived of as democratic and practical even as it went on to be a star with degrees of exclusivity. (By the time Knoll took over production and distribution in 1961, the B3 was an icon that could be distributed in the emergent market of the "accessible" as opposed to original modern design objects.) Moving from industrial to postindustrial reproduction, the B3 signals a transformation of state from the conceptually functional to the iconic. This is a cultural reformulation that reframes the aspirational production and materiality of a "democratic and practical" object, moving it toward reification. It is frozen in a mode of stardom that belies the basic formulation of modularity intrinsic to the B3 design, eliding characteristics of "mobility, variability, and efficiency."[7] If we look for the author of this change of state, it is not the B3 itself, notwithstanding its agency as object. Rather, it is in the cultural ascendance of the Bauhaus from avant-garde to city-maker. In its move to America in the 1940s, the Bauhaus both dissipated as coherent movement and radiated across key urban landscapes, namely the triumphant US cities of a postwar empire. The second and third phases of the Bauhaus (Dessau and Berlin in Germany and then to outposts such as Gropius's at Harvard University or Mies van der Rohe's appointment at Chicago's Armour Institute) moved to city scale. In a sense, it is the shift of scale itself that frames the shift of aesthetic in going from craft to architecture, all under the sign of total design. It is that last part of the equation, good design = good taste, *bon gens bon chic*, good genre (heritage) as the historical precondition of chic, that I disrupt in asking about the B3 club chair genealogy. If the African Chair (directly) and the Elbo chair (in spirit) are pre and post histories of a shared family tree, what more do we know about the family Bauhaus?

A Briefer History of a Not Yet Famous Chair

Philosopher of automation Luciana Parisi points to the postmodern emergence of a "contagious architecture," one that is digitally inflected with forms that speak of folds (Gehry) and blobs (Lynn). These are uncommon forms that move distinctly away from an industrial production of modular building blocks. Under the sway of a computational aesthetic as opposed to a functional one, the design ontology behaves somewhat differently: the algorithmic describes a generative instantiation of space and time. The modular, as the industrial with its concrete, steel, and glass no-frills production, is superseded by an architecture of motion. To be clear, *motion* is not constitutionally better than the mechanically self-replicating of the industrial; it is not more democratic or accessible. Its difference is not one of an ethics but of recursive referentiality of function.

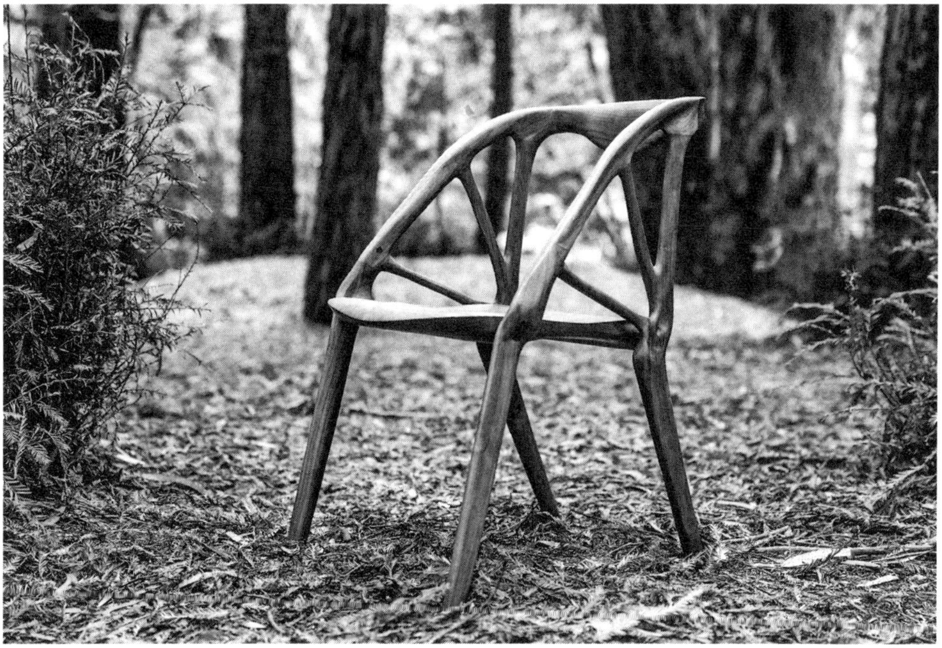

Figure 22.3
Elbo chair, 2017. Arthur Harsuvanakit and Brittany Presten of Autodesk's Dreamcatcher, generative design CAD system.

I am not claiming a triumph of "progress." But I am citing an acceleration of speed (*pace* Virilio). My task here is to point to the meaningful differences of change that interlace technology and aesthetics. It is not only possible to produce structural objects in the world that fold space yet address laws of physics and engineering sufficiently to stand up (the Guggenheim Bilbao is an iconic example); we need to conceptualize a moment in which form equals *generative* function in the sense of motion that algorithmic design embodies. In this sense, materiality and the design aesthetic could not be further apart.

In this framework of a computational aesthetic, there is a recursion of the modernist—and particularly Bauhaus—articulation of "form equals function." In the computational context it is literally function that dictates form: until a generative object is *set in time and material* as a construction, it will continue to recursively shift. The difference rests between the historic modular, as the industrial modernism with its concrete, steel, and glass production, and an architecture of motion that has superseded it: we can recognize the latter's signature in the nonhuman function of software and probability management (the algorithmic). It is important to remember that the nonhuman, in this case the computational, enters into this relationship as collaborator and not simply dumb mechanical. We might identify the important difference of this Bauhaus future in the reversal of function and form, as this computational functionality dematerializes both a human and a material factor in design.

With the Elbo chair, designers Arthur Harsuvanakit and Brittany Presten collaborate with the Autodesk Dreamcatcher software, a generative design CAD system, to produce a functional piece of furniture with charm to attract humans. In a sense, we might claim that a literal "machine for living" is produced with the Elbo, as it enacts a human-machine interaction that replaces the modernist metaphor with actualization. This means that the human agents outline rule sets or constraints (e.g., chair should support up to 300 lbs., chair should support average desk height for user, etc.). Following that, the Dreamcatcher computationally decides what Elbo will actually look like—how thin the legs, how light the wood, and so on. *Wired* writes of the process: "Typically, a designer decides how something should look, what it is made of, and how it is constructed. The emerging field of generative design upends that process by handing over big swaths of design process to software."[8] And yet, despite the Elbo's intertwined sociotechnological engagement, the object produced fails to evidence a level of aesthetic ideology comparable to the B3. Even if Breuer's chair was never positioned as a chair of "the people," its aspirations toward a democratized production already mark a significant shift in design ontology. The Elbo neither negates nor expands such claims on production and dissemination.

If we return to the imitation game of the iconic image of the B3, we find one woman interchangeable with another; with generative software, it is a person interchanged with a machine, the more classic version of the Turing test. With the chair in question, the projected linear plan from design (sketch, blueprint, model, etc.) to execution (object) is disrupted—a conception of planning, Suchman shows, that points to the serendipity of navigating one's way—by an alien intelligence.[9] It is the algorithm that decides what the chair will be. Often with algorithmic production, it is difficult for human agents to comprehensively know how a decision has been made. In the case of Elbo, the human designers set the parameters within which to make such decisions, which are nontrivial: what we feed to our artificial intelligence becomes the stuff of decision-making, regardless of bias. In this case, the input data rests on a priori assumptions about what "good taste" in a chair means, which dictates what images the system "learns." With that said, the quotidian stuff of (industrial) decision-making is left in the dirt. The high-water mark, the threshold for change of state, rests with a computational shift that elicits a generative outcome, where the machine (software in this case) makes aesthetic choices.

To do its work, the program has to learn the constraints of "chair." The designers feed the system 3D models of Hans Wegner's Round Chair and Berkeley Mills's Lambda Chair. In the mode of artificial intelligence, the program needs to have some limits on what it might generate: chair is not table; chair is not ball; chair has x properties, can bear y weight, should stand z tall. Unlike a human designer, Dreamcatcher is able to rapidly prototype thousands of designs, teaching itself modes of optimization (such as load-bearing and structural form). At intervals in the iterative process the human designers make selections, determining what direction the chair will evolve in but not the nature of the evolution. This is a mode of human-computer interaction that shifts the relationship from service closer to something that looks like collaboration. One of the qualities that Dreamcatcher optimizes for is lightweight forms with strength, as the application is more commonly used by Autodesk to produce industrial or medical customized parts.

If industrial production introduced scales of replicability, the algorithmic space demonstrates at least two phenomena: the generative as the singularity of object in a computational production. This is an odd combination of the uniquely handcrafted of the local, "folk" production and the ability to surpass industrial production in distribution. The Elbo is all *function* in the computational sense and not particularly bound to any materiality. It is chair that could be shipped as a set of instructions—the ultimate construction kit?

In the short history of generative computational production, virtual (or software) objects are often output as 3D prints. Working against this tradition of computational synthesis to synthetic print, the Elbo is CNC-milled out of wood, the wood giving it an organic caste. At the same time, as a programmable machine that translates code-based instructions to analog output, the CNC machine is also part of a software production line. In this sense, as a wooden, carved object (and not the more typical ABS plastic or nylon), the Elbo presents itself as a simulacrum of the organic. This turn to a computationally organic structure brings us full circle to Breuer's first chair, the African.

The Return of the Repressed of an Old Chair

The Bauhaus as a school focused on design, art, and craftsmanship when it was first founded, adding architecture as its own course only in 1925 when it moved to Dessau. The focus on craft stemmed from a desire to relate to an emerging working class, with Gropius claiming direct influence of the Berlin-based Arbeitsrat für Kunst (Works Council for Art), 1918–1921.[10] Craft was a mode of social engagement that put one's hand to the task like other laborers, with the twist of the avant-garde: the utopian design of a world in which the house, the clothes, the vessels one lived with signified

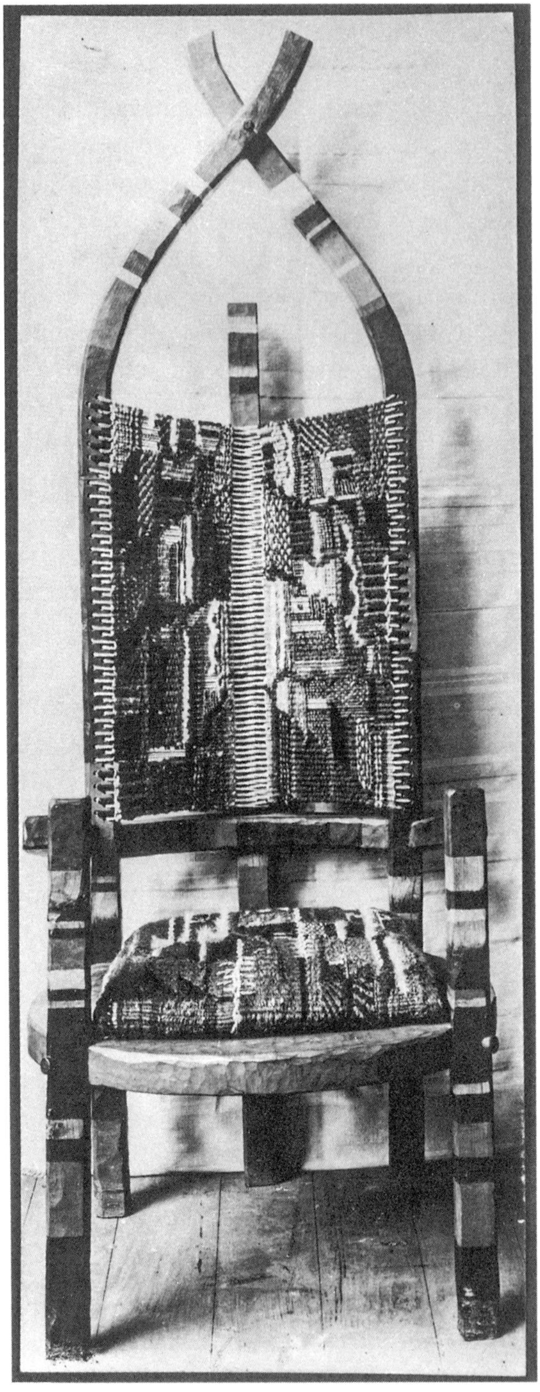

Figure 22.4

Marcel Breuer and Gunta Stölzl, Afrikanischer Stuhl (African Chair), 1921. Bauhaus-Archiv Berlin.

a total artwork of one's life. This conceptual framing had more to do with a romantic expressionism than the later machine aesthetic. And it was expressed through the use of textile, color, organic material, and ritual. As architectural historian Maria Stavrinaki argues, these material forms were brought into a circle of *spiritual* production toward the healing of a wounded, post-World War I Germany.[11]

Out of this context, the African chair, which was originally called the "Romantic Chair," makes sense.[12] It is reported to be Beuer's first known student construction and was made in collaboration with artist Gunta Stölzl.[13] It is a surprising construction, made of five legs, a high back, and a bold textile woven directly to the structure and cushion with additional patterns painted on the wood. Bauhaus historian Christopher Wilk describes the influences on Breuer's production in the following manner: "The design suggests the work of a student responding to a variety of influences; the Magyar folk art of Breuer's native Hungary, the vogue for African art in Europe, and the interest in naive art and the occult."[14] It is a mode of production that disappears in the wake of the industrial. Nonetheless, it performs a particular function that carries on through the evolution of aesthetic: the African chair in its mythic referentiality hails a spirit of German *Volk*. In the course of Bauhaus history, the one-of-a-kind of craft was left behind for mechanical reproduction. But with the computationally generative, we land back in a strange space of both.

After Modernism: The Chair Vanishes

In the poster for "A Bauhaus Movie Lasting Five Years," the film's author is given as "Life demanding its rights"; the film's operator is listed as "Marcel Breuer who recognizes these rights."[15] One clear shift between the modernist industrial (with its echoes of a romantic expressionism) and the algorithmic postmodern is the place of author in relation to object. "Life" as such seizes command, with the designer relegated to the role of "operator." Between these three chairs I point to a triangular relation, where the B3 is the point by which the other two are oriented. The Elbo is not an "improvement" on the B3. Nonetheless, it is contingent on it for its design *Geist*. Similarly, the African Chair tunes a romantic avant-garde imagination toward a construction of *Volk* that influences the industrial turn of the B3. The latter's design worldview absorbs and shifts the desire for a cohesive (German) civic body to an international style of *Baukasten im Grossen*. In relation, what we encounter with the Elbo chair is a computational aesthetic without a worldview as such—to make the Elbo, the software must learn about chairs—but with the recursive *spirit* of the modernist. In this particular instantiation of a Bauhaus future, the shift is from industrial materiality to a dematerialization. The performance of the Elbo is as close as we have come to the 1926 speculative chair made of air. In this sense, I would call it an auratic object, more *Geist*-in-the-machine than material. Breuer's final trick, the vanishing chair.

Notes

1. Herbert Bayer, Walter Gropius, and Ise Gropius, *Bauhaus, 1919–1928* (New York: Museum of Modern Art, 1938), 132.

2. Barry Bergdoll, "Marcel Breuer and the Invention of Heavy Lightness," *Places Journal*, June 2018, https://placesjournal.org/article/marcel-breuer-and-the-invention-of-heavy-lightness/.

3. Luciana Parisi, *Contagious Architecture: Computation, Aesthetics, and Space* (Cambridge, MA: MIT Press, 2013); Patrik Schumacher, *The Autopoiesis of Architecture*, vol. 1, *A New Framework for Architecture* (Chichester, UK: John Wiley and Sons, 2010).

4. For further discussion of generative aesthetics and urban design, see B. Coleman, "Let's Get Lost," in *The Handbook of Civic Technologies*, ed. Eric Gordon and Paul Mihailidis (Cambridge, MA: MIT Press, 2016).

5. Christopher Wilk, *Marcel Breuer, Furniture and Interiors* (New York: Museum of Modern Art, 1981).

6. Michael Siebenbrodt, Jeff Wall, and Klaus Weber, eds., *Bauhaus: A Conceptual Model*, trans. Benjamin Carter (Berlin: BauhausArchiv, Berlin Museum für Gestaltung, Stiftung Bauhaus Dessau, and Klassik Stiftung Weimar, 2009).

7. Ibid., 000.

8. Margaret Rhodes, "So. Algorithms Are Designing Chairs Now," *Wired*, October 3, 2016.

9. Lucy Suchman, *Human-Machine Reconfigurations: Plans and Situated Actions*, 2nd ed. (Cambridge: Cambridge University Press, 2006).

10. Jeffrey Saletnik and Robin Schuldenfrei, eds., *Bauhaus Construct: Fashioning Identity, Discourse and Modernism* (London: Routledge, 2009).

11. Maria Stavrinaki, "The African Chair or the Charismatic Object," *Grey Room*, no. 41 (Fall 2010), 88–110.

12. Ibid.

13. Christopher Wilk, "Marcel Breuer and Gunta Stolzl: 'African' Chair. 1921," in *Bauhaus 1919–1933: Workshops for Modernity*, ed. Barry Bergdoll and Leah Dickerman (New York: Museum of Modern Art, 2009), 100–103.

14. Wilk, *Marcel Breuer, Furniture and Interiors*, 20.

15. Bayer, Gropius, and Gropius, *Bauhaus, 1919–1928*.

23 The Twittering Machine

A Conversation with the Editors of *Logic*

Robert Wiesenberger with Ben Tarnoff and Moira Weigel

Bauhaus master Paul Klee's 1922 drawing *The Twittering Machine* (*Die Zwitscher-Maschine*) has long held a mirror to the human relationship with technology and with nature, coloring it either whimsical or sinister depending on the beholder.[1] Is the birds' song sweet, or do they screech against their shackles? Does the machine obviate the animals, or do they perch triumphant on a defunct device? And who turns the crank? Beyond its subject matter, the work also invites the question of how Klee, a painter and self-styled mystic who satirized the machine, related to the technocratic culture of the Bauhaus, as one of its longest-serving and most influential instructors. The year after Klee completed the drawing, Bauhaus founder Walter Gropius would famously declare the school's aim as a "new unity" of art and technology.

Parallels abound between the interwar avant-garde and the Silicon Valley of our time. They appear in techno-utopian ideology[2] and even in the metaphors underlying today's software interfaces.[3] These links precede the avowed "Bauhaus aesthetic" sought by Apple founder Steve Jobs, or the quasi-playful office culture and simplified visual language of Google.[4] In both contexts as well, the cult of the engineer reigns: function and efficiency, it is said, produce beauty. And whether in code or construction, makers prize elegant simplicity and standardization (one might think of a code library as a kind of digital prefabrication). Function and data supposedly dictate form, and are achieved by tools and systems that are thought to be neutral.

Following Bauhaus master László Moholy-Nagy, the designer-engineer "hacks" the existing and iterates constantly.[5] And as in the student work of Marcel Breuer, there is a deep faith in progress, often an epiphanic origin story behind innovations, and an air of openness combined with canny claims on intellectual property.[6] In both times of manifesto-writing, the world-changing ambitions seem unbounded by borders and generally untroubled by cultural specificity.

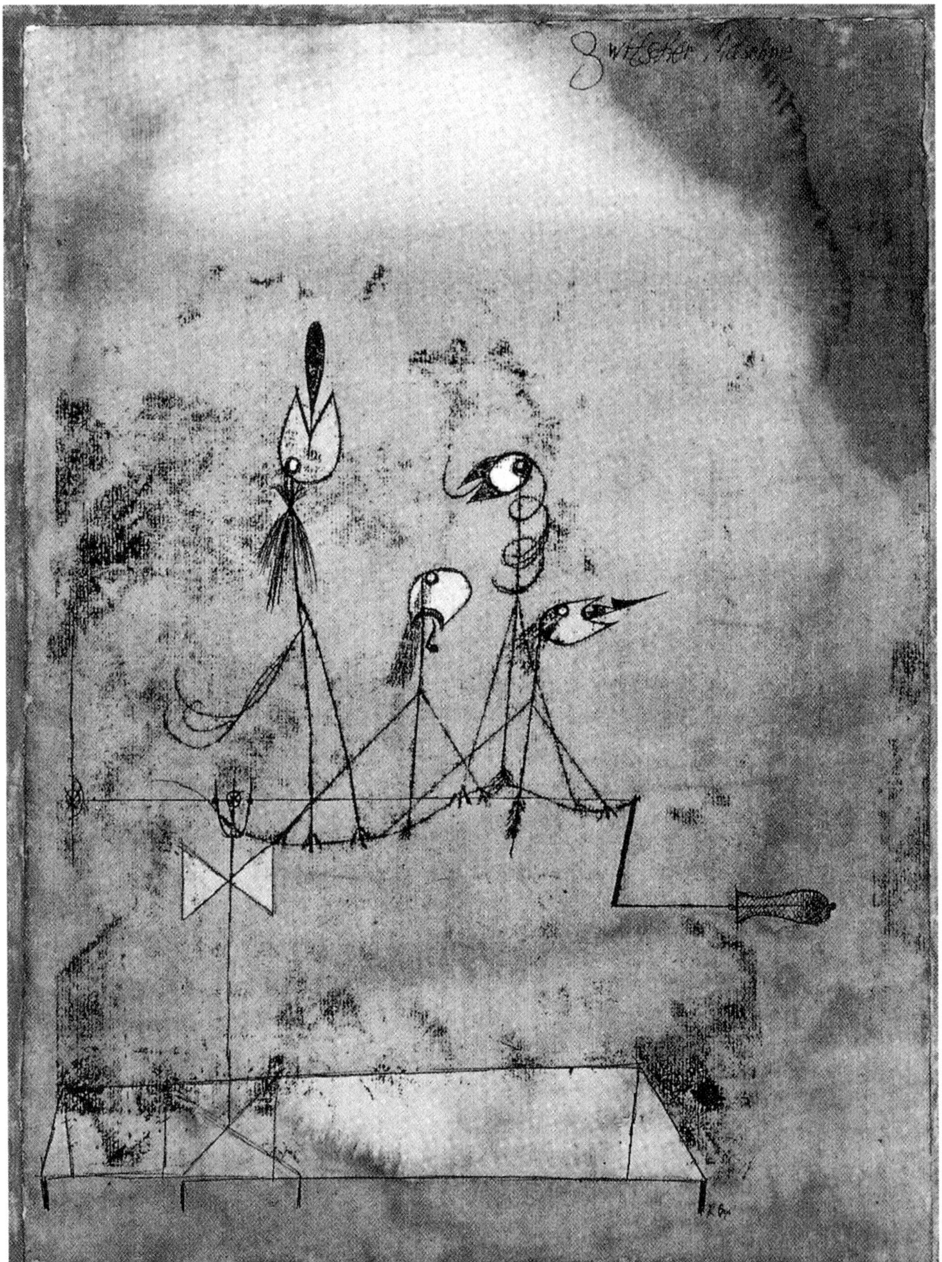

Figure 23.1

Paul Klee, *Twittering Machine* (*Die Zwitscher-Maschine*), 1922. Oil transfer drawing, watercolor, and ink on paper with gouache and ink borders on board. © The Museum of Modern Art/Licensed by SCALA/Art Resource, NY.

The austere culture of research is leavened, in both cases, by a campus-based camaraderie of work-hard-play-hard. There is also a fascination with self-optimization, life-hacking, and augmenting perception—a common denominator across all three versions of the Bauhaus preliminary course. Amidst egalitarian rhetoric, cults of personality hold sway: beyond the resemblance of eyewear and facial hair, shirt collars and vegetarian diets, for example, Bauhaus master Johannes Itten and Steve Jobs also each had their own quasi-religious followings. And in both settings, idiosyncrasy and free-spiritedness aside, organizational survival depends on capital, the grace of government, and studied efforts to appear politically neutral.

Of course, comparing a small school and a massive industry, in two vastly different socioeconomic moments, verges on absurdity. In just over a decade, the Bauhaus delivered on several of its aesthetic and pedagogical promises; in about two decades, Silicon Valley has reshaped our economies, political systems, ecologies, and even psyches, some beyond recognition or obvious repair. The interwar period had its own media buzz about technology, variously self-promotional and self-critical, hagiographic and hostile, just as we have ours. Indeed, tech chatter—the welter of buzz, hype, speculation, and recrimination—sometimes seems like one of the greatest outputs of the industry, a vast twittering machine.

According to the editors of *Logic*, a new journal, our technology discourse is broken. A group of friends from Harvard and San Francisco founded the magazine in 2016, shortly before the US presidential election: Ben Tarnoff, Moira Weigel, Jim Fingal, Christa Hartsock, and Xiaowei Wang are software developers, designers, journalists, and an academic in the humanities. Each of *Logic*'s three issues per year takes on a different theme, such as "Intelligence," "Justice," "Sex," or "Failure," enlisting contributions from a diverse range of voices from within the tech world. For "Intelligence," the editors note at the outset that "a technologized world created the conditions for Trumpism. Social dislocations caused by automation helped create his base, and social media incubated and propagated his fascist rhetoric."[7] And in "Justice," they offer "pieces by and about people who are trying to build new technologies, or use existing ones, to rectify our broken social systems. [The issue] includes people who are being disciplined and punished by technologies—from robo-debt software to racist search engines. And it offers strategies for resistance, whether through little hacks or all-out mutiny."[8] In this conversation, Ben Tarnoff and Moira Weigel cut through the chatter, and stress the urgent need to rethink how we talk about technology.

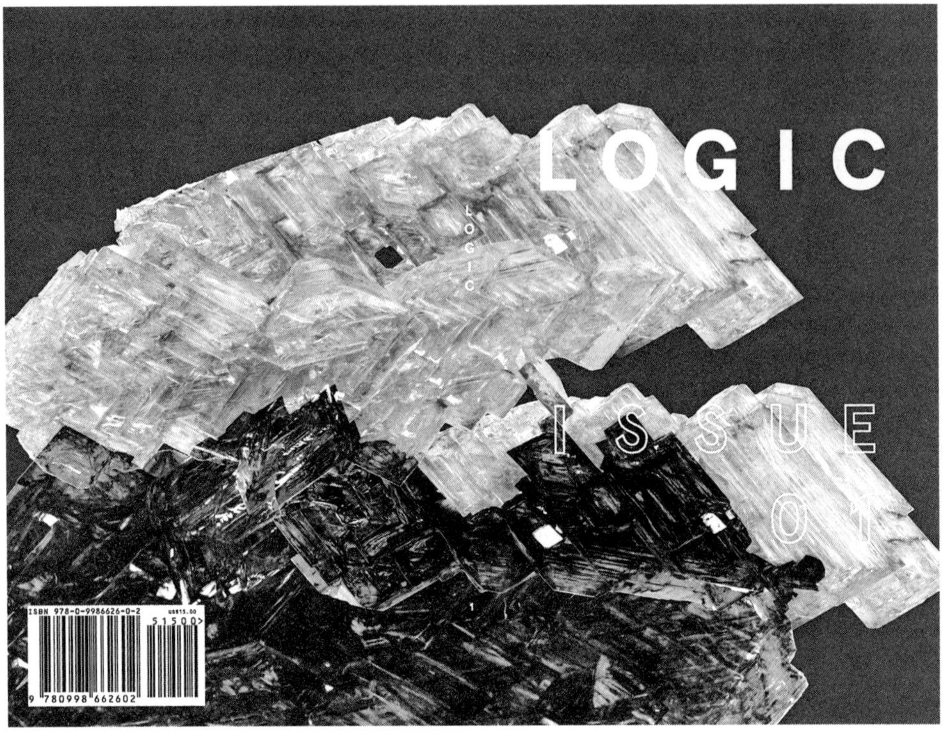

Figure 23.2
Front cover of *Logic*, no. 1, "Intelligence" (Spring 2017), cover art by Xiaowei Wang.

Q: *What is wrong with the discussion of technology today?*

Ben Tarnoff: We started *Logic* because we felt underserved by the existing conversation about technology. Broadly, we saw it as polarized into two camps: the sycophants and the scolds. The sycophants are your standard-issue techno-utopians, the sort who have been dominating the popular discourse about technology since at least the 1990s. They believe that technology, and the internet in particular, is always and everywhere a force for human liberation. This idea has taken a few knocks lately, but its significance can't be overstated: legitimated and amplified by the media, it supplied the ideological ammunition for an intensely deregulatory approach to the tech industry that continues to this day. And while it may take a slightly more sober form now than it did during the total delirium of the dot-com days, it's still broadly shared by industry elites. The notion that tech companies are trying to "make the world a better place" may be a punchline on *Silicon Valley*, but it remains a big part of the culture.

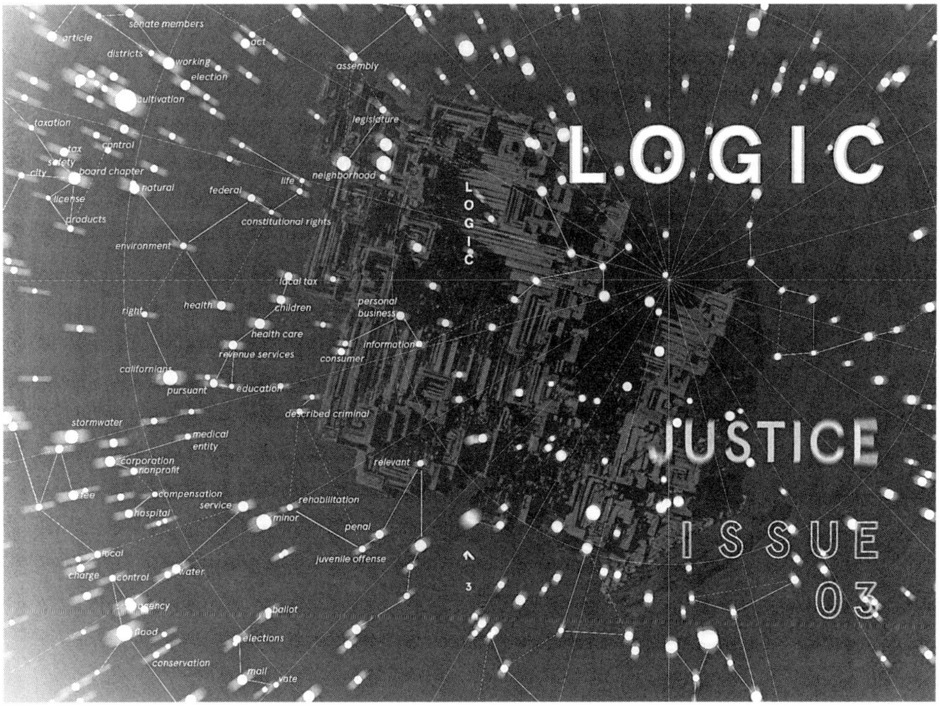

Figure 23.3
Full cover of *Logic*, no. 3, "Justice" (Winter 2017), cover art by Xiaowei Wang.

The scolds, on the other hand, see technology as a moral, spiritual, and social evil. The scolds have always been with us, but their ranks seem to have grown with the "tech backlash" that's emerged in the aftermath of the 2016 election. You can find this point of view widely represented these days: social media and smartphones are making us dumber, meaner, less human; it's killing our relationships, our attention spans, our culture, our individuality, and so on. The scolds are capable of making good points, sometimes, but on the whole they simply invert techno-utopianism to arrive at an equally inadequate techno-dystopianism. Technology becomes always and everywhere a force for human misery—indeed, for *de*humanization. The operating assumption here, of course, is that there's some essential quality called humanity that resides in all of us, and the internet is destroying it. Inevitably, this essential quality is associated with offline activities, like spending face time with loved ones and reading long novels in print.

Frankly, it's insufferable. It reminds me of Thoreau complaining about the telegraph. Perhaps even less forgivable, however, is the scolds' lack of precision. They tend to think in moral terms, not material ones. They tend to think in big idealist narratives where specifics aren't important. In this sense, they're the mirror image of the sycophants. Neither camp pays much attention to how the technology actually works, or who's building it. They're not interested in the technology itself, but in what kinds of stories the technology lets them tell.

Q: *So how are you framing the story?*

Moira Weigel: One thing we observed before founding *Logic* was that a lot of coverage of "tech" treated it narrowly as the subject of a business story. "So and so raised such and such amount of money and then made this or that much more or less." *Zzz*. Technology is not just a business story, we said; it's an *everything* story, and it deserved to be explored as such. We wanted to pull the camera way back—or maybe the better metaphor would be to make it mobile, move it to other places. But creating a new framework required us to start by asking very basic questions. Like: What even *is* technology? It's something Ben and I would walk around San Francisco and talk about for hours.

Q: *And what is it?*

MW: I'm an academic, trained in comparative literature, so I can't help but want to run for Greek roots. *Technology* comes from *techne*, "crafts" and arts. *Logos*, of course, is logic—language, reason, also the set of rules governing how a system operates. In German there is *Technik,* too. As Geoffrey Winthrop-Young indicates in a prefatory note to his translation of the German media theorist Bernhard Siegert's recent book *Cultural Techniques*, "[*Technik*'s] semantic amplitude ranges from gadgets, artifacts, and infrastructures all the way to skills, routines, and procedures."[9] For instance, *Medientechniken* ("media-technics") refer to particular tools—cameras, camcorders, digital editing software and so on—while *Körpertechniken* ("bodily technics") refer to gestures and habits of physical comportment. Siegert himself points out that *Kulturtechnik*, "cultural technics," comes from nineteenth-century agriculture, where it referred to procedures for improving *cultivation*, such as irrigation, drainage, enclosure, and river regulation.

My fellow editors would never let me get away with riffing this way in *Logic*. But I bring it all up for at least two reasons. First, we wanted to broaden what was meant by "tech" or "technology," and think about devices and infrastructures that were not just vehicles for venture capital but created the conditions of possibility of our lives. Second, we wanted to think about technology as everyday. One way of talking about this is demystification.

Q: *Can you say more about the mystique of tech?*

MW: For the past decade there has been so much hype around Silicon Valley, and such an aura attached to the work that goes on there. This mystique is heightened, of course, by all the measures that the industry uses to keep its own secrets. Building their vast campuses in the middle of nowhere, surrounding them with private security, making anyone who comes in or out of the building sign an NDA.

Talking to technologists and tech workers directly is a big part of dispelling that. One thing *Logic* aims to do is to bring those voices into the conversation. Perhaps it's not so different from the Bauhaus impulse to dispel the rarefied aura around the bourgeois work of art—to recreate art as some more democratic kind of category, as something usable, as craft. And to puncture some of the mythologies surrounding the men who made it. Maybe we can take the myth that surrounds these libertarian (supposedly value-neutral) temples of digital capitalism, and use them to make a print magazine that starts aesthetic and political conversations!

Q: *So the scope of Logic seems fairly expansive.*

BT: Generally the "technology" term is taken to be synonymous with the tech industry, itself a somewhat imprecise term that loosely refers to a cluster of big companies on the West Coast, especially Facebook, Amazon, Google, and Apple. This is an extremely important set of firms, no doubt, and their growing power over the infrastructures that shape and sustain our social, political, and economic life deserves close critical attention. But the emphasis on these companies obscures the fact that information technology is rewiring the whole economy, not just a single sector. And its impact tends to be greatest in those industries that we may think of as the *least* high-tech, like manufacturing. So when we talk about technology, we shouldn't just be talking about our social media feeds, or the new iPhone. We should be talking about almost everything.

Q: *How do you cut through the lofty rhetoric?*

BT: Ask a tech executive or their publicist what their company is building, and then ask their engineers the same question. You'll probably get different answers. The people who run the tech industry and the communications departments that speak on their behalf can't be expected to give a truthful, detailed account—it's not strategic, as their reputation and their valuation depends on a good deal of mystification and hype. The engineers, by contrast, can speak more candidly and concretely to a technology's mechanics, potential, and limitations, because they're the ones who are in the trenches every day building it. But their voices aren't the ones represented in the media, for various reasons. If I had to tell the scolds one thing, I'd say: Stop taking everything the tech industry says at face value. Stop thinking in PR narratives, and come down to earth.

Down on earth is where *Logic* tries to live. We try to understand how technology is built, who builds it, how it works, and whom it works for. We try to see technology in terms of power and political economy, as a force that acts through and within capitalism, continuously transforms it, and is in turn continuously transformed by it. While our contributors come from different political traditions within the broad left, ranging from the liberal center-left to the anarchist ultra-left, our editorial outlook embodies the basic insight of historical materialism that how a group of humans make the things they need to survive is typically the most determinant aspect of that group. That what Engels called the "production and reproduction of real life" is the most useful starting point for understanding why a society organizes itself in a particular way.

Q: *Your approach seems pragmatically grounded, and clear-eyed about capitalism.*

BT: Different technologies can open up different utopian or dystopian possibilities. But these possibilities have to be evaluated in relation to the system we currently live in, not as floating thought bubbles untethered from material reality. The material reality suggests that technology is not usually utopian or dystopian. Instead, it's something more ordinary: a force for profit-making or repression, for making capital into more capital or making the world safe for making capital into more capital. If you can't think clearly about capitalism—or won't acknowledge that a historically specific capitalist mode of production even exists—then you're going to have trouble thinking clearly about technology. We need less TechCrunch and more Lenin, in other words; less reckless prognosticating about artificial intelligence and more "concrete analysis of the concrete situation."

Q: *When people say the tech world is apolitical, how do you respond?*

BT: They're partially right. Engineering culture tends to have a certain impatience with politics. Politics is seen as occupying a lower, more animal plane. It's messy, slow, hard to quantify, and it can make people angry, which is awkward. Perhaps most importantly, the measures of success—the "acceptance criteria," to borrow a phrase from agile software development—aren't quite as clear as they are in engineering. As Fred Turner explains in his interview with us, the ethics of engineering are mostly about asking the question, "Does it work?" If it works, you've done the right thing.[10] Full stop.

But this is more a description of engineering culture in its pure form. In the wild, that culture is embedded in companies that absolutely do have a political complexion. Traditionally, information technology as an industry has been heavily Democratic. In the 1980s, the neoliberal "New Democrats" in particular cultivated a close relationship with a rising tech industry. Michael Dukakis, in his 1988 presidential campaign, made much of his role in presiding over the "Massachusetts Miracle" that took place while he was governor, which involved the rapid growth of tech firms along the Route 128 corridor. Today, Route 128 has been eclipsed by Silicon Valley—but Silicon Valley, as everyone knows, is also very close to the Democratic Party. Silicon Valley remains a major donor base for the Democrats, and enjoyed a particularly cozy relationship with Obama.

So overall, I think it's safe to say that the political orientation of the tech industry is largely center-liberal, perhaps best embodied by someone like Sheryl Sandberg, with pockets of more libertarian tendencies associated with a figure like Peter Thiel. However, it's absolutely critical to make the point that the politics of the people running the tech industry are not identical with the politics of the people who work in the tech industry. The former tend to get all the media attention, so it's understandable that the general public tends to think about the politics of tech in terms of [Cheryl] Sandbergs and [Peter] Thiels. Now, both of those political perspectives are certainly represented among the tech rank-and-file—in fact, the center-liberal tendency likely predominates. But there are other perspectives represented as well, including a small but significant left-wing current.

It would be a little overeager to call this current socialist, exactly. It's composed primarily of people who voted for Bernie—tech workers supported Bernie during the Democratic primary in large numbers, as I never tire of pointing out—and who remain available to a more redistributive, more social-democratic agenda. But tech has its militants, too—and more than you might expect.

Q: *Does the tech worker think of themselves that way? Is there a sense of class consciousness?*

BT: I'd say that the level of class consciousness varies widely among tech workers, because there are so many different kinds of tech workers. The term "tech worker" is a useful one, because it makes visible the crucial and oft-concealed fact that tech, like any other industry, is primarily composed of *workers*—not founders, entrepreneurs, and VCs. But it's also a somewhat unwieldy abstraction, because it encompasses not only the workers who belong to what is traditionally seen as tech's core profession—software engineering—but also to those who belong to other white-collar professions represented within tech, such as marketing, *as well as to* the blue-collar workers who perform the labor upon which all of that white-collar work depends: the security guards, the shuttle bus drivers, the food service workers, and so on, who are particularly present at top firms like Google and Facebook.

And the term tech worker is actually even more spacious than that. Because if you dig into each of those categories, you'll find they have all sorts of internal differentiations of their own. For instance, not all software engineers work for the top firms; most, in fact, work for companies you've never heard of, for less money, in far less glamorous settings. Many of them work as contractors, or work from offices in countries with lower labor costs, like India.

So what do we mean when we say "tech worker"? Essentially, all of the above. I'm not making this point to be pedantic—the term's heterogeneity has a very concrete bearing on class consciousness. How likely it is for a tech worker to think of themselves *as a worker* tends to correlate to where they fit into this stack. A cafeteria worker at Facebook is more likely to think of themselves as a worker than a software engineer at Facebook. Someone who does IT for a community college is more likely to think of themselves as a worker than someone who does IT for a big bank. And so on.

When you talk to the people at the Tech Workers Coalition (TWC), an activist organization in the Bay Area that is very active in tech organizing, they'll say that the goal is to get all of these workers to see themselves as workers—even the senior developer at Facebook. But, depending on the worker, that can be a pretty challenging series of conversations. Your average white-collar tech worker is taught to think of themselves in entrepreneurial terms—not as a worker whose labor power helps capital make more of itself. How do you persuade a Facebook developer that they have more in common with the person who drives the shuttle bus that brings them to work every morning than with Zuckerberg?

Q: *So how would you do that?*

BT: Among other things, this requires thinking differently about class. Ellen Meiksins Wood writes that there are two ways of thinking about class. You can think about class as a location or as a relation. To the extent that Americans think about class at all, they tend to think of it as a location—you're located in a particular class because of your income or education level. If that's the way you understand class, then the Facebook engineer is indeed very far apart from the Facebook shuttle bus driver. But the other way to think about class, Wood explains, is the more specifically Marxist way. This is class as a relation, in particular the relation between capital and labor, between those who own the means of production and those who sell their labor power to earn a wage. In this sense, anyone who works for a living is a worker.

It's obviously much more complicated than that. But I think this framing of class might offer a useful starting point for trying to get *all* tech workers to think of themselves as workers. I don't underestimate the difficulty, though. It'll take a lot of talking.

It'll take a lot of what Stuart Hall calls "articulation," forging a political unity out of distinct social elements, persuading people that what they have in common is more important than what they don't, because what they have in common has the potential to make them tremendously powerful.

Q: *Any final thoughts on the techno-utopian chatter?*

MW: The internet creates democratic possibilities, but it is not inevitably democratic. The kind of techno-determinist and techno-utopian language that said computer networks are inherently liberating is precisely the kind of language that *Logic* seeks to challenge—not because we are pessimists, but because we are optimists. The problem with Silicon Valley reason is not that we are too soft or sensitive to handle its rationality. It is that it has not yet become rational enough.

We should probably admit that one of our long-term daydreams is to create a Frankfurt School-like institute, for analyzing technology. We are materialists but fascinated by the psychic investments that we all have in our devices and the narratives around them, too. *Logic* is, hopefully, a start.

Notes

1. For a classic discussion of the work, see Maurice L. Shapiro, "Klee's Twittering Machine," *Art Bulletin* 50, no. 1 (1968), 67–69.

2. See Fred Turner, *The Democratic Surround: Multimedia and American Liberalism from World War II to the Psychedelic Sixties* (Chicago: University of Chicago Press, 2013), 77–113. This is the prequel to Fred Turner, *From Counterculture to Cyberculture: Stewart Brand, the Whole Earth Network, and the Rise of Digital Utopianism* (Chicago: University of Chicago Press, 2006). Turner links the two projects in his lecture "The New Man: From Bauhaus to Silicon Valley" (Projekt Bauhaus, "Preliminary Course: From Bauhaus to Silicon Valley," Haus der Kulturen der Welt, Berlin, December 2, 2017), https://www.youtube.com/watch?v=zc92ntPGPtQ.

3. Lev Manovich has shown how avant-garde strategies of the "new vision," such as montage and mobile viewpoints, have informed the metaphors that structure software interfaces. See Lev Manovich, *The Language of New Media* (Cambridge, MA: MIT Press, 2002), xiv–xxxvi.

4. Jobs, quoted in Walter Isaacson, *Steve Jobs* (New York: Simon and Schuster, 2011), 125–128.

5. Moholy-Nagy, under the heading "Production-Reproduction," called for repurposing the technical apparatus to creative new ends. See László Moholy-Nagy, *Painting, Photography, Film* (Cambridge, MA: MIT Press, 1969), 30–31. Some of his own work, like the *Light Prop for an Electric Stage*, gestated over a long period and underwent various modifications by the artist well after its first display.

6. Breuer, as a student, famously illustrated the progression of his work in the 1925 collage *ein bauhaus film, fünf jahre lang* (A Bauhaus film, five years long), which culminates in an imagined future with the legend "Things improve each year. Ultimately, we'll sit on elastic columns of air." He likewise cited a new bicycle, and the lightness and strength of its bent steel tube handlebars, as the inspiration for his iconic club chair—which went on to be the subject of conflicting intellectual property claims. See Christopher Wilk, *Marcel Breuer, Furniture and Interiors* (New York: Museum of Modern Art, 1981), 37ff.

7. The Editors, "Hello World," *Logic*, no. 1 (Spring 2017).

8. The Editors, "Flying Blind," *Logic*, no. 3 (Winter 2017).

9. Geoffrey Winthrop-Young, "Translator's Note," in *Cultural Techniques: Grids, Filters, Doors, and Other Articulations of the Real* (New York: Fordham University Press, 2014).

10. Fred Turner, "Don't Be Evil: Fred Turner on Utopias, Frontiers, and Brogrammers," interview in *Logic*, no. 3 (Winter 2017).

24 The Bauhaus, the *Colloquy of Mobiles,* and the Meaning of Interaction

Karen Kornblum Berntsen and Paul Pangaro

Interaction design degrees lead to highly sought-after jobs in America[1] and go by many names.[2] Universities are graduating countless numbers of students who become well-employed designers and have a vast impact on our daily lives, worldwide.[3] These students are asked to "bridge the tangible and the intangible" and to create interactions that are meaningful to human beings. What exactly does this mean, and how best can educators achieve it? In a similarly challenging era, the Bauhaus asked students to interact with tangible materials in new ways. By creating the Bauhaus *manifesto* Walter Gropius put a stake in the ground for educators—so isn't it time for a new manifesto for interaction design? In this chapter we lay the groundwork, by explaining Gordon Pask's theory of conversation via his *Colloquy of Mobiles*, originally exhibited in 1968 and recreated in 2018.

The artifacts left behind from any age are living proof of the inseparable three-way relationship among people, raw materials, and technology. Evidence is abundant—museums are filled with enduring remains that exemplify the "present moments" of bygone ages: prehistoric bowls made of local clay fired in ovens, chariots made of local wood hewn with chisels, and pyramids made of local limestone ground into concrete. The *Colloquy of Mobiles* captures and exemplifies Gordon Pask's approach to the three-way relationship, and it can teach us a lot about the fundamental nature of interaction design.

Today, with data as a new raw material, an interaction designer's primary challenge is finding effective ways for people to manage signals, feedback, goals, and responses. (This designing of the intangible is also a form of craft.) Data streams in from many sources and flows out to many others. Any given piece of software is networked across many nodes and many actors, whether individuals, companies, databases, and even other computations. The role of designers transitions from makers of tangible products to makers of systems and services, and therefore, more than ever, influencers of experiences.[4]

Looking to the Bauhaus as a benchmark of success in design education, we see that it emerged in the 1920s and 1930s as the world was still adjusting to the industrial revolution and factories of mass production were displacing artists and craftsmen. It was the first design school in the world. The tangible artifacts that came from it reflect the three-way relationship described above. Artists and designers worked with raw materials that were manufactured through the use of technology. These materials included metal tubing, plywood sheets, and glass. The clean, modern design associated with the Bauhaus can be traced to the creations of artists at the Bauhaus school, and these designs still influence us today. When Marcel Breuer designed his famous chair, nothing resembling its modern aesthetic had ever been seen before. Yet people intuitively knew how to interact with it and found it both beautiful and practical. When Herbert Bayer challenged typographic traditions by using only lower case letters and sans serif typefaces for most Bauhaus publications (he even invented new typographic characters with his *fonetic alphabet*), people still were engaged and eager to consume the messages and information on the posters. "My work seen in its totality is a statement about the integration of the contemporary artist into an industrial society."[5] The machine-age aesthetics (chairs, desk lamps, and buildings) of the Bauhaus are evidence of Walter Gropius's revolutionary approach to the three-way relationship.

Gropius's approach was captured in his Bauhaus *manifesto*.[6] In the manifesto he expressed solidarity with industrial workers, reflecting the ethics and values that were relevant in the context of 1920s Germany. The school broke down the barrier between fine art and applied art, machines and humans, musicians and photographers, as well as other juxtapositions that were newly forged. Evidence of interdisciplinary influence can be seen in the relationship between Kandinsky's 1923 painting (figure 24.1) and Peter Keler's 1922 furniture (figure 24.2).

Unlike traditional art schools that equated expertise with narrowing one's focus, Gropius's curriculum (figure 24.3) required students to maintain a broad (360°) view of the theories, raw materials, and practices offered by diverse faculty through rigorous studio classes. Students themselves were from diverse backgrounds, and the school quickly became a living, breathing community. During a time when mass production was viewed as a threat to artists and craftspersons, Bauhaus students and instructors embraced the industrial revolution while deeply respecting the biological, emotional, and spiritual aspects of being human. They never even considered the possibility that their human needs and responses might be compromised by industrialization and new technology. What emerged was a vibrant culture which unapologetically embraced humor, sexuality, nature, and play.

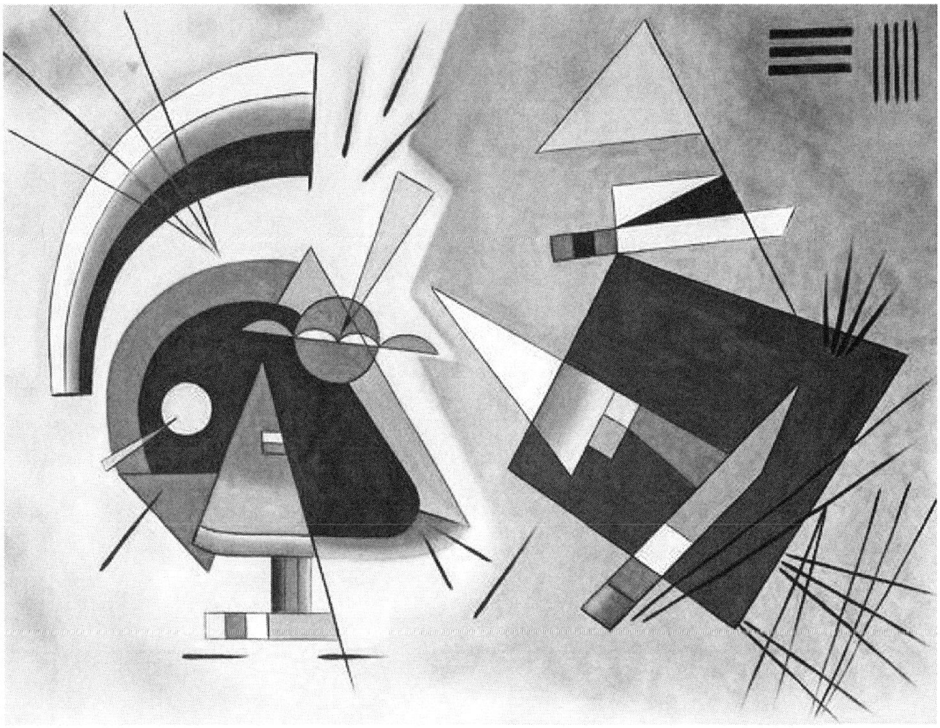

Figure 24.1
Wassily Kandinsky, *Black and Violet*, 1923. (Also plate 17.)

The Bauhaus closed in 1933, but its influence was firmly in place in design culture. Born around this time, Gordon Pask would come to develop his own unique approach to designing interactive systems. He saw no disparity between the technological and the biological. Gordon became an artist—illustrator, lyricist, and producer for the stage. He was also emphatically a tinkerer who developed all of his machines in an iterative dance between concept, materiality, and interaction. In the *Colloquy of Mobiles* Pask unselfconsciously melds signals, feedback, goals, and responses with large organic tangible forms, creating an experience that bridges the tangible and the intangible.

Not long after the Bauhaus closed in 1933, early computers (first analog, then digital) began the explosion of computation that transformed the landscape of industry from factories of mass physical production to factories of "mass computational production," ultimately dubbed the "Information Age."[7] In today's digital world, data and algorithms have taken over the zeitgeist and somehow we have lost our human selves

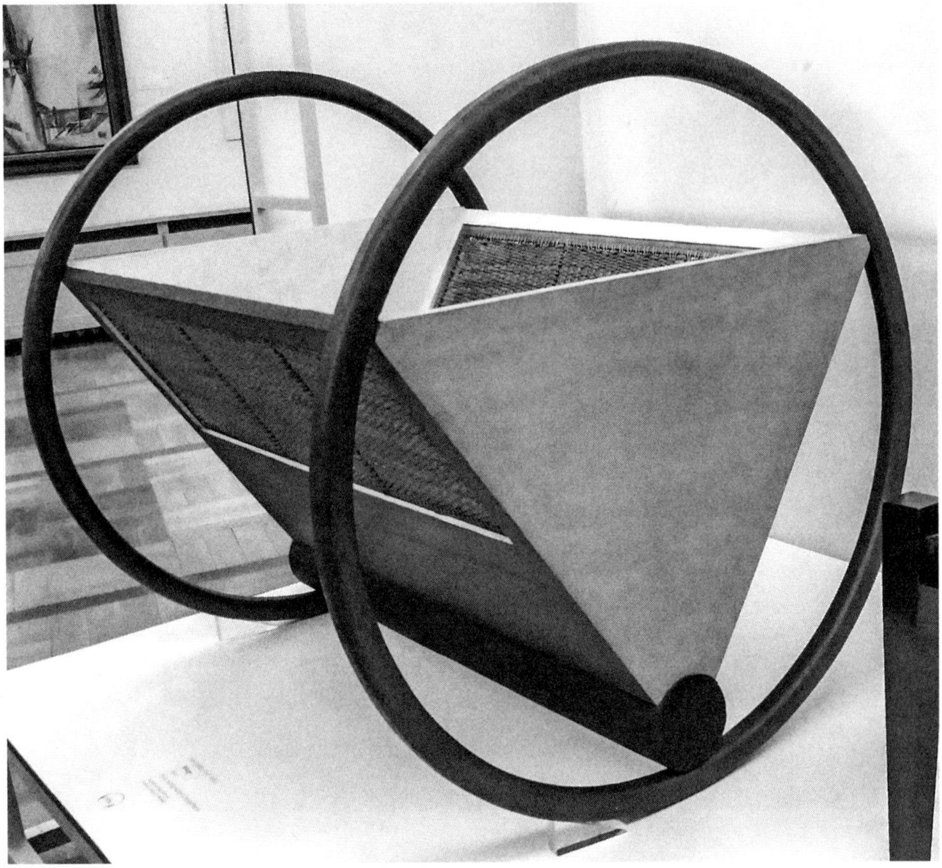

Figure 24.2
Peter Keler, Cradle, 1922.

by substituting digital, logical calculations as the basis for designing interactions—with no regard for biological, organic, analog ones.

Analog lost the battle. Knowingly or not, designers have capitulated to digital advances—the clichéd momentum toward "smaller, cheaper, faster." Nearly all of today's products are screen-based (though this is shifting with voice interfaces, which suffer from the same design issues and lack a human model for interactivity). The physical devices that we carry everywhere and even glue to our bodies are poorly suited to our organic shapes or our biological needs. We want to interact with data, but it comes at the expense of straining our eyes, our wrists, our brains, our social skills, and at times our moral compass.

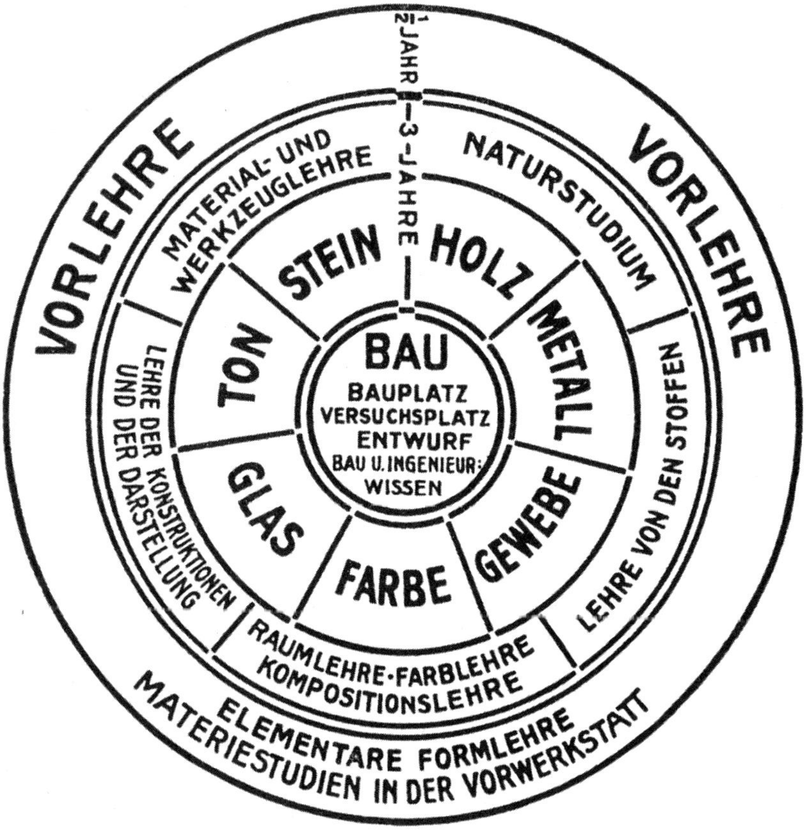

Figure 24.3
Walter Gropius, "Schema zum Aufbau der Lehre am Bauhaus, 1922," published in *Staatliches Bauhaus Weimar, 1919–1923* (Bauhaus-Archiv / Museum für Gestaltung, Berlin), http://folksonomy.co/?permalink=3771.

What would Walter Gropius, Marcel Breuer, or Herbert Bayer think of today's interaction designers? What was it about the Bauhaus manifesto that prepared its students so well for rapid changes in technology without compromising human needs? What might be required in a *manifesto for interaction designers* today? At its core, it needs to educate students about the fundamental nature of designing for interaction.

The *Colloquy of Mobiles* (figure 24.4), designed by Gordon Pask in 1968, is relevant today because it does exactly that—it exposes the fundamental nature of designing for interaction. As a cybernetician, Pask made major contributions to a discipline that

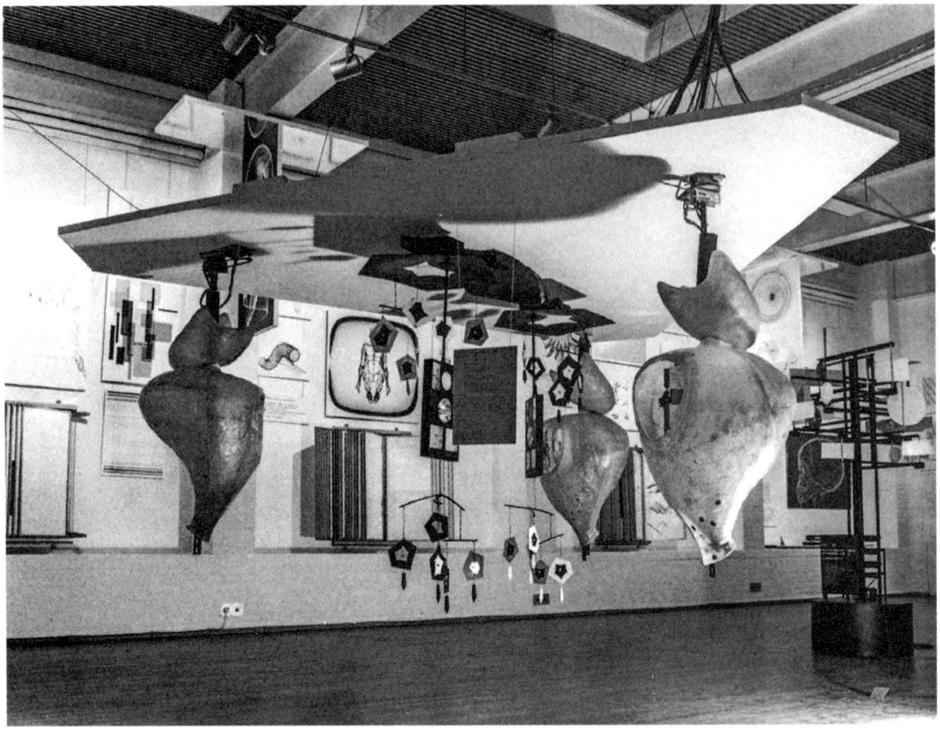

Figure 24.4
Pask's *Colloquy of Mobiles*, part of the exhibition "Cybernetic Serendipity" at the Institute for Contemporary Arts, London: 1968. Credit: MediaKunst.net.

from the 1940s was a revolution in science because it pivoted from focusing on the tangible (physical materials) to the intangible (information and purpose). Cybernetics embraces interaction as the "stuff" between the tangible and the intangible. What is striking and critical to note is that *Colloquy* (created in 1968) is one example of a long lineage of exclusively analog interactive projects that Pask created over the course of his career, starting in the early 1950s.[8] Hence *Colloquy* predates the assumptions of digital's meaning of "interaction."

Created long before laptops or mobile devices, *Colloquy* is an immersive environment consisting of tangible archetypal forms that interact with each other and with human beings in physical space. *Colloquy*'s mobiles are purposeful and autonomous, serendipitous and delightful. They encompass machine-machine interaction and then also human-machine interaction.

Pask referred to *Colloquy*'s mobiles as "male" and "female." Lights, sounds, and geometric shapes offer opportunities for a range of interactions, including conversations. The mobiles interact via light and sound that are used as signals to initiate connections and to give feedback on their responses and preferences, all in service of their goal—in Pask's words, to satisfy their "'drives.'"[9] Even though involving machines, Pask designed *Colloquy*'s interactions to reflect human drives, attraction, and satisfaction. This created opportunities for conversation, seemingly simple in the media he used, but rich in the interactive sense of involving both intentions and actions, competition and cooperation. The result was a novel and unpredictable behavior that human gallery-goers found engaging enough that they spent hours interacting with the mobiles via flashlights, pretending to be mobiles themselves.[10]

In 2018 at the College for Creative Studies, master's students in interaction design participated in the remaking of the full-scale installation of *Colloquy* (figure 24.5). This required a deep investigation into Pask's intentions about the nature of interaction. Students worked from his incomplete prose descriptions of the mobiles' behaviors, his flowcharts, and low-contrast movies of the original. They specified, instruction by instruction, the competitive and cooperative interactions among the males and the females. What emerged was a snapshot of Pask during the development of his "conversation theory," which matured in the mid-1970s.[11] Just as in conversation theory, *Colloquy* expresses the manner by which behaviors may reflect intentions and the means by which conflicts may be resolved. This provides students with an instructional model for precisely the deep understanding of interaction that is missing in many design schools.

The recreation of *Colloquy* in 2018 provided students with an opportunity to grasp the essentials of interaction design in ways that can be applied to many other domains, such as the internet of things and conversational user interfaces. Pask's original *Colloquy* is now seen as an overlooked historical landmark that offers new goals for today's interaction design education. Like the Bauhaus in its time, Pask's approach to interaction design proposes new relationships between people, materials, and technology. The human qualities that were the foundation of Bauhaus culture—humor, sexuality, nature, play, and community—are all present in Pask's masterpiece.

The world is only getting more complicated. Interaction design is both ubiquitous and perilous in its unintended consequences. As we struggle to keep up with social and technological change, interaction designers must deepen their understanding of interactivity. Conversation theory is a powerful way to bridge the tangible and the intangible. It is not enough to design for data streams of sensors and clicks; we must design for the interpretation of information as a means to formulate goals and act toward

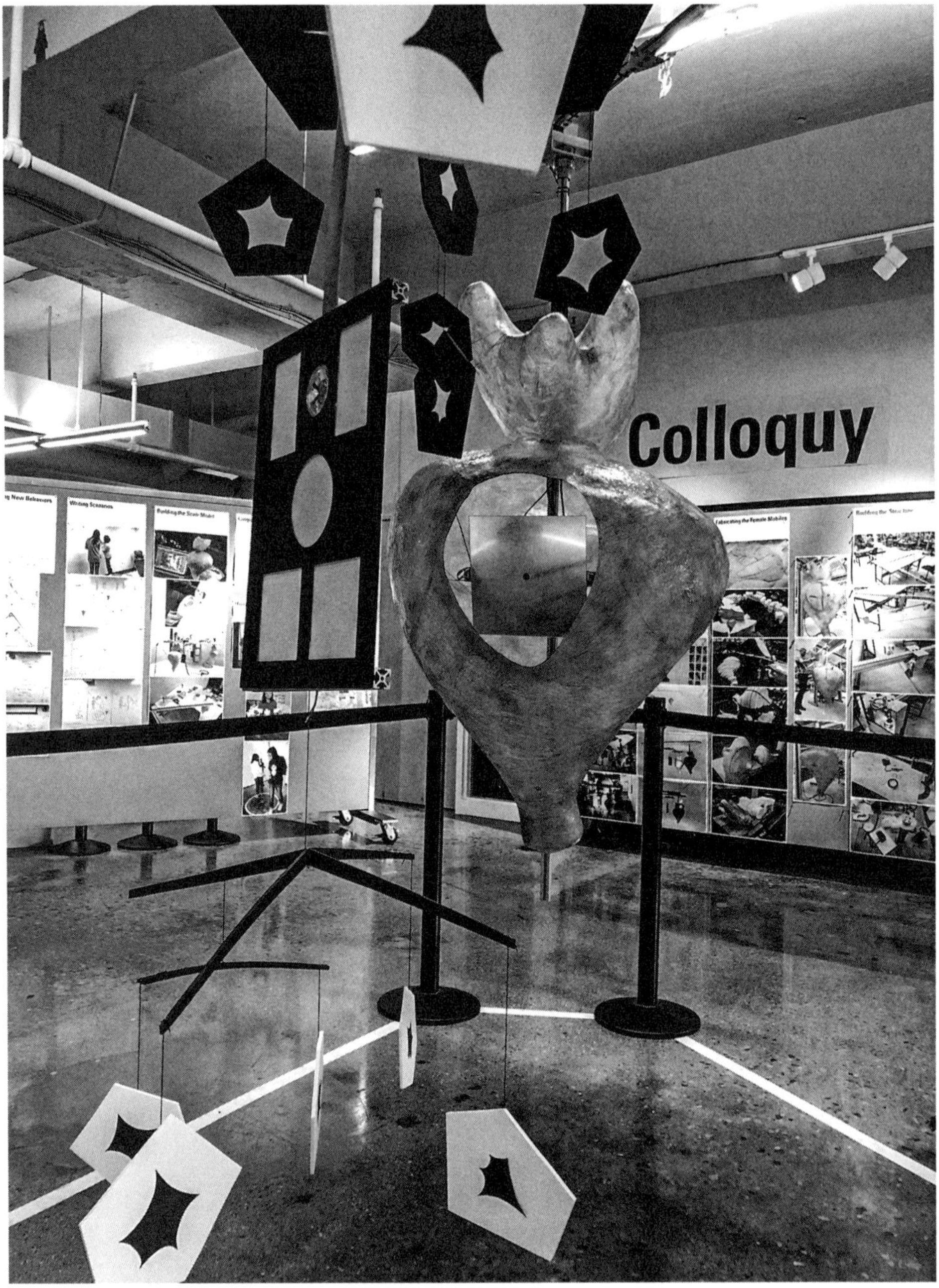

Figure 24.5

Colloquy of Mobiles installation, May 2018, Interaction Design Master's Program, College for Creative Studies, Detroit; full-scale replica of Gordon Pask's original design from 1968 by TJ McLeish, showing completed female mobiles and paper mock-ups of male mobiles, later replaced with finished forms. Photo by Paul Pangaro. (Also plate 19.)

them. A manifesto driving an interaction design curriculum will help students build machines whose logic comes from human sensibilities rather than computational logic alone. This is what Pask helps us to see, and we speculate that he could not have seen without the groundwork laid by the Bauhaus with its prior synthesis of humanism and technology.

Taking inspiration from both the Bauhaus and the *Colloquy of Mobiles*, here we offer discussion points for what might become an updated manifesto about how to teach interaction design.

Interaction Design Manifesto—Initial Discussion Points

Fundamental Design Principles for Our Era

Interaction Frameworks is a required foundation course, as it imparts the deepest understanding of what constitutes successful interactions. *What do models of conversation afford designers of complex interactive systems?*

"Human-centered design" expands ergonomics and decision-making to include the satisfaction of biological drives. *How does our curiosity and drive for "making sense" impact how we use technology and what we want from it?*

The natural world is the basis for student enquiry. We refer to natural forms and processes to influence interaction design. *What exercises (or practicum) would return focus to the riches of the natural world?*

Our human senses are the bases of interaction. Interaction design requires the use of sound, touch, and visual feedforward and feedback.[12] *What is the role of novelty in interaction?*

New rubrics for success are to be developed, based on outcomes that include the achievement of goals, the ability to correct errors, and the ethical consequences of the designed interactions. *Who must be in the conversation to define these rubrics in order to make them comprehensive, realistic, and clear?*

Notes

1. Aimee Picchi, "The Best 11 Jobs in America for 2017," CBS Moneywatch, https://www.cbsnews.com/media/the-best-11-jobs-in-america-for-2017/

2. Adam Dunford, "The Interaction Design Competency Framework," chapter 5, available from https://www.researchgate.net/publication/320353022_The_Interaction_Design_Competency_Framework_A_tool_to_understand_what_industry_wants_from_interaction_design_education.

3. Tristan Harris, "How a Handful of Tech Companies Control Billions of Minds Every Day," TED Talk, 2017 https://www.youtube.com/watch?time_continue=2&v=C74amJRp730.

4. Jodi Forlizzi, "The Product Ecology: Understanding Social Product Use and Supporting Design Culture," *International Journal of Design* 2, no. 1 (2008).

5. Grace Glueck, "Herbert Bayer, 85, a Designer and Artist of Bauhaus School," *New York Times*, October 1, 1985, https://www.nytimes.com/1985/10/01/arts/herbert-bayer-85-a-designer-and-artist-of-bauhaus-school.html.

6. Walter Gropius, "Bauhaus Manifesto and Program," 1919, available at http://mariabuszek.com/mariabuszek/kcai/ConstrBau/Readings/GropBau19.pdf.

7. It remains a point of dispute whether our age encounters "information" in the true sense of "data in context."

8. Gordon Pask, *An Approach to Cybernetics* (London: Hutchinson, 1961).

9. Gordon Pask, "A Comment, a Case History, and a Plan," reprinted in *Cybernetics, Art, and Ideas*, ed. Jasia Reichardt (London: Studio Vista, 1971).

10. Andrew Pickering, *The Cybernetic Brain: Sketches of Another Future* (Chicago: University of Chicago Press, 2010), chapter 7.

11. Gordon Pask, *Conversation Theory* (London: Elsevier, 1976).

12. The authors recognize both the additional term "user experience design" (UXD) as well as its distinctions from user interface design. We view UXD as a sweeping domain of interactions within which interaction design is pervasive.

Editors

Laura Forlano is an Associate Professor of Design at the Institute of Design and Affiliated Faculty in the College of Architecture at Illinois Institute of Technology, where she is Director of the Critical Futures Lab. In 2018–2019, she was Visiting Research Fellow at the Digital Life Initiative at Cornell Tech and Faculty Associate at the Berkman Klein Center for Internet and Society at Harvard University. A writer, social scientist, and design researcher, she has received a Fulbright award as well as funding from the National Science Foundation. Forlano's research is focused on the aesthetics and politics at the intersection between design and emerging technologies. Over the past ten years, she has studied the materialities and futures of sociotechnical systems such as autonomous vehicles and smart cities; 3D printing, local manufacturing, and innovation ecosystems; automation, distributed labor practices, and the future of work; and computational fashion, smart textiles, and wearable medical technologies. Forlano is coeditor with Marcus Foth, Christine Satchell, and Martin Gibbs of *From Social Butterfly to Engaged Citizen* (MIT Press, 2011) and coeditor with Janet Vertesi, David Ribes, Carl DiSalvo, Stephen J. Jackson, Yanni Loukissas, Daniela K. Rosner, and Hanna Rose Shell of *digitalSTS: A Field Guide for Science & Technology Studies* (Princeton University Press, 2019). She received her PhD in communications from Columbia University.

Molly Wright Steenson is the K&L Gates Associate Professor of Ethics and Computational Technologies at Carnegie Mellon University, Senior Associate Dean for Research in the College of Fine Arts, and Associate Professor in the School of Design. A designer, writer, and historian, she is the author of *Architectural Intelligence: How Designers and Architects Created the Digital Landscape* (MIT Press, 2017), a history of artificial intelligence and cybernetics in architecture. The Bauhaus has long been a subject of her research, including its ecological history and *Siedlungen* and the work of Xanti Schawinsky. Steenson was previously Assistant Professor in the School of Journalism and Mass Communication at the University of Wisconsin-Madison, adjunct faculty at Art Center in Pasadena, and Associate Professor of Connected Communities at the Interaction Design Institute Ivrea in Ivrea, Italy. She holds a PhD in Architecture from Princeton University and a master's in Environmental Design from Yale School of Architecture.

Mike Ananny is an Associate Professor at the University of Southern California's Annenberg School for Communication and Journalism and an Affiliated Faculty with USC's Science, Technology and Society research cluster. He studies the public significance of networked news infrastructures. He has held fellowships and scholarships with the Berggruen Institute, Stanford's Center for Advanced Studies in the Behavioral Sciences, Columbia's Tow Center for Digital Journalism, Harvard's Berkman Klein Center for Internet and Society, Stanford's Center on Philanthropy and Civil Society, the Pierre Elliott Trudeau Foundation, LEGO, and Interval Research. He was a founding member of Media Lab Europe, a postdoc with Microsoft Research's Social Media Collective, and has consulted for LEGO, Mattel, and Nortel Networks. He holds a PhD from Stanford University (Communication), SM from the MIT Media Lab (Media Arts and Sciences), and BSc from the University of Toronto (Human Biology and Computer Science). He has published in various academic and popular venues, is the author of *Networked Press Freedom* (MIT Press, 2018), and is writing a book on absence and silence in online journalism (Yale University Press).

Contributors

Alice Arnold is a documentary media maker and an educator. Her work, spanning documentary films and photography, explores the urban environment, from public space issues to visual culture and environmental sustainability. Her documentary films are in the collections of libraries and institutions throughout the United States and have been screened at the Museum of Modern Art and in various festivals worldwide. She is a recipient of a New York Foundation for the Arts Photography Fellowship and a Fulbright Fellowship, among other grants. In addition to making media she is also an Adjunct Professor, currently teaching design and media production, at the City University of New York.

Jeffrey Bardzell is Professor of Informatics and Director of the HCI/Design program in the School of Informatics, Computing, and Engineering at Indiana University–Bloomington. His research contributes to design theory through the study of critical design, research through design, design criticism, and nonprofessional creative practices. A common thread throughout this work is the use of aesthetics—including the history of criticism, critical theory, and analytic aesthetics—to understand how concepts, materials, forms, ideologies, experiential qualities, and creative processes achieve coherence in design objects. He is coeditor of *Critical Theory and Interaction Design* (MIT Press, 2018) and coauthor of *Humanistic HCI* (Synthesis Lectures in Human-Centered Informatics, 2015).

Shaowen Bardzell is Professor of Informatics in the School of Informatics, Computing, and Engineering at Indiana University and the Affiliated Faculty of the Kinsey Institute. Bardzell holds a PhD in Comparative Literature from Indiana University and pursues a humanistic research agenda within the research and practice of human-computer interaction (HCI). A common thread throughout her work is the exploration of the contributions of feminism, design, and social science to support technology's role in social change. Recent research foci have included care ethics and feminist utopian perspectives on IT, research through design, women's health, and posthumanist approaches to sustainable design. Her work is supported by the National Science Foundation, Intel Corporation, and the Mellon Foundation, among others. She is the coeditor of *Critical Theory and Interaction Design* (MIT Press, forthcoming) and coauthor of *Humanistic HCI* (Morgan & Claypool, 2015).

Karen Kornblum Berntsen is a designer who has received numerous national and international awards for her works, some of which were included in the opening of the Museum of Contemporary

Art in Chicago. She has designed museum exhibits, books, websites, and educational materials for students in grades K–12. She is currently an Associate Teaching Professor at the HCI Institute at Carnegie Mellon University, where she teaches students about interaction design, typography, information architecture, and the visual display of complex information. She has developed and implemented a pedagogical framework for teaching interaction design within the HCII. The framework ensures that students learn high-level thinking skills, design methodologies, and design craftsmanship across the curriculum as a whole and within each assignment. She has a BFA in drawing and printmaking and an MS in Interactive Media.

Marshall Brown is a licensed architect, urbanist, and principal of Marshall Brown Projects. He recently joined the School of Architecture at Princeton University as an Associate Professor and Director of their Center for Architecture, Urbanism, and Infrastructure. He was previously an associate professor at the Illinois Institute of Technology, where he directed the Driverless City Project. Brown received his BA from Washington University, St. Louis, and concurrent master's degrees in both architecture and urban design from Harvard University. Among other accomplishments, Brown has been a Graham Foundation grantee, a MacDowell Fellow, and was selected for the US Pavilion at the 2016 Venice Architecture Biennale. His works have been collected by the San Francisco Museum of Modern Art and the Museum of Contemporary Photography. He has also exhibited at the Arts Club of Chicago, the Museum of Contemporary Art Detroit, the Architecture and Design Museum in Los Angeles, and the Chicago Architecture Biennial. His projects and essays have appeared in the *New York Times Magazine, Log, Metropolis, Crain's, Architectural Record, Architect Magazine*, the *Chicago Tribune, Art Papers*, and other publications. Brown has lectured widely at institutions including the Cranbrook Academy of Art, University of Michigan, Northwestern University, Harvard University, the University of Toronto, the Frank Lloyd Wright School of Architecture, Princeton University, and the Rhode Island School of Design. Brown has served as a member of the Chicago Mayor's Cultural Advisory Council and as Vice President of the Arts Club of Chicago.

Stuart Candy, PhD, is an Associate Professor in the School of Design at Carnegie Mellon University. He is recognized as a pioneer of practices at the intersection of design and foresight (experiential futures, design fiction, speculative design, etc.), bringing these idioms to wide attention and application as a writer and educator, and expanding their boundaries as a director and collaborator on numerous transmedia storytelling projects, participatory design events, installations, and guerrilla interventions. He has worked with institutions worldwide including IDEO, the University of Oxford, UNESCO, the Dubai Museum of the Future, the TED Conference, Mexico City's Laboratorio para la Ciudad, Cook Inlet Tribal Council, the United States Conference of Mayors, and the National Film Board of Canada. Candy is a founding member of the Foresight Advisory Board for the International Federation of Red Cross and Red Crescent Societies (Geneva), and a fellow of the World Futures Studies Federation (Paris), INK (Mumbai), the Long Now Foundation (San Francisco), and the Museum of Tomorrow (Rio de Janeiro). With Jeff Watson he is codirector of Situation Lab and co-creator of the award-winning imagination game and worldbuilding tool The Thing From The Future.

Jessica Charlesworth is a British artist, designer, and educator. She is cofounder of the London-based arts salon Alterfutures, and lectures in speculative design in the Designed Objects program at the School of the Art Institute of Chicago. She graduated from the Design Interactions program at the Royal College of Art in London and has collaborated with artists, futurists, and scientists including think tanks Foresight (UK) and the Institute for the Future (US). With her husband Tim Parsons, she is a principal of the art and design studio Parsons & Charlesworth, which explores how object design can play a greater cultural role in the discussion of contemporary issues such as human enhancement, climate change, personal survival, and happiness. The studio has exhibited work at the Museum of Art, Architecture and Technology (Lisbon), Science Gallery Dublin, Chicago Cultural Center, Arts Club of Chicago, Istanbul Design Biennial, Museum of Contemporary Art Chicago, and Aram Gallery (London). Their work is included in the permanent collection at the Museum of Applied Arts, Vienna.

Elizabeth Chin is a Professor at Art Center College of Design in Pasadena, teaching in the MFA program Media Design Practices. Her work spans a variety of topics—race, consumption, Barbie—but nearly always engages marginalized youth in collaboratively taking on the complexities of the world around them. Chin has current projects in Los Angeles, Uganda, and Haiti and has engaged partners including the Los Angeles Police Department, numerous public schools, Jovenes, Inc. in Boyle Heights, and Lekòl Kominotè Matènwa in Haiti. A specialist in Haitian folkloric dance, she has performed professionally and still occasionally teaches dance. Chin's work increasingly investigates the ethnographic voice with an eye toward decolonizing anthropological knowledge as it appears on the page.

Taeyoon Choi is an artist, educator, and activist. His art involves performance, electronics, drawings, and installations that form the basis for storytelling and social practice. He published artist's books, including *Urban Programming 101* and *Anti-Manifesto*. Choi was an artist in residence at the Lower Manhattan Cultural Council's Workspace and at The Frank-Ratchye Studio for Creative Inquiry at Carnegie Mellon University. He was a fellow at the Data and Society Research Institute and Eyebeam Art and Technology Center. He received commissions from Art +Technology Lab, Los Angeles County Museum of Art, and SeMA Biennale Mediacity Seoul. Choi cofounded the School for Poetic Computation in New York, where he continues to organize sessions and teach classes on art and critical theory of technology. He collaborates with various communities to unlearn the boundaries between disability and normalcy and enhance accessibility and inclusion. He is currently working on Distributed Web of Care.

B. Coleman is Associate Professor of Experimental Digital Media at the University of Waterloo where she directs the City as Platform Lab. Her work focuses on smart technology, big data, and civic engagement. Her practice engages research methods and design inquiry toward the creation of public, civic, and aesthetic works. She has published the monograph *Hello Avatar: Rise of the Networked Subject* (MIT Press). Her research affiliations include the Berkman Klein Center for Internet and Society, Harvard University, and expert consultant for the European Commission Digital Futures. She is the cofounder of SoundLab Cultural Alchemy, with an international exhibition history that includes the Whitney Museum of American Art; Recollets, Paris; and Waag Society, Amsterdam. She is a visiting scholar at Data and Society Research Institute, New York.

Carl DiSalvo is an Associate Professor at Georgia Institute of Technology with joint appointments in the School of Interactive Computing and the School of Literature, Media, and Communication. At Georgia Tech he directs the Public Design Workshop: a design research studio that explores socially engaged design and civic media. DiSalvo's scholarship draws together theories and methods from design research and design studies, the social sciences, and the humanities to analyze the social and political qualities of design, and to prototype experimental systems and services. His first book, *Adversarial Design* (2012), is part of the Design Thinking, Design Theory series at the MIT Press. He is also a coeditor of the MIT Press journal *Design Issues*. DiSalvo's experimental design work has been exhibited and supported by the Center for Art and Media (ZKM) in Karlsruhe, Grey Area Foundation for the Arts, Times Square Arts Alliance, Science Gallery Dublin, and the Walker Arts Center.

Michael J. Golec is Associate Professor of the History of Design at the School of the Art Institute of Chicago. His scholarship focuses on histories and theories of modern design, technical images, and data visualization. His publications include "In the Way of Technical Images," *Historical Studies in Natural Science*; "Graphic Visualization and Visuality in Lester Beall's Rural Electrification Posters, 1937," *Journal of Design History*; "Facts between Pictographs and Photographs," *Zeitschrift für Ästhetik und Allgemeine Kunstwissenschaft*; "Visual Style and Forms of *Science* in the Cold War," in *Visual Rhetoric and the Eloquence of Design*; and "A Natural History of a Disembodied Eye: The Structure of Gyorgy Kepes' *Language of Vision*," *Design Issues*. Golec is the author of *Brillo Box Archive: Aesthetics, Design and Art*.

Kate Hennessy is an Associate Professor specializing in Media at Simon Fraser University's School of Interactive Arts and Technology, where she leads the Making Culture Lab. Her research explores the role of digital technology in the documentation and safeguarding of cultural heritage, and the mediation of culture, history, objects, and subjects in new forms. Her video and multimedia works investigate documentary and archival practices to address histories of place and space. Her work has been published in journals such as *Leonardo*, *American Indian Quarterly*, and *Cultural Anthropology* and exhibited at Crane Arts (Philadelphia), the Reach Gallery Museum (Abbotsford), and the Capture Photography Festival (Vancouver). She has co-curated and produced award-winning online exhibits for the Virtual Museum of Canada. She is one of the cofounders of the Ethnographic Terminalia Collective.

Matthew Hockenberry is a Lecturer in Digital Technology and Emerging Media at Fordham University. A media historian and technologist whose research examines critical developments in the epistemology of assembly, his work centers on the history of logistics, tracing the impact of media forms and material practices on decentralized production and the mediation of manufacture throughout the nineteenth and twentieth centuries. He is particularly concerned with how media-archaeological approaches to the networks of production can reveal transitional moments within histories of paperwork, telecommunication, and computation. As a researcher with the MIT Center for Civic Media and Tangible Media Group he developed Sourcemap, a platform for mapping supply chains and sharing "where things come from," and he writes regularly on the state of global supply through the lens of its most emblematic objects.

Joi Ito is the director of the MIT Media Lab, Professor of the Practice of Media Arts and Sciences at MIT, and a visiting Professor of Law from Practice at the Harvard Law School. He received a PhD from the Keio University Graduate School of Media and Governance in 2018 for his thesis "The Practice of Change." He is the author, with Jeff Howe, of *Whiplash: How to Survive Our Faster Future* (Grand Central Publishing, 2016). Ito is chairman of the board of PureTech Health and serves on several other boards, including those of the New York Times Company, the MacArthur Foundation, and the Knight Foundation. He is the former chairman and CEO of Creative Commons, and a former board member of ICANN, The Open Source Initiative, and The Mozilla Foundation. Ito is also a serial entrepreneur and has helped start and run numerous companies, including one of the first web companies in Japan, Digital Garage, and the first commercial internet service provider in Japan, PSINet Japan/IIKK. He has been an early-stage investor in many companies, including Formlabs, Flickr, Kickstarter, littleBits, and Twitter.

Denisa Kera is a philosopher and designer who uses prototypes and prototyping in the context of STS (science, technology, and society) research. Prototypes express the entrepreneurial, educational, participatory, and activist aspirations and promises of the emergent technologies. She uses various creative strategies inspired by artistic and design methods (user experience, critical design, and design fiction) to support the public engagement in these early promissory stages of new technologies. She spent the last decade as an assistant professor at the National University of Singapore, visiting assistant professor at Arizona State University, and senior fellow at Prague College (Future Design program). Currently she is a Marie Curie senior research fellow at the University of Salamanca, researching blockchain, design, and policy issues.

N. Adriana Knouf is an Assistant Professor of Art + Design at Northeastern University. She is a media scholar and artist researching noise, interferences, boundaries, and limits in media technologies and communication. Her book *How Noise Matters to Finance* (University of Minnesota Press, 2016) traces how the concept of "noise" in the sonic and informatic domains of finance mutated throughout the late twentieth century into the twenty-first. Her current research project, tentatively entitled *The Xenology Notebooks*, traces practices of "making strange" in radio, the voice, the search for ghosts, space exploration, and potential extraterrestrial communication. Her current artistic research explores the re-presentation of signals from the cosmos.

Silvia Lindtner is an Assistant Professor at the University of Michigan in the School of Information, with a courtesy appointment in the Penny W. Stamps School of Art and Design. Lindtner's research and teaching interests include innovation and technology entrepreneurship, making and hacking cultures, and shifts in tech work and industries. This work unfolds through a deep engagement with issues of gender, inequality, and masculinity in engineering and design, labor, and contemporary political economy. Lindtner draws from ten years of multisited ethnographic research, with a particular focus on China's position in global tech production. She is currently completing a book on the promise of making and entrepreneurial living. Her research has been awarded support from the US National Science Foundation, Institute of Museum and Library Services, Intel Labs, Google Anita Borg, and the Chinese National Natural Science Foundation. Her work contributes to science and technology studies, feminist anthropology, China studies, human-computer interaction, and design.

Shannon Mattern is a Professor at The New School for Social Research. Her writing and teaching focus on archives, libraries, and other media spaces; media infrastructures; spatial epistemologies; and mediated sensation and exhibition. She is the author of *The New Downtown Library: Designing with Communities*; *Deep Mapping the Media City*; and *Code and Clay, Data and Dirt*, all published by University of Minnesota Press. She contributes a regular long-form column about urban data and mediated infrastructures to *Places*, a journal focusing on architecture, urbanism, and landscape, and she collaborates on public design and interactive projects and exhibitions. You can find her at wordsinspace.net.

Ramia Mazé specializes in participatory and critical practices of design. She is Professor of New Frontiers in Design at Aalto University in Finland. Previously in Sweden, she worked at Konstfack College of Arts Crafts and Design, at KTH Royal Institute of Technology School of Architecture, at the national PhD school Designfakulteten, and at the Interactive Institute. Trained as a designer and architect, she has worked in design consultancies and corporate research, and her PhD is in interaction design. In the areas of sustainable development, design activism, smart materials, and interactive spaces, she has published and exhibited widely through interdisciplinary and international research projects in which she has had leadership roles. Recent relevant collaborative projects include *Feminist Futures of Spatial Practice* (Baunach: Spurbuchverlag, 2017), "Utopia Now Here" (Istanbul Design Biennial, 2014), and *DESIGN ACT Socially- and politically-engaged design today* (Berlin: Sternberg Press / Iaspis, 2010).

V. Mitch McEwen is principal and cofounder of A(n) Office, an architecture collaborative in Detroit, Princeton, and New York City. A(n) Office and McEwen have been commissioned by the 2016 US Pavilion at the Venice Architecture Biennale, the Museum of Contemporary Art Detroit, and the Istanbul Design Biennial. Projects in Detroit include a combined residence and flower incubator for an engineer at 3M and a City of Detroit-commissioned action plan for housing across 160 acres of waterfront and canals in the Jefferson-Chalmers neighborhood. Her work in urban design and architecture began at Bernard Tschumi Architects and the New York City Department of City Planning, and included founding SUPERFRONT in Brooklyn. She joined the faculty at Princeton School of Architecture in 2017, where she teaches studio and building technology and leads A(n)other Lab. McEwen earned her MArch at Columbia and BA at Harvard College.

Oliver Neumann is an Associate Professor in the School of Architecture and Landscape Architecture at the University of British Columbia. Prior to joining UBC in 2003 as an Assistant Professor, he taught at the Hochschule für Wirtschaft, Technik, und Kultur in Leipzig, Germany, at the UBC School of Architecture, and as the 2002/03 Oberdick Research and Teaching Fellow at the Taubman College of Architecture and Urban Planning at the University of Michigan. Oliver's interdisciplinary research projects build on collaborations with wood scientists, engineers, fabricators, and material suppliers. His research focuses on the role of digital technology in the building process and in broader speculations of emerging material culture. His building research and teaching projects explore contemporary fabrication technologies, mass customization processes, and their implications for ecological design concepts, design methodology, and construction. His design research projects explore the potential of digital wood fabrication.

Paul Pangaro is Professor of the Practice in the Human-Computer Interaction Institute at Carnegie Mellon University, and previously was Chair and Associate Professor of the MFA Interaction Design program at the College for Creative Studies. He has published and presented widely on applications of conversation in interaction design, organizational change, and design methods. His career spans teaching, research, startups, and consulting. He has lectured and published on "designing for conversation" from his research and his design and implementation of software and organizational processes. Pangaro has worked with and within software startups in New York, Boston, and Silicon Valley in product and technology roles. As a consultant, he has been hired by multinational tech companies, nonprofits, and incubators, focusing on organizational development or future-casting. He is a recipient of the American Society for Cybernetics Warren McCulloch Award.

Tim Parsons is an Associate Professor and Chair of the Designed Objects programs in the Department of Architecture, Interior Architecture and Designed Objects at the School of the Art Institute of Chicago. He studied industrial design before earning a Master of the Arts degree in Design Products at London's Royal College of Art in 2000. He has gone on to teach product design for fifteen years at universities in Britain and America, including University of the Arts London and Manchester Metropolitan University. As a designer, he has worked with manufacturers in Britain and Europe and exhibited widely, including at the Design Museum, London and the Museum of Contemporary Art Chicago. As a writer he has contributed articles and essays to publications including *Blueprint*, *ICON*, *Crafts*, and Phaidon's Design Classics; his book *Thinking: Objects: Contemporary Approaches to Product Design* was published in 2009 by AVA Academia.

Nassim Parvin (formerly JafariNaimi) is an Assistant Professor of Digital Media in the School of Literature, Media, and Communication at Georgia Tech, where she also directs the Design and Social Interaction Studio. Parvin's research explores the ethical and political dimensions of design and technology, especially as related to values of democratic participation and social justice. Integrating methods of humanistic scholarship and design-based inquiry, her research answers pressing questions about the influence of digital technologies on the future of social and collective interactions. Her papers have appeared in premier publication venues in design studies, science and technology studies, and human-computer interaction. She is an award-winning educator and serves on the editorial board of the journal of *Catalyst: Feminism, Theory, Technoscience*. Parvin received her PhD in Design from Carnegie Mellon University. She holds an MS in Information Design and Technology from Georgia Tech and a BS in Electrical Engineering from the University of Tehran.

Joanne Pouzenc is an architect, curator, and educator based in Berlin. After 10 years of architectural practice in southern France, she entered the Bauhaus postgraduate program in Dessau and launched a curatorial career. Among her projects are "City Inc" (Bauhaus Dessau Foundation, 2011), SAM Basel (2011); "Post Capitalist City—International Competition for Society Design" (2012); "Berlin Unlimited," first festival for arts, architecture, and urban research in Berlin (2014); co-curator of Make City Festival, Berlin (2015); Atelier d'Architecture Itinérant (2015, featured in the 2016 Venice Biennale); communication manager for the German Pavilion at the Venice Biennale (2016); co-curator of "Fights and Fictions / 36h Factory of Thoughts" at the Akademie der Künste, Berlin with the Goethe Institut (2016); artistic direction and program coordination of projekt bauhaus, Berlin (2017–2018). She is currently teaching in the Ecole Nationale Supérieure d'Architecture in Toulouse, France, and a lecturer at the NODE center for curatorial practices.

Luiza Prado de O. Martins engages with material and visual culture through the lenses of decolonial and queer theories. In her doctoral dissertation (awaiting publication) she examined technologies and practices of birth control and their entanglements with colonial hierarchies of gender, race, ethnicity, class, and nationality, offering the idea of "technoecologies of birth control" as a framework for observing and intervening in biopolitical articulations. Her current artistic research project, titled "A Topography of Excesses," starts from a call to reappropriate the perception of excess attributed to gendered and racialized bodies through the modern/colonial gender system. Through installation, net-art, video, and text, the project looks into the transmission of indigenous and folk knowledges about herbal birth control as decolonizing practices of radical care that allow communities to forge new paths by accessing the poetic dimensions of the pluriversal.

Daniela K. Rosner is an Assistant Professor in Human Centered Design and Engineering (HCDE) at the University of Washington and codirector of the Tactile and Tactical Design (TAT) Lab. Her research critically investigates ways people work with materials to imagine more socially responsible technological futures, focusing on practices historically marginalized within engineering cultures such as electronics maintenance and needlecraft. Rosner's work has appeared in *Public Culture*, *New Media and Society*, and other journals, conference proceedings, and edited volumes. She is the author of *Critical Fabulations: Reworking the Methods and Margins of Design* (MIT Press). Her work has been supported by multiple awards from the US National Science Foundation, including an NSF CAREER award. Rosner earned her PhD from the University of California, Berkeley. She also holds a BFA in Graphic Design from the Rhode Island School of Design and an MS in Computer Science from the University of Chicago.

Natalie Saltiel is the Program Manager for the Ethics and Governance of Artificial Intelligence Initiative at the MIT Media Lab, a collaboration between the Media Lab and the Berkman Klein Center for Internet and Society at Harvard University. She has an MSc from the Oxford Internet Institute at Oxford University and was previously the Coordinating Editor of the *Journal of Design and Science*. Her work focuses on bridging the gap between the humanities and social sciences and computing and the ethical implications of technology.

Trudi Lynn Smith is an artist and anthropologist with an Interdisciplinary PhD from the University of Victoria. Her research addresses political and material entanglements between photography, archives, and places. She reworks formal aspects of photography—a relationship between durable images and electromagnetic radiation—to emphasize the materiality of the unfixed image in everyday life. Her place-specific works have been installed in locations across Canada and the United States, and she has exhibited work at Third Street Gallery (Easton), Crane Arts (Philadelphia), Open Space Gallery (Victoria), and Southern Alberta Art Gallery (Lethbridge). Her work has been published in journals such as *Cultural Anthropology*, *c-theory*, *Anthropologica*, and *Imaginations*. She is one of the cofounders of the Ethnographic Terminalia Collective.

Carol Strohecker is dean of the University of Minnesota College of Design. Having earned her doctorate at the MIT Media Lab, she directed learning research and learning environment design at Mitsubishi Electric Research Laboratories (MERL) and Media Lab Europe. She was director of the UNC Center for Design Innovation and vice provost at the Rhode Island School of Design (RISD). Strohecker was a presidential nominee on the MIT Corporation Visiting Committee for Media Arts and Sciences, and a selected delegate at the World Summit on the Information Society. Her work in interactive media tools and methods resulted in four US patents. An alumna of Complex Systems programs at the Santa Fe Institute and a cofounder of the NSF-funded network for Sciences, Engineering, Arts, and Design (SEAD), Strohecker received fellowships from the Massachusetts Council for the Arts and Humanities, the US National Endowment for the Arts, and the Harvard Graduate School of Design.

Alex S. Taylor is a sociologist working in the Centre for Human Centred Design at City, University of London. Showing a broad fasciation with the entanglements between social life and machines, his research ranges from empirical studies of technology in everyday life to speculative design interventions—both large and small. Across these realms, he draws on a feminist technoscience to ask questions about the co-constitutive roles human-machine composites play in forms of knowing and being, and how they might open up possibilities for fundamental transformations in society. Most recently, he's begun to wonder about the abilities of humans and nonhumans, together, and to speculate on hybrid compositions that enlarge capacity and offer the chance of something different-than, something more-than.

Martin Thaler is a Studio Professor at the IIT Institute of Design where, since 2008, he has been teaching graduate-level courses in product and environmental design. He also teaches early-stage prototyping in Mexico and China, expanding his global cultural perspective on design. Previously, for twelve years he led multidisciplinary teams at the IDEO Chicago office, working with companies in the consumer electronics, medical, and furniture industries, including Motorola, Baxter, and Steelcase. Before this, he cofounded the award-winning consulting firm Design Logic in Chicago. His clients included Bang & Olufsen and View-Master. Martin's work has been exhibited and published in books and periodicals such as *ID*, *Blueprint*, and *Time*. Martin holds a master of fine arts from the Royal College of Art, London, and a bachelor of fine arts from the Rhode Island School of Design.

Fred Turner is Harry and Norman Chandler Professor of Communication at Stanford University. He is the author of several books, including the award-winning history *From Counterculture to Cyberculture: Stewart Brand, the Whole Earth Network, and the Rise of Digital Utopianism* and its prequel, *The Democratic Surround: Multimedia and American Liberalism from World War II to the Psychedelic Sixties*, in which he traced the influence of Bauhaus refugees on American multimedia. Prior to Stanford, he taught Communication at Harvard's John F. Kennedy School of Government and MIT's Sloan School of Management. He also worked for ten years as a journalist. He has written for newspapers and magazines ranging from the *Boston Globe Sunday Magazine* to *Harper's*.

Andre Uhl is a PhD candidate at Harvard University's Department of Visual and Environmental Studies, and project lead at the Global Council on Extended Intelligence (CXI) of the MIT Media Lab and the Institute of Electrical and Electronics Engineers (IEEE). His doctoral research explores participatory design practices for the ethics and governance of artificial intelligence. He is a current Fellow at the MIT Dalai Lama Center for Ethics and Transformative Values, and co-chair of One Harvard for Sustainable Peace, a program to integrate spiritual and ethical formation into leadership preparation at Harvard University. Before coming to the United States, Andre received an MA in New Media from the National University of the Arts in Tokyo and a dual BA in Visual Art and East Asia Studies from Free University in Berlin. He is an alumnus of both the MEXT Fellowship Program of the Japanese Ministry of Education, Culture, Science and Technology, and the German National Academic Foundation.

Jeff Watson, PhD, is an Assistant Professor of Interactive Media and Games at the University of Southern California School of Cinematic Arts, and a director of the Situation Lab. An interdisciplinary scholar-designer, Watson uses a range of methods to investigate the relationships among play, technology, creativity, and politics. His written works have appeared in journals such as the *Journal of Transformative Works and Cultures*, the *International Journal of Learning and Media*, and *Well Played*; and in books such as *Alternate Reality Gaming and the Cusp of Digital Gameplay* (Bloomsbury, 2018) and *Game Design Workshop* (CRC Press, 2014). His artistic and design efforts have reached international audiences, receiving coverage from publications such as *Wired* and *Fast Company* and winning awards including the 2012 Impact Award at the IndieCade International Festival of Independent Games, and the 2015 Most Significant Futures Award from the Association of Professional Futurists. Watson is currently completing a book about play, technology, and power after the internet.

Robert Wiesenberger is Associate Curator of Contemporary Projects at the Clark Art Institute in Williamstown, Massachusetts, where he also teaches in the graduate program in art history at Williams College. For 2019–2020 he is an associate in the Department of Visual and Environmental Studies at Harvard University. From 2013 to 2018 he was Critic at the Yale School of Art, teaching in the MFA program in graphic design. From 2014 to 2016 he was the Stefan Engelhorn Curatorial Fellow at the Harvard Art Museums, where he was responsible for the museums' Bauhaus collections. He is the coauthor of *Muriel Cooper* (MIT Press, 2017). He holds a BA in history and German from the University of Chicago and a PhD in art history from Columbia University.

Index